THE GEFILTE VARIATIONS

200 INSPIRED RE-CREATIONS OF CLASSICS FROM THE JEWISH
KITCHEN, WITH MENUS, STORIES, AND TRADITIONS FOR THE
HOLIDAYS AND YEAR-ROUND

JAYNE COHEN

SCRIBNER
NEW YORK LONDON TORONTO SYDNEY SINGAPORE

Scribner
1230 Avenue of the Americas
New York, NY 10020

SCRIBNER and design are trademarks of Macmillan Library Reference USA, Inc.,
used under license by Simon & Schuster, the publisher of this work.

Designed by Abby Weintraub

Set in Fournier

Manufactured in the United States of America

1 3 5 7 9 10 8 6 4 2

Library of Congress Cataloging-in-Publication Data
Cohen, Jayne.
The gefilte variations : 200 inspired re-creations of classics from the Jewish kitchen,
with menus, stories, and traditions for the holidays and year-round / Jayne Cohen.
p. cm.
Includes bibliographical references and index.
1. Cookery, Jewish. I. Title.
TX724.C54 2000
641.5'676—dc21   99-054353

ISBN 0-684-82719-0

Owing to limitations of space, permissions and previously published materials appear on page 416.

*To the memory of my parents, Joan and Max Cohen, who
instilled in me a voracious appetite for the banquet of life.
And to Howie and Alex, for passionately eating there with me.*

CONTENTS

YEAR-ROUND FAVORITES

THE HOLIDAYS

A LIST OF THE RECIPES

MEATS AND POULTRY   **103**

DAIRY DISHES   **134**

NONDAIRY AND PAREVE GRAINS AND VEGETABLES   **158**

THE HOLIDAYS

INTRODUCTION

This book was written for cooks who approach the rich tapestry of Jewish foods as an exciting cuisine—filled with nostalgia, yes, but still very much alive, and above all, delicious. Characterized by homey techniques and tastes, like slowly braised stews and soft, caramelized onions, this family cuisine serves here as a departure point, much the way Italian pasta and pizza have been explored by innovative cooks, and American Southwestern cuisine has been transformed and infused with new life.

Jewish food was meant to be *potchkehed*, or played with. Jews are constantly encouraged to question and reinterpret the accepted, as no one who has read the Passover Haggadah can forget. There, the learned rabbis argue over the number of plagues God visited on the Egyptians, starting with the traditional ten, and going through many variations, including ten times ten (one for each finger of God's hands) and then that figure taken to the tenth power. The possibilities, considered from various perspectives, are always infinite.

Delicate matzoh balls, for instance, whose flavors—roasted fennel, sweet potato—change with the seasons. Or simple staples like hummus that become a sensuous feast when prepared with quick-cooking lentils perfumed with pomegranate and mint and served with toasted za'atar matzoh.

But you need not pay for such culinary forays with kitchen servitude. Use ready-made kosher wonton wrappers to make paper-thin kreplach filled with tart sour cherries and crystallized ginger, then glossed with sour cream; or stuff them with leftover pot roast and beets and set them afloat in a tangy winter cabbage soup. Fashion airy knishes from store-bought phyllo dough and spoon in luscious garlic-mashed potatoes. Jews have always assimilated the exotic ingredients and cooking methods they encountered in trade, travel, and the many new homelands they were forced to find.

WHAT KIND OF COOKBOOK IS THIS?

Earthy and elegant, these delectable improvisations are foods I love to cook and eat. My preferences and predilections are the sole determinants for including a recipe. You won't find every delicious Jewish dish here—or its reinterpretation. For that, many excellent, authoritative books on Jewish cuisine already exist (a partial selection is listed in the bibliography), whose recipes, when carefully read, will evoke a history of the people who cooked and ate this food.

This is instead that other kind of cookbook: a highly subjective selection. Revealing the ingredients, combinations, methods, and refinements I am drawn to and the culinary influences that nourished me, this book tells a more personal story, the autobiography of one palate.

It is written in my culinary mother tongue—Jewish—and for that reason, these improvisations are inextricably bound to the foods of my childhood and my family. My grandmothers were superb traditional home cooks, but both my parents were particularly inventive in the kitchen. Although each holiday appeared at our table cloaked in its customary set of enticing aromas, when my parents cooked the meal it was a safe bet that the foods would somehow taste different every time.

With the possible exception of politics, no topic ever inspired so much passion in our house as food. The meals we had eaten and those we talked—and argued—about sharing in the future were a metaphor for all that we had relished together, for everything that was delicious in life.

Our gastronomical selves, of course, are constantly evolving, and in the transition from eager palate to curious cook, I've also experimented with ideas derived from traveling and eating, from talking and reading. Here I mean not just cookbooks—though I confess to savoring piles of them late at night like secret sweets—but food tasted in fiction and in poetry. I might bring to life, for example, a tantalizing breast of veal from a forgotten novella by Armand Lunel, a Jew from Provence. Perhaps you will taste the recipes in this book first in reading their introductions, which are intended to provoke and excite your "mind's tongue" to get you cooking.

These improvisations are firmly rooted in Jewish tradition, and while playful, they remain faithful to its spirit and soul. I am not creating silly, culturally perverse combinations here, like matzoh balls made with butter and destined for a meat soup, or gourmet hybrids, like jalapeño–sun dried tomato gefilte fish. Nor am I after chili, Jewish simply because it is prepared with kosher ground meat. Rather, my recipes are all integrated interpretations of foods I think of as Jewish, and all are kosher.

W H A T   I S   J E W I S H   F O O D ?

Can the food of a people dispersed all over the world centuries ago, cooking the many disparate foods of their adopted homelands, be described as a cuisine? A cuisine that would find common elements in a beef kibbe, tart-sweet with apricots and tamarind, and a tender brisket, heady with onion gravy? Or delicate gefilte fish dumplings and bellahat, Egyptian spicy ground fish balls?

There *is* a Jewish cuisine. But it cannot be defined as simply any food cooked by Jews. By that logic, pasta primavera and Mexican salsa, now made with kosher ingredients by Jewish cooks, are Jewish foods.

Nor are the only true Jewish foods matzoh, haroset, the Passover fruit-nut paste that commemorates the mortar the Jews used in ancient Egypt, and long-simmering Sabbath dishes, like hamins and cholents. We cannot deny chopped liver or the oniony hard-cooked eggs, huevos haminados, because they are not eaten by all Jews. Jewish cooking is perhaps the original regional cuisine, with a purview that nearly spans the globe.

Blintzes may first have been prepared in a Russian kitchen as round pancakes meant to evoke the winter sun at Shrovetide. But haven't Jews, who welcome summer with them at Shavuot, adapted and adopted them long enough to call them their own? When does an immigrant food become natural-ized? Surely baked beans are solid New England fare, though many food historians believe that either the Pilgrims borrowed their overnight Sabbath stews from Jewish versions during their sojourn in Holland or seafaring captains brought the Jewish dish back from North Africa.

THE VARIED WORLD OF JEWISH CUISINE

Comprising the largest segment of world Jewry, the Ashkenazim (from Ashkenaz, the Hebrew word for Germany) are descended from the Jews who originally settled in France and Germany, later emi-grating east and north to Poland, Russia, the Baltic, and Central Europe. While their cuisine was far from homogeneous—contrast the Hungarian stews spicy with paprika and hot peppers with sweet Polish dishes like raisin-studded stuffed cabbage or a honey-sweet tsimmes of meat, fruit, and vegeta-bles—there is a recognizable commonality. Most Ashkenazim came from cool climates and worked with similar ingredients: beets, carrots, cabbage, potatoes. Few had access to the sea, so collectively they developed a love for freshwater fish. Their shared food traditions were also a by-product of the interaction among the various Ashkenazi communities through trade, marriage, and the constant migrations resulting from persecution and expulsion (an integration made easier because they spoke the same language, Yiddish). Later the cuisine became further standardized in the apogee of such intermingling, namely, the American melting pot.

Sephardim (from the Hebrew *Sepharad,* meaning Spain) refers technically to those Jews and their descendants expelled from the Iberian Peninsula beginning in 1492, but it has come to mean as well all the Jews from the diverse communities of the Balkans, the eastern Mediterranean, North Africa, the Middle East, and parts of Asia. There had been a Jewish presence in all these lands for centuries: Jews have made Morocco home, for instance, at least since Roman times, and the Jewish community in Iraq dates back to antiquity when King Nebuchadnezzar brought Jews to Babylonia as captives after he destroyed the First Temple in 506 B.C.

Many of these Muslim areas welcomed the Spanish and Portuguese Jews—indeed, the Ottoman Sultan Bayazid II invited them, avowing, "[Ferdinand] is impoverishing his country and enriching my kingdom"—and they brought with them not only their language, Ladino, but their foods and cooking techniques as well. These in turn influenced and became influenced by all the different culinary traditions of the new lands they settled.

Sephardi cooking then is really a constellation of disparate cuisines, revolving, to some extent, around similar ingredients like sun-soaked vegetables and fruits, lamb, saltwater fish, oils, herbs, and aromatic spices. While the boundaries are permeable, at least four very general types of cooking styles can be distinguished: the cuisines of the eastern Mediterranean Jews (Greece, Turkey, and the Balkans), where the cooking of the Iberian Jews had the greatest influence; the Maghreb (North Africa) Jews; the various Jewish communities of the Middle East: Egypt and the Levant; and Iran and Iraq.

Although it is often classified as Sephardi by Ashkenazi Jews, Italian cuisine is quite distinct. Jews have lived in Rome continuously for twenty-one centuries: *la cucina ebraica* is an amalgam of the foods of the ancient Jewish communities, the Sephardi and Ashkenazi émigrés and their Italian-Christian neighbors.

The third largest group of Jewry, the Yemenite Jews, trace their ancestry to the celebrated union of Solomon and Sheba in the ninth century B.C. Because they were fairly isolated from other Jews, not only their customs but their fiery hot cuisine developed differently.

Separate mention should also be made of the Asian Jewish communities. Many Jews who settled in the stops along the Silk Route—the fabled names out of Coleridge, like Samarkand, Bukhara, Tashkent—originally came from Iran. Cut off from their forebears, they developed a rich, festive cuisine greatly influenced by their Central Asian and Russian neighbors. The cuisines of two of the three far-flung Jewish settlements in India—the Bene Israel in Kerala and later Bombay, and the Cochini Jews from the Malabar Coast—bear strong resemblance to the Hindu and Muslim cooking there. The Baghdadis, who make up the third community, centered in Bombay and Calcutta, were Iraqi and Syrian Jews. Their unique foods blend elements of the Jewish Middle East with Indian and, to a lesser extent, British cooking.

Some time ago I was in the home of a Jewish woman originally from Kerala, on the southwestern coast of India. Accustomed to celebrating Rosh Hashanah during the furious monsoon season there, in New York, on a soft September morning, she prepared the same traditional foods with which she welcomed the New Year back home. The apartment was filled with the aromas of chicken curry simmering on the stove and platters of *halwah*, sweet puddings enriched with coconut milk (in avoidance of the dairy that would contravene kosher law), cooling on the dining table.

Such strong smells are intensely evocative. And I was indeed transported—but not to a place of pink palaces, golden caparisoned elephants, and silk saris in rainbow colors. Instead, I was back in my Polish grandmother's apartment on Davidson Avenue, in the Bronx, the one with the sealed-up dumbwaiter, inhaling the same warm, homey smells of sizzling onions, sweet cinnamon, and toasted poppy seeds, from the Rosh Hashanah brisket, tsimmes, and honey cookies she used to cook in the old white Formica kitchen.

Was the food the same—or the grandmothers? Probably a little of both. Jewish cooking is, after all, "bubbe cuisine," created by grandmothers and served up family-style. The most festive—and delicious—meals are centered around home celebrations, whether with the immediate family at quiet

Sabbath dinners or the whole raucous extended *mishpocheh* at the Passover seder. And table ceremonies like dipping challah and apples in honey to ensure a sweet new year appear invented to engage the family and delight the children.

There are no trained chefs, educated on elegant, codified recipes, who prepare Jewish banquet dishes in royal kitchens or luxe restaurants. The best Jewish restaurants mimic fine Jewish home cooking—not the other way around.

This homeyness that informs every aspect of the cuisine, from the favored ingredients to the cooking techniques to the family-centered style of eating, is born of an ancient religion, deeply rooted in ritual and the rhythms of the natural world.

Take brisket and beef kibbe, for example. They are both carefully braised over gentle fires—one of the long, slow meat-cooking methods, like stewing, oven- or pan-roasting, that have for centuries warmed Jewish kitchens from Beirut to Bialystok and the Bronx.

Such cooking methods are no accident. Jewish dietary laws require that meat be soaked and salted to remove the blood so it no longer resembles the flesh of a live animal. By tradition, it is usually cooked well-done enough that no trace of blood remains visible. For the blood of any being is sacred to God: "Ye shall eat the blood of no matter of flesh" (Leviticus 17:14).

Kashrut, the dietary laws, also proscribe eating—in addition to pork, rabbit, and any other animal that does not chew its cud and have split hooves—many of the tender cuts of kosher animals, like cows and lamb. Because Jacob had injured his thigh during his fight with the angel (Genesis 32:33), meat from the hindquarters, like filet mignon, sirloin, and leg of lamb, is taboo, unless the sciatic nerve is removed first—a difficult and expensive process. (Some non-Western Jews do remove the sciatic nerve from animals: in Kaifeng, China, where a flourishing community of Jews settled in the tenth century, Jews were called *Tiao Kia Kisou*, "sect which extracts the sinews.") So long, patient simmering is also necessary to tenderize the tougher cuts that are permissible.

And the word "gefilte" may belong to Eastern European Jews, but the process of separating fish from its bones and grinding it up is common to much of Jewry. On Sabbath and religious holidays, Jews are not permitted to work. For some, meticulously removing the flesh from tiny fish bones was a labor that swallowed up some of the joy of the holy day. And yet, one is encouraged to eat fish on these days as it is a symbol of fruitfulness and a mystical means to taste a bit of Paradise and ward off the evil eye. The solution: ground fish balls, which also stretch the supply of fish and can be prepared in advance.

Foods that can be readied ahead characterize much of Jewish cookery. Since Jews are not permitted to kindle fires on the Sabbath, but are exhorted to feast then, foods like kugels, tagines (Moroccan stewlike dishes), and yes, curries, are fixed in advance, and then simply heated through, or like cholents and dafinas, slow-cooked overnight, on previously lit fires. And from diverse Jewish communities come imaginative cold dishes, especially well-seasoned fish, developed with the injunction against Sabbath cooking in mind. Because no last-minute cooking is permitted, the whole family can sit down together to eat.

An ancient people, Jews have a taste for ancient foods. The onions and garlic that nourished the Hebrew slaves in Egypt are relished today by Jews everywhere. Those well-done meat dishes would lie leaden on the tongue without garlic, roasted or sautéed, and crisply browned or gently stewed onions to provide the requisite aromatic lift.

The pomegranates that quenched the thirst of the Israelites as they wandered forty years in the desert are still sought out by Jews regardless of how difficult they are to find in their new homelands, especially for the fall holidays, when the fruit is at its peak. And biblical ingredients like lamb, figs, dates, barley, lentils, almonds, and pistachios still locate a dish as Jewish for many.

Dairy- and grain-intensive foods are central to the Jewish culinary universe. Dairy or vegetarian meals assume more significance when obtaining meat slaughtered according to kashrut has proven difficult. The legendary beauty Queen Esther, wife of the Persian King Ahasuerus, relied on legumes like chickpeas and lentils for sustenance, since no kosher meat was available at the court where the wicked Haman held sway. And during the Inquisition, when it would have been perilous for them to kosher their meat, many "secret" Jews depended on eggs and dairy for protein.

The biblical injunction "a kid must not be seethed in its mother's milk" means that meat and dairy (any food containing milk or milk products, including butter and cheese) may never be eaten at the same meal—and observant Jews wait one, three, or six hours (depending on local custom) after eating any meat before swallowing a dairy product. (There is no waiting period, however, between eating dairy— except for hard cheeses—and subsequently eating meat. One must simply cleanse the palate with a drink or a piece of bread.) When dairy foods are eaten, like blintzes slicked with rich sour cream, cheesy fritadas, and creamy puddings—they become the focus of the meal, rather than simply flavoring adjuncts to the meat dishes.

Although many dishes derived from humble foods like kasha and lentils, even the poorest Jewish kitchens had exotic sweet-smelling spices available—usually cinnamon, cloves, and nutmeg at least— because they were integral to the Saturday night Havdalah ceremony, evoking the fragrance of the hereafter as Queen Sabbath is escorted out. (The need for special spices, fruits, and nuts for ceremonial use, like Havdalah, Passover haroset, and the Sukkot bouquet, is one reason Jews became important international traders in such foodstuffs.) Cinnamon and other aromatic spices are frequently called for in both Ashkenazi and Sephardi savory and sweet recipes.

The spice of Sabbath became a metaphor for its unique flavor, and preparing especially fragrant and sapid foods was a means of honoring the festive days. Glistening fresh fish and vegetables just plucked from the garden need little adornment, but foods prepared ahead for a holiday and either kept heated or eaten chilled require exuberant seasoning to make them sparkle. Some Jews added sweetening, some spicy or savory flavoring. And many, in disparate communities from Morocco and Italy to

Germany and Poland, added both. After all, the taste for sweet and sour or sweet and savory has potent resonance for a people whose every joy is tinged with bittersweet: whose wedding laughter is momentarily shattered by the traditional breaking glass, who punctuate their most joyous festivals with poignant allusions to their enemies' sorrows, and their own.

The Jewish kitchen revolves around the Sabbath and the seasonal cycle of holidays. Though the specifics of a dish may differ, according to local availability of ingredients, cooking traditions, and customs, all foods prepared for holidays and other life-cycle events speak to the same ritual and symbolic concerns. Ashkenazi Jews may fry latkes in oil, and Israelis their *sufganiyot,* jelly doughnuts, but both foods are inspirited with the miracle of the oil that burned in the holy lamp for eight days at Hanukkah. Although the permissible foods vary from community to community, all Jews have a unique Passover cuisine rooted in the absence of leavening to commemorate the unleavened bread the Hebrews ate during their hasty exodus from Egypt.

Everyday fare too resonates with that abiding Jewish love for symbolism. "Soul food" in its most basic sense, Jewish dishes are routinely used to explain and reinforce the mysteries of life. Most Jews in mourning commonly eat round foods, such as eggs, bagels, and lentils, which reflect the eternal cycle of life. Symbolic of abundance, stuffed dishes, whether made from grape leaves or cabbage, are especially enjoyed at harvest time.

Are these foods to be appreciated only by Jews involved in their traditions or nostalgic for their people and their past? Or would they intrigue other food lovers too?

Many people, when they learned the subject of this book, reacted with smug smiles and suppressed giggles. And those were the polite ones.

Partly, of course, such responses are a telling commentary on the deteriorated quality of contemporary Jewish cooking. But more to the point, I think, is what they reveal about the stereotyped perception of Jewishness.

Can you be too Jewish to be beautiful? In her provocative silkscreen *Four Barbras,* from *The Jackie Series,* Deborah Kass answers the question even as she asks it. Kass's work, part of the controversial exhibit "Too Jewish? Challenging Traditional Identities" at The Jewish Museum, New York, March to July 1996, proudly celebrated Barbra Streisand's frankly ethnic face as transcendent cultural icon, akin to Jacqueline Kennedy Onassis, in the format the artist borrowed from Andy Warhol's famous series.

But it was rare until recently for artists to celebrate their Jewishness in their work. In aesthetics, Jews strove for the universal; Jewish beauty was assimilationist. To a child growing up in the 1950s and '60s, "Oh, you don't look Jewish," was a compliment more often than not, whether delivered by Jews or non-Jews: it meant you were pretty. And by inference, looking Jewish meant you were not.

The same aesthetics applied to food. My mother, a superb, imaginative cook, could not help but leave her imprint on the Jewish food she prepared for our everyday and Jewish holiday tables. But her real flights of fancy were reserved for the Italian meals she whipped up for company or other special occasions. Jewish food was, well, too *Jewish* to be beautiful.

Like many American Jews who came of age while actively involved in the civil rights movement, I began to appreciate my own roots as I explored other minority cultures. Not only were these diverse ethnic groups beautiful, so was mine: we too were a vivid patch in the exciting crazy-quilt of multiculturalism.

I was not alone. Today Jewish chefs around the country express their Jewishness in their dishes, challenging the marginalized, exclusionary concept of Jewish food as nongourmet; that is, dreary and unrefined.

The culture serves as inspiration, however, not imprisonment. For only by rethinking, questioning, and reinventing—in the best midrashic tradition—can we guarantee it will remain meaningful to us.

Jews have always believed, in a very real sense, that you are what you eat: foods remain forever in our bodies, transformed into blood, brains, heart, and even soul. More than mere corporal nourishment, the proper food keeps both body and soul healthy. The physical becomes the spiritual, as we approach God through eating, worshiping at this unique altar, the table.

For food is truly magical. Through the simple act of eating, Jews partake of a mystical but very real communion with their families, their traditions, and the world itself. In improvising in this culinary universe, I have varied the ingredients and experimented with different styles, but always the essential—the magic—endures.

N O T E S   T O   T H E   C O O K

Good cooks are good eaters. Excited by delicious food, they keep sampling and adjusting their work until that charmed moment when flavors, texture, temperature, and appearance coalesce and, like the girl with the golden tresses said, "it tastes just right."

Throughout this book I give approximate cooking times for various stages in a recipe. But ultimately, these are only guidelines. The exact time it will take you to caramelize onions, for instance, will depend on many factors: the onions themselves (how much moisture and natural sugar they contain, how finely you have cut them); the type and size of the pan; the degree and kind of heat you are using; other ingredients, like salt, you may have added; as well as your own personal preferences. In the end you decide whether the onions are sweetly browned enough.

By all means, adjust the seasonings to suit your ingredients and your tastebuds. Recently I prepared Honeyed Quince–Apple Blintzes (page 252), using fruit from the fragrant centerpiece that had graced my table for a couple of weeks. The fruit looked ripe and fresh and bore no telltale signs of discoloration. Yet it tasted singularly dull and lackluster with the seasoning called for in the recipe, quantities that, the six or seven times I had previously made the blintzes, had always produced beautifully flavored fruit. Perhaps I had let the quinces and apples languish too long, unchilled, in my steam-heated apartment. Perhaps they were insipid to begin with. I should have tasted the raw fruit first. Luckily, I did sample the cooked fruit before I filled the blintzes, and by adding another quarter teaspoon or so of cinnamon and vanilla, an extra teaspoon or two of honey and a squeeze of lemon, I was able to revive the tired flavor.

Use these recipes as departure points for your own explorations, changing flavorings or making other substitutions as your tastes and the seasons dictate. Often suggestions for variations are given in the "Cook's Note" at the end of a recipe. If a dish is not in your food memory—if you are not sure what it is supposed to taste like—use the descriptions and your mind's tongue to determine what you want it to taste like when you begin experimenting.

A lot of Jewish cooking can be rather filling for contemporary tastes. Many Ashkenazi dishes are based on dairy (sour cream, butter, and cream cheese), heavy starches, and rich meats. Sephardi food, while lighter in general, relies on generous quantities of oil. And both cuisines make lavish use of eggs.

I have reduced unnecessary amounts of oil in recipes, I trim off the meat fat, and thoroughly skim soups and gravies (detailed instructions for removing fat from gravies is given in the introduction to "Meats and Poultry"). But many recipes frequently call for real butter, real sour cream, whole milk, and other rich foodstuffs—not substitutions.

Certainly, you are not going to eat blintzes and brisket every day. And when you do serve them, round out the meal with fresh salads, seasonal vegetables, and fruit (either a light compote or beautiful uncooked fruit, artfully arranged on dessert plates). For centuries, Jews ate their Saturday lunch cholent (a heavy, meat-and-starch meal-in-a-pot) accompanied by a starchy kugel, or pudding. They probably had no choice, given the scarcity of other foods, especially vegetables. But we do. To best enjoy a rich cholent or *dafina* (the Sephardi equivalent), eat it with a salad of fresh-tasting tart and bitter greens. (The suggested menus for holidays and life-cycle events will further assist you in planning meals.)

Here are some ways to "lighten up" in the kitchen:
• Fresh fruit, barely cooked and sweetened, adds a flavorful burst to the top of rich noodle puddings and as filling for blintzes. Fresh fruit sauces, like Fresh Raspberry Applesauce (page 178) or Fresh Persimmon Sauce (page 282), provide a lighthearted but full-flavored counterpoint to fried latkes, blintzes, and brisket.

• Dried fruit, like tart apricots, dates, and especially prunes, round out flavors in recipes and contribute body to a variety of foods, including soups and sauces.

• Intense fat-free fruit concentrates (such as pomegranate molasses and temerhindi, or tamarind) and full-bodied fruit juices, like apple-cranberry and prune, reduced over high heat to deepen their flavors, add clean-tasting zest and decrease reliance on added sugars.

- Fruits and vegetables, soft-cooked or pureed, can fill out soups, gravies, and sauces. And they can be used to replace butter and eggs, lightening and enriching pâtés and grains. I substitute some pureed caramelized onion for part of the hard-boiled egg in a chopped liver variation, and use meltingly tender cubes of eggplant instead of gobs of butter to moisten kasha.

- Reduce, reduce, reduce soups, sauces, and gravies to concentrate flavors and thicken them.

- Vary the textures in a dish to create the impression of lightness. For example, I combine both sautéed and crisp raw onions in the Chopped Chicken Liver recipes (pages 47 and 51) and Chopped Eggs and Onions (page 312). To make latkes, I grate most of the potatoes coarsely, ensuring a crunchy crust; I puree the remainder for a creamy interior.

H O W   T O   U S E   T H I S   B O O K

The Gefilte Variations is divided into two parts. The first, organized by menu category, features techniques and imaginative renditions of year-round Jewish favorites, like Marinated Brisket with Chestnuts; Potato-Onion Kreplach, Pot Sticker Style; and Peach-Raspberry Blintzes.

The second section offers new takes on holiday standards as well as international Jewish dishes that are particularly appropriate for holiday tables: Double Ginger–Caramelized Pear Noodle Kugel to break the Yom Kippur fast, Cheese Latkes with Fresh Persimmon Sauce to celebrate Hanukkah. Additional recipes from the first section that make excellent holiday matches are cross-referenced.

I've devised a variety of suggested menus for holidays (including several nonmeat meals) and life-cycle celebrations, like the bar/bat mitzvah. Arranging these foods (many of them quite rich and filling) into appealing, well-balanced meals requires a graceful tango between, on the one hand, the exigencies of Jewish traditions, and on the other, contemporary demands for lighter, fresher tastes. To round out these menus, I have added some simple dishes for which no recipe is given. These straightforward foods—mostly salads and vegetables—are in the repertoire of most home cooks or easily prepared from the descriptions given. Feel free to supplement the menus with your own favorite dishes. And after you become familiar with the cuisine, you will find it easy to compose delectable menus of your own.

Because the dietary laws proscribe eating foods containing meat or meat products with foods containing milk or its derivatives, I have designated recipes as meat, dairy, or pareve. (Pareve foods, considered "neutral," contain neither meat nor dairy and so may be eaten with either, and are suitable for vegetarian diets. However, though dairy-free, many pareve foods include eggs, so vegans will need to check the ingredients list.) If a recipe may be categorized in more than one way, depending on your choice of ingredients (for example, butter instead of margarine, chicken versus vegetable broth), it bears all possible labels.

PANTRY AND PROCEDURES

MATZOH   (For a fuller discussion of matzoh, other varieties around the world, and more ways to use it, including as a flavored, toasted flatbread, see "Passover," page 305, and Toasted Za'atar Matzohs, page 54.)

The regular matzoh that Jews are commanded to eat on Passover instead of bread is a thin, crisp cracker made simply of wheat flour (there is a special ritually prepared oat variety for those who are wheat-intolerant) and water—no yeast or other leavening and no salt. To prevent fermentation, the entire preparation, from mixing flour and water to baking the matzoh, should take no more than eighteen minutes. According to Eve Jochnowitz, a culinary historian who has done extensive research on the subject, matzoh is currently sold in many supermarkets in Poland—despite the fact that few Jews have remained there since the Holocaust. The Jewish cracker is marketed there as a pure and wholesome health and diet food for everyone.

Plain matzoh *is* pure and elemental, wheaty-tasting without the spongy, yeasty quality of bread or the flavorings or additives of crackers, and is an ideal substitute for these starches in recipes. I use matzoh not only in Passover recipes, but year-round, for matzoh brie, in some stuffings and kugels, and to make home-ground matzoh crumbs for crunchy coatings.

Why grind your own matzoh when perfectly acceptable matzoh meal is available in most supermarkets? Packaged matzoh meal is very finely ground, perfect for fluffy matzoh balls, meat loaf, latkes, and most kugels. But if you want a coarse, crumbly topping, particularly one combined with butter or oil and toasted until golden and crunchy, you need to grind your own. And for crumb coatings, I find texture and flavor are superior when the crumbs are not ground uniformly. Also, there are times when fresh matzoh meal is not available, when you know that matzoh meal has been sitting on the grocer's shelf—or yours—for far too long.

Then there are the flavored matzoh, especially egg matzoh: terrific, but unavailable ground unless you do it yourself.

To make matzoh crumbs and homemade matzoh meal: Whirl matzoh in a blender or food processor using the pulse motion until desired texture is achieved. A medium grind, with a slightly uneven texture, is best for crumb coatings. Blend to the texture of sand for matzoh meal with a powdery consistency (and, if necessary, rub the fine crumbs through a sieve to remove any remaining coarse pieces).

25

To toast matzoh crumbs or matzoh meal: Preheat the oven to 350°F. In a baking pan, melt some butter, warm a little olive oil, or use a combination of both. Add matzoh crumbs or meal, season to taste with salt and pepper, toss to combine, and spread out in an even layer. Toast in the oven until fragrant and golden, about 15 to 20 minutes, stirring every once in a while to redistribute the oil and prevent burning. Stir in other seasonings, if you like: spices and herbs (such as paprika, cumin, rosemary, or thyme), minced garlic, grated cheese (about 2 to 3 tablespoons of Parmesan, hard cheddar, or other well-flavored variety for every cup of matzoh crumbs or meal).

Flavored matzoh (including egg, whole wheat, and egg and onion, etc.): Check the ingredients on the package. Some contain zesty seasonings like onion or garlic and are excellent served as crackers or used in cooking, as flavorful crumbs or savory stuffing. Egg matzoh, made simply of flour, egg yolks, and apple cider, is superb as a cracker (divine with cream cheese) or matzoh brie. And it makes delicious crumbs—the slight sweetness from the cider provides an almost caramelized edge to the crumbs when they are toasted or fried.

But other flavored matzoh contain positively bizarre or inappropriate ingredients, like malt, rye, white and brown sugar, as well as additives and preservatives. So read the labels carefully.

Availability and storage: Plain and several flavored kinds are available year-round in most supermarkets. (Although during Passover many Jews enjoy flavored matzoh, like the egg and whole wheat varieties, which have been produced under stringent rabbinic supervision, strictly Orthodox Ashkenazi Jews eat only plain matzoh on Passover, reserving the flavored kinds for the rest of the year.)

Egg matzoh can usually be found for only a couple of months close to Passover. It sells out quickly and manufacturers often don't make more until the next season. I buy several extra boxes when I find them and store them for later use.

Matzoh meal can usually be purchased year-round. In January or February, freshly produced matzoh meal for Passover makes its appearance in supermarkets. But if you find a box in December stamped for Passover use, it's probably almost a year old and you might consider grinding your own from fresh matzoh.

Although matzoh and matzoh meal are generally not made with added oil (some flavored varieties might be), there is, of course, oil in the flour itself, which can turn rancid and musty after prolonged exposure to air. And moisture can make matzoh soggy. As with preservative-free crackers and bread crumbs, both matzoh and matzoh meal must be well wrapped to keep them from going stale. Unless you will be using up an opened box of matzoh within four or five days (fewer in very humid areas), it's a good idea to store the matzoh in an airtight plastic container or resealable plastic bag instead of the cardboard box it comes in. Don't leave a box of matzoh meal in the pantry, its perforation seal pushed open and left yawning. Keep it tightly closed in an airtight glass jar or plastic container, and store in the refrigerator, especially if it is not used on a regular basis. And if you trot out that same box of meal for two or three short appearances a year, consider keeping it in the freezer.

Let your nose be your guide in determining freshness: like crackers, matzoh and matzoh meal should smell fresh and wheaty. Discard any that smell musty, stale, or off. If matzohs have become soggy, you can recrisp them in the oven at 350°F for a few minutes. And read the Passover section about toasting matzoh for superb, fresh-from-the-oven flavor.

SCHMALTZ, OLIVE OIL, BUTTER, AND OTHER FATS

> This part of Fifth Avenue always seemed fat to him, fat
> and prosperous: like chicken *schmaltz.*
> — HENRY ROTH, *MERCY OF A RUDE STREAM*

More, perhaps, than they longed for the pomegranates, the dates, and the figs, the Jews of Central and Eastern Europe missed the olives and the rich, green-gold oil made from them in *eretz* Israel. In Europe, olive oil was expensive to import; when the Jews could buy it, they reserved it for ritual lamps or medicinal purposes.

For their daily cooking needs, they adopted the butter of their Gentile neighbors for dairy meals, and they turned to schmaltz, fat, rendered from geese or chickens and flavored with onions, for meat meals.

My grandmother served schmaltz often when I was little—sometimes spread thick as butter on corn-rye bread with *griebenes* (the bits of crackling skin and onions formed in rendering the fat) and coarse salt. But as she grew older and more concerned with cholesterol counts, she substituted corn oil, often disguised with onion flavoring to better resemble the golden schmaltz she adored. Myself, I find corn oil a rather dowdy replacement for schmaltz. I prefer the lush yet grassy-clean taste of intensely aromatic extra-virgin olive oil. *Plus ça change. . . .*

There are, however, certain foods in the Ashkenazi kitchen that were really developed for schmaltz, that rely on it not just for its rich flavor, redolent of onions and poultry, but for its texture as well: solid when chilled, semi-solid at room temperature. Because it is never completely liquid, like oil, schmaltz, like butter, combines differently with foods than oil does. Matzoh meal mixed with schmaltz forms clumps, while matzoh meal and oil crumble together. A dough made with schmaltz produces fluffier and more tender matzoh balls than one made with oil. (Butter too makes a wonderful matzoh ball, scrumptious in dairy or pareve soups—see Fresh Borscht with Dilled Onion-Butter Matzoh Balls, page 75).

So I make a flavorful fat with some texture that I use to prepare matzoh balls and other dumplings, and often to enrich chopped liver, chopped eggs and onions, grated black radish, and grains like kasha. Do *not* use it for sautéing foods; this schmaltz contains too much water because of the pureed onions.

OLIVE OIL SCHMALTZ

½ pound onion, finely chopped (2 cups)
¾ teaspoon salt
¼ cup olive oil

1. In a strainer, toss the onions with the salt. Cover them with a paper towel and weight down with a bowl or plate topped with a heavy object, like a large can of tomatoes. Let the onions drain for at least 30 minutes, tossing them occasionally. Place the onions in fresh paper toweling or a clean kitchen towel and squeeze out as much liquid as possible.

2. Warm the oil in a heavy 8- or 9-inch skillet. Add the onions and cook, uncovered, over the very lowest heat. As their moisture evaporates, the onions will shrink considerably and the ever-deepening gold oil will appear to increase. Stir occasionally, spreading the onions out in the skillet and making sure that they do not stick or color past gold. After cooking for 60 to 75 minutes, they should be very soft and have exuded most of their liquid. Let the mixture cool slightly, then scrape all the onions and oil into a blender (a food processor won't work well here).

3. Blend to emulsify the ingredients, stopping to scrape down the contents of the blender when necessary. Continue blending until you have a smooth, rich puree.

4. Store tightly covered in the refrigerator. It will thicken and become more "schmaltz"-like when chilled. It will keep for at least 3 to 5 days.

YIELD: About ⅔ cup

For frying foods well-seasoned with onions, garlic, or herbs, like potato latkes (pancakes), I use a good-quality olive oil. It doesn't taste like the traditional schmaltz, but like schmaltz, it does have a rich, flavorful taste that enhances foods. And, after all, it was olive oil that burned in the lamp for eight days in the Temple—not chicken fat. In dishes where the taste of olive oil is important, as in the Green Olive Sauce (page 60), I use an excellent-quality extra-virgin oil.

I also use other fine vegetable and nut oils: the toasty, popcorn flavor of unrefined corn oil for a more nuanced mamaliga (Romanian cornmeal mush), but also marvelous for American corn bread and muffins; a delicate sunflower or sesame oil when a light touch is required in a nondairy dish; or even better, avocado oil, which imparts a wonderful buttery taste to food and is excellent for frying. To prevent butter from burning at high temperatures, I often combine it with a little avocado oil. (Most people think the cholesterol content of avocado oil is astronomical. They are wrong: its cholesterol content is zero. Its price, however, can be astronomical.)

Pricey—but worth it—fragrant nut oils, like walnut or hazelnut, make stellar salad dressings and are particularly appealing in baking with nondairy ingredients, when using butter would render the dish inappropriate for a meat meal.

Because I don't use these delicate oils as frequently as I do olive oil, after opening, I store them tightly sealed in the refrigerator, where they will keep for months. Any cloudiness or congealing disappears when the oil returns to room temperature. These oils are available in health food and specialty shops, as well as many well-stocked supermarkets.

For dairy dishes, I always use sweet (unsalted) butter. Despite the ads, no margarine will ever taste as good as pure butter. Besides, margarine contains as many calories as butter, and processing techniques and preservatives render any benefits garnered from the reduced cholesterol levels questionable at best.

SOUR CREAM, YOGURT CREAM, AND LABNEH

> And her face always looked strained and worried,
> as if her shipload of sour cream had just sunk.
>
> —I. L. PERETZ, "IN THE MAIL COACH"

Slathered on blintzes and onion-laced herring, spooned over strawberries, whisked into fruit soup—Jewish food can be extravagant with thick, luscious sour cream.

Delicious? Yes. Fattening? Absolutely. But real sour cream is a sensational splurge.

And there are alternatives.

You *can* substitute reduced-fat sour cream. But personally, I tend to stay away from most such products—either the taste itself is strange or the ingredients list contains too many weird, unwholesome additives. I'd rather eat the real stuff, just less frequently. And between-times, I use the Sephardi counterpart made of drained yogurt, sometimes referred to as yogurt cheese, here called yogurt cream.

Many cookbooks claim plain yogurt is a good alternative to sour cream. It is not: it's watery and flat-tasting. But when most of the liquid whey is removed, the sweet, tangy flavors become more concentrated and the yogurt develops more body. Then even plain low- and nonfat yogurt can taste rather creamy and make a perfectly acceptable substitute for sour cream where fat is not essential to the dish. And sometimes the tart clean taste of yogurt cream actually works better than sour cream in a dish, such as Sautéed Chive Mamaliga with Feta-Yogurt Cream (page 156).

Labneh, Middle Eastern drained yogurt, usually made from whole milk or cream, is a sensuous treat. The most delicious *labneh* I ever tasted was made by a Palestinian New Yorker, who used equal parts of half-and-half (or light cream) and whole milk. Eating it was bliss. Prepared *labneh* can be bought in Middle Eastern markets, many specialty stores, and supermarkets. Substitute it for either sour cream or yogurt cream in any recipe.

For a rich-tasting yogurt cream, use whole-milk yogurt. Or for the best of the Ashkenazi and Sephardi worlds, stir a spoonful or two of sour cream into thick yogurt cream made from whole or low-fat milk.

To prepare yogurt cream: Line a strainer or colander with uncolored paper towels or a double thickness of cheesecloth. Or place a coffee filter in the drip funnel of a coffeemaker like Melitta or Chemex. Spoon in whole, low-, or nonfat yogurt. Set strainer, colander, or funnel over a bowl or cup to catch the liquid whey, and let drain in a cool place until the yogurt is as thick and creamy as desired, from 30 minutes to 2 hours, or more. (One quart, 4 cups, of yogurt will yield about 2 cups of yogurt cream.)

Tangy yogurt cream lends itself to many seasonings: honey or maple syrup and finely chopped dates, vanilla, or fragrant spices for a sweet taste; garlic mashed to a paste with salt, dried mint, fresh dill, etc., for a fresh, savory flavor.

If you allow the yogurt to continue to drain for about 24 hours, it becomes a wonderful soft yogurt cheese. Season the cheese with a few drops of extra-virgin olive oil, salt, and either garlic or fresh herbs or both.

Store covered in the refrigerator for up to one week.

WONTON WRAPPERS   When I first began buying wonton wrappers in New York City's China-town, I noticed a kosher seal on several brands. Apparently, using paper-thin wonton wrappers to make kreplach was not a novel idea. But it is a delicious one, an elegant, easy, inexpensive timesaver. And even if I had time enough to make my own dough, I doubt it would turn out as delicate and thin as these egg-enriched little pasta squares.

If you can't find wonton wrappers in Asian stores, look for them in health-food and specialty stores and most supermarkets (often they are kept in the refrigerated section of the produce department). The non-Asian ones may be somewhat thicker and less delicate, but they too will work well as kreplach wrappers.

To prepare wonton kreplach: Thaw wonton wrappers if frozen and bring to room temperature. These fragile little squares dry out easily, so keep them covered with plastic wrap or a slightly dampened kitchen towel. Remove wrappers as needed, leaving the rest covered to prevent cracking and drying.

Prepare an egg wash: in a small bowl, beat an egg with 1 teaspoon of water. (You can use plain water to seal the kreplach, but the egg creates a more permanent "glue.")

Put a wrapper on a lightly floured surface. Mound 1 heaping teaspoon of filling in the center of the wrapper. Dip your finger in the egg wash and "paint" the edges all around the filling. Or use a small pastry brush to paint. Fold the krepl (singular of kreplach) in half by pulling one corner of the square over to the opposite corner, forming a triangle. Carefully press down all around the filling to force out all the air and seal the edges firmly. It's important to push out the air, otherwise the krepl may fill up with water as it is being poached. Trim away any excess dough around the filling with a sharp knife. Or curl the two opposite corners together, dab with egg wash, and pinch tightly closed.

You can also make larger kreplach, as called for in Poached Prune Kreplach with Honeyed Cream and Pecans (page 298). Place 1 heaping tablespoon of filling in the center of a wrapper, paint the edges with egg wash, and cover with a second wrapper. Press out air, seal, and trim. Or trim off the excess dough using cookie cutters in fanciful shapes—great fun to do with children.

Place filled kreplach on a dry kitchen towel and cover with plastic wrap. Let them rest for about 15 to 20 minutes so the egg wash seal can dry (turn them occasionally).

To poach, bring a large, wide pot of salted water to a gentle boil. Add the kreplach, in batches as necessary, and cook for 3 to 7 minutes, depending on the brand of wrapper you are using, or until they float to the surface and are tender. Never let the kreplach boil rapidly: they will fill with water or explode, or both! And don't try to save time by cooking the kreplach in soup—inevitably one will rupture and ruin your broth.

Use a skimmer to transfer the kreplach as they are done to a dry kitchen towel or paper towels to drain briefly. They are too fragile to be dumped into a colander. If you aren't serving them soon, moisten them with a little broth, sauce, butter, or oil, and keep them warm until needed.

After they are poached, kreplach can be served in soup, or sautéed or baked with butter or oil. For an unusual preparation, make them pot sticker–style (follow the instructions for Potato-Onion Kreplach, Pot Sticker Style, page 152).

I find it is easier to stuff kreplach with a filling that has been chilled: it is firmer and less runny. Use the fillings in this book to start, then improvise some of your own. Try the cheese blintz filling and its savory variation—or any of the fruit blintz fillings. Ground liver works well, as does kasha, or even mashed chickpeas or pumpkin sauced with yogurt cream, crushed garlic, mint, and olive oil. And don't forget your refrigerator full of leftovers.

Storing the wrappers: Fresh wonton wrappers tend to dry out quickly after only a few days in the refrigerator, so make sure they are very well sealed. Wonton wrappers can be frozen in airtight packages for about two to three months (after that, they tend to dry out); don't refreeze them.

POMEGRANATE MOLASSES AND TEMERHINDI, OR OURT I am crazy about pomegranate molasses (sometimes called pomegranate concentrate or syrup), the thick, tangy-sweet concentrate of reduced pomegranate juice, and usually sugar and lemon juice. It has a myriad of uses in the kitchen, from barbecue sauces, marinades, and gravies, to flavoring dips like hummus and even guacamole. I call for it in several recipes, and you'll find it in Middle Eastern markets and some specialty stores. Once opened, it should be stored tightly covered in the refrigerator, where it will keep almost indefinitely. (For more on pomegranate molasses, see Spiced Pomegranate Molasses Applesauce, page 180.)

Temerhindi, also known as *ourt,* a concentrate of tamarind, lemon juice, and sugar, is usually prepared at home by Middle Eastern Jews in a rather time-consuming process. It is available ready-made at Middle Eastern Jewish groceries. *Temerhindi* is delectably tart and sweet, like pomegranate molasses, which makes a good substitute for it. If neither is available, a fair stand-in can be made by boiling together a mixture of 1 part prune butter (lekvar), 1 part sugar, and 2 parts lemon juice until it has the consistency of thick tomato sauce. In a pinch, mix equal parts of lekvar and apricot butter with a bit of lemon juice and simmer together for a few minutes until well combined.

SALT   I use kosher salt for cooking and at table. I prefer its pure, clean flavor and coarse texture. Because of its large crystals, it doesn't melt into foods, and is essential for certain recipes, like curing Pastrami-Style Salmon (page 250), topping the Onion-Crusted Light Potato Kugel (page 169), or salting eggplant. But if it is not specified in a recipe, feel free to substitute your own favorite salt, bearing in mind that kosher salt is somewhat milder than most other kinds.

A note on salting: I usually add salt at several stages in a recipe. I find it flavors the food better than when added all at once at the conclusion of the cooking. And I usually wind up adding less salt in all.

Even humble kitchens had exotic, sweet-smelling spices necessary for the Saturday night Havdalah ceremony. (Silver spice container. Turkey, 19th century.)

BREAKFASTS AND BRUNCHES

For most Americans, a "Jewish Breakfast" conjures up visions of bagels—or even better, hot oniony bialys—and rich cream cheese, accompanied by a panoply of smoked fish, from paper-sheer slices of lox to whitefish salads.

But some mornings want the gentle aromas of warm, comforting foods to begin the day. In this chapter, I've included several recipes for matzoh brie, a delicious, homey blend of matzoh and eggs that is endlessly variable, and a fruit-filled challah French toast.

Scattered throughout the book are other wonderful breakfast and brunch ideas, like delicate cheese latkes with fresh persimmon sauce and luscious blintzes. They are listed below.

OTHER BREAKFAST AND BRUNCH SUGGESTIONS

Fruit and Cheese Blintz Recipes (check Index)
Sorrel-Onion Noodle Kugel (page 148)
Spinach-Cheese Squares (page 150)
Sautéed Chive Mamaliga (page 156; see variations with cheddar and syrup)
Rich Noodle Kugel Baked with Fresh Plums and Nectarines (page 186)
Roasted Apple–Walnut Noodle Kugel (page 189; dairy version)
Peach-Buttermilk Kugel (page 191)
Double Ginger–Caramelized Pear Noodle Kugel (page 254)
Cheese Latkes with Fresh Persimmon Sauce (page 282)
Black Grape, Goat Cheese, and Noodle Latkes with Fragrant Honey (page 286)
Poached Prune Kreplach with Honeyed Cream and Pecans (page 298)
Huevos Haminados (page 314)
Turkish Silken Rice Pudding with Fresh Raspberry Sauce (page 357)

MAKING MATZOH BRIE

You can prepare matzoh brie in several different ways, from crisp French toast–style to fluffy matzoh omelets to batter fried as pancakes. Like most breakfast food mavens, matzoh brie lovers tend to claim there is only *one* correct way to make it (theirs, of course). But I have found that personal preferences aside, different flavorings are often better suited to one method of preparation than another: tender, delicate artichoke hearts, for example, are best savored in a matzoh brie that is light and fluffy, not thin and crisp.

All else being equal, my favorite is the combination matzoh brie, known as scrambled egg–style: a jumble of buttery crisp, well-flavored, chewy, and creamy egg-rich pieces—all in one mouthful.

When I merely want to soften the matzoh, I use cold water. Hot water leaches out the matzoh flavor. When I want a liquid, like apple juice, to impart flavor as well as soften, I often warm it first so it is better absorbed.

For crisp, French toast–style matzoh brie: Soak the matzoh in cold water just long enough to soften it, then gently but thoroughly press out the liquid with your hands, or place in a colander and press with the back of a spoon. Heat a generously greased, heavy, well-seasoned, preferably cast-iron, skillet, rather than a nonstick one. Add the matzoh all at once to the hot, sizzling pan, and spread it out in a thin layer. (If necessary, fry in batches: if you fry too much at once, it won't be crisp.) Fry over medium to medium-high heat until browned on the bottom. Now decide whether you want to keep the matzoh brie in one piece—it will be more attractive, certainly, but rather tricky to do, perhaps more trouble than this homey dish calls for. To keep the matzoh in one piece, try using two spatulas to carefully flip it. Or turn it like a frittata; that is, slide it out onto a platter, and then invert the platter over the skillet. Or cook it in batches in a smaller skillet, so it will be easier to flip. If looks don't count, simply cut it in half or in quarters and turn each piece using two spatulas.

For fried pancakelike matzoh brie: Soak the matzoh in cold water until it is quite soft, almost falling apart. Squeeze out as much liquid as you can with your hands, or place in a colander and press with the back of a spoon. Then stir in the eggs and beat well until the mixture is well combined. Drop the batter by heaping tablespoonfuls into the hot, greased skillet, flatten slightly with a spatula, and fry, flipping once, over medium to medium-high heat until browned on both sides.

For either fluffy or combination (scrambled egg–style) matzoh brie: Soak the matzoh in cold water until soft but not mushy, and gently press out moisture. The less liquid it holds, the more egg it will absorb and the fluffier it will be. Let the matzoh drink in the beaten eggs for about ten minutes or longer to produce the fluffiest matzoh brie. (The egg may or may not be completely absorbed by the matzoh— it will not matter.) Use either a large, heavy, well-seasoned skillet or a nonstick one (nonstick would be preferable if the matzoh brie contains dried fruit, such as raisins or prunes). Add the matzoh mixture all at once to the hot, greased pan. Spread it out evenly, and let it cook over medium heat until it is set and golden on the bottom. Now you have a choice: For attractive matzoh brie, resembling a frittata, turn the matzoh in one piece (see For crisp, French toast–style matzoh brie, page 34) or cut the matzoh brie into halves or quarters and then turn to brown each section. Cook until still fluffy inside or more well-done, as you prefer. Known as scrambled egg–style, your alternative is matzoh brie that is homelier, but more varied in texture and taste. After the bottom is set, break the matzoh brie into sections with the spatula. Keep lifting and turning the sections as they brown until you have a superb mélange of lightly crisp, chewy, moist, and fluffy pieces. Don't overcook the matzoh brie or it will be dry and hard.

SAVORY ARTICHOKE MATZOH BRIE

DAIRY OR PAREVE

And then there was the great classic, matzoh brie, pieces of matzoh soaked in milk, squeezed into a delectable mess, and fried to golden curls and flakes—one of the dishes that evokes piercing darts of nostalgia in every Jewish breast and stories of childhood Passovers complete with lightly drunken uncles.

—KATE SIMON, *BRONX PRIMITIVE*

Not just for Passover. Like matzoh balls and potato latkes, matzoh brie now makes regular appearances at the table year-round.

And not just for breakfast. One tony Manhattan restaurant features entrées of fluffy matzoh brie, chockablock with smoked salmon and sautéed sweet onions, fragrant with dill or layered with exotic wild mushrooms.

Like the best soul-satisfying starchy foods, matzoh brie is a chef's canvas, reflecting the image and nuances you choose: served like French toast, flavored with vanilla, cinnamon, or almond extract and doused with maple syrup; or frittata-style, sautéed with onions, mushrooms, and sapid tender vegetables like artichokes or asparagus. In fact, I often add some soaked and drained matzoh to frittata recipes—it stretches the number of eggs used, reducing that insistent egginess that spells breakfast to so many of us.

This well-seasoned matzoh brie is delicious any time of the day.

¾ pound onions, very thinly sliced (3 cups)

5 tablespoons olive oil, or 4 tablespoons olive oil and 1 tablespoon unsalted butter

1½ cups (about 4½ ounces) lightly precooked fresh or thawed frozen artichoke hearts, sliced (if using frozen artichokes, pat them dry first between layers of paper towels)

½ teaspoon minced fresh garlic (optional)

Salt and freshly ground black pepper

1 tablespoon balsamic vinegar or fine-quality red wine vinegar

4 whole plain or egg matzohs

5 large eggs

3 tablespoons finely chopped fresh dill, plus additional for garnish (also delightful and fresh-tasting with finely chopped mint leaves added to or in place of the dill)

1 teaspoon dried oregano

Optional accompaniments: yogurt cream (page 30) or yogurt, plain or mixed with some finely chopped scallions

---

1. In a 10- to 12-inch heavy skillet (preferably well-seasoned cast-iron or nonstick), sauté the onions in 2 tablespoons oil over medium heat, lifting and turning them occasionally, until soft and golden at the edges, 10–15 minutes. Add the artichokes and garlic, if using, and continue lifting and scraping for 5–7 minutes, or until the artichokes are cooked through and the onions are dotted with dark gold. Generously season with salt and pepper and add the vinegar. Cook for a few minutes over high heat, stirring, until the vinegar is completely evaporated and just a soft, acidic sparkle remains. Taste again for seasoning, then remove from the heat and let cool to room temperature.

2. Break the matzohs into 2- or 3-inch pieces and place in a bowl. Cover with cold water and soak for 5 minutes. Meanwhile, beat the eggs in a large bowl until light and foamy. Drain the matzoh in a colander, pressing out all the water with your hands or the back of a spoon, and add to the eggs. Add the dill and oregano, and season with salt and pepper to taste. Stir in the artichokes and onions and combine thoroughly.

3. Please read "Making Matzoh Brie" on page 34 and choose the cooking style you prefer. Wipe out the skillet thoroughly, add the remaining 3 tablespoons olive oil or 2 tablespoons oil and 1 tablespoon butter and heat until sizzling. Add the matzoh batter all at once, and cook either frittata-style (in one piece, waiting until the whole is golden brown before turning, or break it into sections with the spatula in order to turn it) or scrambled egg–style (lifting and turning pieces as different egg-soaked matzohs begin to set). Or drop it in by heaping tablespoonfuls, like pancakes, and fry over medium heat, until golden brown on the bottom, then turn and fry until done to taste on the other side (either golden and fluffy or more well-done and crisp).

4. Serve matzoh brie as soon as it is done, accompanied, if desired, by the yogurt cream or yogurt and sprinkled with additional fresh dill or mint.

YIELD: 4 servings

CINNAMON MATZOH BRIE WITH TOASTED PECANS AND WARM VANILLA MAPLE SYRUP

DAIRY

Homey matzoh brie takes so well to flavorful additions it's easy to turn this simple breakfast treat into something special. Here I bathe the matzoh in apple juice and sweet spices before frying, then serve it with warm, vanilla-scented maple syrup to accent the crunchy pecan studding. Other suggestions for improvisations follow.

3 whole plain or egg matzohs	3 tablespoons chopped toasted pecans
½ teaspoon ground cinnamon	2 tablespoons unsalted butter
⅛ teaspoon salt, or to taste	
1 cup apple juice	**VANILLA MAPLE SYRUP**
½ teaspoon vanilla extract	⅓ cup pure maple syrup
3 large eggs	½ teaspoon vanilla extract

1. Break the matzohs into small pieces in a bowl. Sprinkle with the cinnamon and salt.

2. Combine the apple juice and vanilla in a wide saucepan and boil over high heat until reduced to about ½ cup. Pour it over the matzohs and toss until all the liquid is absorbed. Beat the eggs until light and foamy and add to the matzoh mixture. Stir well and set aside for a few minutes to soak the matzohs. Stir in the pecans.

3. Make the syrup. Warm the maple syrup and vanilla in a small saucepan until heated through. Keep warm until ready to serve.

4. Please read "Making Matzoh Brie" on page 34 and choose the cooking style you prefer. In a 9- or 10-inch heavy skillet (nonstick works well here), heat the butter over medium heat until it sizzles. Add the matzoh batter, either dropping it in by heaping tablespoonfuls, like pancakes, or all at once, like an omelet or frittata. Fry until golden brown on the bottom, then turn and fry until done to taste on the other side: either golden and fluffy or more well done and crisp.

5. Serve at once, accompanied by the warm syrup.

YIELD: 2 servings

COOK'S NOTE: This simple, sweet matzoh brie should inspire some flavor variations of your own. For soaking, use warm milk or cream flavored with ¼ teaspoon almond extract, generous pinches of nutmeg and cloves, and honey or molasses to taste. Or dampen the matzohs instead with undiluted thawed orange juice concentrate, then serve the matzoh brie drizzled with orange blossom honey and a sprinkle of sliced toasted almonds. And sweet matzoh brie is delicious accompanied by lightly stewed fruits, like Fresh Raspberry Sauce (page 357), Fresh Berried Fruit Compote (page 355), or any of the fruit sauces on pages 175–183.

Man and woman with matzohs. Matzoh brie was originally served as a Passover treat. (Passover Haggadah, 15th century.)

MATZOH BRIE WITH PRUNES AND WINE

DAIRY

At the Terezin concentration camp, a vibrant but surreal cultural life was played out against the horrific backdrop of starvation, disease, and death. There, children teeming with lice watched performances of the opera *Brundibar,* and elderly Jews, bodies wracked with enteritis, scavenged for potato peels before attending lectures on theology.

A holding pen where Jews—largely from Moravia and Bohemia, as well as prominent Jews from Germany, Austria, and Western Europe—were kept before being sent to death camps, Terezin, or Theresienstadt, as the Germans renamed it, was held up to the world as a Ghetto Paradise, evidence of the Führer's decency to the Jews.

The cultural activity, extraordinarily prodigious because of the sheer density of talented artists and scholars imprisoned there, and feverishly intensified by the pervasive sense of mortality, was exploited by the Nazis, who trotted out the artists for a propaganda film before shipping them out to Auschwitz.

But, as Cara De Silva points out in her remarkable book, *In Memory's Kitchen,* such fierce cultural pursuits were also a form of revolt. As the Nazis tried to dehumanize them, the children produced poetry and art (later collected in a book, *I Never Saw Another Butterfly*). While the Nazis systematically blotted out their culture, the Jews of Terezin taught philosophy and circulated tens of thousands of books in a camp lending library. And they transcended their hunger by "cooking with the mouth"—talking constantly about food—and writing cookbooks. *In Memory's Kitchen,* "a memoir of life in Terezin, written in recipes," is not the only cookbook to come out of the concentration camps. According to Cara De Silva, there are five more that she knows of, and certainly others exist.

Cocooned in a warm Amtrak berth coming home from the Holocaust Museum in Washington, I read De Silva's description of one of these manuscripts, authored by Malka Zimmet, an inmate in a work sub-camp of Mauthausen. She mentioned a matzoh brie with wine and prunes, and I conjured up the dish and the vanished life that had savored it. I haven't seen the recipe yet—the manuscript is in Yad Vashem, Israel's repository of Holocaust research—so I made up my own version, cooked scrambled egg–style.

The interplay of tastes and textures—crisp, tender, and eggy matzoh pieces sandwiching tart-sweet juicy prunes—made this an instant family favorite. It is even better with a dollop of sour cream or yogurt, which underscores the richness of the prunes.

2 cups unsweetened apple juice, or 1 ¼ cups
   unsweetened Concord grape juice
1 ½ cups pitted prunes, halved or quartered if
   large
1 teaspoon vanilla extract
4 whole plain matzohs
1 teaspoon ground cinnamon
¼ teaspoon salt, or to taste

¾ cup traditional sweet Jewish wine or
   Concord grape juice
4 large eggs
1 ½ teaspoons brown sugar
3 tablespoons unsalted butter
Accompaniments: plain yogurt, yogurt cream
   (page 30), or sour cream; if additional sweetening is desired, maple syrup, preserves, or honey

1. Prepare the prunes. In a medium saucepan, boil the apple juice over high heat, until reduced to about 1 ¼ cups. (If using grape juice, warm it without reducing.) Add the prunes and vanilla and cook over medium heat until very tender, 10–15 minutes. You should have no more than about ¼ cup of liquid left in the pan; if needed, reduce the liquid for a few minutes over high heat.

2. Meanwhile, break the matzohs into small pieces in a bowl. Sprinkle with ½ teaspoon cinnamon and the salt. Pour the wine or grape juice over the matzohs and stir until all the liquid is absorbed. Beat the eggs until light and foamy and add to the matzoh mixture. Stir well and set aside for a few minutes to soak the matzohs (the eggs will not be totally absorbed). In a small bowl, combine the remaining ½ teaspoon cinnamon and the brown sugar and set aside.

3. Please read "Making Matzoh Brie" on page 34 and choose the cooking style you prefer. In a 10- to 12-inch heavy skillet (preferably nonstick—the sugar from the prunes will make this matzoh brie somewhat sticky) heat the butter until it sizzles. Add the matzoh and egg mixture all at once. As it begins to set and brown, break it up into largish pieces with a spatula, turning and browning them on both sides. Spoon the stewed prunes and their liquid over the cooked matzoh brie, as a topping. Or you can incorporate the prunes into the matzoh brie: when the matzoh brie is nearly browned, add the prunes and their liquid. Continue lifting and turning until all the matzoh pieces are golden brown and well combined with the prunes. If you prefer a fluffier matzoh brie, lightly fry the matzoh sections until just cooked through on all sides, adding the prunes about halfway through the cooking process.

4. Sprinkle with the cinnamon sugar. Top with plain yogurt or, if you prefer something richer, yogurt cream or sour cream. It really needs no additional sweetening, but if you wish, serve it with maple syrup, preserves, or honey.

YIELD: 3–4 servings

OVERNIGHT CARAMELIZED APPLE MATZOH BRIE

An evil apple may have done the trick for Snow White's wicked stepmother, but no apple caused Adam's downfall. Though mentioned several times in ancient Hebrew literature, the apple plays no part in Genesis. Adam and Eve sin simply by eating "fruit"—the generic kind—from the Tree of Knowledge.

Was the actual culprit the sensuous, many-seeded pomegranate? Perhaps the luscious golden apricot or the flesh-soft fig? Scholars continue to debate. Though the apple was first used by early translators of the Bible, it was Renaissance painters who popularized it, burnished an enticing red, to concretize our fall from grace.

The caramelized apples here certainly reek of temptation, but there's no need to lose any sleep over this matzoh brie. Prepare it the night before, then pop it in the oven the next morning while you shower and dress. It's ready when you are, for breakfast or brunch. And it's splendid too for a teatime treat.

CARAMELIZED APPLES

4 medium-large (about 2 pounds) flavorful apples (an assortment of sweet and tart, such as Wine-sap, Northern Spy, or Mutsu combined with Jonathan, Gala, Braeburn, or the lovely heirloom apple Golden Russet, works particularly well; if possible, search out local, seasonal varieties—and avoid Rome apples, which will turn to mush)

3 tablespoons unsalted butter

⅓ cup pure maple syrup

½ teaspoon ground cinnamon

⅓ cup evaporated milk, half-and-half, or cream

2 teaspoons fresh lemon juice

⅛ teaspoon salt

MATZOH BRIE

Unsalted butter for greasing the pan, plus 2 tablespoons, melted and cooled

4 whole plain matzohs

½ cup evaporated milk, half-and-half, or cream

4 large eggs

¾ teaspoon vanilla extract

⅛ teaspoon salt

1 teaspoon granulated brown or white sugar

Optional accompaniments: sour cream or yogurt cream (page 30)

---

1. Make the caramelized apples. Peel, core, and cut each apple into small chunks. In a large, heavy skillet, melt the butter over medium-high heat. Add the apples and cook, lifting and turning occasionally, for about 3 minutes. Add the maple syrup and cinnamon and continue cooking until the apples are just tender, 4–6 minutes, depending on the variety of apples. Using a slotted spoon, transfer the apples to a bowl and set aside.

2. Boil the syrup remaining in the skillet until it becomes a thick, luscious, golden caramel. Stir it frequently while it cooks, taking care that it does not burn. (Although its aroma will be tantalizing, do not taste it—the syrup is scorching hot and will badly burn your tongue.) Off the heat, very carefully add the milk, half-and-half, or cream, the lemon juice, and the salt and stir well. Return the skillet to the heat and simmer the sauce, stirring, until smooth and somewhat thickened. Return the apples to the skillet and stir until thoroughly coated with caramel sauce. Set aside to cool slightly.

3. Generously butter the bottom and sides of a large, shallow baking pan (approximately 13-by-9-inch, or its equivalent).

4. Make the matzoh brie. Break the matzohs into small pieces and spread them evenly in the prepared pan. In a large mixing bowl, whisk together the milk, half-and-half, or cream, the eggs, vanilla, salt, and sugar. Beat in the cooled, melted butter. Pour this mixture over the matzohs and let the matzohs soak up the liquid for about 15 minutes. Then smooth out the matzoh mixture, evening the top as best you can. Spread the caramelized apples—with all of their delicious sauce—evenly over the matzoh mixture. Cover the pan with foil and refrigerate overnight.

5. Remove the pan from the refrigerator and bring the dish to room temperature. Preheat the oven to 425°F. Bake, uncovered, for about 20 minutes, or until thoroughly cooked and the top is light golden brown. To finish off the matzoh brie, turn the broiler on and briefly brown the apple topping, rotating the pan as necessary so it's a rich, even brown all over.

6. This is excellent served as is, but if you'd like, accompany the matzoh brie with fresh sour cream or yogurt cream.

YIELD: 4 servings

CHALLAH FRENCH TOAST STUFFED WITH MANGO AND GINGER MAPLE SYRUP

DAIRY

> Fresh breezes wafted scents of tropical plants and
> fruits for which I had no name in Yiddish.
> —ISAAC BASHEVIS SINGER, "THE IMPRESARIO"

I am a pushover for the bracing heat of both fresh and candied ginger. So when I first tasted maple syrup infused with ginger, brainchild of Deep Mountain Farms in Vermont, I knew I had to devise a recipe to showcase it. This French toast, with its mango filling, plays up to the syrup's fresh, sweet bite.

Maple partners well with spicy hot flavors as I learned from tasting Deep Mountain's maple candies laced with jalapeño and ginger at New York City's Union Square Greenmarket. Later I experimented so I could replicate the syrup whenever theirs was not available.

Steeping the ginger for an hour will lend the syrup a warm glow with a bit of heat; longer infusion releases deep, spicy undertones. I like to start the syrup the night before I need it, and prepare the French toast, up to the point of frying, the night before as well.

GINGER MAPLE SYRUP

1 cup pure maple syrup

1 tablespoon peeled and finely chopped fresh
  ginger

FRENCH TOAST

1 medium-large ripe, fragrant mango

⅛ teaspoon nutmeg, preferably freshly grated

4 large eggs

½ cup heavy cream, half-and-half, or whole
  milk

1 teaspoon vanilla extract

3 tablespoons pure maple syrup

¼ teaspoon salt

8 slices day-old challah, cut about ½ inch thick

About 4–8 tablespoons (2–4 ounces) cream
  cheese, softened

Unsalted butter, for frying

1. Make the syrup. Combine maple syrup and ginger in a glass jar and cover tightly. Let stand at least 1 hour or as long as overnight at room temperature. Strain before using.

2. Prepare the French toast. Working over a bowl to catch the juices, peel the mango, then cut it into small cubes. Appearance doesn't matter here—the mango will be hidden inside the challah. Stir the nutmeg into the mango, and let the flavor meld for a few minutes.

3. Beat together the eggs, cream, half-and-half, or milk, vanilla, maple syrup, and salt in a shallow bowl until smooth.

4. Spread a slice of challah with about 1 tablespoon of cream cheese (if your challah slice is very large, you may need more cream cheese). Top with one-quarter of the cubed mango, then cover with a second slice of challah. Gently pat the challah sandwich together so it is neat and compact. Repeat with remaining challah, cream cheese, and mango.

5. Place the stuffed challahs in a baking dish just large enough to accommodate them in one layer (I use a glass 13- by 9-inch baking dish). Pour the egg mixture over them evenly and let soak for about 10 minutes. Using a spatula, carefully turn them and allow the other side to absorb the egg mixture for 10 minutes; at this point, you can either cover the pan with foil and refrigerate until the following morning or make them right away.

6. Preheat the oven to 400°F.

7. In a 10- to 12-inch heavy skillet, fry the stuffed challahs (two at a time, so you don't crowd the pan) in sizzling butter until golden brown on both sides. Transfer to a baking sheet and bake for 12–15 minutes, or until the mango is hot and bubbling.

8. Serve the French toast with the syrup—even better when the syrup is warmed.

YIELD: 4 servings

COOK'S NOTE: Fresh blueberries make a marvelous substitute for the mango.

STARTERS AND NOSHES

Special delicacies are known as *nasheray*,[1] and the
pleasant exercise of eating them is *nashn*,[2] to nibble.
—Description of the shtetl world in MARK ZBOROSKI
and ELIZABETH HERZOG'S *LIFE IS WITH PEOPLE*

OTHER STARTER AND NOSH SUGGESTIONS

Savory Artichoke Matzoh Brie (page 36)
Mishmash Kreplach with Sautéed Mushrooms (page 111)
Fried Onion and Chicken Kreplach (page 130)
Potato-Onion Kreplach, Pot Sticker Style (page 152)
Garlic Mashed Potato Knishes (page 154)
Leek Croquettes from Rhodes (page 223)
Smoked Whitefish and Fennel Salad (page 249) on Celery Root—Potato Latkes (page 276)
Pastrami-Style Salmon (page 250)
Stuffed Vegetables: Cabbage Stuffed with Mushrooms and Meat (page 261);
Mujadderah-Filled Roasted Red Peppers in Tomato-Garlic Sauce (page 263);
Chard Stuffed with Artichokes and Rice (page 266)
Chickpeas with Garlic and Barbecue Spices (page 296)
Chopped Eggs and Onions (page 312)
Mozzarella in Matzoh Carrozza (page 344)

[1] Yiddish, variant of *nosheray* (from the German *nachen*, "to eat on the sly"): snack food, a tidbit, a small portion.
[2] Variant of *noshn*, nosh: to eat or feed with nosheray.

46

CHOPPED CHICKEN LIVER
FROM THE RUE DES ROSIERS

Not through Proust or Camus, Colette or Chanel. Not even through French food. I became a Francophile early by way of Toni home permanents.

On Sunday nights in the days before cream rinse, my mother attempted to distract me as she wielded her comb through the chewing gum, wisteria blossoms, and weblike tangles that inhabited my hair. And she had to find a way to keep me cooperative through the longer process of applying vile-smelling lotion to my unfashionably straight locks, then rolling them up in the doll-size pink rubber curlers that left me with hair like stiff radish sprouts. So she taught me French.

And I loved it. I loved the way the words sounded. I loved her accent. Later on, I learned she mispronounced half the words, her definitions were off, her accent execrable. No matter. I loved her, and because of her, I loved everything French.

I didn't get to France until I finished college, but after that I returned as frequently as my finances would allow. One of my favorite areas was the former Jewish ghetto around the rue des Rosiers, now the site of some very *à la mode* designer boutiques and a number of stores still selling Judaica as well as Ashkenazi and Sephardi foods.

On one visit, I took my daughter to Sacha Finkelstajn, an Eastern European delicatessen with a refined Gallic touch. As in the *cave* of a *grand château de vins,* the *vendeuses* ply you with generous samples until you finally decide what to purchase. The spicy golden onion rolls are ethereal, and the chopped herring is whipped to a mousselike froth and garnished with delicate lingonberries. But to Alexandra, my husband, and me, the silken chopped liver is the finest of the treasures.

Unfortunately, Blueberry, our little Yorkie-poodle, devoured the sandwiches in the car while we were out touring Monet's gardens at Giverny. We returned to Paris the next Passover and this time we left Blueberry home. I had written to the *patronne* at Finkelstajn's for the recipe but received no response. Now I pleaded with her but *non,* she never gave it out. "Just one ingredient. What makes it so airy, what packs that subtle bite?" I persisted. Little by little, she told me things. There was no secret ingredient. It was simply a matter of proportion. Then she drew me a diagram: equal amounts of liver, egg, and onion, plus sufficient oil to make it creamy. And another diagram of the onions: two-thirds sautéed lightly, one-third raw. Simple Cartesian logic.

Haunted by the taste memory, I weighed it out at home and came up with this recipe, much eggier than more familiar versions. For all of us—including Blueberry—it has become an edible souvenir of our beloved Paris.

7 large eggs

Approximately 6 tablespoons olive oil, or 3 tablespoons olive oil plus approximately 3 tablespoons Olive Oil Schmaltz (page 28)

1 pound onions, diced (about 4 cups)

1 pound fresh (not previously frozen) chicken livers, rinsed, fat and any green spots removed

Coarse kosher salt

Freshly ground black pepper

Accompaniments: soft lettuce, Belgian endive, or radicchio leaves; radishes, scallions, ripe tomatoes, black olives; thinly sliced rye, matzoh or other crackers, or challah; Grated Black Radish and Endive Salad in Shallot Vinaigrette (page 50)

1. Preheat the broiler.

2. Hard-boil the eggs, cool, and peel (see Cook's Note). Cut the eggs into eighths. In a heavy, 10-inch skillet, heat 3 tablespoons oil over medium heat. Add 2 ⅔ cups of the onions and cook, stirring from time to time, until soft and rich gold, about 15 minutes. Do not let the onions brown or they will make the texture chewy.

3. Meanwhile, prepare the liver. Line the broiler rack with either heavy brown paper sprinkled with water, or foil. Pat the livers dry with paper towels and spread them out on the broiler rack. Sprinkle them lightly with salt and broil about 4 inches from the flame until lightly browned on top, 3–4 minutes. Turn, sprinkle the other side with salt, and broil for another 3–4 minutes. Add the broiled livers to the onions in the skillet, season generously with salt and pepper to taste, and sauté for about 1 minute, tossing and turning the ingredients. Let cool slightly.

4. Transfer the contents of the skillet to a food processor and pulse on and off to chop coarsely. Add the eggs and 1 tablespoon of either oil or schmaltz. Pulse. Add the remaining 1 ⅓ cups raw onions and pulse on and off a few more times until the desired texture is achieved. I prefer it slightly coarse—a rustic rather than fine-textured pâté, but some like a smooth spread. (Alternatively, you can chop all the ingredients by hand in a wooden bowl with a hand chopper. Chop the liver and sautéed onions first, then add the eggs and additional oil or schmaltz. Finally, add the raw onions and chop again.)

5. Scrape the mixture into a large bowl. Adjust the seasoning and add 1–2 tablespoons (or to taste) more oil or schmaltz as needed to make it moist and rich. Mix again so the ingredients are well combined. Refrigerate covered until thoroughly chilled.

6. Serve cold, on lettuce, Belgian endive, or radicchio leaves for an elegant presentation. Accompany the liver with the suggested vegetables and breads. It is terrific served with a condiment of grated black radish.

YIELD: 6–9 generous appetizer servings

COOK'S NOTE: For a foolproof method for hard-boiling eggs so that they're tender and moist, without chalky greenish yolks or tough, rubbery whites: Place the eggs in a heavy saucepan large enough to accommodate them in a single layer. Add ½ teaspoon salt (to prevent cracking) and enough cold water to cover them by at least two inches. Partially cover the pan and bring the water to a full boil over medium heat. Immediately turn off the heat. Cover the pan, remove it from the heat, and allow the eggs to stand for 15 minutes. Pour off the water and cover the eggs with fresh, cold water until they are cool, to prevent further cooking. To remove the shells easily, peel the eggs under cold running water or submerged in a bowl of very cold water.

Fish-shaped silver Sabbath candlesticks.
(Russian, late 18th century.)

GRATED BLACK RADISH AND ENDIVE
SALAD IN SHALLOT VINAIGRETTE

PAREVE

For the Sabbath, I have to prepare a radish with chicken fat for my husband. If I
don't, as far as he's concerned, the Sabbath just isn't the Sabbath.

— CHAIM GRADE, *MY MOTHER'S SABBATH DAYS*

½ pound black radish (available at many green-grocers, specialty and ethnic markets, and some well-stocked supermarkets)

Coarse kosher salt

5 tablespoons finely chopped shallots

About 1 tablespoon plus 2 teaspoons fresh lemon juice

¼ teaspoon grated lemon zest

About 4 tablespoons excellent-quality extra-virgin olive oil or Olive Oil Schmaltz (page 28)

Freshly ground black pepper

2 small Belgian endives

2 tablespoons chopped fresh parsley, preferably flat-leaf

---

1. Peel the radish and grate it coarsely in a food processor or using the large holes of a hand grater. Place in a colander or strainer, sprinkle with 1 teaspoon salt, and mix well. Weight the radish down with a plate and heavy object, like a can of tomatoes, and allow to drain for about 1 hour, stirring it every 15–20 minutes. Squeeze all moisture from the radish, rinse with fresh water, and squeeze thoroughly dry again.

2. Meanwhile, in a small bowl, combine the shallots, lemon juice, zest, and olive oil or schmaltz; season well with salt and pepper. Stir in the grated radish and allow the flavors to mingle and meld for at least 20 minutes.

3. Cut the endives into fine shreds, then toss with the grated radish and shallot mixture. Taste and adjust seasonings (it takes quite a bit of salt), adding more oil or schmaltz and lemon juice as needed. Sprinkle with the parsley. Serve with Chopped Chicken Liver (pages 47 and 51) or Chopped Eggs and Onions (page 312).

YIELD: About 6 servings

CHOPPED CHICKEN LIVER
WITH CARAMELIZED ONIONS

I often prepare a variation on the preceding Parisian chicken liver using fewer eggs. It derives its exceptional lightness—and slightly sweet taste—from a puree of caramelized onions.

4 large eggs

6–8 tablespoons olive oil, or 5 tablespoons olive oil plus approximately 1–3 tablespoons Olive Oil Schmaltz (page 28)

5 cups very thinly sliced onions, plus 1 cup coarsely chopped (about 1½ pounds total)

Salt and freshly ground black pepper

1–2 tablespoons balsamic vinegar (if the vinegar is rough or if you must substitute instead 1 tablespoon mild red wine vinegar, you will also need ¼ teaspoon brown sugar)

1 pound fresh (not previously frozen) chicken livers, rinsed, fat and any green spots removed

Accompaniments: soft lettuce, Belgian endive, or radicchio leaves; radishes, scallions, ripe tomatoes, black olives; thinly sliced rye, matzoh or other crackers, or challah; Grated Black Radish and Endive Salad in Shallot Vinaigrette (page 50)

1. Preheat the broiler.

2. Hard-boil the eggs, cool, and peel (see Cook's Note on page 49). Cut the eggs into eighths.

3. In a 10- to 12-inch heavy skillet, warm 3 tablespoons of the oil over medium heat. Add the sliced onions, salt and pepper them lightly, and sauté, lifting and turning them occasionally, until softened and translucent, about 10 minutes. Cover tightly and cook the onions over the lowest heat setting, stirring occasionally to prevent burning, for 40–45 minutes, or until meltingly tender. Uncover, add the vinegar and additional salt and pepper to taste, and cook over high heat, lifting and tossing, until moisture is evaporated and the onions are colored a rich brown, about 15 minutes. Taste to adjust seasoning: The mixture should be just slightly sweet, but well salted and peppered, and the vinegar scent should be almost gone. If necessary, add the brown sugar and additional seasoning, then continue sautéing until thoroughly incorporated. Transfer about three-quarters of the mixture to a food processor, add 2 tablespoons oil, and puree.

4. Meanwhile, prepare the liver. Line the broiler rack with either heavy brown paper sprinkled with water, or foil. Pat the livers dry with paper towels and spread them out on the broiler rack. Sprinkle

them lightly with salt, and broil about 4 inches from the flame until lightly browned on top, 3–4 minutes. Turn, sprinkle the other side with salt, and broil for another 3–4 minutes. Add the broiled livers to the cooked onions remaining in the skillet and sauté for a minute or two. Let cool slightly, then add to the onion puree in the food processor. Pulse on and off to chop coarsely. Add the eggs. Pulse. Add the remaining 1 cup chopped raw onions and pulse on and off until desired texture is achieved. Transfer to a large bowl, taste for seasoning, and add 1–3 tablespoons more oil or schmaltz as needed to make it moist and rich. Mix well and refrigerate, covered, until thoroughly chilled.

5. Serve cold, on lettuce or, for a sophisticated presentation, Belgian endive or radicchio leaves. Accompany the liver with the suggested vegetables and breads. It is particularly good with grated black radish served alongside.

YIELD: 6–9 generous appetizer servings

LENTILS "HUMMUS STYLE," WITH POMEGRANATE AND MINT AND TOASTED ZA'ATAR MATZOHS

PAREVE

Round as the wheel of life so it has no "mouth" to scream out against iniquities, the lentil, like other legumes, has been a food of mourning since Jacob consoled grieving Isaac with lentil soup after Abraham's death.

Is it to hoodwink the Evil Eye then that Ashkenazi Jews feature mourning foods on the menu at a Shalom Zahar, the joyous celebration held the Friday night after a male child is born?

Perhaps. But I prefer another explanation. In the womb, the *neshama*, or soul, of the baby boy has total knowledge of the Torah, but all that wisdom is left behind when he enters the world. And it is this grave loss the infant mourns at his Shalom Zahar.

Although "hummus" actually means "chickpea," quick-cooking lentils are a delicious alternative in the garlicky spread. In this version, sesame tahini is replaced by other tastes from the Middle East, pomegranate and mint, which freshen the bean puree with fragrant, sweet-sour grace notes.

The aromatic za'atar, a Middle Eastern herb blend crusting the toasted matzoh, underscores the tart, fruity flavors in the hummus.

---

1 ¼ cups (about ½ pound) brown lentils
Salt
1 ½–2 tablespoons coarsely chopped garlic, according to taste
About 6 tablespoons best-quality extra-virgin olive oil
6 tablespoons fresh lemon juice, or to taste
1 tablespoon pomegranate molasses, or to taste
¼ cup fresh mint leaves, plus additional leaves for garnish

Freshly ground black pepper
Garnish: 3 tablespoons fresh pomegranate seeds (optional)
Accompaniments: trimmed fresh raw vegetables, such as fennel, celery, carrots, red and yellow pepper strips, etc.; Toasted Za'atar Matzohs (page 54), plain matzoh, or hot pita quarters

---

1. Pick over the lentils carefully, discarding any stray objects or discolored beans, and rinse well in fresh cold water. Drain and place in a medium saucepan. Add enough cold water to cover generously and bring to a boil. Lower the heat to moderate and cook, covered, for about 30 minutes, or until very soft. About 5–10 minutes before the cooking time has elapsed, add salt to taste.

STARTERS AND NOSHES

53

2. While the lentils are cooking, sauté the garlic in 2 tablespoons olive oil until just tinged with pale gold. (You only want to eliminate the raw taste.)

3. Drain the lentils, reserving about ½ cup of the cooking water, and put them in a food processor, together with the garlic and its cooking oil, 3 tablespoons oil, the lemon juice, pomegranate molasses, mint leaves, and salt and pepper to taste. Process to a smooth puree. Add some of the reserved cooking water if necessary to achieve a soft and creamy consistency. Taste and adjust the salt, pepper, lemon juice, pomegranate molasses, and oil as needed. Spread the hummus on a large platter and drizzle with the remaining 1 tablespoon oil. Garnish with pomegranate seeds, if using, and mint leaves.

4. Serve with fresh vegetables and Toasted Za'atar Matzohs or warm pita, for dipping.

YIELD: About 6 servings

TOASTED ZA'ATAR MATZOHS

PAREVE

1 tablespoon plus 2 teaspoons sesame seeds	½ teaspoon dried mint
1 tablespoon plus 1 teaspoon sumac (available at Middle Eastern and specialty stores)	Coarse salt to taste (start with ½ teaspoon)
	Matzohs
2 tablespoons dried thyme	Extra-virgin olive oil
2 teaspoons dried oregano	

1. Preheat the oven to 400°F.

2. Prepare the sesame seeds. In a small (about 7-inch), heavy, ungreased skillet, toast them over moderately high heat, stirring or shaking the pan constantly, just until they release their nutty fragrance and turn light gold. Don't allow them to brown, or they'll be bitter. Remove the skillet from the heat.

3. Transfer to a mortar, add the sumac, thyme, oregano, mint, and salt, and crush coarsely with the pestle. Or pulse a few times in an electric spice grinder, or put the seasonings in a plastic bag (let the sesame seeds cool slightly first) and pound well with a mallet. Taste and adjust the salt. Brush the tops

of the matzohs with olive oil, then sprinkle generously with the za'atar (I use 2½–3 teaspoons for each matzoh). Bake until hot and crisp. The matzoh should be very fragrant, puffed slightly, and just beginning to curl at the deep brown edges. Serve hot.

YIELD: 4–6 servings

COOK'S NOTE: Some companies now package their own za'atar blends. Check the spice department of well-stocked specialty or Middle Eastern groceries. Store any leftover za'atar in a tightly closed jar. Za'atar is also delicious sprinkled on other breads: pita, lavash, nan. Brush breads lightly with oil before sprinkling with za'atar and bake until hot and fragrant.

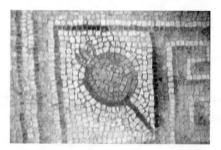

Jews have treasured pomegranates since ancient times; the many-seeded fruit quenched their thirst in the desert. (Floor mosaic from 5th-century synagogue, Khirbet Susiya, Israel.)

MY MOTHER'S FRIED CAULIFLOWER

PAREVE

My mother always fried up cauliflower late at night. Long ago she had decided it—or her fluffy buttermilk pancakes—was the perfect antidote to flagging appetites, so she would make a batch after she noticed one of us had eaten very little at dinner.

During school holidays or when one of us lay afflicted with some childhood bug, it was often past eleven o'clock when she carried the tray into the TV room, piled high with bronzed cauliflower nuggets and golden lemon quarters. We ate fast, lest we miss Zacherley pulling up his wife's hair or the Mummy's response when offered thirteen tanna leaves.

Because we polished it off so quickly, I always assumed it took no time to prepare. Not so. The cauliflower must be boiled until tender before being breaded and fried—necessitating another large pot to wash. I once tried to skip this step, but the whole purpose of fried foods is the contrast of the crisp and crunchy coating the soft and yielding.

I have come upon a technique, though, that works with fresh young cauliflower. If you pour boiling water over small florets and let them steep awhile in a bowl, you can eliminate the parboiling.

To coat the cauliflower, my mother usually used matzoh meal, which falls somewhere between bread crumbs and flour in terms of thickness. Because it is so bland—it lacks even salt—it must be generously seasoned. She used lots of garlic, lemon peel, and, when she had them on hand, finely minced anchovies for a zesty nuance not readily identifiable by anchovy haters.

For perfectly fried cauliflower, I rely on two simple tricks. When possible, let the coated florets set at least fifteen minutes (before frying) to allow the egg dip to dry to a gluelike paste, so that the matzoh meal is less likely to fall off and burn in the oil while frying. And divide the seasoned coating mixture into two piles. After a while, dredging the egg-dipped florets into the matzoh meal renders the meal ragged with little wet eggy clumps. So, when the matzoh meal is just too lumpy to coat the cauliflower, I replace it with a fresh supply.

---

1 medium head of cauliflower, preferably young and fresh

Salt

About 1½ cups matzoh meal

1 tablespoon dried oregano

1 tablespoon grated lemon zest

2–3 teaspoons pressed or very finely minced fresh garlic

2–3 anchovies, finely minced (optional)

Freshly ground black pepper

2 large eggs

2 tablespoons fresh lemon juice

Olive oil, for frying

Accompaniment: lemon wedges

---

1. Break the cauliflower into small florets and put them in a large, heatproof bowl. Sprinkle with 1 teaspoon of salt. Bring a large pot of water to a rapid boil and pour over the cauliflower, covering it by at least an inch. Cover the bowl and allow the cauliflower to steep in the water for 5–8 minutes. Stir it around a bit so all of the pieces are sloshed by the water. If the florets test fork-tender (but before they are soft and mushy), drain them well. If not, let them steep for a few more minutes. (Alternatively, if you have a very mature head of cauliflower, boil the florets in salted water until just tender and drain them.)

2. In a bowl, stir together the matzoh meal, oregano, lemon zest, garlic, anchovies, if using, and plenty of salt and pepper. (Use the greater amounts of garlic and anchovies for a zippier taste.) Divide the mixture in two, spreading half out on a plate or sheet of wax paper and setting the other half aside. Beat the eggs well with the lemon juice in a wide shallow bowl or pie pan.

3. Taking one floret at a time, dip it into the beaten egg, coating well on all sides. Let the excess egg drip back into the bowl. Dredge the florets all over with the matzoh meal mixture. When the matzoh meal mixture gets lumpy with bits of egg, discard and replace with the reserved fresh mixture. To prevent loose crumbs from falling off and burning in the hot oil, pat the coated florets firmly so the matzoh meal adheres. Then, if possible, place them on a rack and let stand for about 15 minutes to set the coating.

4. Heat ½ inch of olive oil in a heavy 10- to 12-inch skillet over medium-high heat until hot but not smoking. Add the florets, and sauté them in batches until golden brown on all sides. Drain on paper towels or brown paper bags.

5. Salt and pepper the cauliflower generously, like French fries, and serve with the lemon wedges. They are best hot, though they are still delicious, if somewhat greasy, at room temperature.

YIELD: 4–6 servings

COOK'S NOTE: For a lovely variation, omit the anchovies and season the matzoh meal with about ¼ cup grated Parmesan.

CHICKEN GEFILTE BALLS (FALSHE FISH) AND GREEN OLIVE SAUCE

MEAT

Jewish cuisine is full of make-believe. Many dishes are kosher analogues of foods Jews around the world found enticing. Italian Jews devised *chazirello*, breast of veal redolent of rosemary and garlic to mimic roasted piglets, and silken *prosciutto d'oca*, "ham" fashioned from goose, a delicacy relished today as much by Gentiles as by Jews. Turkish Jews make a rich milk pudding that does not break the laws of kashrut as a substitute for *tavuk gogsu*, a sweet dessert comprising an unlikely amalgam of milk and pureed chicken breast, served with ice cream in summer.

Other foods, like falshe fish, where ground chicken poses as gefilte fish, were improvised when the real thing was either unavailable or too expensive. To prepare it, most cooks followed their regular gefilte fish recipes, substituting water and vegetables for the fish broth—no bones and scum to skim, no fish smells, so the dish was a snap to prepare. I learned to add chicken wings from talented home cook Esther Taubenfeld so the broth is richer, especially important here because chicken breast is so bland. The wings also help the broth to gel when cold.

I've played around a bit with the texture, and since I prefer the fresher taste that comes with a brief poaching, the "fish" is simmered for only forty minutes, rather than the two hours traditional gefilte fish recipes require. You may substitute moistened matzoh or matzoh meal for the challah, but you must have *some* filler—it keeps the balls from turning hard and tough.

If you like, serve the falshe fish with real horseradish to complete the masquerade, but I love it with this delicious green olive sauce I devised to accentuate, rather than overpower, the delicate chicken.

CHICKEN GEFILTE BALLS

½ pound onions, chopped (2 cups)

Salt

2 thick slices challah, crusts removed and
   discarded, bread torn into small pieces
   (about 1½ cups packed)

1 large garlic clove

1½ pounds skinless, boneless chicken breasts (if
   you prefer, have the butcher grind the chicken
   for you)

¼ teaspoon freshly ground black pepper, or to taste

½ cup grated carrot (optional)

3 large eggs

POACHING STOCK

4 chicken wings (about 1–1½ pounds)

2 large or 3 medium onions, peeled and cut into
   quarters

2 celery stalks

3 large carrots, scraped and cut into chunks

Salt and freshly ground black pepper

Sugar

Accompaniments: soft lettuce, Belgian endive,
   or radicchio leaves for lining serving plates;
   Green Olive Sauce (page 60) or prepared
   horseradish

1. Prepare the chicken balls. Toss the onions in a strainer with 1½ teaspoons salt. Let stand for about 10 minutes. Add the challah and toss again. Transfer to a food processor and process to a coarse puree (the moisture from the onions will wet and soften the bread). Add the garlic and process to a paste. Scrape the mixture into a wooden chopping bowl (or onto a chopping block). If the chicken is not ground, pulse in the food processor until it is coarsely chopped. Place the chicken in the bowl (or on the block) with the other chopped ingredients. Add 2 teaspoons salt, the pepper, carrot, if using, and 1 egg. Chop, using a hand-chopper or cleaver, until well-combined. Continue chopping, adding the remaining 2 eggs, one at a time, until the mixture is finely chopped, smooth, and fluffy. Cover the bowl and refrigerate for 1–2 hours.

2. Meanwhile, prepare the poaching stock. Place the wings in the bottom of a large, deep pot. Arrange the vegetables on top. Add cold water to cover, a little salt and pepper, and a pinch or two of sugar. Bring to a simmer, skimming off any foam, if necessary, as it rises to the top. Continue simmering, partially covered, for about 45 minutes. Taste and adjust the seasoning, adding another pinch or two of sugar if needed to erase any trace of bitterness.

3. Form the chicken into egg-size balls or large walnuts if you prefer them smaller, wetting your hands if needed to prevent the mixture from sticking. Bring the stock to a gentle boil and add the chicken balls, placing them one at a time on top of the vegetables. Cover the pot, reduce the heat to very low, and simmer for about 40 minutes, or until the chicken balls are completely cooked through. Let them cool in the liquid, then transfer with a slotted spoon to a large, deep dish. Over high heat reduce the poaching liquid to about 1 cup, then pour through a strainer over the chicken balls and let cool to room temperature. Cover and refrigerate for at least 8 hours.

4. To serve, line plates with lettuce, endive, or radicchio and arrange the chicken balls on top. Pass the green olive sauce or horseradish separately.

YIELD: 8 servings

GREEN OLIVE SAUCE

½ cup meaty, brine-cured green olives (look for
  olives with a deep, fruity olive oil flavor, like
  Sicilian green), pitted and sliced

2 tablespoons chopped shallots

2 tablespoons fresh lemon juice

1 tablespoon Dijon mustard

1 teaspoon grated lemon zest

4 tablespoons extra-virgin olive oil

Salt and freshly ground black pepper

In a food processor or a blender, process the olives, shallots, lemon juice, mustard, and zest to a coarse puree. With the machine on, add the olive oil in a slow steady stream through the feeder tube or blender top. Season to taste with salt and pepper. Allow the flavors to meld together for at least ½ hour before serving. The sauce will keep for about 5 days, refrigerated.

YIELD: About ⅔ cup

COOK'S NOTE: This sauce is wonderful with real fish as well: poached fillets or steaks or the Oven-Fried Smoked Salmon Croquettes (page 101). It is also delicious diluted with a few spoonfuls of broth or mayonnaise and paired with the Veronese Rolled Turkey Loaf (page 323).

SOUPS AND GARNISHES

From the savory red pottage of lentils for which Esau exchanged his birthright to the golden chicken nectar touted as magical elixir ever since the time of Maimonides, Jewish soups have always been highly treasured. Tucking into a brimming bowlful, you are at once deeply nourished and nurtured.

And perhaps even better than the soups are their enticing accompaniments, especially knaidlach (dumplings) and kreplach (stuffed pasta pockets), both of which provide superb canvases for inspired flavor designs.

Here you'll find, in addition to classic chicken soup, selections like wintry Russian cabbage soup, thick with pot roast and beet kreplach, as well as vegetarian soups like mushroom barley, tangy with sorrel and buttermilk. Additional soup recipes are listed below.

OTHER SOUP AND GARNISH SUGGESTIONS

Mishmash Kreplach (page 111)
Fried Onion and Chicken Kreplach (page 130)
Golden Soup from Iranian Stuffed Chicken (page 232)
Pumpkin and Sweet Potato Soup with Sweet Potato Knaidlach (page 259)
Chicken Soup with Asparagus and Shiitakes, Served with Roasted
Fennel Matzoh Balls (page 316)
Warm Shav with Salmon Kreplach (page 351)
Grandmother's Cold Fruit Soup (page 353)

CLASSIC CHICKEN SOUP

MEAT

Do you think there will be any yellow rings on the soup? I saw the chicken soup the women from the sick-visiting society brought old Rachel when she was sick, and it was all yellow on top—fat!—and smelt so good!
— MARY ANTIN, "MALINKE'S ATONEMENT"

From Maimonides on, much has been made of the curative powers of Jewish chicken soup—"Jewish penicillin," "the doctor who makes house calls," and so on. Now it seems, the doctor often needs doctoring—and not just in America. A friend in Verona, Italy, confessed that Italian Jews too at times enhance their homemade soups with imported Israeli bouillon cubes for a needed jolt of flavor.

Broth is no more than the simmered essence of its ingredients, and the problem here, of course, is the weakened flavor of the chicken itself. Traditional Jewish chicken soup was always made from a tough old hen with plenty of character. Today's battery-feeding produces picture-pretty birds with lots of fat and little flavor. And those "yellow rings" extolled in Antin's story from 1911 have lost their appeal now—to us they taste merely of grease, not of chicken. So how do you coax out enough flavor from a lackluster bird to make a splendid soup?

Over the years I've gleaned some *trucs* for preparing excellent Jewish chicken soup.

1. Start with the best-quality fowl available, and if at all possible, buy feet, or at least some extra wings, to give the soup extra body. I find that, although chicken backs are fine for making chicken stock, they are too fatty and lack the requisite clarity of flavor for a soup meant to be served solo. It may seem extravagant to use a large hen for soup—after all, the cooked chicken cannot be served later as an entrée (you've already extracted all the flavor from it). However, the meat is perfectly good for chicken salad, sandwiches, Fried Onion and Chicken Kreplach (page 130), and *dayenu* (matzoh balls with snippets of chicken, page 66), or served cut up in soup.

2. To compensate for the often anemic taste of today's chickens, I add lots and lots of earthy, aromatic vegetables to provide the soup with strength and character.

3. It's a struggle, but I resist the temptation to use a lot of water. And if the soup tastes too watery when I'm finished, I reduce it as much as necessary, even though it pains me to see the fruits of all my labor just boiling away.

4. Long, slow cooking will extract every bit of flavor from both chicken and vegetables. Using a huge stockpot—about 20- or even 24-quart size, far larger than the contents would warrant—and a tiny flame, so there is no danger of the soup boiling, I cook it for at least four hours, and more often, overnight.

5. To prepare the chicken, I remove every bit of fat and some of the excess skin, since they don't add any flavor and later I'll just have to discard the grease they produce.

6. Skim, skim, skim. Froth and scum taste bitter and look terrible.

7. To prevent the precious flavors from evaporating, after I have finished skimming the soup, I cover the surface with a layer of the green part of the leeks used in the soup. If I have no leeks, I use the outer leaves of a mild lettuce.

8. And lastly, I *never* bring the soup to a boil. That roiling bubble action traps fat and scum beneath the surface, bonding them to the liquid, so that the soup becomes clouded, murky, and impossible to clarify. Instead, I let it simmer gently the entire cooking period, "smiling," as the French say of the tiny bubbles that open and close along the edge of the pot. (Boiling the finished soup—strained and defatted—to reduce it is, of course, another matter.)

One 5- to 6-pound fowl or stewing hen (not a roaster) and its giblets (reserve the liver for another use)

2 chicken feet, or 1 pound chicken wings

4 quarts cold water (quality is important here, so if you use bottled water to make coffee or tea, use it here)

Salt

2 large onions, 1 peeled and quartered, 1 washed, roots trimmed but left unpeeled, and quartered

2 parsnips (about ½ pound), scraped and cut into chunks

3 celery stalks, cut into large chunks

½ cup celery leaves

5 large carrots (about 1–1¼ pounds), scraped and halved

2–3 garlic cloves, peeled

6 fresh parsley sprigs

1 parsley root (petrouchka), peeled and cut into chunks (often found in greenmarkets and specialty stores, as well as supermarkets with well-stocked produce departments; optional)

2 large leeks, trimmed (reserve long green leaves), washed of all traces of sand, and cut into large pieces, or if absolutely necessary, 1 sweet red onion, peeled and quartered

10–12 peppercorns, lightly crushed

1 bay leaf

Several leaves of mild-flavored lettuce, such as Boston or iceberg, if no leek greens are available

About ½ cup snipped fresh dill

Accompaniment: kreplach, matzoh balls (page 66), cooked thin egg noodles, or rice

---

1. Prepare the chicken. I find it easier to work with the chicken (remove the fat, cover it completely with water and vegetables, skim thoroughly, etc.) when it is cut up, so I divide it roughly into quarters. Remove all visible fat from the chicken and giblets. Remove the skin from the neck and the neck and tail openings. Wash all the pieces thoroughly, including feet or wings, and place in your largest stockpot, which should be tall and straight-sided. Add the water and about 1½ teaspoons salt to begin with.

2. Turn the heat to medium and bring to a simmer. As the soup cooks, keep skimming off any scum and fat that rises to the surface. When the soup begins to "smile," that is, tiny bubbles open and close along the edge of the pot, turn the heat down to very low. Skim the soup constantly—at this point, you really need to fret over it. When the soup is just about clear, add the remaining ingredients (except the leek greens or lettuce and the dill) and raise the heat slightly to bring it back to a simmer. Continue skimming any froth or scum.

3. When the soup is again clear, turn the heat down to as low as possible. Cover the surface of the soup with the leek greens or lettuce leaves, and put the pot lid on, leaving it slightly askew. Simmer the soup for at least 2½ to 4 hours—overnight is better still. Never let the soup boil; if necessary, use a flame-tamer, or *blech,* or put it on top of two burner grates stacked together. (But do make sure the bubbles are breaking very gently on the surface. If there is no surface movement at all, the soup might spoil.)

4. Adjust the seasonings. Using a slotted spoon, remove the chicken and carrots and set aside. Let the soup cool to room temperature in the pot, *uncovered.* (Hot soup in a covered pot may turn sour.)

5. While the soup is cooling, pick over the reserved chicken and discard the bones, skin, and other inedible parts. Reserve the chicken for another use or refrigerate, along with the carrots, to be served later in the soup.

6. Strain the cooled soup through a fine sieve, pressing down on all the vegetables to extract as much of their juices as you can, then discard the vegetables.

7. Refrigerate the soup, covered, overnight or until all the remaining fat has congealed on the top. Carefully scrape off the fat and discard it. If the soup still seems fatty, line a fine sieve with a layer of paper towels and pour the soup through it into a clean bowl or pot (if the soup has jelled from chilling, bring it to room temperature first). If the paper towels become thickly coated with fat, you might want to change them once or twice during the process.

8. Before serving, reheat the soup. Taste for salt and pepper and add lots of snipped dill. If you feel the soup is not strong enough, reduce it over high heat to concentrate the flavors. Serve the soup very hot, with additional fresh dill, the reserved carrots, and if desired, shreds of the soup chicken. It is delicious with kreplach or matzoh balls, egg noodles or rice, or just plain.

YIELD: 2½–3 quarts

MATZOH BALLS

✶✶✶✶✶✶✶✶✶✶✶✶✶✶✶✶✶

MEAT

I was stumped by the name *dayenu* that Ester Silvana Israel, avid cook and secretary of the Jewish community of Verona, Italy, used for matzoh balls—either traditional Ashkenazi knaidlach or more uniquely Italian kinds, incorporating bits of chicken or other meats.

I questioned her as we walked through the pink marble columns of her exquisite synagogue. Smiling, she wondered whether I remembered the song from the Passover service?

"Of course," I replied. "Each miracle God performed would have been *dayenu*, enough; each would have sufficed to show God's love. Nothing else was necessary."

"Well, so too with the matzoh balls," she explained. "Each one is so filling it would be enough; each could suffice for the entire meal. But there is always more and still more yet to come."

Some recipes for matzoh balls and variations follow, including matzoh balls made of whole matzoh instead of matzoh meal. To make *dayenu*, matzoh balls Italian style, add up to three-quarters cup cooked chicken, finely shredded and then cut into bits, to this recipe. For additional matzoh ball recipes, see the index.

---

4 large eggs
1 recipe Olive Oil Schmaltz (page 28; see
  Cook's Note)
About 3–5 tablespoons chicken broth, preferably
  homemade (page 63) or good-quality low-
  sodium canned
About 1 teaspoon salt, or to taste
Freshly ground black pepper

1 teaspoon baking powder
  (optional; see Cook's Note)
1 cup matzoh meal (you can substitute up to ¼
  cup finely ground skinned almonds for an
  equal quantity of matzoh meal)
3 tablespoons finely minced fresh dill or parsley
  and/or 2 pinches of ginger (optional)
1 recipe Classic Chicken Soup (page 63)

---

1. In a large mixing bowl, beat the eggs and schmaltz well until light and foamy. Whisk in 3 tablespoons broth. Stir the salt, pepper to taste, baking powder, if using, and matzoh meal into the egg mixture. Stir in the optional seasonings, if using. Let the batter stand for a few minutes; the matzoh meal will begin to absorb the liquids. Stir well but don't overbeat. The batter should be rather soft. If it seems too dry, stir in another 1–2 tablespoons broth. Cover the mixture and refrigerate for at least 2 hours or up to 24 hours, so the matzoh meal can fully absorb the liquids and seasoning.

2. Bring 4 quarts of water and 1½ tablespoons salt to a boil in a large wide pot.

3. The balls formed from the soft batter may not hold their shape well, especially those made without baking powder. Not to worry: they will be very tender. Shape the batter into walnut- or olive-size balls, and place on a platter. When the water comes to a rapid boil, reduce the heat. Carefully slide the balls in one at a time. Or you can form the balls using two spoons and drop them right into the water. Don't crowd the pot—if necessary, prepare the matzoh balls in two batches or use two pots. When the water returns to a gentle boil, immediately cover the pot tightly and lower the heat to a simmer. Cook over low heat for 35–45 minutes, without removing the lid. (They will cook by direct heat as well as by steam, which makes them swell up—lifting the lid will reduce some of that steam.) Test for doneness: remove a matzoh ball and cut it in half. It should be tender, fluffy, and completely cooked through. If it isn't, continue cooking for a few more minutes.

4. Remove the matzoh balls gently with a skimmer or a large slotted spoon—they are too fragile to pour into a colander. To serve, heat the chicken soup, add the matzoh balls, and simmer until they are heated through. Ladle into warmed shallow bowls and serve immediately. Or cover the drained matzoh balls with some broth and set aside for a few hours until you are ready to heat them.

YIELD: 6–8 servings

COOK'S NOTE: Olive oil schmaltz, a puree of oil-stewed onions, provides not only flavor but also a texture approximating a semi-solid fat, which makes the matzoh balls fluffy and light. If you want a substitute, similar aromatic blends, like purees of roasted garlic or mushrooms sautéed or braised until soft, combined with some oil (add a chopped fresh herb, for extra flavor, if you'd like), also work well. And I've made exquisite matzoh balls using the above recipe but substituting ¼ cup jarred artichoke puree mixed with 2 tablespoons olive oil for the schmaltz and decreasing the broth to 2 tablespoons. For another delicious variation, see Roasted Fennel Matzoh Balls (page 316).

Baking powder, of course, would not be used on Passover. I think of it here as insurance—with it, you are much less likely to experience serious Knaidlach Failure: matzoh balls that fall apart, that won't swell up, that are too tight or too tough. When carefully prepared, however, these matzoh balls made without baking powder will be tender and buttery tasting too. To keep them light and fluffy, remember not to lift the lid at all until you suspect they are ready, that is, not before at least 30–35 minutes have elapsed.

SAVORY HERBED MATZOH KLEIS (MATZOH BALLS MADE FROM WHOLE MATZOH)

MEAT

I saw once more...the soup with dreamily swimming dumplings—
and my soul melted like the notes of an enamoured nightingale.

—HEINRICH HEINE, *THE RABBI OF BACHERACH*

Homey dumplings have been a hallmark of German cuisine ever since the Middle Ages, and the Yiddish words *knaidl* (a variant of *knoedl*) and *kleis* (which began as *klosse*) reveal their German ancestry. Jewish cooks in Central and Eastern Europe incorporated dumplings into their repertoire, fashioning them from bread, rolls, flour, and potatoes.

And for Passover they made fluffy balls out of matzoh. I have found that the Alsatian, German, and Czech matzoh ball recipes, often called kleis, created from soaked pieces of whole matzoh, are frequently more imaginatively and assertively flavored than the familiar variety made of matzoh meal. And I love the way the matzoh pieces seem to inhale the seasonings far more lustily than matzoh meal does.

In my rendition, generous lacings of fresh herbs and lemon zest, along with a delicate, traditional ground-almond thickener, make for kleis that are vibrant yet gossamer-light.

---

6 whole plain matzohs

2 cups chicken or beef broth, preferably homemade (pages 63 or 78), or good-quality low-sodium canned

½ pound onions, finely chopped (2 cups)

3 tablespoons mild olive or vegetable oil

2 teaspoons minced fresh garlic

2 tablespoons finely chopped fresh parsley

2 tablespoons finely chopped fresh chives

1 tablespoon finely chopped fresh dill

2 teaspoons grated lemon zest

3 large eggs

About 3 tablespoons ground blanched almonds or matzoh meal, plus additional, if desired, for dredging kleis

Salt and freshly ground black pepper

1 recipe Classic Chicken Soup (page 63)

---

1. Break the matzohs into small pieces in a large bowl. Heat the broth until it is very hot and pour it over the matzoh. Set aside to allow the matzoh to drink up the broth.

2. In a large skillet, sauté the onions in the oil over medium heat, stirring, until soft and translucent, 7–10 minutes. Add the garlic and cook for 2–3 minutes. Stir in the parsley, chives, dill, and lemon zest.

Add the soaked matzoh and cook, stirring constantly, until the mixture becomes dry and pastelike. Return it to the bowl and let cool until you can handle it.

3. Your fingers will do the best job mixing this, but if you're really averse to using them, try a potato masher, ricer, or just a heavy fork. Knead and mash the matzoh pieces until you have a fairly smooth, homogeneous mixture.

4. Beat in the eggs, one at a time, and the ground almonds or matzoh meal, and season well with salt and pepper. Cover and refrigerate for at least 2 hours to allow the mixture to absorb all the seasoning and liquid.

5. Bring 4 quarts of water and 1½ tablespoons salt to a boil in a large wide pot.

6. Place a bowl of cold water and a large platter or tray near you as you work. Now try rolling a little batter into a walnut- or olive-size ball. It should be somewhat sticky, but fairly easy to roll into very soft balls, with hands moistened with the cold water as needed. If the batter is too soft to roll, or the balls don't hold their shape on the platter, add just enough ground almonds or matzoh meal to achieve the right consistency. (Too much will make the kleis heavy, as will packing them too densely into a ball. A light touch is essential. Eventually you'll know quite easily when they feel just right.)

7. If you'd like the kleis to look more finished, without homey, ragged edges (it's a slight tradeoff—they won't be quite as light), spread additional ground almonds or matzoh meal on a sheet of wax paper or a plate, and very lightly dredge the rolled balls in it. Put the finished balls on the platter or tray, and continue making the kleis until all the batter is used up.

8. When all the kleis are rolled and the water is boiling furiously, turn the heat down to a gentle boil. Quickly and carefully slide the balls in, one by one, nudging them in with a spoon or your finger, and cover the pot tightly. Don't crowd the pot—if necessary, prepare the matzoh balls in two batches or use two pots. Temperature is important here: If the water is boiling with too much force, the matzoh balls may break up or disintegrate into thick sludge. If the water is not hot enough, the protein won't coagulate and the hapless balls will also fall apart. Aim to keep the water, as the French say, "smiling"—perhaps even "laughing softly," the bubbles breaking slowly and gently on the surface of the water. (You can best check the water temperature if the pot lid is glass; otherwise, listen for sounds of rapid boiling, but don't lift the lid.)

9. Simmer over low heat for 30–40 minutes, without removing the lid. (They will cook by direct heat as well as by steam, which makes them puff and swell, and peeking will dissipate some of that steam.) Take out a dumpling and cut it in half. It should be tender, fluffy, and completely cooked through. If it isn't, continue cooking until the kleis test done.

10. Remove them gently with a skimmer or large slotted spoon—they are too fragile to pour out into a colander. Add them to the soup and simmer slowly until piping hot. Ladle the kleis and steaming soup into warmed shallow bowls and serve immediately. Or cover the drained kleis with some broth and set aside until you are ready to heat them.

YIELD: About 6 servings

Grandparents blessing children on the Sabbath. (*Friday Night*. Lithograph. Cologne, Germany, c. 1860.)

TANGY RUSSIAN CABBAGE SOUP WITH POT ROAST–BEET KREPLACH

Long ago, kreplach were more than mere ravioli: They were savory edible amulets. According to Patti Shosteck, author of *A Lexicon of Jewish Cooking,* Jews in seventeenth-century Germany inscribed the outside of the pasta with mystical incantations and messages intended to bring God's favor to them and their chaotic universe.

Kreplach continue to make magic in this recipe. Instead of raw meat simmered along with the cabbage in the soup, ready-cooked brisket or pot roast, combined with sweet beets for flavor and moistness, are enclosed in the kreplach, adding unexpected layers to the eloquent balance of tastes and textures here. And because the soup is made with beef broth, not meat, there is no fat to remove or skimming needed.

CABBAGE SOUP

1 medium green cabbage (about 1½–2 pounds)

1 pound onions, chopped (4 cups)

3 tablespoons olive oil

Salt and freshly ground black pepper

1 small parsnip, diced (about ½ cup) (optional)

About ¾ pound carrots, chopped (2 cups)

2 tablespoons finely chopped garlic

1 tablespoon peeled and minced fresh ginger

6 cups homemade beef broth (page 78)
  or good-quality low-sodium canned

1 cup canned Italian plum tomatoes, coarsely
  chopped, and their juice

1 bay leaf

2 tablespoons tart dried apricots, minced (for an
  added subtle sour-sweet note) (optional)

1 cup sauerkraut, rinsed well

2 tart green apples, peeled and diced

About 3 tablespoons brown sugar

About 3 tablespoons fresh lemon juice

POT ROAST–BEET KREPLACH

1 cup shredded cooked pot roast or brisket,
  plus 2–3 tablespoons gravy (if you have no
  leftover gravy, substitute some rich broth—
  that is, good broth that has been reduced by
  about half)

¾ cup cooked, peeled, and very finely diced
  beets

3 tablespoons finely chopped fresh dill, plus
  additional for garnish

1 tablespoon grated onion

1 large egg yolk

Salt and freshly ground black pepper

30–40 wonton wrappers (it's a good idea to have
  some extra in case of tearing)

Egg wash (1–2 large eggs, as needed, each
  beaten with 1 teaspoon of water)

1. Start the soup. Discard the tough outer leaves of the cabbage, then cut it into quarters and cut out and discard the core. Shred the cabbage coarsely or cut it into thin slices.

2. In a very large, wide, heavy saucepan or 5- to 6-quart Dutch oven, sauté the onions in the olive oil over medium heat until softened, about 15 minutes. Salt and pepper lightly, then cover and simmer over low heat until very soft and sweet and almost translucent, 20–25 minutes. Add the parsnip, if using, the carrots, and the garlic, and raise the heat to moderately high. Sauté, stirring, until some of the vegetables are tinged dark-gold around the edges. Stir in the ginger and the cabbage, and season with salt and pepper. Continue sautéing, lifting and turning the vegetables, until the cabbage begins to soften, 7–10 minutes. Add the broth, tomatoes and juice, bay leaf, apricots, if using, and sauerkraut. Bring the soup to a slow boil, set the cover slightly askew, then simmer gently for 2 hours. Stir the soup occasionally.

3. Add the apples, brown sugar, lemon juice, and salt and pepper to taste. If needed, adjust the lemon and sugar until you reach the perfect sweet-and-sour balance. Cook for an additional hour. Remove the bay leaf. Taste again and adjust the seasoning if needed.

4. While the soup is simmering, prepare the kreplach. Stir together all the ingredients except the wonton wrappers, seasoning generously with salt and pepper. Refrigerate for at least 30 minutes. Fill and seal the kreplach, using 1 heaping teaspoon of filling, 1 wrapper, and egg wash for each krepl, then folding into a triangle shape. Poach the kreplach. (See pages 30–31 for procedures.)

5. To serve, place 4–5 cooked kreplach in each warmed, shallow soup plate. Ladle in the soup along with some of the vegetables. To freshen the flavors, sprinkle with some chopped dill.

Even better the next day.

YIELD: 6–8 servings

SORREL-FLAVORED MUSHROOM BARLEY SOUP

"A bread of affliction," the Passover Haggadah calls it. And the first matzoh probably was. Made of barley flour, like the Hebrew breads at that time, it was dense and tooth-defying. As the lighter, more delicate wheat flour became available, baked goods made of barley flour took on an air of poverty and deprivation, gradually losing favor among Jews.

Not so fluffy barley kernels. For soups and pilafs, where it offers a creamy, risottolike richness, barley has remained a kitchen staple. Jewish cooks classically combine it with earthy dried mushrooms to accent the grain's toasted nut taste.

Meaty mushrooms provide the base for this full-bodied vegetarian soup. I use tart sorrel to play up the sweet barley and dairy flavors. Add buttermilk for a fresh light dish; rich palates will choose instead a dollop of sour cream.

½ cup pearl barley

About 2 ounces dried porcini mushrooms

¾ pound onions, chopped (3 cups)

1 tablespoon unsalted butter

3 tablespoons oil

Salt and freshly ground black pepper

About ½ pound carrots, finely chopped (1 cup)

2 celery stalks, including leaves, coarsely chopped, or 2 cups coarsely chopped fennel

6 large garlic cloves, peeled

½ pound fresh shiitake mushrooms

½ cup dry red wine

A few fresh thyme sprigs, or ½ teaspoon dried thyme

½ cup finely chopped shallots, or 1 cup chopped onions plus 2 teaspoons minced garlic

2 tablespoons soy sauce

3 cups tightly packed fresh sorrel (about 6 ounces), washed well, stems removed, and leaves coarsely shredded (sorrel leaves should be crisp, bright, and unwilted—avoid torn or yellow leaves or those with wet or soft spots; sorrel can be stored 1–2 days in perforated bags in the refrigerator)

Sour cream or buttermilk

Chopped fresh dill, for garnish

---

1. The night before, or several hours prior to starting the soup, soak the barley in a bowl with 1 ½ cups of cold water. (Barley soaked for 5–6 hours will cook in about 15 minutes in the soup. Unsoaked barley will absorb a great deal of the soup liquid while cooking, so if you don't have time to soak it, parboil it in about 3 ½ cups of water for about 20 minutes, then drain and add to the soup when called for in the recipe.)

2. Start the mushroom stock. Put the porcini in a large, heatproof bowl and add 4 cups of hot water. Cover and set aside for about 45 minutes to soften. Drain the mushrooms through a strainer lined with paper towels or a coffee filter, reserving all the soaking liquid. Wash the mushrooms under cold water to remove any remaining grit, then chop them coarsely and set aside.

3. While the porcini are soaking, in a 6-quart Dutch oven or large, heavy saucepan, sauté the onions in the butter and 1 tablespoon of the oil over moderately high heat. Stir occasionally at first, then more frequently as they begin to caramelize, until they are very fragrant and colored a rich butterscotch gold, about 15 minutes. Salt and pepper lightly, then add the carrots, celery or fennel, and garlic and sauté until the vegetables are softened and dotted with gold and deep bronze, 10–15 minutes. Wipe the shiitakes clean with a damp paper towel. Cut off the stems flush with the caps. Slice the caps thinly and set them aside, covered with plastic wrap, for finishing the soup. Trim off and discard the tough woody end of the stems. Slice the stems and add them to the sautéed vegetables along with the wine, and cook for 3–4 minutes. Add the porcini soaking liquid, thyme, and salt and pepper to taste, bring to a boil, and then simmer gently, partially covered, for about 1 hour. Strain the mixture through a wire mesh strainer into a large bowl, pressing down hard on the solids with the back of a spoon to extract as much liquid as possible. Discard the solids and set the strained mushroom stock aside.

4. Wash out the saucepan and dry it thoroughly. In it heat the shallots (or alternatively the onions and garlic) in the remaining 2 tablespoons of oil (or use 1 tablespoon each of butter and oil) until golden, about 5 minutes. Add the reserved sliced shiitake caps and sauté over moderately high heat until they're nutty and aromatic and bronzed at the edges. Stir in the soy sauce and chopped porcini and cook over high heat for about 3 minutes, evaporating all the liquid. Add the reserved mushroom stock. Drain the barley and add it, along with the sorrel and salt and pepper to taste. Bring to a boil and simmer for 15–20 minutes, or until the barley is very tender. Taste and adjust seasonings.

5. To serve, spoon a dollop of sour cream into each bowl, then ladle in the soup, stirring until smooth. Or gently warm some buttermilk (don't let it boil or it will curdle) and stir 3–4 tablespoons of it into each bowl of hot soup. When enriched with buttermilk, the soup is also delightfully refreshing served tepid, so you need not go to the trouble of heating the buttermilk on sultry summer days. Garnish with chopped dill.

YIELD: About 6 servings

COOK'S NOTE: The barley will literally drink up all the broth if allowed to remain in the soup. To reserve any leftover soup, be sure to separate the solids from the broth and refrigerate both individually.

FRESH BORSCHT WITH DILLED ONION-BUTTER MATZOH BALLS

> A broth of beet is beneficial for the heart and good for the eyes, and needless to say for the bowels.... This is only if it is left on the stove till it goes tuk, tuk.
> — BABYLONIAN TALMUD: BERAKOT 39A

The lovely caterer Arlette Lustyk shared the recipe for this simple delicious soup with me in her Paris office while my husband and daughter entertained themselves poring over photographs of the giant challahs that line the tables at her fabulous weddings and bar mitzvahs.

Madame Lustyk and her husband, Claude, recommend serving the borscht hot in winter, accompanied by *klops,* Polish-Jewish meatballs bursting with onions; for the summer, they combine it with crème fraîche and offer it chilled, ladled over a hot boiled potato. But it was spring when I was playing around in my kitchen and I decided to compromise. I enriched the broth with sour cream and served it warm, a supernal hot pink complement to my buttery matzoh balls.

To draw out all the fresh beet essence for the soup, the raw beets are soaked first in cold water for several hours or overnight, then slow-simmered in the liquid. The resulting borscht (the catchall Yiddish name for soups containing the ubiquitous beet) is more deeply flavorful than most meatless beet broths. I find that the plain borscht, without eggs or cream, also doubles quite successfully as an easily prepared *rosl,* a fermented beet juice, to be used for braising (see Beet-Braised Pot Roast on page 326).

BORSCHT

About 2½ pounds fresh beets (weight without leaves)

7 cups cold water (quality is important here, so if you use bottled water for coffee or tea, use it here)

Salt and freshly ground black pepper

About 1 teaspoon sour salt, or to taste (available in specialty stores and those that cater to European and Middle Eastern clientele)

About 2 tablespoons brown or white sugar, or to taste

2 large egg yolks

MATZOH BALLS

¼ pound onion, finely chopped (1 cup)

3 tablespoons unsalted butter

Salt and freshly ground black pepper

3 large eggs

½ cup matzoh meal

½ teaspoon baking powder

2 tablespoons finely chopped fresh dill

Optional accompaniments: sour cream, yogurt cream (see page 30), or crème fraîche; chopped fresh dill, for garnish

1. A day before you plan to serve the borscht, peel the beets and slice them thinly. Place them in a non-reactive stockpot and add the water. Cover the pot tightly and let it sit at room temperature overnight or up to 24 hours. Don't peek.

2. Start the matzoh balls. In a medium skillet, sauté the onion in the butter over moderate heat until soft and golden, about 7 minutes. Salt and pepper lightly and let cool. Beat the eggs in a bowl until foamy. Add the sautéed onion mixture and beat again. Whisk in the matzoh meal, baking powder, salt (about ¾ teaspoon, or to taste), and some pepper. Stir in the dill. Cover with plastic wrap and refrigerate for at least 2 hours to allow the mixture to absorb the seasonings and liquids.

3. When ready to cook the borscht, remove the pot lid and carefully skim away all the foam that has risen to the top. Add 2 teaspoons salt and about ⅛ teaspoon pepper, or to taste, and cook over moderate heat for 1½ hours, vigilantly skimming off any foam and scum as it accumulates.

4. About 10 minutes before the borscht has finished cooking, stir in the sour salt and sugar. Season generously with salt and pepper. Adjust sour salt and sugar until a happy balance between tart and sweet is achieved.

5. Meanwhile, poach the matzoh balls. In a large, wide pot, bring 3 quarts of water and 1 tablespoon salt to a furious boil. Form the batter into balls the size of large walnuts. (You can also make them smaller, as you prefer.) Slip them in, one at a time, then turn down the heat to a simmer. Cover the pot tightly, and don't lift the lid at all until you are ready to test them. Begin testing after 35–40 minutes of cooking. They should be light, fluffy, and completely cooked through. If necessary, continue cooking until the matzoh balls test done. To test, remove a matzoh ball and cut it in half: the interior should have no raw or dark spots. Remove them gently with a large slotted spoon or skimmer.

6. Strain the borscht, reserving the liquid and returning it to the pot. (If the beet slices still retain their shape and flavor, toss them with a distinctive vinaigrette—and serve at another meal. Try walnut vinaigrette: Whisk together 1 teaspoon Dijon mustard, 1 tablespoon fresh lemon juice, salt, and freshly ground pepper. Slowly beat in 3 tablespoons walnut oil and 1 tablespoon mild olive oil until well blended and thick. Adjust seasoning to taste. Shower the beets with chopped toasted walnuts and fresh, finely minced chives. If all the flavor has cooked out, discard the beets.)

7. In a medium bowl, whisk the egg yolks until light and foamy. Ladle in about a cup of hot soup, stirring to prevent curdling. (This is "tempering" the egg yolks—adding them all at once to the hot soup

would result in curdling.) Gradually stir this mixture into the soup pot, and cook, stirring, over low heat, just until the ingredients are well incorporated and the soup is hot and slightly thickened.

8. When ready to serve, if the matzoh balls are no longer hot, place them in the hot soup to reheat. If needed, warm the soup gently, but do not allow it to boil or it will curdle. Put a few matzoh balls in each heated shallow soup bowl and ladle the hot soup over them. If desired, add a dollop of sour cream, yogurt cream, or crème fraîche to each bowl and garnish with dill. Or pass these accompaniments separately so that guests can add their own.

YIELD: About 6 servings

BEEF STOCK

By setting aside a cup or two of clear chicken soup for the freezer every time I make it, I usually have sufficient chicken stock available for most cooking needs. Using good homemade chicken stock does beef recipes no injustice, in most cases. But there are times when only a full-bodied beef stock will do—for simmering flanken (page 108) or adding dimension to Tangy Russian Cabbage Soup (page 71), for instance.

These dishes call for deep, rich flavors, so first I caramelize the meat, bones, and aromatics. Because I have a very large, wide, heavy pot (an 8-quart Dutch oven), I can do everything—browning and simmering—in one pot, on top of the stove. A regular stockpot is neither wide nor heavy enough to brown the ingredients well. If you don't have a large enough saucepan or Dutch oven, use a 5- to 6-quart pot for browning, then transfer everything to a stockpot. Either way is simpler and less messy than caramelizing the ingredients by oven-roasting them.

About the bones. While marrow bones are often suggested, I find they give the stock an almost greasy quality that can be quite unpleasant in many dishes. Many butchers will not charge for soup bones—knuckle, shank, shoulder, and neck are good choices—if you request them when placing a large meat order. If you buy meat infrequently, request bones whenever you do make a purchase and store them in the freezer until you are ready to prepare the stock.

1–2 tablespoons mild olive or vegetable oil	3 large, fat garlic cloves, peeled
3 pounds lean stewing beef, such as chuck or neck meat, trimmed and cut into 3-inch pieces	½ cup dry red or white wine
2 pounds knuckle, shank, shoulder, or neck bones (if bones are very meaty, you can reduce the amount of beef to 2 pounds), trimmed of as much fat as possible	4 quarts cold water (quality is important here, so if you use bottled water for coffee or tea, use it here)
½ pound onions, cut into coarse chunks (2 cups)	20 peppercorns, crushed
About ½ pound carrots, cut into coarse chunks (1½ cups)	1 teaspoon salt
About 1 parsnip, cut into coarse chunks (½–1 cup)	1 small rutabaga or white turnip, cut into chunks (about 1–1½ cups)
	About 3 celery stalks, including leaves, if available, coarsely chopped (1 cup)
	1 cup fresh parsley sprigs

1. In an 8- to 10-quart Dutch oven or heavy saucepan, heat 1 tablespoon oil. Working in batches so you don't crowd the pan, lightly brown the meat over moderately high heat (don't let it get too crusty), and transfer it to a platter. In the same pan, brown the bones on all sides, then transfer them to

the platter. Add another tablespoon of oil, if necessary, and the onions, carrots, parsnip, and garlic. Brown them in the dark meat residue, stirring and scraping them as they begin to bronze around the edges, about 10 minutes. Add the wine and stir constantly with a wooden spoon to scrape up the browned bits. Add 1 quart of the water and boil for 3 minutes, stirring, to pick up any remaining meat and vegetable bits. (If using a smaller size pan, transfer everything now to a stockpot.)

2. Add the meat, bones, remaining 3 quarts water, peppercorns, and salt. Turn the heat to medium and bring to a slow bubble. As the soup cooks, keep skimming any froth and scum that rises to the surface. When the soup begins to "smile," that is, tiny bubbles break along the edge of the pot, turn the heat down to very low. Let the soup simmer for about 30 minutes, skimming it frequently. Add the rutabaga, celery, and parsley and raise the heat slightly to bring it back to a simmer. Turn the heat down as low as possible, put the lid on, leaving it slightly askew, and continue skimming any froth or scum occasionally. Simmer the soup for at least 2–2½ hours longer—3–5 is even better. Do *not* let the soup boil. If necessary, use a flame-tamer, or *blech,* or put it on top of two burner grates stacked together. (Make sure the soup *is* bubbling, though ever so gently. If there is no movement on the surface at all, the soup will spoil.) Add more salt if you want, but remember this is a stock: the other dishes in which you will use it may be salty enough, and besides, the stock's flavors will become more concentrated when you boil it down.

3. Let the soup cool to room temperature in the pot, *uncovered*. (Hot soup in a covered pot may turn sour.)

4. Strain the cooled soup through a fine sieve, pressing down on all the meat, bones, and vegetables to extract as much of their flavorful juices as you can, then discard the solids. (If desired, you can save the meat—and the carrots—and dice them finely to serve in the stock. Most of the flavor will, however, have been extracted from them already.)

5. Refrigerate the soup, covered, overnight or until all the fat has congealed on top. Carefully scrape off the fat and discard it. If the soup still seems fatty, line a fine sieve with a layer of paper towels and pour the soup through into a clean bowl or pot (if the soup has jelled from chilling, bring it to room temperature first). If the paper towels become thickly coated with fat, you might want to change them once or twice during the process.Store the stock in the refrigerator (it will keep for about one week) or freeze for up to 3 months.

YIELD: 2½–3 quarts

VEGETABLE STOCK

PAREVE OR DAIRY

Because vegetable stock is pareve, or neutral, that is, it contains neither meat nor dairy, according to the dietary laws, it may be eaten with either. But meat dishes generally rely on meat stocks; in Jewish cooking, it is foods glossed with butter or topped with cream that give vegetable stock its reason for being. Only vegetable stock can jazz up a plain pilaf destined to partner a butter-gilded fish. It is the sole stock base for a soup that will be enriched with sour cream or yogurt. And kasha, often insipid when prepared with plain water, turns inspired with a stock that permits generous lacings of genuine sweet butter instead of margarine.

You can purchase acceptable ready-made, even canned, versions of chicken and beef stock that will do nicely in a pinch for sauces, stews, and so on, but good-quality vegetable stocks are harder to find. Fortunately, they are much quicker to make than the meat-based kind (in fact, lengthy cooking will ruin, not improve, a vegetable stock).

This is one of those recipes for which I am reluctant to provide exact ingredients and measures because it can be varied endlessly according to availability of produce and how the stock will ultimately be used. So think of this recipe as a guide.

Some of the optional ingredients here will give you bigger flavors. Use them when you desire a stronger, darker stock. Tomatoes make everything sing, but with a rather full-throated voice. Soy sauce and the liquid from soaking dried mushrooms can be insistent too. You may want to start with smaller quantities of these ingredients, and keep tasting as you go along, adding more as necessary. If you have the corncobs leftover from scraping the kernels for another use, they will provide an earthy sweetness.

And by all means, add other vegetables: anything in the onion family, a little sweet red pepper, more fresh mushrooms (parings are fine), fennel, pea pods, a small potato, celery root, fresh herbs. Aim for balance and complexity—no one ingredient should overwhelm the others. And avoid strong or bitter-tasting vegetables, like broccoli, members of the cabbage family, eggplant, and pungent greens.

---

1 tomato (optional)

2 tablespoons olive oil or unsalted butter, or
  1 tablespoon of each

2 large onions, 1 coarsely chopped, 1 sliced
  rather thin

2 medium carrots, scraped and diced

2 celery stalks, coarsely chopped

1 small parsnip, peeled and coarsely chopped

1 small turnip, scraped or, if waxed or thick-
  skinned, peeled and coarsely chopped

½ pound fresh mushrooms, wiped clean (pieces
  and stems are fine; choose regular
  cultivated or shiitake mushrooms)

6–8 garlic cloves, peeled and smashed

About 1 teaspoon soy sauce (optional)

4–6 fresh thyme sprigs, or ¼ teaspoon dried thyme

5 peppercorns, crushed

1 teaspoon salt

10 fresh parsley sprigs

1 bay leaf

¼ cup celery leaves, or 1 teaspoon celery seed,
   crushed lightly

Optional additions:

   Up to 1 cup zucchini or summer squash chunks,
   strips of mild lettuce, green Swiss chard
   leaves or stalks

   2 corncobs

Up to ¼ ounce dried mushrooms (soaked in 2
cups hot water for 30 minutes, or until soft,
then rinsed for grit and finely chopped)

Some liquid from soaking dried mushrooms
(you can use leftover liquid from another
recipe; just make sure you have strained the
liquid through a sieve lined with a paper towel
or a coffee filter to remove any remaining grit)

2 quarts cold water (quality is important here,
so if you use bottled water for coffee or tea,
use it here)

1. If you are using the tomato, char it to give it some character and to remove the peel easily: Rinse and pat it dry first, then spear it through the stem end with a long-handled fork and lightly blacken the skin on all sides over an open gas burner, as you would roast a pepper. Let it cool until you can handle it, then pull off the peel with your fingers. Cut the tomato in half, scoop out the seeds and the core and discard. Chop the pulp coarsely and set it aside.

2. In a 6-quart Dutch oven or very wide, heavy saucepan, heat the oil and/or butter until sizzling. Add all of the onions and sauté over moderately high heat for about 15 minutes, frequently lifting and scraping the pieces from the bottom of the pan as the onions caramelize into a deep golden bronze, speckled all over with nutty brown.

3. Add the carrots, celery, parsnip, and turnip, and cook over moderately high heat until the edges of the vegetables are tinged with brown. Add the mushrooms and garlic and cook until the mushrooms give up their liquid. Sprinkle with the soy sauce, if using, thyme, peppercorns, and salt. Add the tomato pulp and sauté for 5 minutes. Add the parsley, bay leaf, celery leaves or seeds, optional zucchini, squash, lettuce, and chard and sauté for 1–2 minutes. Add the optional corncobs, soaked dried mushrooms, and/or mushroom soaking liquid. Add the water. Bring to a gentle boil, so the bubbles just begin to break along the edges, then reduce to a simmer. Cook, partially covered, for 45–60 minutes until the vegetables are very soft. Strain immediately through a sieve or colander fitted with paper towels, pressing hard against the solids with the back of a wooden spoon to extract all of the flavorful liquids. Taste and adjust seasonings. If the stock lacks character, concentrate the flavors by reducing the liquid slightly. (Don't reduce this stock too much—it will turn bitter.)

4. Let cool completely, *uncovered*, then cover and refrigerate. The stock will keep for up to 5 days refrigerated or for up to 3 months frozen.

YIELD: About 6 cups

FISH

And in Rome, Poland, and New York too. Throughout the Diaspora and in Israel, fish has been a cardinal fixture of Jewish cuisine.

Fat golden carp, set thrashing in bathtubs on Thursday, metamorphosed into savory gefilte fish come Friday morning. Gleaming red and gray mullet and sweet-fleshed sole were fried and marinated for elegant cold Sabbath lunches. Stewed or roasted, sauced with fresh green plums or spicy gingersnaps, the choicest fresh fish graced the festive meals.

And during the workday week, there were barrels of preserved fish, smoked, salt-crusted, or brined—herring, mostly, and anchovies. Later there was salmon in all its permutations, including canned, which in America was quickly adopted for the ubiquitous dairy meal, salmon croquettes.

Not all fish are kosher. Permissible fish must have fins and scales that are visible to the naked eye, that overlap, and that can be detached from the skin. So not only are all shellfish like shrimp, lobster, clams, and oysters forbidden, but also swordfish, catfish, skate, and shark, among others, because they lack true scales. Rabbis have debated for centuries whether the scales of the sturgeon conform to the strict laws of kashrut; today most observant Jews refrain from eating it.

But fish that are kosher require no special treatment in the Jewish kitchen. They are free from the stringent laws of slaughter and preparation that govern meat and poultry. Anyone—fishmonger or home cook—can kill a permissible fish, and it needs no soaking and salting to ritually purify it. And fish are considered pareve; like vegetables and grains, they may be eaten at meat or dairy meals and cooked and served in either meat or dairy pots and dishes. (However, observant Jews refrain from eating fish and meat together in the same dish, like veal seasoned with anchovies, or gefilte fish poached in chicken broth. Traditionally, after a fish appetizer, they will cleanse their palates with a bit of bread, a sip of wine or whiskey, or, in more luxurious surroundings, even a tart sorbet, before tucking into a meat course.)

> ...the feast was worthy of a king. There was fish that
> brought to mind the biblical verse about the great whales.
> —CHAIM N. BIALIK, "THE SHORT FRIDAY"

According to Jewish mystical tradition, eating fish is not merely practical—it is fraught with magical optimism. Ever since the biblical blessings in Genesis to "be fruitful and multiply" and "fill the waters of the sea," fish have symbolized fertility and immortality, abundance, and prosperity.

Dining on fish brings a taste of Paradise, a mystical means to preview the exquisite serenity of the Messianic Age. For, according to the legend in the Book of Job, the Leviathan, a monstrous fish embodying evil, will be defeated when the Messiah arrives and the righteous will feast upon its flesh.

> Wherewith does one show delight in the Sabbath...
> with beets, a large fish, and garlic.
> —BABYLONIAN TALMUD: SHABBAT 118ʙ

The numerical value of the letters in the word *dag* (Hebrew for fish) adds up to seven, and Sabbath is the seventh day of the week. And so whoever ate *dag* on the Sabbath was thought to be safe from the judgment of *Gehenna,* the hellish afterlife for the damned.

Although prepared differently in the myriad kitchens of the Diaspora, a special fish dish usually appears at one or more meals on every Jewish Sabbath: Friday night, the hearty Saturday lunch, or the light meal at Sabbath's close. In fact, two widely divergent chopped fish recipes, gefilte fish and Middle Eastern ground fish balls, like Egyptian bellahat, may both owe their origins to the injunction against

Sabbath work, which includes *borer,* or picking over bones. Removing the bones from the fish and chopping it up in advance afforded Jews from Eastern Europe and North Africa a delicious, pleasurable way to enjoy their Sabbath fish.

The fish recipes that follow no longer require a day's devotion. You'll find short—and long—versions of gefilte fish here, and variations of other ground fish, as well as terrific salmon croquettes and a vervy make-ahead Venetian fish. Additional fish recipes are listed below.

OTHER FISH SUGGESTIONS

GOLDEN GEFILTE FISH WITH GOLDEN HORSERADISH (LONG AND SHORT VERSIONS)

PAREVE

Hashed onions and soaked challa fill the fish with new blood.... The smell tantalizes us, tickles our noses. It brings us the first taste of Sabbath.

—BELLA CHAGALL, *BURNING LIGHTS*

"We also put in saffron, to make the fish yellow," adds my mother.

—CHAIM GRADE, *MY MOTHER'S SABBATH DAYS*

My father's mother baked whitefish smothered with chopped tomatoes, onions, and peppers, and served it cold for Sabbath meals. The only fish I remember my maternal grandmother making was canned tuna, mixed with hard-boiled eggs and onions.

So I've had to invent my own family recipe for gefilte fish—for many, the defining dish of Ashkenazi cuisine. I'd eaten some very good versions at dairy restaurants, and tasted even more delicious ones in the evocative prose of Yiddish writers. I knew what I was after.

Most important is a soft, tender texture. In place of the matzoh meal filler, which might make the mixture dense, I choose bits of fresh challah, as Bella Chagall's family had done in *Burning Lights,* her charming memoir of growing up in Vitebsk, Russia, before she married the legendary artist.

There's a play of flavors in the seasoning, from a jot of mellowed garlic to a tart citrus splash and the fresh, clean bite of heaps of freshly ground pepper blossoming on the tongue. And to pull all the flavors into balance, I steal a little sweetness from carrots and onions that I sauté first and then puree. These vegetables also add softness and moisture, and dab the pale fish with tiny threads of color.

But I want color that will tantalize, so, like the overworked mother in Chaim Grade's novel of World War II Vilna, *My Mother's Sabbath Days,* I gild the fish with golden saffron.

When I prepare a broth for the fish, I simmer it long with sweet root vegetables and poach the fish balls short, to maximize their flavor and keep them quenelle-light. For a quick version, I dispense with the broth and bake the fish in individual custard cups in a hot water bath; the resulting flavor and texture are a shade more delicate, if less intense.

The golden horseradish, made with cooked carrots and moistened with carrot juice for the barest suggestion of sweetness, is a beguiling, festive departure, but if you don't have time to prepare it, serve the fish with the ready-made variety.

FISH BALLS

¾ pound onions, chopped (3 cups)

1 medium carrot, diced (½ cup)

2 tablespoons mild olive or vegetable oil such as
  avocado or sesame

1 large garlic clove, peeled

Salt and freshly ground black pepper

½ cup packed fresh challah pieces
  (crusts removed) or, for Passover, replace
  the challah with an equal quantity of egg
  or plain matzoh, moistened with white wine
  or water

¼ teaspoon packed saffron threads, crushed and
  dissolved in 2 tablespoons hot water

3 pounds skinless fish fillets (stray bones
  removed), rinsed to remove any scales, patted
  dry, and cut into 1-inch pieces, or ground by
  the fishmonger (see Cook's Note)

½ cup ice water

2 pinches of sugar

4 large eggs

2 tablespoons fresh lemon juice

IF PREPARING WITH FISH STOCK

About 3 pounds fish bones, skin, and heads

4 large carrots, scraped and quartered

2 large onions, peeled and quartered

2 celery stalks, including leaves, quartered

2 parsnips, peeled and quartered (they add a
  subtle whisper of sweetness) (optional)

3–4 parsley sprigs

Salt and freshly ground black pepper

Sugar, if needed

IF OVEN-POACHING

1 medium carrot, scraped

Mild oil, for greasing the custard cups

Boiling or scalding-hot tap water, for hot water
  bath

Accompaniments: soft lettuce, Belgian endive,
  or radicchio leaves, for lining serving plates;
  Golden Horseradish (page 89) or freshly
  grated or prepared horseradish

Very finely minced fresh flat-leaf parsley or
  chives, for garnish (optional)

1. Prepare the fish balls. In a heavy, 10-inch skillet, sauté the onions and carrots in the oil over moderate heat, stirring occasionally, for about 10 minutes. Don't let the vegetables brown: you just want to soften and sweeten them. Add the garlic and season with salt and pepper lightly. Cover the pan, reduce the heat, and cook, stirring occasionally, until the carrots are soft enough to mash roughly with the back of a metal spoon, 10—15 minutes.

2. Transfer the vegetables and oil in the skillet to a food processor and pulse just until the ingredients are thoroughly combined. Add the challah and saffron and process until smooth. Transfer the mixture to a large wooden chopping bowl (the kind used with a crescent-shaped chopping tool, like the half-moon-shaped Jewish *hockmeisser* or crescent-shaped Italian *mezzaluna*) or a chopping board.

3. If the fish was not purchased ground, place half of the pieces in the food processor (don't bother rinsing it out) and pulse until it is chopped medium-coarse. Add to the challah mixture. Process the

remaining half of the fish in the same way, and add it to the mixture. If the fish is already ground, add it now to the challah mixture.

4. Chop the ingredients, using a hand chopper with the bowl or a sharp cleaver with the board, gradually adding the ice water as you work. Continue chopping while adding 2 teaspoons salt, 1½–2 teaspoons pepper, or to taste (the fish should be quite peppery), and the sugar. Chop in the eggs, one at a time, and the lemon juice. Keep chopping until the mixture becomes very smooth, light, and fluffy. (All this hand-chopping incorporates lots of air into the ingredients, which will make the fish balls light and delicate. Using a food processor or blender will simply puree the ingredients to liquefaction.) Refrigerate until thoroughly chilled and firm, at least 2 hours.

5. If stovetop-poaching the gefilte fish in fish stock, prepare the stock. Rinse the fish bones, skin, and heads and place in a very large, wide, heavy saucepan. Add 2 quarts of cold water and bring to a boil, skimming constantly to remove all the bitter froth and scum as they rise to the top. Continue skimming the broth while it cooks at a gentle boil for another 10 minutes. Add the vegetables and salt and pepper to taste, then reduce the heat and simmer, partially covered, for about an hour. Skim occasionally, as needed. Strain the broth through a fine strainer, pressing down hard on the solids with the back of a spoon to extract as much flavorful liquid as possible. Discard the solids (if you want to serve the carrots with the fish, save them and set them aside). Rinse out the saucepan and pour in the strained broth. Bring the broth to a simmer and adjust the seasonings. Add a pinch or two of sugar to remove any trace of bitterness, if needed.

6. Wetting your hands with cold water as necessary, form the fish mixture into ovals, using about ⅓–½ cup of fish for each gefilte fish ball. Place the balls on one or two platters as you finish making the rest. Using a spatula, carefully lower the balls one by one into the simmering broth. Add only as many fish balls as will fit comfortably in a single layer. If they are not covered with stock, baste them with a few spoonfuls. Cover tightly and simmer over low heat, without peeking, for 30 minutes. Remove a fish ball and cut it in half to test for doneness: it should be completely cooked through, with no dark or raw spots. Cook a bit longer, as needed, but don't overcook. Remove the balls with a slotted spoon and place in a single layer in a deep dish or two. Poach any remaining balls in the same way, and transfer them to the same dish. Reduce the liquid in the pan over high heat by at least half. Pour a shallow layer of the liquid over the gefilte fish and refrigerate any remaining liquid. It should gel nicely. Refrigerate the gefilte fish for at least 6 hours, preferably overnight. To serve, arrange the chilled fish on the lettuce, endive or radicchio, surrounded by some of the fish gelatin, if desired, and any reserved carrots. Accompany with golden horseradish or prepared beet horseradish.

7. If oven-poaching, boil the carrot in lightly salted water until tender. Drain. Preheat the oven to 350°F. Grease the bottom and sides of twelve 1-cup custard cups. Cut the carrot into very thin slices

and decoratively arrange 1, 2, or 3 slices in the center of each custard cup. Spoon the prepared fish mixture into the cups, then tap the cups sharply on the side with a butter knife to remove any trapped air bubbles and even out the mixture. Use the butter knife or the back of a spoon to smooth the tops. Cover the cups with foil. Fold a dish towel flat on the bottom of a large baking pan. Place the custard cups on the towel and pour in enough boiling or scalding tap water to come halfway up the sides of the cups. Place in the oven and bake for about 30 minutes, or until cooked through (they should feel solid in the center). Remove the custard cups from the hot water bath and cool, uncovered, to room temperature. Keep the cups covered with foil and refrigerate for at least 6 hours, or preferably overnight. To serve, run a knife around the edges and unmold onto plates lined with lettuce, endive, or radicchio. If desired, after inverting, dust the tops (avoiding the carrot slices in the center) with the parsley or chives. (Alternatively, before baking, you could sprinkle the custard cups with the herbs after you have added the carrot, but before spooning in the fish mixture.) Accompany with golden horseradish or prepared beet horseradish.

YIELD: About 12 servings

COOK'S NOTE: For the fish, choose an equal quantity of carp, pike, and whitefish; equal parts pike and whitefish (my preference); or your own or your fishmonger's favorite mixture. You can mix fresh and saltwater varieties, if you'd like, such as carp with halibut. Avoid very strong flavored fish, like bluefish or mackerel. For the best taste, you should have some combination of fat and lean fish. (See chart below.)

MODERATE- TO HIGH-FAT FISH	LEAN FISH	
Arctic char	cod (scrod)	pollock
buffalofish	flounder	red snapper
carp	grouper	sea bass or striped bass
Chilean sea bass	haddock	sea trout
lake or rainbow trout	hake or whiting	sole
pompano	halibut	
sablefish or black cod	ocean perch	
salmon	perch (yellow)	
whitefish	pike (pickerel, muskellunge)	

GOLDEN HORSERADISH

⅓ cup peeled carrots, cut into small chunks
Enough fresh horseradish root, peeled, to yield
  about 1 cup when grated (about 2 cups of
  peeled chunks)
About ¼ cup cider vinegar

About 1 teaspoon salt
½ cup fresh carrot juice (see Cook's Note)
Sugar (optional)

1. In a small saucepan, boil the carrots in lightly salted water until very tender. Drain and rinse with cold water until cool. Pat dry and set aside.

2. Place horseradish in a food processor and grind until coarsely grated. With the machine on, add through the feed tube ¼ cup vinegar, 1 teaspoon salt, and ¼ cup of the carrot juice. Continue processing just until the horseradish is finely grated but not reduced to a puree. Averting your face when removing the processor lid (to avoid the noxious fumes), scrape down the bowl. With the machine on, add the cooked carrots, alternating with the remaining ¼ cup carrot juice. Remembering again to avert your face, transfer the contents (including the liquid) to a bowl. Mix very well, cover tightly, and refrigerate for at least 3 hours so the flavors mingle.

3. Stir well and if needed, adjust the vinegar and salt before serving. The combination of the cooked carrot and carrot juice brings a delicate, vegetal sweetness to the sauce without added sugar. If you prefer a sweeter-tasting sauce, add a pinch or two of sugar.

Store in a tightly covered glass jar. Serve leftover sauce with beef or mix with mayonnaise for cold poultry; combined with mayonnaise or sour cream it is a perfect foil for richly flavored poached, smoked, or fried fish.

YIELD: About 1¼ cups

COOK'S NOTE: If you cannot get fresh carrot juice, boil down the carrot cooking water until reduced to ¼ cup. Let it cool, then substitute it for the juice in the recipe. (Since the cooking water is thinner and not as deeply flavored as the carrot juice, using an equal quantity of it would dilute the taste of the sauce too much.)

Like Ginger-Beet Horseradish (page 94), golden horseradish marries well with a little freshly grated ginger. Add the ginger to taste when first grating the horseradish.

GEFILTE FISH QUICKLY STEAMED BETWEEN CABBAGE LEAVES

PAREVE

Inspired by the Chinese method for preparing tender, soft dumplings, I cushion these wonderfully delicate fish balls between cabbage leaves for a gentle twenty-minute steam bath. The wet vapor helps preserve all the subtle flavors of the fish while the nutty-sweet cabbage wrapper keeps it moist as it steams, and later as it chills, without broth, in the refrigerator.

The fish mixture here is particularly delicious. Extra egg yolks and a little pureed carrot and parsnip bring added flavor and a lush softness. No fish broth but a bit of the liquid from cooking the sweet vegetables moistens the matzoh meal filler.

The result is gefilte fish brimful of flavor yet light and fresh tasting. To complement it, mellow the horseradish's fire with some mayonnaise seasoned with fresh dill.

FISH BALLS

⅓ cup carrots, scraped and diced

⅓ cup parsnips, peeled and diced

3 tablespoons matzoh meal

2 tablespoons mild olive or vegetable oil

1½ cups onions, coarsely chopped

Salt and freshly ground pepper

1 tablespoon chopped shallots

2 tablespoons chopped fresh dill, plus
  16 additional sprigs of dill

2 pounds fish fillets, skin and any bones
  removed and discarded (either have the fish
  ground by your fishmonger or rinse it to remove
  any scales, pat dry, and cut into 1-inch
  pieces)(see Cook's Note)

2 large eggs

2 large egg yolks

2 tablespoons fresh lemon juice

DILL-HORSERADISH MAYONNAISE

1 cup mayonnaise

⅓ cup finely minced dill

⅓ cup plus 1 tablespoon prepared white
  horseradish, drained

About 12 large cabbage leaves, washed (the cabbage bed is discarded before serving, so you can
  use slightly imperfect or dark green outer leaves)

Soft lettuce leaves, endives, or radicchio for
  lining plates

1. Prepare the fish balls. In a small saucepan, bring one cup lightly salted water to a boil. Add the carrots and parsnips, and simmer until the vegetables are very tender. Drain, reserving the cooking water, and transfer the vegetables to a food processor. Put the matzoh meal in a small bowl and stir in ⅓ cup of the reserved cooking water. Let this mixture sit so that the matzoh meal can soften as it soaks in the liquid.

2. Warm the oil in an 8-inch skillet. Add the onions, sprinkle them lightly with salt and pepper, and sauté, stirring, over medium heat until soft, shiny, and just beginning to color palest gold, 8–9 minutes. Don't let them brown. Transfer the onions and any oil remaining in the skillet to the food processor. Add the shallots and the chopped dill to the food processor and puree until fairly smooth. Transfer the mixture to a large wooden chopping bowl or a wooden chopping board. (Don't wash out the food processor if you are grinding your own fish.) If your fish is not ground, put it, about 2 teaspoons salt, and ⅛ teaspoon pepper in the workbowl of the food processor and pulse just until the mixture is chopped fine, but not pasty. Add the fish to the wooden bowl or board. (If you are using preground fish, add it now, seasoned with salt and pepper.) Add the soaked and softened matzoh meal mixture. Beat the eggs and the yolks in a bowl until thick and lemon-colored. Using a hand chopper or a cleaver, work the beaten eggs and the lemon juice into the fish mixture, a little at a time. (Hand-chopping at this point incorporates air into the mixture, making it lighter and fluffier than pulsing in the food processor.)

3. Test for seasoning. Poach a teaspoon of the fish mixture in lightly salted boiling water for a few minutes. Taste, and if needed, add additional salt and pepper. Chill the fish mixture, covered, for at least 1 hour or up to 4 hours. It will be easier to mold and the fish balls will cook up fluffier.

4. While the fish is chilling, combine the ingredients for the dill-horseradish mayonnaise. Cover and refrigerate.

5. Steam the fish balls. You'll need a large, wide pot, like a 5- to 6-quart Dutch oven or heavy casserole with a tight-fitting lid, and a rack that stands at least 2 inches high. A simple round cake rack works well. If it is not high enough, set it over 2 custard cups or empty tuna cans in the pot. Fill the pot with water to a depth of 1 inch.

6. Line the rack with a layer of cabbage leaves. Wetting your hands with cold water if necessary, form the fish mixture into 16 ovals, using a scant ¼ cup for each. Depending on the variety of fish used, the mixture may be very soft, but it will firm up as it cooks and later, as it chills. Bring the water in the pot to a boil. Gently put as many ovals on top of the cabbage leaves as will fit comfortably in a single layer without touching. Place a sprig of dill on each fish oval. Top the fish with another layer of cabbage leaves and cover the pot tightly. Turn the heat down to medium and steam the fish ovals for 20–25 minutes, or until they are completely cooked through at the center. (When steamed in raw cabbage leaves, the fish will probably take closer to 25 minutes; when steaming the second batch in the now cooked cabbage leaves, it will probably take about 20 minutes.) Line a platter with some of the cooked

cabbage leaves and carefully put the cooked fish on top of them. Using additional cabbage leaves as needed, cook any remaining fish ovals in the same way, transferring the fish as it is done to the cabbage-lined platter. Remove and discard the dill sprigs from all the cooked fish ovals, then cover the fish with a layer of cooked cabbage leaves to keep them moist. Let everything cool to room temperature. Wrap the platter with plastic wrap and chill the fish until cold.

7. For best flavor, serve the fish chilled but not icy cold. Remove the fish from the cabbage leaves and arrange the ovals attractively on platters or individual plates lined with lettuce, endive, or radicchio and accompany with dill-horseradish mayonnaise.

YIELD: About 8 servings

COOK'S NOTE: I like a combination of half salmon and half red snapper or lemon or grey sole. And I've made a terrific, plush-tasting gefilte fish with half Chilean sea bass and half flounder. Or use your own or your fishmonger's favorite mixture. Avoid very strong flavored fish, like bluefish or mackerel. Be sure to use a combination of fat and lean fish. (See the chart on page 88 for some fat and lean fish options.)

SALMON GEFILTE FISH POACHED IN FENNEL-WINE BROTH WITH GINGER-BEET HORSERADISH

PAREVE

Preparing gefilte fish from scratch no longer seems so daunting, with food processors and the wide availability of a variety of gleaming fresh fish fillets besides the noble triad of carp, pike, and whitefish.

Except for the broth. That still requires real commitment.

You'll need bones, of course, so you will have to befriend a fishmonger who will remember to save the trimmings. If you don't have a high-tech air filtration system, you can resign yourself to a kitchen (and perhaps living room and bedrooms too) smelling for several days like old Marseilles without the charms of Panisse and Marius. Not to mention constantly skimming all that fish foam.

Which is why I sometimes prefer to use a simple but intensely flavored vegetable stock made of wine and aromatic vegetables like fennel that complement the fish beautifully.

Forget the fish jelly, though: no bones, no gelatin. I don't miss it—it always seemed kind of a food oxymoron anyway. But the broth is delicious, and if enough is left over, use it to slow-braise potatoes for an intriguing accompaniment to simple grilled or poached fish. Oded Schwartz calls the recipe "fish potatoes" in his book *In Search of Plenty*. Cover quartered peeled potatoes with the broth, add knobs of butter, and season with salt and pepper. Bring to a boil; then simmer slowly until most of the liquid is evaporated and the potatoes are brown and fragrant. Serve hot with sour cream.

FENNEL-WINE BROTH

¾ pound onions, coarsely chopped (3 cups)

About ½ pound carrots, coarsely chopped
 (1 ½ cups)

2 tablespoons mild olive or vegetable oil

1 small fennel bulb, coarsely chopped (include
 stalks and some of the fennel fronds)

1 parsnip, coarsely chopped (about 1 cup)
 (optional)

3 garlic cloves, peeled

Salt

3 cups dry white wine

1 teaspoon peppercorns

1 teaspoon fennel seeds, crushed

1 bay leaf

½ cup coarsely chopped fresh parsley leaves and
 stems

FISH

1 ½ pounds salmon fillets, cut into 1-inch pieces,
 skin and any bones removed and discarded

½ pound sole, flounder, or any other soft white
 fish fillets, cut into 1-inch pieces, skin and any
 bones removed and discarded

2 large garlic cloves, peeled

Sautéed onion and carrot reserved from preparing the broth (about 1 ½ cups chopped onions
 and ¾ cup chopped carrots)

2 large eggs

1 tablespoon fresh lemon juice

1 ½ teaspoons salt

⅛ teaspoon freshly ground black pepper

⅛ teaspoon ground cinnamon

3 tablespoons finely ground blanched almonds

GINGER-BEET HORSERADISH

1 tablespoon peeled and finely grated fresh
  ginger, or to taste

1 cup prepared beet-horseradish

Soft lettuce, endive, or radicchio leaves, for
  lining plates

1. Prepare the broth. In a large, wide, heavy saucepan or 5- to 6-quart Dutch oven, sauté the onions and carrots in the oil over medium heat until the onions are softened and the carrots are tender, about 15 minutes. Using a slotted spoon, transfer about half the mixture to a food processor and let cool (you'll be using it later for the fish balls). To the saucepan, add the fennel, parsnips, if using, and garlic. Mix well and cook over medium-high heat for 5 minutes, stirring, until the vegetables begin to wilt and soften. Add salt to taste and 1 cup of the wine, cover the pan, and let sweat gently for 10 minutes. Stir occasionally to prevent sticking. Add the remaining 2 cups wine, 5 cups of water, the peppercorns, fennel seeds, bay leaf, and parsley. Bring to a boil, then simmer for about 45 minutes. Taste and adjust the seasoning. If the broth seems weak, raise the heat to high and boil briefly to concentrate the flavors. Cool slightly, then strain the broth through a fine sieve, pushing down on the solids to extract all the flavorful juices. Discard the solids. Rinse out the pan and return the strained broth to it.

2. Make the fish balls. Add the salmon, sole, and garlic cloves to the sautéed onion and carrot in the food processor. Chop fine, using the pulse motion, but don't puree. Put the mixture in a chopping bowl or on a chopping board. Using a hand-chopper or cleaver, work in the eggs, lemon juice, salt, pepper, and cinnamon. (Hand-chopping at this point incorporates air into the mixture, making it lighter and fluffier than pulsing in the food processor.) Stir in the ground almonds.

3. It's a good idea to do a test for seasoning. Poach a teaspoon of the fish mixture in lightly salted boiling water for a few minutes. Taste, and if needed, add additional salt and pepper. Refrigerate the fish, covered, for at least 1 and up to 4 hours (this step makes it easier to mold and the result is fluffier fish balls).

4. Prepare the ginger-beet horseradish. Stir the ginger into the horseradish, adding more or less according to preference. Cover and let stand for at least 30 minutes to allow the flavors to meld.

5. Bring the strained broth to a gentle boil. Wetting your hands with cold water if necessary, form the fish mixture into 16 ovals, using about ¼ cup for each. Place the ovals on a platter lined with wax

paper. Carefully slip the fish ovals into the broth and reduce the heat to a simmer. If the fish is not completely covered by the broth, baste with several spoonfuls of the broth. Cover the pot and poach the fish ovals for about 20 minutes, or until an inserted toothpick tests clean and the ovals are completely cooked through at the center. Remove the pot from the heat and let the fish cool in the broth. Then, for maximum flavor, cover and refrigerate in the broth overnight or, preferably, for 24 hours.

6. To serve, line platters or individual plates with lettuce, endive, or radicchio. Arrange two ovals of the chilled, drained fish attractively on top and accompany with the ginger-beet horseradish.

YIELD: About 8 servings

Spice container shaped like a fish. (Silver and amethyst. Germany, 18th century.)

EGYPTIAN GROUND FISH BALLS WITH TOMATO AND CUMIN (BELLAHAT)

PAREVE

Favored by Egyptian Jews as a prelude to Sabbath and holiday meals, this easy-to-prepare, well-seasoned alternative to gefilte fish requires no poaching in fish stock and can be made with any white-fleshed fish. The pungent cumin that flavors bellahat tastes like today, but it is an ancient spice, sold by the Hebrews during biblical times in herb markets, and used in their soups, stews, and breads.

Simple tomato sauce, galvanized by extra-virgin olive oil and lemon, cloaks the fish balls in this version from Corinne Rossabi, an excellent home cook raised in Egypt. When summer collides head-long with fall, I prepare a tomato and pepper sauce variation from the explosion of red, orange, and yellow at my local greenmarket (page 96).

FISH BALLS

1½ pounds flounder, haddock, cod, scrod, sole, hake, sea bass, snapper, grouper, or other nonoily white fish fillets, skin and any bones discarded

½ cup matzoh meal

2 large eggs

1 tablespoon minced fresh garlic

1 teaspoon kosher salt

½ teaspoon ground cumin

Cayenne (I usually use about ¼ teaspoon—I like this rather spicy, the traditional Egyptian way—but season to your taste)

Olive or vegetable oil, for frying

SAUCE

2 cups good-quality canned whole tomatoes with their juice, seeded and chopped

2 tablespoons fine-quality extra-virgin olive oil

Juice of 1 large lemon

Salt and freshly ground black pepper

Soft-leafed lettuce, for lining the platter

Optional accompaniments: chopped fresh parsley or cilantro, lemon quarters

1. Make the fish balls. Cut the fish into 1-inch pieces. In a food processor, puree them with the matzoh meal, eggs, garlic, salt, cumin, and cayenne until the mixture is smooth. Transfer the puree to a large bowl and refrigerate it, covered, for 1 hour. With moistened hands, shape the mixture into 16 slightly flattened logs, using a scant ¼ cup for each, and transfer them as they are formed to a sheet of wax paper. Heat ¼ inch of oil over high heat in a large, heavy skillet until it is hot but not smoking. Add the fish balls in batches, and fry, turning them once, until pale golden. Transfer the balls as they are fried to paper towels to drain.

2. Make the tomato sauce. Wipe out the skillet thoroughly. Add the tomatoes and their juice, olive oil, lemon juice, and salt and pepper to taste and cook over high heat for 8 to 10 minutes, stirring occasionally, until the tomatoes break up and the sauce is thickened. Add the fish balls and simmer the mixture over low heat, covered, for 15 minutes, turning the fish balls once or twice. Remove the skillet from the heat and allow the bellahat to cool in the sauce.

3. Line a platter with the lettuce leaves, arrange the bellahat on them, and spoon the sauce over the fish. Sprinkle with parsley or cilantro and accompany with lemon quarters, if desired. Serve the fish chilled or at room temperature.

YIELD: About 8 servings

TOMATO AND SWEET PEPPER SAUCE

PAREVE

Try this cilantro-scented sauce when beautifully fresh tomatoes and peppers are in season.

2 pounds fresh plum tomatoes (if you have access to a farmers' market, look for heirloom varieties; I've particularly enjoyed a deep-flavored, juicy yellow plum tomato)

2 tablespoons olive oil

1½ cups chopped onions (scant ½ pound)

1½ cups diced sweet red peppers (look for the long, narrow, thin-fleshed frying peppers, such as Cubanelle, or, even better, local heirloom varieties; if unavailable, substitute finely diced red or yellow bell peppers; or add a little finely chopped thin-fleshed mildly hot red pepper, like Hungarian wax pepper)

Salt and freshly ground black pepper

1 tablespoon excellent-quality extra-virgin olive oil

Juice of 1 lemon

2 tablespoons chopped fresh cilantro

1. Prepare the tomatoes. Bring a 6-quart saucepan of water to a boil. Add the tomatoes and cook for 60–90 seconds. Using tongs, transfer them one by one to a large bowl to cool slightly. Peel off the skins (they should come off quite easily). Cut off and discard the stem end of each tomato and chop the tomatoes coarsely.

2. Heat the 2 tablespoons regular olive oil in a heavy 10- to 12-inch sauté pan or deep skillet. Add the onions and sauté, stirring occasionally, over medium heat until softened, 5–7 minutes. Add the peppers, raise the heat to moderately high, and sauté, scraping and stirring the vegetables, until the peppers are soft and slightly caramelized, 7–8 minutes. Add the tomatoes and salt and pepper to taste and continue cooking, taking care to stir and scrape the bottom of the pan so the vegetables don't burn, until the tomatoes are very tender and melting. The exact time will vary depending on the juiciness of the tomatoes, but figure on 10–15 minutes. If you prefer a sauce with a smooth texture, puree it in the pan using an immersion blender, or transfer to a blender, food processor, or food mill to puree. (If you want to reuse this pan to fry the fish balls, transfer the sauce to a bowl, then clean out the pan thoroughly.) Before adding the fish balls to the sauce, rewarm the sauce gently in the pan and stir in the extra-virgin olive oil and lemon juice. After the fish balls are cooked, sprinkle them with the cilantro and allow them to cool in the sauce before refrigerating.

ITALIAN-JEWISH MARINATED FRIED FISH (PESCE IN SAOR)

PAREVE

Above the night music, the Venetian skies boom and burst into explosive color, sending showers of rainbow meteors skittering across the heavens, their shimmering reflections dancing in the inky canals.

It is the Festa del Redentore, Feast of the Redeemer, celebrated every July 19 since 1576 to commemorate the end of a plague that devastated the city. Among the traditional ritual foods eaten before the blaze of spectacular fireworks is an ancient Venetian-Jewish dish, sole in a sweet-and-sour sauce of onions, raisins, and pine nuts, served cold.

Unlike some Italian-Jewish foods whose names betray their provenance—artichokes *alla giudea* and several others with a "Sara" or "Rebecca" appended to the title come readily to mind—the Jewish origins of *pesce in saor* are not always acknowledged. But culinary historians, both those with an Italian focus and those with a Jewish one, trace the dish to the traditional methods Jews devised to preserve fish for the Sabbath. In Italy, Jewish cooks doused fried fish with hot vinegar, then to counteract the acidic taste, added sweet fried onions, raisins, and sugar. (This pattern—using vinegar or lemon as a preservative, then sweetening to eradicate the resulting sour taste—may explain why so many vastly different Jewish communities throughout the world developed their own sweet-and-sour fish dishes.) A fondness for raisins and pine nuts was acquired in Sicily, where Jews had dwelled from ancient times until they were expelled at the end of the fifteenth century.

The result is a well-flavored, make-ahead fish excellent for holidays and company buffets. I round out the flavors by caramelizing the onions and bedding the fried fish on fresh sliced oranges—their sweetness, and the concentrated sugars in the soaked raisins, obviate the need for any added sugar. This dish is especially good accompanied by a salad of marinated roasted red peppers (see page 125).

---

2 pounds lemon sole, grouper, red snapper, perch, or similar nonoily, fairly firm fleshed fish fillets (choose fillets no more than ½ inch thick)

About 1 cup unbleached all-purpose flour

Salt and freshly ground black pepper

Olive oil, for frying, plus 2 tablespoons additional

1 large, juicy orange, preferably thin-skinned, very thinly sliced

1 ½ pounds onions, very thinly sliced (6 cups)

¼ cup pine nuts

¼ cup raisins

½ cup balsamic or red wine vinegar

2 anchovies, finely chopped (optional)

1 cup orange juice

1 bay leaf

Bright green leaves of parsley, curly endive, frisée, or other greens, for garnish (optional)

FISH

1. Cut the fillets in half lengthwise and, if necessary, remove the thin bony strip that runs through the middle of many fillets. Now cut the fillets into 4-inch pieces. If time permits, soak the fish in a pan of cold, lightly salted water for about 20 minutes. (This centuries-old technique not only seasons the fish, but also helps it to stay firm when fried.)

2. Pat the fish dry with paper towels. Spread the flour on a sheet of wax paper or a platter and season with salt and pepper. Dredge the fish pieces thoroughly in the seasoned flour, then shake lightly to remove all excess. Heat ¼ inch of oil in a large heavy skillet until hot but not smoking. Fry the fish in batches until nicely golden on both sides. Drain well on paper towels.

3. Choose a casserole or nonreactive baking dish just large enough to accommodate the fish in one layer and line it with the orange slices. Place the fish on top, overlapping the pieces slightly if necessary.

4. Wipe out all the oil in the skillet, then warm the 2 tablespoons of fresh oil in it. Add the onions and toss until completely coated with the oil. Salt and pepper lightly, cover the pan, and cook slowly over very low heat for 35–40 minutes, until the onions are meltingly tender. Stir from time to time to make sure the onions don't burn.

5. While the onions are simmering, toast the pine nuts on a baking sheet in a preheated 350°F oven for 7–10 minutes, until fragrant and lightly golden. Shake the baking sheet from time to time to ensure even toasting. Set the toasted nuts aside to cool. Soak the raisins in the vinegar.

6. When the onions are very tender, stir in the optional anchovies (they add an elusive, subtle depth), and cook for 2 minutes, stirring to dissolve them. Add the vinegar with the raisins, the orange juice, and bay leaf. Turn the heat up to high and cook, uncovered, until the liquid is reduced by half and the onions are caramelized and richly colored, 15–20 minutes. Be sure to stir frequently to redistribute the syrupy juices and, if necessary, turn the heat down a bit to prevent the onions from sticking and burning. Season generously with salt and pepper and remove the bay leaf.

7. Spread the caramelized onion mixture evenly over the fish. Scatter the toasted pine nuts on top. Wrap well with plastic and refrigerate for at least 6 hours or overnight (even better when served after 48 hours). It will keep very well for at least 4 days.

8. The fish is best at room temperature, so remove it from the refrigerator at least 1 hour before serving. Brighten the dish with a garnish of parsley, curly endive, frisée, or other greens, if desired.

YIELD: 6–8 servings

OVEN-FRIED SMOKED SALMON CROQUETTES

PAREVE

My mother had her own way of doing things. On New Year's Eve, the former Miss Greenwich Village of 1928 (she was disqualified when it was learned that she was only fourteen) would dust golden glitter over her red hair and Vaseline-glossed brows. No Donna Reed at home either, there she *potchkehed* the mundane into the marvelous. She painstakingly sewed green and bronze sequins all over our Davy Crockett T-shirts; she painted our names in Revlon's "Coral Vanilla" nail polish on tin lunch boxes. And when sore throats stole our appetites at breakfast, she served us steaming oatmeal with a scoop of coffee ice cream.

Her salmon croquettes too were special: humble canned salmon fishcakes given luxury treatment with slivers of buttery smoked salmon and lemon zest. I have gently reworked her recipe, replacing the matzoh meal coating with crumbs crushed from egg matzoh, which, made with apple cider, provides a slightly caramelized crunch to the crust. But other matzoh crumbs or matzoh meal will work well too.

CROQUETTES

About 1 pound canned salmon, drained, bones and skin removed, or, even better, an equal amount of poached fresh salmon

2 large eggs, beaten

2 tablespoons chopped fresh dill

3 tablespoons finely chopped shallots, or ¼ cup finely minced onions

1 tablespoon grated lemon zest (for an eloquent contrast to the rich smoked salmon) (optional)

5–6 ounces smoked salmon or lox, cut into fine shreds (about ½–⅔ cup)—by all means, use the less expensive "ends," if available

¼ cup matzoh meal or all-purpose flour

Salt and freshly ground black pepper to taste

COATING

3 tablespoons mayonnaise

2 tablespoons Dijon mustard

1 tablespoon fresh lemon juice

½–¾ cup toasted matzoh crumbs, preferably made from egg matzoh, or use toasted matzoh meal (see pages 25–26 for making and toasting matzoh crumbs; crumbs will give you a crunchier texture)

Olive or vegetable oil, for oven-frying

Lemon wedges

1. Preheat the oven to 450°F.

2. In a large bowl, flake the salmon well. Add the eggs, dill, shallots or onions, lemon zest, if using, smoked salmon or lox, and matzoh meal or flour, and combine thoroughly. Season to taste with salt (none may be needed, especially if the lox is salty) and pepper. Form the mixture into 4–6 hamburger-shaped patties.

3. Prepare the coating. In a shallow bowl, whisk the mayonnaise, mustard, and lemon juice together. Put the toasted matzoh crumbs or meal on a large sheet of wax paper or a plate. Using your fingers, spread each croquette on all sides with the mayonnaise mixture. Roll each in the crumbs or meal to coat well. To make the coating adhere better, pat it firmly on both sides of the croquettes and refrigerate the croquettes for 15–20 minutes, if you have the time.

4. With the oil, generously grease a baking sheet large enough to accommodate the croquettes without touching. Heat it in the oven until the oil is sizzling. Gently shake off any excess crumbs or matzoh meal from the croquettes, then arrange them on the hot baking sheet at least ½ inch apart (so they will cook crisply around the edges too). Bake until the bottoms are crisp and golden, 5–7 minutes. Turn and bake until golden on the other side, 3–4 minutes longer. Serve with lemon wedges.

YIELD: 3–4 servings

COOK'S NOTE: Lush with smoked salmon, these croquettes need only a squirt of lemon, but if you really want to serve a sauce, try ½ cup mayonnaise whisked with 4 teaspoons fresh grapefruit or orange juice, 1–2 teaspoons capers, drained and chopped, 3 tablespoons chopped fresh dill, and 2 teaspoons minced shallots. For a lighter sauce, thin with 2–4 tablespoons plain yogurt. Or try the delicious Green Olive Sauce (page 60).

According to the Talmud, one shows delight in the Sabbath by eating fish. (*Family at the Sabbath Table,* by Nahum Ischacbasov. Oil on canvas. New York, 1946.)

MEATS AND POULTRY

There is no joy without meat and wine.
—BABYLONIAN TALMUD: PESACHIM 109ᴀ

The best of milky foods is a meat dish.
—SHOLEM ALEICHEM

A BRIEF DISCUSSION OF KOSHER MEAT AND POULTRY

Just like humankind, animals too are sacred to God, and while permission to partake of their flesh was finally granted to Noah (Genesis 9:3), there has always been a pervasive sense among Jews that meat is at once imbued with God's holiness and tainted by the profanity of blood.

A precious gift, meat is so highly esteemed that it will grace the Sabbath and holiday feasts that honor God. It is a food so special it should be eaten only if it is craved. But before it can be savored, meat—more God's food than any other—must be strictly regulated more than any other food. These regulations are kashrut, the Jewish dietary laws that determine what is kosher, or fit to eat.

Many reasons have been suggested for the specifics of kashrut—why certain animals are permitted and not others, why meat and milk may not be eaten together, and so on. A few of these explanations are economic and environmental (the pig would not flourish in the arid Middle East; it is more likely to cause trichinosis in warm climates, etc.); some are cultural (the Jews wanted to differentiate themselves from the surrounding people and their pagan practices). Some or all of this may be valid. But I believe the initial restrictions derived from the simultaneous sense of wonder and revulsion at consuming flesh and the concomitant need to reconcile meat eating with God's universe by subjecting it to God's laws.

Kashrut determines not only what meats—indeed, even what *cuts* of permissible meats—may be eaten, but also, to some extent, how they are to be prepared. So to fully understand Jewish cuisine, it is worthwhile briefly examining these dietary regulations.

The permitted mammals include only those that have split hooves and chew their cud: cattle, sheep, goat, deer, antelope, gazelle, and buffalo. Prohibited are the pig, horse, hare, rabbit, and camel, among others. Of poultry, no bird of prey may be eaten.

These permitted animals must be healthy; the *shochet* (ritual slaughterer) checks before and after slaughter to make sure there are no signs of sickness or damage. If, for example, it is found after slaughtering an animal that it had lesions on its lungs, the animal would be considered *treyf,* or unfit to eat.

The strict procedure for ritually slaughtering meat and poultry was designed to be less painful to the animal. An extremely sharp, smooth knife is drawn across the throat. Poultry, of course, is easier to slaughter this way than mammals. It is joked that the giraffe, a kosher animal, has never been eaten by Jews because it is impossible to determine where to draw the knife on the throat. Because all animals must be slaughtered according to kosher ritual, hunting is forbidden: deer, buffalo, quail, and pheasant must be farm-raised. (The Israelites used nets to catch the large flocks of quail that fell, exhausted by their long, migratory flight, near the camp in the wilderness.)

While all parts of poultry may be eaten, only certain parts of mammals are allowed. The sciatic nerve, located in the thigh area, must be removed—a very difficult and costly process that would necessitate hacking up the tenderest, most expensive cuts, rendering them impossible to sell as prime meat. So Ashkenazi and most Sephardi butchers do not sell the meat from the hindquarters; instead, it is sold to nonkosher butchers. Tender cuts, like leg of lamb, porterhouse, and sirloin steaks, which come from the hindquarters, are proscribed.

Animal blood is strictly prohibited ("No soul of you shall eat blood." Leviticus 17:12). To purge meat and poultry of blood, they must be soaked in cold water for 30 minutes and covered with coarse salt for one hour (a process usually carried out today by kosher butchers). Instead of being soaked, the liver, an extremely bloody organ, must be sprinkled with salt and broiled until it changes color before it is eaten or cooked further in a recipe. (These processes will draw out most of the blood; the residue of blood in the tissues will provide moisture to the meat.) The brief brining imbues kosher meat with an appealing lightly seasoned taste and concentrates the meat flavor.

Kosher meats are sold very fresh: the koshering process is performed no longer than seventy-two hours after slaughtering. Unlike nonkosher meats, they do not develop the full-bodied flavor and tenderness that comes with aging.

COOKING JEWISH MEATS

The Jewish cook, faced with the least tender cuts of meat, made tougher still by lack of aging, often gravitated to parts with lots of connective tissue that would soften with slow braising, like brisket and flanken. Long, gentle cooking produced meats that were completely cooked through, with no trace of blood. If meats were roasted, broiled, or sautéed, they were usually served well done, not rare. (Kashrut does *not* require that meats be cooked until well done. After the meat has been properly soaked, salted, and rinsed, it may be cooked any way—or not at all. Served in fine kosher steakhouses, like Le Marais in Manhattan, steak tartare, chopped raw beefsteak, is perfectly permissible. But, perhaps because of the strong taboos against consuming blood, most traditional Ashkenazi Jews have refrained from eating rare meat.)

Sometimes ornery cuts of meat were minced, then combined with sautéed fennel, eggplant, masses of shimmery onions, or other imaginative ingredients to make them tender and tasty.

Jewish cooks concocted beautifully flavored sauces, savory with garlic, onions, and leeks, or sweet and sweet-sour from fragrant spices, such as cinnamon, ginger, and cloves, and exotic, fleshy fruits like prunes, pomegranates, and quinces. They coaxed the tough and dry to aromatic succulence.

THE GRAVY BOAT

Flavorful sauces remain to this day an integral part of Jewish meat cooking; brisket and similar cuts want a mantle of gravy to keep them moist and tasty. These are simple pan sauces, developed organically in the course of slow-cooking the ingredients together. I reduce the pan liquids to concentrate the flavors. Then I add body by pureeing some of the aromatic vegetables, like carrots and onions, and the sweet, mellow chestnuts or other special ingredients braised with the meat.

You'll find delicious pan sauces here, derived, for example, from the whole garlic cloves, tomatoes, and honey used in preparing the meat.

But there will be times, of course, when you need to stretch—or even create—a pan sauce, or just improve a lackluster one. Here are some suggestions to help with your improvisations.

Start with a generous amount of aromatics. Caramelized onions are terrific; so are roasted garlic or shallots, if you have some on hand, or a combination of members of the garlic-onion family and coarsely chopped carrots, fennel, celery or celery root, mushrooms, etc. Sauté slowly in olive oil until softened. Add a little lemon juice, or some good red vinegar or wine, and reduce quickly until almost evaporated.

Choose a flavorful liquid. Add beef or chicken broth, any leftover gravy or meat juices (even a tablespoon will contribute integrity). And try small amounts of rich fruit juices, like prune, pomegranate, and apple-cranberry to round out liquids. Reduced over high heat, they bring dimension to sauces that complement both meat and poultry. Season with salt, pepper, and fresh herbs.

Rely on vegetables and fruits to thicken a sauce. The aromatics will provide most of the needed body. If more thickening is needed, a charred tomato (see step 1, page 81) or a tart apple will enhance and fill out a sauce. Carrot puree works well too, but it is quite sweet, so use a judicious hand, and taste as you go; a few prunes simmered until soft will add a complex tangy-sweetness and also provide body.

Simmer until the vegetables are very tender. Strain the vegetables, reserving the liquid, and puree them in a blender. Reduce the reserved liquid well over high heat to concentrate the flavors, then stir in the puree, a bit at a time, until the gravy is the right consistency. (If you have an immersion blender, puree as many of the solids as needed right in the pan.)

Brighten the flavors of the finished sauce with seasonings. I find that slow-cooking sometimes flattens the flavor of a sauce. Rejuvenate just before serving by stirring in more of the fresh herbs starring in the dish, or chopped parsley or chives, some grated lemon zest or a drop of juice, a bit of raw garlic puree, a tart-sweet jolt of pomegranate molasses, even a generous grind of fresh pepper. Reheat just to combine flavors. To add silkiness, try a little artichoke puree (available jarred).

To reheat meats, bring the sauce to a simmer, add the meat slices, and warm slowly until the meat is heated through. If you have only a small amount of sauce, reserve it for serving, and heat the meat in a little simmering broth.

R E M O V I N G   F A T S

Many Jewish cuts contain a fair amount of fat. And slow, moist cooking methods like braising draw out the fats in the meat and distribute them in the pan sauce.

To defat this sauce, take the meat out of the pan and keep it warm. Strain the cooking liquids from the solids, like carrots, garlic, and other aromatics. If the liquid looks fatty, you might want to line the strainer first with a few sheets of paper towels (this will also blot up some of the grease from the cooked vegetable solids with which you will be thickening the gravy later).

If you have the time, you can cool this liquid, then refrigerate it or pop it into the freezer for a while, until the fat solidifies—then you can scrape off the fat.

In the real world—mine at least, of last-minute everything—that is rarely practical. So pour the strained liquid into a tall glass or two or a special gravy skimmer, if you have one. Allow it to rest a moment, and you'll notice most of the clear, light fat rising to the top. Carefully dip a small ladle or large spoon into the layer of clear fat and discard it. Continue until you have spooned out as much of the fat as possible. (Or pour out the fat through the top spout of your gravy skimmer.)

If you accidentally stir the top layer of grease into the gravy, let stand briefly until separated again, then continue removing the remaining fat. Should the gravy still be fatty, strain it again through a couple of thicknesses of paper towels. For desperate degreasing measures, fill the strainer with ice (you'll want whole cubes here, which will melt less, not ice pieces). Quickly pour cooled gravy through—the fat should be trapped on the ice.

Not all the meats in this chapter are braises and simmers. *Carnatzlach*—quickly grilled garlicky Romanian beef patties—a simple Italian fried chicken, Sephardi vegetable-stuffed meatballs, and a succulent breast of veal inspired by the Provençal-Jewish writer Armand Lunel round out the offerings. And two kreplach recipes using wonton wrappers make superb use of the leftovers.

Of course, nothing beats a warm brisket sandwich on sour rye, savored in a quiet, clean kitchen after the maelstrom has been set to rights. So remember to put aside enough gravy and meat for late-night noshing.

OTHER MEAT AND POULTRY SUGGESTIONS

Lemon-Roasted Chicken (page 203)
Duck and White Bean Cholent (page 212)
Herbed Beef Cholent with Onion Gonifs (page 214)
Garlicky Lamb and Lima Hamin with Little Eggplant Boats (page 217)
Brisket Braised in Pomegranate Juice with Onion Confit and Pomegranate Seeds (page 225)
Syrian Apricot-Stuffed Meat Rolls with Tart-Sweet Cherry Sauce (page 228)
Iranian Stuffed Chicken with Fresh Green Herbs and Golden Soup (page 232)
Cabbage Stuffed with Mushrooms and Meat (page 261)
Apricot- and Orange-Scented Goose with Roasted Garlic (page 290)
Braised Lamb with Artichokes, Lemon, and Fresh Herbs (page 321)
Veronese Rolled Turkey Loaf (page 323)
Beet-Braised Pot Roast with Horseradish and Potato Knaidlach (page 326)
Lemon-Fried Chicken with Tart Salad Topping (page 340)

FLANKEN WITH TART GREENS

My grandmother had flanken.

I don't mean she consumed prodigious amounts of it, or that she served up her superb version often, though both are true.

I refer, instead, to her arms.

Her dark olive skin was perfectly smooth and taut across her elegant face. But the soft flesh from her gently sloping shoulders to her wide, tired feet hung in rounded folds like an old shower curtain.

When she left the house, every bit of that loose flesh was constrained: in heavy, pink satin brassiere and matching girdle, strong support hose, and then, beautifully tailored clothes with long or three-quarter-length sleeves.

But not when she was cooking. At her apartment in the Bronx or at our house, preparing the delicacies that marked our holiday feasts, my tiny grandmother permitted herself to wear a sleeveless housedress with extra-large armholes to accommodate her upper arms.

One such morning, my brother, my sister, and I sat eating the lumpy but delicious farina she had made, our sleepy eyes hypnotically fixed on the huge pleats of flesh flapping rhythmically, the identical color of the boiled beef she was cutting up.

"Flanken," my brother whispered. "Look at Grandma's flanken. She has flanken on her arms."

But she got the last laugh. Now that my sister and I are in our forties, we know just how hard it is to keep arms free of flanken.

This dish is commonly translated as "boiled beef," but it is actually beef that is long-simmered in water with aromatic vegetables. My grandmother's method uses instead a full-bodied beef broth as the cooking medium, along with plenty of earthy vegetables, producing lusty-flavored, succulent meat as well as a luscious soup. Though eight cups of broth may seem extravagant, in effect, you are borrowing it and returning it, deepened by the vibrant flavors of the meat and vegetables, as a husky soup that really sings, ready to be served at another meal. To garnish it, use the leftover flanken to make the kreplach in the recipe that follows (see page 111). Or ladle the soup over egg noodles and sprinkle with lots of chopped fresh dill. Offered solo, the broth is wonderfully restorative on frosty days, and it makes a refined opener to a rich meat dinner.

Flanken is a bony Jewish cut of beef made by cutting short ribs across the bone. It is available in kosher butcher shops and from many nonkosher butchers in areas with large Jewish populations. If it's unavailable, you can substitute chuck short ribs.

Horseradish, the traditional accompaniment to flanken, can overpower the almost-sweet meat. I prefer broccoli rabe, whose gentle bitterness plays well against the richness of the beef. But I have both horseradish and mustard available for guests who insist.

FLANKEN

4 pounds lean beef flanken

8 cups beef broth, preferably homemade
  (page 78), or good-quality low-sodium
  canned

1 large onion, peeled and thickly sliced

3 large garlic cloves, peeled and crushed

2 carrots, scrubbed or peeled and quartered

1 parsnip, peeled and quartered

1 parsley root, peeled (optional)

2 celery stalks, including leaves, if available,
  quartered

1 bay leaf

Salt and freshly ground black pepper

GREENS

1 pound broccoli rabe, cleaned, stems trimmed
  and cut into bite-size pieces, leaves and florets
  coarsely chopped (or an equal amount of kale,
  mustard or turnip greens, or escarole)

2–3 teaspoons minced fresh garlic

2 tablespoons olive oil

⅛ teaspoon crushed red pepper (optional)

Salt

About 3 tablespoons broth from the flanken

Accompaniments: kosher sour dill pickles,
  coarse salt, grated horseradish, and sharp
  mustard (for traditional tastes, if desired)

1. Put the beef and broth in a 6-quart Dutch oven or wide, heavy saucepan, partially cover, and bring to a bare simmer: the liquid shivering, occasional bubbles breaking gently and noiselessly on the surface. Don't allow the liquid to come to a boil—that will make the broth cloudy and the meat tough. Regulate the heat as necessary. Use a skimmer to remove as much foam and scum as possible from the surface.

2. After the flanken has simmered for about 30 minutes, add the onion, garlic, carrots, parsnip, parsley root, if using, celery, and bay leaf. Season to taste with salt and pepper, bearing in mind that if you started with a salted broth, it will get saltier as it cooks down. Place the lid slightly askew and continue cooking over very low heat for 2½–3 hours, or until the meat is fork-tender. Let the flanken rest in the broth for about 15 minutes, then take it out and arrange it on a serving platter. Spoon a little of the broth over the meat to keep it moist. (If you need to reheat the flanken, simmer it in enough broth to cover.)

3. Strain the soup, discarding or reserving the cooked vegetables according to preference (they will be quite soft; I usually discard all but the carrot and sometimes the parsnip and parsley root). Remove as much fat as possible from the broth by refrigerating it thoroughly until the fat solidifies, then just lifting it off. (You can deal with the soup at your leisure, of course, if you are in a hurry to get the flanken on the table.) Reserve 3 tablespoons of the broth for the greens.

4. About 30 minutes before you are ready to serve the flanken, prepare the greens. Bring a large pot of well-salted water to a boil. Add the broccoli rabe, cover, and cook, stirring occasionally, until tender but not mushy, about 4 minutes. Drain thoroughly.

5. In a large heavy skillet, sauté the garlic in the oil over medium-low heat, stirring, for 1 minute, until pale golden (do *not* let it brown). Add the cooked greens, raise the heat to medium, and sauté for about 3 minutes, stirring occasionally. Add the reserved flanken broth, the optional red pepper flakes, and salt to taste, and continue cooking for another 3 minutes, lifting and tossing the greens, to meld the flavors.

6. Slice the flanken across the grain. Serve each guest a portion of broccoli rabe topped with slices of flanken. If desired, ladle a little hot broth over the meat to moisten it. Pass the pickles and coarse salt, and for the tradition-bound, horseradish and mustard.

YIELD: 4–5 servings

The author's grandmother, Rebecca Suffin, holding the author's brother, Steven.

MISHMASH KREPLACH (BEEF, POTATO, AND FRIED ONION KREPLACH)

They started out in three separate piles, our weekday trinity: brisket, skirt steak, or sometimes a thick beef patty (it only became a hamburger when surrounded by a roll); one hill of fluffy mashed potatoes; and another of shimmering, bronzed onions. Under my grandmother's tutelage, I learned the correct way to combine them in a sublime mishmash.

First, of course, stir the onions into the potatoes, adding little spoons of gravy or meat juices to make the mixing easier. Impale the meat on your fork and bury it deep in the potato pile. Withdraw and lick it like a lollipop, flavored if necessary with copious quantities of additional gravy and judicious sprinkles of pepper—there was probably too much salt to begin with.

Years later I found out that we were not the only family that engaged in mishmashing this classic trio. In these kreplach, a paean to the combination, I fashion the same ingredients into a simple but lush pasta package. Including mashed potatoes in a filling for pasta may seem an overload of starch. But as in my grandmother's original mishmash, smooth, rich potatoes lend a creamy sumptuousness to the golden onions and savory shards of beef, especially when encased in thin, silky kreplach like these made from wonton wrappers.

Float the kreplach in homemade beef or chicken broth. They also make an outstanding appetizer or side dish, sauced with beef gravy or topped with sautéed mushrooms. Or pat the cooked kreplach dry, then panfry them lightly in oil with sizzled onions.

---

10 ounces onions, chopped (2½ cups)

3 tablespoons olive oil

1 teaspoon minced fresh garlic

Salt and freshly ground black pepper

1 cup mashed potatoes (leftover is fine)

1½ cups shredded cooked beef (leftover flanken, pot roast, or brisket)

1 large egg yolk

About 50 wonton wrappers

Egg wash (1–2 large eggs, as needed, each beaten with 1 teaspoon of water)

Accompaniments: chicken or beef broth (page 63 or 78), leftover brisket or other beef gravy, fried onions, or fried mushrooms (see Cook's Note)

---

1. In a large skillet, sauté the onions in the oil over medium-high heat, tossing them frequently, until soft and golden, about 15 minutes. Add the garlic and continue sautéing until the mixture is tinged a rich caramel color in spots. (Good fried onions should be an amalgam of several degrees of doneness: from nearly clear to butter yellow to speckles of deep bronze.) Salt and pepper to taste and scrape into

a large bowl. Add the mashed potatoes and the meat and combine well. Season generously to taste and stir in the egg yolk. Cover and refrigerate until cold, about 1 hour.

2. Fill and trim the kreplach (see page 30), using about 1 heaping teaspoon of filling per krepl, and then folding it into a tight triangle and sealing it with the egg wash.

3. Poach the kreplach. In a large, very wide pot, bring at least 5 quarts of lightly salted water to a boil. Slip in the kreplach, one by one, being careful not to overcrowd the pot (if necessary, cook them in batches or use two pots). Lower the temperature slightly (the kreplach might explode if the water is boiling furiously) and poach until tender, 3–6 minutes (exact time will depend on the brand of wonton wrapper used). Lift the kreplach out, a few at a time, with a large skimmer, gently shaking the skimmer so the water drains back into the pot (the kreplach are too fragile to pour into a colander).

4. Serve the poached kreplach in broth, sauced with leftover brisket or pot roast gravy, or topped with fried onions or sautéed mushrooms.

YIELD: About 50 kreplach

COOK'S NOTE: To prepare a cloak of fried mushrooms, sauté 1 cup chopped onions and 2 teaspoons minced garlic in 2 tablespoons oil over moderately high heat, stirring, until deep gold, 5–7 minutes; add 3 cups thinly sliced mushrooms (fresh shiitakes would be heavenly, but cremini or regular button mushrooms will do very well) and cook over high heat until the mushrooms smell fragrant and release their juices; add 1 tablespoon soy sauce and 2 teaspoons fresh lemon juice, and cook another 2 minutes; season to taste with salt and freshly ground pepper; garnish, if desired, with chopped parsley, scallions, chives, or dill.

BRAISED BRISKET WITH THIRTY-SIX CLOVES OF GARLIC

You could smell the brisket all over the house, it had so much garlic in it.
A roast like that, with a fresh warm twist, is a delicacy from heaven.
—SHOLEM ALEICHEM, "TIT FOR TAT"

In my take on the French classic, chicken with forty cloves of garlic becomes brisket with thirty-six cloves. All that feisty garlic turns sweet and mellow with gentle braising; when pureed, it forms a seductive gravy, which is finished with a zing of chopped raw garlic and lemon zest.

Why thirty-six cloves? Beginning with *aleph,* which equals one, each letter of the Hebrew alphabet stands for a number, and so every word has a numerical value. All multiples of eighteen, the numerical value of the Hebrew word *chai,* life, are considered especially auspicious, which is why donations to charity and wedding and bar mitzvah gifts are often given in multiples of eighteen.

---

36 fat garlic cloves or an equivalent amount of smaller cloves, plus 1 teaspoon minced garlic

3 tablespoons olive oil

A first-cut beef brisket (about 5 pounds), trimmed of excess fat, wiped with a damp paper towel, and patted dry

2 tablespoons red wine vinegar

3 cups beef or chicken broth, preferably home-made (page 63 or 78), or good-quality low-sodium canned

3–4 fresh thyme sprigs, or 2 teaspoons dried thyme

2 fresh rosemary sprigs, plus 1 teaspoon chopped rosemary

Salt and freshly ground black pepper

1 teaspoon grated lemon zest

---

1. Preheat the oven to 325°F.

2. Drop the garlic cloves into boiling water for 30 seconds. Drain immediately. Peel as soon as the garlic is cool enough to handle. Set aside on paper towels to dry.

3. Heat the olive oil over medium-high heat in a heavy-bottomed roasting pan or casserole large enough to accommodate the meat in one layer. Use two burners, if necessary. Add the brisket and brown well on both sides, about 10 minutes. Transfer the brisket to a platter and set aside.

4. Pour off all but about 1 tablespoon of fat remaining in the pan and add the garlic cloves. Cook over medium heat, stirring occasionally, until the garlic edges are tinged with gold. Add the vinegar and deglaze the pan, scraping up all the browned bits from the bottom with a wooden spoon. Add the stock, thyme, and rosemary sprigs and reduce the heat to a simmer. Salt and pepper the brisket to taste on all sides, and add it to the pan, fat side up. Spoon the garlic cloves over the meat.

5. Place the brisket in the oven, cover (if you have no lid, use heavy-duty foil), and cook, basting every half-hour, until the meat is fork-tender, 2½–3 hours or longer. (As the meat cooks, periodically check that the liquids are bubbling gently. If they are boiling rapidly, turn the oven down to 300°F.)

6. Transfer the brisket to a cutting board and tent it loosely with foil.

7. Prepare the gravy. Strain the braising mixture, reserving the garlic and discarding the thyme and rosemary sprigs. Skim and discard as much fat as possible from the liquid. Puree about one-half of the cooked garlic and 1 cup of the defatted braising liquid in a food processor or a blender. Transfer the pureed mixture, the remaining braising liquid, and the rest of the cooked garlic to a skillet. Add the reserved chopped rosemary and minced garlic and the lemon zest. Boil down the gravy over high heat, uncovered, to the desired consistency. Taste and adjust the seasoning. (If you want a smooth gravy, puree all of the cooked garlic cloves.)

8. Cut the brisket into thin slices across the grain at a slight diagonal. Arrange the sliced brisket on a serving platter. Spoon some of the hot gravy all over the meat and pass the rest in a separate sauce-boat.

YIELD: 8 generous servings

AROMATIC MARINATED BRISKET
WITH CHESTNUTS

Back in biblical days, wily Jacob knew the value of adding chestnut to foods. After he put chestnut twigs in the water he fed to his father-in-law Laban's strongest cattle, they gave birth to spotted calves. Good news for Jacob: he had just cut a deal with Laban—all the spotted cattle in the flock now belonged to him. (The tale lives on in the beautiful spotted heirloom beans known as Jacob's Cattle.)

Today, chestnuts continue to lend their charms to many Jewish dishes. As they do for the French and the Japanese, sweet chestnuts serve as New Year's food for Jews from Transylvania, who eat them when reciting the Sheheheyonu, a prayer for new fruits at Rosh Hashanah. At Sukkot, Hungarian Jews cook them in a special tsimmes, and I have seen several variations for a Passover haroset recipe from Padua, Italy, all calling for chestnuts.

Here the chestnuts break up, imparting a nutty sweetness to the brisket. To build additional layers of flavor, I stud the meat first with garlic, then bathe it in a pomegranate molasses and balsamic vinegar marinade. Sensational anytime, it would be ideal for one of the fall holiday meals.

---

5 large garlic cloves, peeled

A first-cut beef brisket (about 4–5 pounds), trimmed of excess fat, wiped with a damp paper towel, and patted dry

¼ cup pomegranate molasses or temerhindi (see page 31)

¼ cup balsamic vinegar

12 peppercorns, crushed

2 tablespoons olive or vegetable oil (if you brown the meat on the stovetop, you will need 5 tablespoons oil)

1½ pounds onions, chopped (6 cups)

Salt and freshly ground black pepper to taste

8–10 medium carrots, scraped and quartered

3 fresh thyme sprigs or 1 teaspoon dried thyme

2 cups chestnuts, blanched and peeled (see Cook's Note), or use canned (packed in water), frozen, or rehydrated dried chestnuts

Optional accompaniment: Spiced Pomegranate Molasses Applesauce (page 180)

---

1. Cut half the garlic into thin lengthwise slivers and set the rest aside. Make a little slit in the fat side of the brisket with the point of a small, sharp knife. Insert a garlic sliver into the slit, using your fingers and the knife tip to push it in as far as possible. In the same way, insert the remaining slivers all over the top and bottom of the brisket, spacing them as evenly as you can.

2. If you have a plastic food storage or roasting bag large enough to hold the brisket, put the meat in the bag and place it on a baking sheet. Otherwise, just put the brisket in a large nonreactive pan or

bowl. Combine the pomegranate molasses or *temerhindi,* balsamic vinegar, and crushed peppercorns in a small bowl. Chop the reserved garlic and add it to the bowl. Pour the mixture over the brisket. Close the plastic bag or cover the pan with foil and marinate the meat in the refrigerator for a minimum of 2 and a maximum of 4 hours, turning the meat occasionally.

3. Remove the meat from the refrigerator and bring it to room temperature. Take out the brisket and pat it dry with paper towels. Reserve the marinade.

4. Because the brisket tends to splatter somewhat from the marinade (even if patted dry), and because it is so large, I find it easier to brown the meat under the broiler. Just cover the broiler pan well with foil to minimize cleanup. If you prefer, sear the brisket on top of the stove. I offer both methods.

Method one: Preheat the broiler. Place the brisket under the broiler, fat side up, on a foil-lined broiler pan. Broil for 5–6 minutes on each side, or until browned. Don't allow it to develop a hard, dark crust, which might make the meat tough or bitter. Move the meat around as necessary, so it sears evenly on the back and front portions. Transfer the brisket to a platter and set aside.

Method two: Heat 3 tablespoons of the oil over medium-high heat in a heavy-bottomed roasting pan or casserole large enough to hold the brisket snugly. Use two burners, if necessary. Add the brisket and brown well on both sides, about 10 minutes. Sear it to caramelize the meat and seal in the juices, but don't let it develop a hard, dark crust. Transfer the brisket to a platter and set aside.

5. Preheat the oven to 325°F.

6. If you browned the meat under the broiler, heat the 2 tablespoons oil in a large roasting pan or casserole. If you pan-seared the meat, pour off all the fat remaining in the pan, then heat 2 tablespoons fresh oil. Add the onions and sauté over medium-high heat until the edges are golden, about 10 minutes. Add salt and pepper to taste, turn the heat down to very low, and cook until quite softened, stirring occasionally, 15–20 minutes (time will vary depending on type of pan used). Add the carrots, thyme, and reserved marinade, and bring to a simmer, scraping any browned bits from the bottom of the pan with a wooden spoon.

7. Salt and pepper the brisket to taste on both sides, and add it to the pan, fat side up. Spoon the vegetables over the meat. Cover tightly and place in the oven.

8. Braise the meat for 1½ hours, basting with the pan sauce and vegetables every 30 minutes. Add the chestnuts. Cover the pan again and continue cooking and basting for 1–2 hours longer, or until the

meat is fork-tender. (When you baste, check that the liquids are bubbling gently. If they are boiling rapidly, turn the oven down to 300°F.)

9. Transfer the meat, chestnuts, and carrots to a platter and keep warm, loosely covered with foil (reserve a couple of carrots—and some chestnut pieces, if desired—for thickening the gravy). Remove the thyme sprigs and strain the braising mixture, reserving the solids. Skim and discard as much fat as possible from the liquid. In a food processor or blender, puree *most* of the solids, including the reserved carrots and chestnuts, with 1 cup of the defatted braising liquid. (Alternatively, if a completely smooth gravy is desired, puree *all* of the solids.) Put the pureed mixture, the remaining braising liquid, and the rest of the solids into a clean saucepan, and cook until the ingredients are well combined and hot. Taste and adjust the seasoning. If the gravy is too thin, boil it down to the desired consistency over high heat.

10. Cut the brisket into thin slices across the grain at a slight diagonal. Arrange the sliced brisket on the serving platter with the carrots and chestnuts. Spoon some of the hot sauce all over the meat and pass the rest in a sauceboat. Spiced pomegranate molasses applesauce makes a smashing accompaniment.

YIELD: 8 generous servings

COOK'S NOTE: Here's how to blanch and peel chestnuts. Using a sharp knife, cut an "x" on the flat side of the shell. If possible, pierce deeply enough to go through both the peel and the thin brown inner skin. Put the chestnuts in a big, heatproof bowl or pot. Pour in enough boiling water to cover them by an inch or two, cover the bowl, and let soak for about 10 minutes. Chestnuts are easiest to peel when hot, so take them out of the water one at a time. Pull off both the shell and the papery skin. Removing the skin can be tedious; if necessary, pour more boiling water over the nuts to loosen it. They are now ready for the recipe. Cut them into bite-size chunks or, if small, leave whole.

EGGPLANT-STUFFED BRISKET BRAISED WITH TOMATOES, SAFFRON, AND HONEY

"Jews' food," they called eggplant in mid-nineteenth-century Florence, according to Italian food historian Pellegrino Artusi in *The Art of Eating Well* (1891).

They were right, of course. Introduced first into Italy by the Sephardim, who had fallen in love with the meaty vegetable in Arab Spain, eggplants later came to be prized as well by Jews throughout the Balkans, Romania, and in whatever parts of Russia they would grow.

Rich and substantial, satin-skinned eggplants made ideal meat substitutes at dairy meals, and Jewish cooks lightened them with showers of fresh herbs to create refreshing appetizers and salads.

Because eggplant turns succulent and creamy to the point of butteriness when fried in oil, I find it makes an especially appealing filling for tender, but somewhat dry, brisket, so I run a velvet-luscious eggplant ribbon through the meat. A sumptuous sauce of tomatoes, saffron, honey, and cinnamon further moistens the brisket, in keeping with the exotic Middle Eastern origins of the vegetable.

---

1 medium-large eggplant (about 1 ¼ pounds), peeled and cut into 1-inch cubes

Coarse kosher salt

¼ teaspoon saffron threads

About 6 tablespoons olive oil

2 large onions, coarsely chopped (about 4 cups)

Freshly ground black pepper

¼ cup aromatic honey (an herb flower honey, like thyme or rosemary, would be superb)

2 tablespoons red wine vinegar or balsamic vinegar

¼ teaspoon ground cinnamon

One 28-ounce can Italian plum tomatoes, packed in their juice

2 teaspoons peeled and finely minced fresh ginger

3 dried apricots, diced (a tart variety especially—these are usually the ones available in specialty or appetizing stores from California, not Turkey—will point up the sweet and tangy nuances) (optional)

1 tablespoon minced fresh garlic

A first-cut beef brisket (about 5 pounds), trimmed of excess fat, with a deep, wide pocket for stuffing (have your butcher cut along one of the short sides, extending nearly to the edge along the other three sides)

Accompaniments: Steamed rice, mamaliga (polenta), or couscous

---

1. Start the stuffing. Put the eggplant in a colander and sprinkle evenly with 2 teaspoons coarse salt. Weight the eggplant down (I use a plate or bowl topped with a heavy can, like a large size of plum tomatoes), and let drain for about 1 hour, stirring the pieces around after 30 minutes. Rinse the eggplant with water and press it dry with paper towels.

2. While the eggplant is draining, prepare the sauce. Dissolve the saffron threads in 1 tablespoon hot water and set aside. Heat 3 tablespoons of the oil in a 10- to 12-inch heavy skillet over medium-high heat. Add the onions and sauté, stirring, until they are translucent and the edges are tinged with gold, about 10 minutes. Season with salt and pepper and add the honey, vinegar, and cinnamon. Turn the heat up to high and boil the liquid in the pan, stirring, until it evaporates, about 5 minutes.

3. Cut each tomato into 4 or 5 pieces and add them, along with their juice, to the skillet. Stir in the ginger, saffron, and apricots, if you are using them. Cook over high heat, uncovered, until most of the liquid has evaporated and the tomatoes have dissolved into a thick and pulpy sauce, 10–15 minutes. Be sure to stir from time to time and, if necessary, turn the heat down a bit so the mixture doesn't scorch or burn. Season to taste with salt and pepper and set aside.

4. Heat the remaining 3 tablespoons oil in another large, heavy skillet (nonstick would work well here) over medium-high heat until hot but not smoking. Add the eggplant in a single layer without crowding the pan, and sauté until tender and lightly browned on both sides. Work in batches as necessary, transferring the eggplant to a platter as it is done. Add more oil as needed, but always make sure the oil is very hot before adding a new batch of eggplant—this will prevent the pieces from absorbing too much oil. When all the eggplant is browned, return it to the pan, add the garlic, and cook, tossing constantly, for 2 minutes, to marry the flavors. Drain the cooked eggplant lightly on paper towels and let cool to room temperature. Season with salt and pepper.

5. Preheat the broiler.

6. Wipe the brisket with a damp paper towel and pat dry. Fill the brisket pocket with the eggplant mixture, patting the meat to distribute the stuffing evenly. Don't overpack—save any leftover eggplant for another use (delicious in sandwiches). Sew the pocket closed with kitchen twine or dental floss, using a large embroidery needle, as I do, or a trussing needle. Skewers don't work as well here. Season the brisket all over with salt and pepper and transfer it, fat side up, to a foil-lined broiler pan, about 4 inches from the heat. (I sear stuffed briskets under the broiler because there is less handling involved and the stuffing is less likely to seep out.) Brown the top for about 5 minutes, then turn and brown the other side. Reduce the oven temperature to 325°F.

7. Choose a baking or roasting pan or casserole just large enough to hold the brisket. Spread some of the tomato sauce over the bottom, then add the brisket and top with the remaining sauce. Cover the pan tightly (use heavy-duty foil if you have no lid) and braise in the oven, basting every 30 minutes,

until the meat is very tender, 2½–3½ hours. (When you baste, make sure that the sauce is bubbling gently; if you find it is really boiling, turn the oven down to 300°F.) Transfer the brisket to a cutting board, cover loosely with foil, and prepare the gravy. Skim and discard as much fat as possible from the sauce, then put it through a food mill or press through a sieve. (You can also puree it in a blender, although this will result in a much denser mixture.) Reheat the gravy and, if necessary, boil it to reduce to the desired consistency. Taste and adjust the seasoning.

8. Carefully slice the brisket medium-thin across the grain at a slight diagonal, so that each slice encloses a strip of eggplant stuffing. Ladle the hot sauce over the meat and serve with rice, mamaliga, or couscous to sop up the sauce.

YIELD: 8 generous servings

ROASTED GARLIC–BRAISED BREAST OF VEAL WITH SPRINGTIME STUFFING (SPINACH, CHARD, AND FRESH HERBS)

This recipe began with a tattered French novella I read in the library. It led me to medieval towns in the south of France better known for ambrosial melons than Jewish cooking, and took me to bookstores and museums throughout Paris. It tells the story of a vanished cuisine.

I stumbled on *"les juifs du Pape"* (the Pope's Jews) while researching early French-Jewish cuisine at the New York Public Library. Although the Jews were expelled from France in 1394, they were allowed to remain—with restrictions—in four small areas comprising the Comtat Venaissin under papal jurisdiction: Avignon, Carpentras, Cavaillon, and L'Isle-sur-La-Sorgue (in Hebrew, *Arba Kehilloth*).

Tantalizing snippets along the paper trail intrigued me. The French poet Frédéric Mistral, for instance, claimed that the evocative vocabulary and enchanting folklore of the Comtat Jews had enriched the lyrical language of his native Provence. These Jews had their own Judeo-Provençal dialect, their liturgy was unique, and, by all accounts, their cuisine distinctive.

But although French Jews have written scores of cookbooks, I could find no recipes at all from this community. I was about to give up, when a fellow researcher, eyeing the books spread-eagled around me, made an offhand remark about Armand Lunel, a Comtat Jew who, he claimed, wrote evocatively about food in his fiction.

In his charming novella *Jérusalem à Carpentras* (1937), Lunel limned with gentle humor the hot *coudoles* from the ancient Passover oven in Carpentras—matzohs so exquisite that Christians, defying the Bishop's interdiction, came banging on the gates of the Juiverie to purchase them. But it was Lunel's lavish praise for *le prin,* which he called *"le ne plus ultra de l'art culinaire judéo-carpentrassien, "* that convinced me. Served on Passover, this meltingly tender breast of veal is, as he described it, the essence of spring: stuffed with a mixture of chard and spinach and a scant fistful of rice, intensely refreshing and fortifying at the same time. It sounded so delightfully contemporary, and so delicious, I had to have the recipe—or something equally enchanting from this elusive cuisine.

In Cavaillon, where a museum dedicated to the Comtat Venaissin Jews is housed in an old matzoh bakery, I inquired about recipes or cookbooks detailing what must have been a scrumptious cuisine. None existed. In the beautiful old synagogues of Cavaillon and Carpentras, now French landmarks, I couldn't locate any members of the old Comtat community, which had been assimilated and replaced by new waves of French Jewry.

In Paris it was the same story. Even Lunel's book was out of print.

It was Passover, I was in France, and in my mind's eye, I could taste Lunel's *prin*. Like Proust's admirers dreaming of madeleines, I had fallen in love with a food from reading a book. But in the end, this love could be requited only through an act of imagination.

This is how I envisioned the recipe. I include it here in the meat chapter, not the Passover section, because Ashkenazi Jews refrain from eating rice on that holiday.

Fresh herbs are essential to this dish.

---

1 large bunch of Swiss chard (about 1½ pounds), washed, white stems removed and reserved for another purpose, green leaves coarsely chopped (5–6 tightly packed cups)

1 large bunch of spinach (about 1 pound), washed, coarse stems discarded, and leaves coarsely chopped (about 5 tightly packed cups), or 10 ounces frozen leaf spinach, thawed

4 large garlic cloves, minced (1–1½ tablespoons), plus 1 large head, unpeeled

½ cup plus 2 teaspoons olive oil

Salt and freshly ground black pepper

1 very large onion, finely chopped (about 2 cups)

½ cup medium- or short-grain rice, preferably arborio (medium- or short-grain is called for because you want a creamy texture, like a risotto; long-grain rice will give you fluffy, separate grains)

1½ cups chicken broth, preferably homemade (page 63), or good-quality low-sodium canned

1 teaspoon plus 1 tablespoon fresh thyme leaves

2 tablespoons fresh rosemary leaves

Juice and zest of 1 large lemon

1 cup firmly packed fresh flat-leaf parsley leaves

1 cup firmly packed fresh mint leaves

1 large egg, beaten

One 5- to 6-pound veal breast (see Cook's Note)

1 cup Sauvignon Blanc or other dry white wine

---

1. Prepare the stuffing. Bring a 5- to 6-quart nonreactive Dutch oven or saucepan full of lightly salted water to a boil. Add the chard and spinach, bring the water back to a boil, then cook for 2–3 minutes, or until thoroughly wilted. Drain and squeeze out as much moisture as possible, pressing the greens against a colander with a wooden spoon. Or, for a more thorough job, use your hands when the greens have cooled somewhat. Finely chop, either by hand or by pulsing in a food processor.

2. In a large skillet, sauté the minced garlic in 3 tablespoons of the oil over moderate heat until pale gold, 2–3 minutes. Add the chopped drained chard and spinach. Cook, stirring, over medium heat, until the liquid is evaporated and the garlic is thoroughly distributed, 5–7 minutes. The greens should be very tender. Season to taste with salt and pepper. Transfer to a large bowl and set aside.

3. Preheat the oven to 375°F.

4. Sauté the onion in a heavy, medium saucepan over medium heat in 3 tablespoons of the oil until softened, 7–10 minutes. Add the rice and stir to coat the grains with the onions. In another saucepan, bring the broth to a simmer. Add the broth to the rice a few spoonfuls at a time, as if making risotto. Keep the heat medium-low, and stir, waiting until the broth is nearly absorbed before adding another spoonful. Cook the rice until just tender, about 15–20 minutes in all. If you finish adding the broth and the rice is not yet tender, add a tablespoon or two of hot water, as needed. Season the rice with salt and pepper (taking into account the saltiness of the broth you are using), add it to the chard and spinach, and set aside to cool.

5. Prepare the garlic head. Break the head into single cloves and put them, unpeeled, into a small baking dish in which they fit snugly (I use a 5-inch square porcelain ramekin). Drizzle with 2 teaspoons of the oil and 1 teaspoon of the thyme. Cover tightly (use foil if you don't have a lid) and roast for 30–45 minutes, until a soft puree is formed when you squeeze a clove. Avoid overcooking, which turns the garlic bitter. Squeeze the puree out by hand or run the unpeeled cloves through a food mill to trap the peels. Put the roasted garlic puree in a small bowl and add 1 tablespoon of the rosemary and the lemon juice. Stir well and set aside. Turn off the oven—you will be pan-braising the meat.

6. While the garlic is roasting, finish the stuffing. In a food processor, pulse the remaining 1 tablespoon each of rosemary and thyme, the parsley, mint, and lemon zest until finely chopped. Add to the rice mixture in the bowl. Stir in the egg until well combined.

7. Trim the veal of gristle and as much fat as possible. Sprinkle salt and pepper all over, including the inside pocket. Fill the pocket with the stuffing, pushing the mixture as far in as possible, but don't overfill—it will expand somewhat while cooking. Sew the pocket closed. A large embroidery needle and dental floss work very well here. Or use a trussing needle and kitchen twine. I find skewering not as successful here—the stuffing is more likely to ooze out into the pan gravy.

8. In a 6-quart Dutch oven or heavy casserole just large enough to accommodate the veal, heat the remaining 2 tablespoons oil until hot but not smoking. Add the veal and brown it slowly on all sides, turning carefully with wooden spoons so you don't pierce the meat. When it is thoroughly browned, arrange the meat so that the fat side is up. Spread the roasted garlic mixture all over the top. Add the wine and bring to a slow bubble. Place the lid slightly askew and braise at a slow simmer over very low heat for 2½–3 hours, or longer, if necessary, until the meat is very tender. Use a flame tamer or *blech* or stack two stove burner grates if you must to keep the flame very low. Every 20 minutes or so, baste with the pan juices. If possible, turn the meat a few times; don't worry about losing the roasted garlic coating on top—it will add delicious flavor to the cooking juices.

9. Transfer the veal to a platter and let it stand for 10 minutes, tented with foil to keep warm. Boil up the cooking juices for a few minutes to concentrate the flavors, taste for seasoning, then transfer to a sauceboat.

10. Slice the veal about ½ inch thick, making sure the slices enclose some of the filling. Nap with some of the juices. Pass the remaining sauce separately.

YIELD: 6–8 servings

COOK'S NOTE: Veal breast is a delectable but somewhat fatty cut of meat. I have my butcher bone it because it is easier to remove most of the fat that way. But leave the bones in, if you prefer—they will add flavor. Just trim most of the fat carefully. The weight listed in the recipe is before boning. In either case, have your butcher cut a large pocket for stuffing.

ROMANIAN GARLICKY GROUND MEAT SAUSAGES (CARNATZLACH) WITH SOUR PICKLE VINAIGRETTE AND ROASTED RED PEPPERS

MEAT

With several helpers, she brought platters of cold sweet-and-sour fish, stewed meat, and roasted chicken, flasks of lemonade, baskets filled with rolls and hard white pretzels, bowls of sauerkraut sprinkled with sugar, and plates filled with freshly pickled cucumbers as cold as ice.

—CHAIM GRADE, "THE REBBETZIN"

I love pickles, though they never live up to their smell: a sirensong of heady garlic, spicy peppercorns, and other enticing aromatics. Crunchy and cold, they provide refreshing respite from the dryness and density of unsauced meats, especially in sandwiches and simple grills.

Eating *carnatzlach*, I grew tired of alternating one bite of barbecued meat with a juicy chew of pickle, so I turned the pickle into this sauce.

This garlicky Romanian grill is wonderful anytime, but it is particularly appealing for casual summer meals. If you're cutting down on beef, well-seasoned turkey is a good substitute here.

2–3 tablespoons coarsely chopped garlic, or to taste

2 teaspoons sweet paprika

1 teaspoon salt, or to taste (you'll need more if using ground turkey)

1 teaspoon dried oregano or marjoram

½ teaspoon ground allspice

¼–½ teaspoon freshly ground black pepper, or fresh hot but not searing chile to taste (preferably Fresno or Serrano, but Hungarian wax, jalapeño, or other varieties will do fine), roasted (see Cook's Note), peeled, and finely chopped (be sure to use rubber gloves when preparing)

1½ pounds lean ground beef (you can substitute ground turkey—the ground thigh meat will work best—with fine results, but you may want to increase the seasoning slightly)

Oil for greasing the broiler rack or pan, if necessary

Accompaniments: 2 large red bell peppers, roasted (see Cook's Note), cut into strips, and seasoned well with salt, pepper, extra-virgin olive oil, and a little vinegar or lemon juice to taste; chopped scallions (both white and green parts); Sour Pickle Vinaigrette (page 127); half-sour or garlic dill pickles, sliced lengthwise, and/or dill tomatoes

1. In a food processor, combine the garlic, paprika, salt, oregano, allspice, black pepper or chile, and ¼ cup water and pulse until the garlic is chopped very fine. Add a third of the meat and process until

thoroughly incorporated with the seasoning. Add another third of the meat and pulse a few times. Add the final third and continue pulsing, stopping to scrape down the bowl if necessary, until the mixture is well combined, very soft, and almost pasty.

2. Transfer to a bowl, cover, and refrigerate for at least 4 hours or overnight so that all the vibrant flavors will meld together.

3. When ready to cook the *carnatzlach,* set out a small bowl of cold water and a large platter. Moisten your hands with water, then take a small lump of the meat mixture and roll it into a sausage, about 3 to 4 inches long and 1 inch wide (about the size of your middle finger, but a little wider). Place shaped *carnatzl* on the platter and continue making more, wetting your hands as necessary, until all the meat is rolled. You'll have approximately 14 to 17 sausages.

4. Preheat the broiler, outdoor grill, or (my choice) a heavy, ridged cast-iron skillet on top of the stove, to high temperature. (Spray rack or pan lightly with oil first, if necessary.) Grill or broil the sausages until beautifully browned, crusty, and cooked to desired doneness, 5–7 minutes per side.

5. To serve, arrange some roasted red pepper strips and chopped scallions on a plate. Nestle a few *carnatzlach* attractively over them, and spoon a generous amount of sour pickle vinaigrette over everything. Garnish with pickles and dill tomatoes.

YIELD: 4–5 servings

COOK'S NOTE: To roast peppers, spear them with a long-handled fork, and roast like marshmallows over an open flame (a gas burner or outdoor fire). Keep turning the peppers until the skins are lightly charred on all sides. You can also roast them under the broiler: Place the peppers on a foil-lined rack under a preheated broiler, as close as possible to the heat source. Turn the peppers as the skins blister and blacken.

Put the charred peppers in a paper bag and twist the bag closed. Or put them in a covered bowl. Let them steam until cool enough to handle—this will make them easier to peel. Rub the skins off with your fingers (if preparing chiles, make sure you are wearing rubber gloves). Don't worry if you don't remove every piece of charred skin—a few bits here and there will add smoky flavor. Although this is messy and the peel will stick to your fingers, I don't recommend peeling the peppers under water, as some cookbook authors suggest, because it washes away the flavorful oils, making the peppers soggy and flat-tasting. Instead, dip your hands into a bowl of water every so often or wipe them on a paper towel to clean them. Pull out and discard the stem, seeds, and ribs. The peppers are ready to be used in a recipe.

SOUR PICKLE VINAIGRETTE

Enough half-sour or garlic-dill pickles to yield
  1 cup coarsely chopped pickles
2 tablespoons liquid from pickle jar (include
  peppercorns and other flavorings, if desired)

3 tablespoons fine-quality extra-virgin olive oil
Salt and freshly ground black pepper to taste
Fresh lemon juice to taste

Place the pickles and the liquid from pickle jar in a blender and process at high speed until pureed. With the machine on, slowly add the oil. Continue processing another minute or two, until the mixture is smooth and emulsified. Transfer the vinaigrette to a bowl, adding the salt, pepper, and lemon juice as needed. You can serve the sauce right away, but it's best to allow the flavors to mellow for a while in the refrigerator. Stir the vinaigrette before serving.

YIELD: 4–5 servings

Horseradish (the Passover "bitter herb") and tangy pickles add savor to many Jewish meals. (Man in top hat, wheeling cart. Silver container for bitter herbs. Germany, 19th century.)

SEPHARDI-STYLE STUFFED MEATBALLS
WITH CELERY ROOT AND CARROTS

In both Sephardi and Italian-Jewish cooking, there is a wealth of recipes for ground meat or poultry cooked with vegetables. Most familiar, of course, are meat-stuffed vegetables, baked or braised; meat is also mounded between sliced vegetables, then breaded and fried; or it is prepared as in this recipe, combined with chopped vegetables, formed into meatballs, fried, and then braised.

I've cooked these meatballs over braised celery root and carrots, a favorite Sephardi combination. If you can't find celery root—or if the knotted bulbs appear too daunting—substitute fennel or celery, perhaps intensifying their flavors with a generous pinch of crushed fennel or celery seeds.

And instead of the green olives or roasted red peppers I've combined with the meat here, you can experiment with other cooked vegetables as well, like chopped spinach, fried eggplant, or braised fennel. Adding vegetables to the meatballs both flavors and lightens them, making this method a particularly good choice when you are using ground chicken or turkey.

---

1 thick (about 1-inch) slice challah or good-quality white bread or semolina, crust removed

2½ cups chicken broth, preferably homemade (page 63), or use good-quality, low-sodium canned

1 tablespoon chopped garlic, plus 2 teaspoons minced garlic

5 tablespoons chopped fresh parsley

1 large egg

1 pound ground chicken, turkey, or beef

1 cup pitted green olives, chopped (use good-quality brine- or oil-cured), or ½ cup minced roasted red pepper (see Cook's Note, page 126, for method)

Salt and freshly ground black pepper

1½ pounds celery root (also called celeriac)

1 pound carrots

Olive oil, for frying

Juice of 2 lemons

1 teaspoon grated lemon zest

---

1. Tear the bread into 2-inch pieces and put it into a small saucepan. Add ½ cup broth and cook over medium heat until the bread has absorbed all the liquid. Transfer the mixture to a food processor, together with the chopped garlic, 2 tablespoons parsley, and the egg and process until well combined. Put the meat in a large bowl and add the pureed bread mixture, the olives or red peppers, and salt and pepper to taste. Knead with your hands until all the ingredients are thoroughly amalgamated. If you have time, refrigerate for at least 30 minutes to let the flavors blend.

2. Prepare the vegetables. Peel and trim the celery root and cut it into large cubes—you'll have 3½–4 cups. (To facilitate the peeling, cut it into largish pieces first, then trim and peel.) Cut the carrots into pieces roughly the same size as the celery root—you'll have about 2 cups.

3. Wetting your hands as needed, form the meat into walnut-sized balls. Heat about ¼ inch oil in a large, heavy, deep-sided sauté pan until hot but not smoking. Add the meatballs and sauté in batches until lightly browned on all sides but not cooked through. (This is the one-pot method. If time is a problem or you don't have a deep-sided sauté pan, fry the meatballs in a regular skillet and braise the vegetables at the same time in a Dutch oven or heavy casserole.) Transfer the meatballs to a platter as they are done.

4. Wipe out the skillet, add 3 tablespoons oil, and heat until hot. Add the celery root and carrots and sauté over medium-high heat, in batches if necessary, until the vegetables turn golden brown at the edges. Keep lifting and turning with a spatula so the vegetables color on all sides. If you worked in batches, return all vegetables to the skillet. Add the lemon juice, remaining 2 cups broth and 2 teaspoons minced garlic, and salt and pepper to taste. Stir well, then simmer over low heat, covered, for about 10 minutes. The vegetables should be almost tender at this point.

5. Add the meatballs to the pan, and spoon the pan liquid and vegetables over them. Cover and simmer gently for 10 minutes, or until the vegetables are very tender and the meatballs are cooked through. Adjust the salt and pepper and stir in the lemon zest and the remaining 3 tablespoons parsley.

6. Transfer the meat and vegetables to a serving platter and ladle some of the pan juices over them. Pass the remaining pan sauce separately. (If you want a more concentrated pan sauce, reduce it for a few minutes over high heat after you have removed the meatballs and vegetables.)

YIELD: 4–5 servings

FRIED ONION AND CHICKEN KREPLACH

What should I be doing? Eating kreplach?

—ISAAC BASHEVIS SINGER, "GIMPEL THE FOOL"

Throughout this book, onions are cooked in many ways, depending on the texture and taste desired—soft and sweet, rich and caramelized, golden and crispy. In this recipe, they are salted first to draw out the moisture, and then fried. If you are pressed for time or don't want to bother, omit the soaking and fry the onions a little longer over medium heat.

Using a high proportion of savory fried onion to the chicken ensures that the filling for the kreplach won't be dry—even if the chicken left its flavor in the soup pot.

---

2 large onions, very thinly sliced (about 4 cups)

Coarse kosher salt

1 cup cooked chicken (use light and dark meat; leftover from preparing chicken soup is fine)

A few tablespoons of chicken broth, as needed

2 tablespoons mild olive or vegetable oil

1 large garlic clove, minced

1 large egg, lightly beaten

1 tablespoon finely chopped fresh dill

Freshly ground black pepper to taste

About 30 wonton wrappers (see page 30; it's a good idea to have some extra in case of tearing)

Egg wash (1–2 large eggs, as needed, each beaten with 1 teaspoon of water)

Accompaniments: Classic Chicken Soup (page 63), gravy, or fried onions or mushrooms from Mishmash Kreplach (page 111)

---

1. Separate the onions into rings. To draw out the moisture, toss in a bowl with 1½ teaspoons salt. Set aside for about 20 minutes, stirring from time to time. Then place the onions between sheets of paper towels, pressing down to soak up as much onion water as possible.

2. Meanwhile, prepare the chicken. Roughly shred it (preferably using your fingers, so you can easily find any little bits of gristle or bone) and place in a bowl. If the chicken is very dry—usually the case if you are using chicken left over from making soup—spoon some broth over it, mix well, and let it drink in the liquid for at least 15 minutes.

3. Heat the oil in a large, heavy skillet over medium-high heat. Add the onions, and keep tossing with a spatula as they soften and begin to turn golden, about 10 minutes. Stir in the garlic and continue cooking and turning, until the mixture is a deep caramel color, but before it turns crispy, about 5 minutes.

4. Stir the onions into the chicken and let cool slightly. Add the egg, dill, and salt and pepper to taste. Refrigerate the mixture, covered, for at least 1 hour.

5. Fill and trim the kreplach (see pages 30–31), using about 1 heaping teaspoon of filling per krepl, and then folding into a tight triangle and sealing them with the egg wash.

6. Poach the kreplach. In a large, very wide pot, bring at least 5 quarts of lightly salted water to a boil. Slip in the kreplach, one by one, being careful not to overcrowd the pot (if necessary, cook them in batches or use two pots). Lower the temperature slightly (the kreplach might explode if the water is boiling furiously) and poach until tender, 3–6 minutes (exact time will depend on the brand of wonton wrapper used). Lift out the kreplach, a few at a time, with a large skimmer, gently shaking the skimmer so the water drains back into the pot to dry the kreplach (the kreplach are too fragile to pour into a colander).

7. Serve the kreplach in soup. Or serve poached or sautéed kreplach with gravy, fried onions, or fried mushrooms as a side dish or appetizer.

YIELD: About 30 kreplach

FRIED CHICKEN CUTLETS,
ITALIAN-JEWISH STYLE

The logs of Jerusalem were of the cinnamon tree, and when lit,
their fragrance pervaded the whole of Erez Israel.

—BABYLONIAN TALMUD: SHABBAT

Fried chicken lightly flavored with cinnamon is a traditional Hanukkah specialty in Italy. Used without any sweetening, the cinnamon acts in concert here with savory garlic and lemon to produce a very fragrant yet subtle marinade.

To accentuate the delicacy of the dish, I dip the chicken in egg after dusting it lightly with matzoh meal. And I fry each batch with a few pieces of celery—a trick sent in to *Cook's Illustrated* magazine by one of its readers—which makes the chicken beautifully golden and more flavorful.

¼ teaspoon ground cinnamon

*4 large garlic cloves, finely chopped (about
    1 ½ tablespoons)*

3 tablespoons fresh lemon juice

1 tablespoon olive oil, plus additional for frying

Salt and freshly ground black pepper

*1 ½ pounds skinless, boneless chicken cutlets,
    trimmed of fat and gristle*

*About 1 cup matzoh meal (use commercially
    ground—you'll need a very fine, powdery
    consistency here)*

2 large eggs

*2–3 celery stalks, including leaves, washed,
    dried well, and cut into 4- to 5-inch lengths*

Lemon wedges

Fresh parsley sprigs, for garnish (optional)

---

1. In a large mixing bowl or nonreactive baking dish, whisk together the cinnamon, garlic, lemon juice, olive oil, and salt and pepper to taste. Add the chicken and toss to coat thoroughly. Cover and marinate for 2–3 hours in the refrigerator, turning the chicken occasionally.

2. Set up a work station near the stove. Spread 1 cup matzoh meal on a large sheet of wax paper or a plate and season it with 1 teaspoon salt and ⅛ teaspoon pepper, or to taste. Next to it, in a wide shallow bowl or pie pan, beat the eggs with a few drops of water until well blended and smooth.

3. Dredge the cutlets well with the matzoh meal, rubbing it lightly into the chicken. Make sure each cutlet is covered all over with meal. If necessary, add more matzoh meal, remembering to add more seasoning.

4. Heat about ½ cup olive oil in a 10- to 12-inch heavy skillet over medium-high heat until hot and fragrant but not smoking. Shake a cutlet to remove all excess matzoh meal, then coat it thoroughly with the egg and slip it quickly into the hot oil. Being careful not to crowd the pan, add more chicken, dipping each piece in the egg just before placing it in the pan. Slip a few pieces of celery in between the cutlets as they fry. Using two spatulas (tongs would ruin the delicate egg coating), carefully turn the chicken when it is light golden, 2–3 minutes. Sauté the other side for 2–3 minutes longer, or until cooked through. Turn the celery pieces when you turn the chicken. Transfer the cutlets to a platter lined with paper towels so they can drain. Discard the cooked celery. Keep the chicken warm in a 200°F oven until the remaining pieces are done. Continue frying any remaining chicken in batches, in the same way, adding fresh celery to the pan with each batch. Wipe out the skillet and replace the oil if some of the coating falls off and burns.

Serve the chicken right away, accompanied by the lemon wedges and garnished, if you'd like, with fresh parsley. It really needs no sauce.

YIELD: 3–4 servings

DAIRY DISHES

We tramped in, sandy-footed and salt-haired, a fine sweat pushing past remnant streaks of tanning lotion on our lightly baked bodies.

"We're having dairy tonight," my mother said, as she nudged us into showers before we could collapse on the sofa.

Set out on the table were fragrant berry soup, hot fruit-filled blintzes and varenikes or oniony potato and cheese kreplach, golden mamaliga dotted with pools of melted butter and scallion flecks, trays of scarlet-edged radishes in paper-thin slices—absolutely everything slathered with a thick layer of cool, rich sour cream. Except the butter. Cold, sweet butter to spread on fat slabs of corn-rye bread, in case such ethereal fare proved too meager to fill our tummies. And before the fireflies beckoned from the falling night, there was warm, sweet cheese-filled noodle pudding with vanilla ice cream.

A dairy meal—which embraced anything from cheese blintzes to salmon croquettes—was always thought of as *light,* simply because no meat was served. Often lavish in butterfat and frequently followed by a rich dessert, the dairy meal was a fixture not only of steaming summer nights but Thursday and pre-holiday evenings too, when the stomach needed rest before the next day's meat-based Sabbath or festival dinner.

Dairy recipes, whether Ashkenazi or Sephardi, are among the stars of the Jewish kitchen. They are not simply sauces or side dishes playing second fiddle to traditional main-course meats or chicken. Because of the dietary regulations, when dairy products are served, no meat or poultry may be eaten. The meals are rounded out with a host of wholesome pareve foods (those which are neither meat nor dairy): fish, grains, vegetables, and fruits.

Of course for many children—and adults—the delight of a dairy meal is its promise of dessert. Because all desserts rich in cream, butter, cheese—or all three together—become possible.

You'll find a diverse selection of dairy dishes here, suitable for any time of day. And be sure to check the noodle puddings in "Sweet Kugels and Desserts" and the other luscious dairy recipes that are listed below.

O T H E R   D A I R Y
S U G G E S T I O N S

Honeyed Quince–Apple Blintzes with Sour Cream–Date Sauce (page 252)
Cheese Latkes with Fresh Persimmon Sauce (page 282)
Greek-Inspired Cheese Latkes (page 284)
Black Grape, Goat Cheese, and Noodle Latkes with Fragrant Honey (page 286)
Poached Prune Kreplach with Honeyed Cream and Pecans (page 298)
Mozzarella in Matzoh Carrozza (page 344)
Cheese Blintzes with Fresh Berried Fruit Compote (page 355)
Turkish Silken Rice Pudding with Fresh Raspberry Sauce (page 357)

Blintzes may seem complicated, but they are as easy to prepare as crepes. Easier, in fact, since they are cooked on one side only. They are the ideal pastry for the rolling pin–challenged.

Like strawberry shortcake and Wallis Simpson, they were meant to be rich. On the other hand, such hefty doses of butter, cream, and cheese are best enjoyed in the company of more pristine flavors, like gently treated fresh or dried fruit.

Devise your own combinations for fillings from the liveliest fruits at the market, and feel free to *potchkeh* with the more detailed recipes that follow. Cooking the fruit just long enough to bring out its natural sugars (or macerating delicate raw fruits, such as blueberries, in hot liquids, like reduced fruit juice) and avoiding fillers like cornstarch will keep the flavors brisk and fresh-tasting. If you find that your fruit is too wet for a filling, stir in a few tablespoons of ground blanched almonds or cream cheese to soak up the juices.

MAKING THE BLINTZ LEAVES (THE BASIC CREPE)

1–1 ¼ cups milk, preferably whole	*2 tablespoons unsalted butter, melted and*
3 large eggs	*cooled*
¾ cup unbleached all-purpose flour	*Additional butter or, less preferable, a mild,*
¼ teaspoon salt	*flavorless oil (like avocado), for frying*

1. In a blender, mix 1 cup of the milk, the eggs, flour, salt, and butter until smooth. Transfer the batter to a bowl. (To prepare the batter by hand, beat the eggs and butter together in a bowl; mix in ½ cup of the milk; gradually add the flour and salt, whisking until smooth, then add another ½ cup of milk; whisk until well-blended.)

2. Let the batter rest for at least 30 minutes or up to 2 hours at room temperature. If refrigerated, the batter should rest for at least 2 hours or up to 12 hours (overnight is fine).

3. Stir the batter well (don't rebeat it because you want to avoid foamy bubbles). It should have the consistency of light cream. If necessary, thin it with some of the reserved milk. You may have to add more milk if the batter thickens as it stands.

4. Heat a very lightly buttered 6- or 7-inch skillet or crepe pan over moderately high heat until sizzling. (A nonstick pan works particularly well, but I find you do have to butter the pan, at least for the

first blintz, to avoid a slightly rubbery texture.) Pour about 2 tablespoons of batter into the hot pan (a coffee measure is good for this), and immediately tilt the pan from side to side to distribute the batter evenly over the bottom. You may find it easier both to add the batter and swirl while holding the pan off the heat. Don't allow the batter to extend up the sides of the pan when tilting or the blintz edges will become too thin and crackly.

5. Cook just until the top of the blintz is slightly dry and the edges start to curl. The bottom should be pale gold, not brown. Do **not** cook the other side. Loosen the blintz with a spatula and turn it out onto wax paper or a large platter, fried side up. Repeat until all the batter is used up. Pile the finished blintz leaves on a platter, separating each with sheets of wax paper or a clean kitchen cloth, and keep the exposed leaves covered to prevent them from drying out. Brush the pan with additional butter or oil only if necessary, and remember to stir the batter periodically. To avoid tears, let the freshly prepared blintz leaves cool to room temperature before filling. (And the wax paper is easier to remove when the blintz leaves are cool.)

6. Blintz leaves may be prepared ahead. Let them cool to room temperature, keeping them separated by wax paper, then wrap well with foil. Refrigerate for up to 3 days, or freeze them for up to 1 month, separated by the wax paper and well-wrapped with heavy-duty foil or in a freezer-proof container. Bring them to room temperature before filling to prevent tearing them.

TIPS

1. Add very little butter or oil to the pan when preparing the leaves. The batter already contains butter, so if you use a nonstick pan, you may not need to add any, after the first blintz. To grease the pan, dip a paper towel *very* lightly in melted butter or oil and quickly film the pan. If you put too much in or if the butter burns as you fry the leaves, wipe the pan clean with a paper towel so as not to transfer any burned butter taste.
2. Work quickly greasing the pan, adding the batter, and turning out the finished leaf. The pan should always be hot before you add the batter.
3. Allow the batter to rest, and stir, don't beat, to eliminate most of the bubbles. Occasionally, bubbles will form on top of a cooking blintz leaf, and generally they are superficial and will cause no damage. But if a bubble looks like it will create a real hole through the finished leaf, I immediately smooth over it with some of the still wet batter from another part of the blintz or I dab on a smidgen of fresh batter to cover it, letting the leaf continue cooking until it seems dry. (Because the leaves are very thin, cooked only on one side, and most fillings are rather wet, even fairly small holes could mean fillings oozing out while blintzes are frying.)

YIELD: 16–18 blintz leaves

FILLING THE BLINTZES

Spread 1 heaping tablespoon of the filling across the middle of the cooked side of each blintz. (Tempting as it may be to use up that extra bit of filling, do **not** overfill blintzes or they might explode.) Fold in the sides, then fold the bottom of the blintz over the filling, and roll up, jelly-roll fashion, pulling the top over tightly. You should have a neat package. Place filled blintzes seam side down, so they don't open up.

At this point, you can refrigerate the blintzes for a couple of days or freeze them for up to one month, if you want to, and fry them just before serving. Don't bother to thaw frozen blintzes, but adjust the cooking time accordingly.

TIP: Fillings should always be cooled at least to room temperature. I find it is often easier to work with chilled fillings: they are firmer and less runny.

COOKING THE FILLED BLINTZES

To fry the blintzes, heat butter, a mild oil, or a combination, in a heavy skillet over medium heat until sizzling. Add the blintzes seam side down, without crowding the pan. Cook, turning once, until golden brown on both sides, 2–3 minutes per side. Adjust the heat if necessary, and watch that the butter does not scorch.

Or you can bake them, for a slightly lighter taste. Preheat the oven to 450°F. Melt a generous quantity of butter or butter mixed with a little oil on a rimmed baking sheet or in a shallow baking pan. Add the blintzes and turn to coat well on all sides. Spread the blintzes out seam side down on the sheet so their sides are not touching. Bake for 10–15 minutes, or until crisp and golden brown on both sides. I usually find it is not necessary to turn them; if they seem slow to brown on top, however, I flip them over for a few minutes. When preparing a large number of blintzes for company, it is usually easiest to bake them.

RASPBERRY-PEACH BLINTZES

DAIRY

> I would tell you that the Garden of Eden is in Menashe the Doctor's
> orchard.... What fruits wouldn't you find in this orchard? Apples and
> pears and cherries, plums and gooseberries and currants, peaches, raspberries,
> rough cherries, blackberries.
>
> —SHOLOM ALEICHEM, "WHAT WILL BECOME OF ME"

For very poor Jews in Eastern Europe, summer fruits from such Edens were not meant for casual indulgences. The orphaned hero of Aleichem's story recalls longingly the one peach he ate years before—a Sabbath treat. The entire harvest of Menashe's beautiful pink-streaked peaches was destined for the jam pot. Other Jews reserved their precious fruits—especially berries and cherries—for juice to be drunk strictly for medicinal purposes.

Here the irresistible combination of syrupy peaches and fragrant raspberries delivers summer's extravagance in a blintz.

To retain the fresh, pure fruit taste of the blintz filling, I steep the peaches and raspberries in hot, reduced, unsweetened berry juice, rather than a sugar syrup. This gentle "cooking" deepens and enriches the intrinsic flavors of not just perfect peaches, but even those that will never ripen properly to slurpy goodness. Now mingled with sunny peach and raspberry notes, the steeping liquid is further cooked down for a refreshing unsweetened syrup to set off the blintzes.

Present the blintzes with dollops of sour cream or yogurt cream for an ethereal play of flavors and textures.

---

*2 cups unsweetened berry-flavored fruit juice
  (for example, apple-raspberry, raspberry-
  cranberry, apple-strawberry)
One 2-inch piece of vanilla bean, split and scraped
About 2¼ cups peeled, sliced fresh peaches
  (5–7 medium)
¾ cup fresh raspberries*

*Sugar, if desired
1 recipe blintz leaves (page 136)
Unsalted butter, mild oil, or a combination, for
  frying or baking
Optional accompaniments: sour cream or yogurt
  cream (page 29), Fresh Raspberry Applesauce
  (page 178)*

---

1. In a wide, heavy saucepan, bring the fruit juice and vanilla bean to a boil over medium heat, and continue cooking until the liquid is reduced to a little more than a cup. Place the peaches in a bowl and pour the boiling liquid over them. (Don't bother to wash the pan—you'll be boiling the juice in it

again for the syrup.) Cover and cool to room temperature. Remove the vanilla bean (rinse and dry it, if you wish to reuse it or bury it in granulated sugar for vanilla sugar). Stir in the raspberries.

2. Place a colander over a large bowl and drain the fruit for at least 15 minutes, reserving the juice. Taste the fruit, and if desired, add a bit of sugar.

3. Fill the blintz leaves with a heaping tablespoon of filling for each blintz (do not overfill), and bake or fry them (see page 138).

4. Prepare the syrup. Pour the reserved fruit juices into the saucepan and boil down until reduced to a maple syrup consistency.

5. Serve the blintzes piping hot, accompanied by the syrup and, if desired, a dollop of sour cream or yogurt cream and/or fresh raspberry applesauce.

YIELD: 16–18 blintzes

STRAWBERRY-RHUBARB BLINTZES

The classic pie mates team up to fill a buttery blintz. The mellow tang of the sour cream or yogurt topping points up the bright flavors of the sassy fresh fruit.

Because the berries are barely cooked, look for fragrant, perfectly ripe berries to make an ambrosial blintz.

About 10 ounces rhubarb, peeled and cut into
1-inch chunks (2¼ cups)
½ cup plus 2 tablespoons packed or granulated
light brown sugar
About 15 ounces (2½ cups) fresh, ripe strawber-
ries, washed, hulled, and halved (or quartered
if large)

1 recipe blintz leaves (page 136)
Unsalted butter, oil, or a combination, for
frying or baking
Accompaniment: sour cream or yogurt cream
(page 29)

---

1. Place the rhubarb in a bowl and sprinkle it with the brown sugar. Let the fruit macerate for about 20 minutes to release its juices, stirring it every once in a while.

2. Put the rhubarb and all its juices in a saucepan, and bring to a boil over medium heat. Reduce the heat and simmer until the rhubarb is very tender, being careful not to let it turn to mush.

3. Stir in the strawberries, remove the pan from heat, cover, and let the fruit and its liquid cool completely. This will take at least 30 minutes.

4. Once cool, drain the fruit for 15–20 minutes in a colander set over a large bowl to capture the juices. Transfer the drained fruit to another bowl. Fill the blintz leaves with a heaping tablespoon of filling for each blintz (do not overfill), and bake or fry them (see page 138).

5. Prepare the syrup. In the same saucepan used for the fruit, boil down the reserved fruit juices (and any leftover filling) until reduced by about one-third, or until as thick as desired. This syrup is also excellent drizzled over pancakes, waffles, ice cream, or frozen yogurt.

6. Serve the blintzes piping hot, accompanied by the syrup and a dollop of sour cream or yogurt cream.

YIELD: 16–18 blintzes

APRICOT BLINTZES WITH TOASTED
PISTACHIOS AND YOGURT CREAM

"If you are going to be in the hospital for five days, I'll bring the sheets."

"No, Ma," I said. I had to undergo yet another procedure in my quest to become pregnant and I was irritable.

"Sweetface, I always had the silk and lace sheets on my bed when my friends came to visit me in the hospital. And an orchid. Your father always brought me an orchid to pin to the pillowcase. I want you to have one too."

"That was different. They were coming to visit you when you had babies. I don't need orchids for this." She stopped talking about orchids and I continued having surgeries.

Then in November 1984, I gave birth to a big beautiful baby girl.

My father put down the bag, redolent of hot, spicy-sweet smells from New York's Lower East Side, where they had stopped on the way to the hospital. We walked down the hall to the nursery, and I pointed out Alexandra, born with a full head of her grandmother's red hair and the ability, rare in neonatals, to cry real tears.

We walked back to my room. Halvah, pistachios, and sour apricots were crowded together on my bed tray. The starched white sheets were now covered with ecru silk trimmed on either side with rows of baroque cream-colored lace.

She smiled her radiant smile, and tears sparkled in the corners of the big, blue-gray eyes.

She walked toward me, arms outstretched.

Then I saw it. The little lump of hospital pillow, swimming in lace. And firmly anchored to the top, a huge, fresh orchid, frilly white edges, vibrant magenta within.

A month later, we still had the leftovers. When friends came to bill and coo and rock Alex, I relaxed in the kitchen, rhythmically turning out these blintzes in the energized haze of euphoria and sleep deprivation peculiar to new parents. The blintzes are reminiscent of luscious *palatschinken* (Hungarian apricot crepes), but the stuffing—plumped tart fruit infused with vanilla and almond—provides more nuanced flavor and texture than the traditional jam filling. I scattered the leftover toasted pistachios over the blintzes for color and a pleasant buttery crunch. Later we swirled the remains of the halvah with vanilla ice cream.

2 cups apple-apricot juice, apple juice, apricot
  nectar, or other apricot- or apple-flavored juice
10–12 ounces dried apricots, preferably tart,
  cut in half or, if large, in quarters (about
  1 ¾ cups)
A 2-inch piece of vanilla bean, split, or
  ½ teaspoon vanilla extract
½ teaspoon almond extract
1 recipe blintz leaves (page 136)

Unsalted butter, oil, or a combination, for
  frying or baking
Yogurt cream (page 30) or labneh (available
  at Middle Eastern and specialty stores),
  sweetened to taste, if desired, with fragrant
  honey
⅓ cup toasted pistachios (see step 1, page 342,
  for method)

1. Put the juice in a wide, heavy, nonreactive 6-quart Dutch oven or saucepan and boil it over medium-high heat until reduced by one-third, to about 1 ⅔ cups. Add the apricots, vanilla, and almond extract, reduce the heat, and simmer, covered, until the apricots are very tender, about 25 minutes.

2. Uncover the pan and boil over high heat, stirring, to evaporate all remaining liquid. (If you used a vanilla bean, remove it, and if desired, dry and save it for another use or bury it in granulated sugar to flavor it). Let the apricots cool in the pan for 15–20 minutes, then refrigerate, covered, for another 20 minutes or up to 24 hours, if you want to fill the blintzes later.

3. Fill the blintz leaves with a heaping tablespoon of filling for each blintz (don't overfill), and bake or fry them (see page 138).

4. Serve the blintzes hot, topped with yogurt cream or *labneh* and a sprinkle of toasted pistachios.

YIELD: 16–18 blintzes

APPLE-CRANBERRY BLINTZES WITH MAPLE-RICOTTA CREAM AND SUGARED WALNUTS

DAIRY

Every place you go, act according to the custom of that place.

—LADINO PROVERB

These tantalizing blintzes are an unabashed ode to the Diaspora. Autumn-scented apples and cranberries form the sweet and tangy filling. For the luscious cream topping, simply sieve ricotta sweetened with maple and vanilla. Finish with a crunch of lightly sweetened toasted walnuts.

APPLE-CRANBERRY FILLING

3 tablespoons unsalted butter

About 3½ cups flavorful apples, peeled, cored, and cut into small chunks (use sweet, local, seasonal, varieties with lots of character, like Gravenstein, Gala, Braeburn, Jonathan, Stayman Winesap, and the heirloom Golden Russet, which will contrast nicely with the cranberries)

⅓–½ cup packed brown sugar

½ teaspoon ground cinnamon

¾ cup cranberries, washed and picked over

2 tablespoons dried cranberries (optional)

Salt

MAPLE-RICOTTA CREAM

1½ cups (about 11 ounces) whole-milk ricotta cheese (you can use part-skim, if desired)

1 tablespoon pure maple syrup

¼ teaspoon vanilla extract

⅛ teaspoon freshly grated nutmeg (optional)

SUGARED WALNUTS

¼ cup walnuts, toasted

1 teaspoon maple or white sugar

1 recipe blintz leaves (page 136)

Unsalted butter, oil, or a combination, for frying or baking

1. Make the apple filling. Heat the butter over medium-high heat in a large, heavy skillet until sizzling. Add the apples and sauté for about 5 minutes, lifting and turning them as they begin to turn golden. Sprinkle with ⅓ cup brown sugar and the cinnamon and mix well to coat the apples evenly on all sides. Add the cranberries, optional dried cranberries, and a pinch of salt, and cook, stirring, until the cranberries have popped and the apples are very tender. Let the fruit cool in the pan, then taste and add more sugar, if necessary, depending on your preference and the sweetness of the apples.

2. Transfer the fruit to a bowl and refrigerate, covered, for at least 20 minutes or up to 24 hours.

3. Meanwhile, make the maple-ricotta cream. Push the ricotta through a fine-mesh strainer, rubbing with the back of a spoon. Using an egg beater or electric mixer, beat in the maple syrup, vanilla, and nutmeg, if using, until smooth and light. Cover and refrigerate to allow the flavors to marry. Rewhip briefly just before serving.

4. To prepare the walnuts, coarsely chop them with the sugar.

5. Fill the blintz leaves with a heaping tablespoon of filling for each blintz (don't overfill), and bake or fry them (see page 138).

6. Serve the blintzes hot, topped with maple-ricotta cream and sprinkled with sugared walnuts.

YIELD: 16–18 blintzes

An orchid in her hair, the author's mother, Joan, and her father, Max, walk her uncle Bernie down the aisle.

GOLDEN CHERRY-CHEESE VARENIKES

The ripest sour cherry popped into the mouth raw—even when heavily sugared—cannot compete with the sweet kind. Just finding a sour cherry requires real detective work. So why bother? Because when they are cooked, sour cherries are unsurpassed. It's then that their fresh, tart-acid taste leaves their sweet cousins in the dust, fleshy and flat in comparison.

Eastern European Jews relished the bright tangy-sweet taste of sour cherries in preserves for sweetening dark Russian tea and in cold summery soups. My father's father macerated them in the fiery plum brandy Slivovitz and doled out a few to his family each Friday night, a grownup Sabbath treat especially appreciated by his young sons. But they are at their best when paired with cream, like hot cherry blintzes or varenikes (fruit-filled kreplach), mellowed with sour cream, *labneh*, or rich yogurt cream.

Here almond extract highlights the nutty undertones of the cherries and cream cheese soaks up the flavorful juices they release. Although fresh cherries work best, canned sour cherries packed in water will do fine.

This filling would also be luscious in a blintz. Because the blintz will be cooked only a short time, however, I recommend poaching fresh sour cherries first for a few minutes in sugared water or fruit juice.

Sugar, as needed (if you have vanilla sugar, by all means substitute it—it is lovely here)

Crystallized ginger to taste, cut into bits (1–2 tablespoons)

About 1 pound sour red cherries, stemmed and pitted (about 2 cups; if you don't have a cherry pitter, a hairpin works well), or if fresh are not available, 2 cups canned sour cherries packed in water, drained

4 ounces (½ cup) cream cheese, softened

½ teaspoon almond extract

35–40 wonton wrappers, plus extra in case of tearing

Egg wash (1–2 large eggs, as needed, each beaten with 1 teaspoon of water)

3 tablespoons unsalted butter, plus additional for greasing the pan

Ground cinnamon to taste

Accompaniments: sour cream, yogurt cream (page 29), labneh, or Honeyed Cream (page 298)

---

1. In a blender, process about ⅓ cup sugar with crystallized ginger to taste until the ginger is very finely minced. Add enough of the mixture to sweeten the cherries to your liking (start with about ¼ cup and keep tasting). Let macerate for at least 20 minutes. Reserve any extra ginger sugar for later.

Drain the cherries of any juice they may have thrown off, saving it to flavor the sour cream or other topping you'll be serving.

2. Mash together the cream cheese and almond extract. Dab a little of the mixture in the center of a wonton wrapper. Set about 2 cherries on top (depending on the size of the cherries). Dipping your finger in the egg wash, moisten the wonton all around the filling. Fold the wonton over to make a triangle. With your fingers, press all air out around the filling, then press the edges very firmly together to form a tight seal. Trim away any excess dough with a sharp knife (see page 30.)

3. Continue making varenikes until all the cherries are used up. Preheat the oven to 400°F and butter a baking sheet generously. In a large, very wide pot, bring at least 5 quarts of lightly salted water to a boil. Slip in the varenikes, one by one, being careful not to overcrowd the pot (if necessary, cook them in batches, or use two pots). Lower the temperature slightly (the varenikes might explode if the water is boiling furiously) and poach until tender, 3–6 minutes (exact time will depend on the brand of wonton wrapper). Meanwhile melt the butter. Remove the varenikes, a few at a time, with a large skimmer, gently shaking the skimmer over the pot to dry them (they are too fragile to pour into a colander). Place the varenikes on the prepared baking sheet and brush generously with the melted butter. Sprinkle to taste with cinnamon and whatever sugar you are using: the reserved ginger sugar, vanilla sugar, or plain white sugar. Bake for 15 minutes, or until golden.

4. Stir the reserved cherry juice into the sour cream, yogurt cream, *labneh,* or Honeyed Cream and serve with the hot varenikes.

YIELD: 35–40 varenikes

SORREL-ONION NOODLE KUGEL

They erupted in early spring, their arching dark-green curlicues and hollow stems betraying them among the lawn grasses long before their pungent waft of onion. My sister and I called these wild chives "onion grass," and we ate shafts and shafts as we foraged outside our New Jersey home for four-leaf clovers and cowering purple and yellow violets.

One day my grandfather pointed out the easily recognized arrow shape of wild sorrel, a lemony green fix to cleanse the mouth of onion and too much sun. I was hooked for life.

I find the fresh tart flavor of sorrel extraordinarily refreshing, especially with rich or stodgy foods—a sour taste, like arugula, that I adore. I no longer have access to sorrel foraged or from a garden, but I am extremely fortunate to live within blocks of the Union Square Greenmarket in Manhattan, where beautiful fresh sorrel is usually available spring, summer, and fall, not just trimmed but completely washed as well.

The intriguing medley of flavors in this suave noodle pudding—tart sorrel and sweet, caramelized onions, mellowed by cream—was inspired by Deborah Madison's opulent Sorrel-Onion Tart in *The Greens Cookbook* (which was, in turn, inspired by Richard Olney's *Simple French Food*). It makes an elegant lunch or brunch or a fine, light summer supper. Or serve it as a starter in a special dairy dinner.

---

2 tablespoons unsalted butter

1 tablespoon mild vegetable oil, plus additional for greasing the pan

2 large onions (about 1½ pounds), thinly sliced

Salt

4 cups packed (6–8 ounces) sorrel, stems removed, leaves cut into shreds or torn into 1-inch pieces (when buying sorrel, it should be crisp and unwilted—avoid torn leaves or those with wet or soft spots; store sorrel in perforated plastic bags in the refrigerator)

½ cup whole milk

4 ounces wide flat egg noodles (not the twisted spiral kind, which won't absorb as much of the flavoring)

4 ounces (½ cup) cream cheese, softened

1 cup sour cream

3 large eggs

Freshly ground black pepper

1 tablespoon grated lemon zest

2 tablespoons grated Parmesan (optional)

---

1. In a 10- to 12-inch nonreactive, heavy skillet, melt the butter in the oil. Add the onions, sprinkle with 1 teaspoon salt, and cook, covered, over moderately low heat, stirring from time to time, until the onions are almost clear and very soft, about 25 minutes. Remove the lid, turn the heat up to high, and

sauté, tossing, until the onions are a rich gold, 5–10 minutes. Don't let the onions brown. Add the sorrel, a little at a time, and cook, stirring, until completely melted down, about 5 minutes. Stir in the milk, lower the heat, and simmer until the milk is well incorporated and the sorrel becomes a puree. (Don't be alarmed when it turns an unattractive gray-green—it will taste delicious.)

2. Preheat the oven to 350°F.

3. Bring 2–3 quarts of water and 1 teaspoon of salt to a rapid boil in a large pot. Add the noodles and cook until almost tender but a bit firmer than al dente. Drain, then rinse lightly under cool water. In a large bowl, whisk together the cream cheese, sour cream, and eggs until smooth. Add the sorrel mixture and cooked noodles and combine well. Season to taste with salt and pepper.

4. Generously grease a shallow 2- to 2½-quart baking dish (such as an 8- or 9-inch square pan) and sprinkle the bottom with the lemon zest. Spoon in the sorrel mixture and smooth the top. Sprinkle evenly with Parmesan, if using.

5. Bake for about 1 hour, or until firm and golden brown on top. Remove from the oven and let rest for at least 20 minutes, or until the kugel is set. Slice the kugel in the pan, or if you prefer, run a knife around the edges and invert onto a serving plate. Serve warm (reheat if necessary).

YIELD: 6–8 servings

SPINACH-CHEESE SQUARES

DAIRY

> Any city where there are no green vegetables—a sage may not dwell therein.
> —BABYLONIAN TALMUD: ERUVIN 55B

Mediterranean Jews so adore fresh spinach that little mountains of the leftover emerald "tails" are a hallmark of their holiday cooking. Called *ravikos* by Sephardim and *testine di spinaci* by Italian Jews, these stems are slow-braised until they turn almost red. They are usually served Thursday nights, when it is customary to eat lightly in preparation for the next day's feasting, and a large stockpile of them has accumulated from the Sabbath preparations.

The leaves often end up in light, eggy vegetable gratins, a Sephardi specialty, especially popular at the *desayuno,* a festive brunch served after morning services on Sabbath and holidays.

Notwithstanding spinach's bad rap, even kids seem to love these crustless, cheesy squares, here freshened up with plenty of green herbs. Good hot, warm, or at room temperature, they make a fine lunch, brunch, or light supper. Or cut them into bite-size pieces for a marvelous hors d'oeuvre. They freeze beautifully.

---

2 pounds fresh spinach, or two 10-ounce packages frozen leaf spinach, thawed

3 tablespoons unsalted butter, plus additional butter or oil for greasing the pan

½ cup chopped shallots, or 1 cup chopped onion

½ cup finely chopped fresh parsley

½ cup finely chopped fresh dill

Salt and freshly ground black pepper

1 cup (8 ounces) small-curd cottage cheese

4 ounces (½ cup) cream cheese, softened

4 large eggs

⅓ pound sharp cheddar cheese, grated into shreds (1½ cups)

1 ounce Parmesan cheese, grated (about ¼ cup)

3 tablespoons matzoh meal

3–4 tablespoons pine nuts, lightly toasted (optional)

---

1. If using fresh spinach, wash it thoroughly to remove all traces of sand. Cut off any tough stems and either trim them for *ravikos,* or discard them. Place the spinach with just the water that clings to its leaves in a large saucepan. Cover and cook over medium heat, stirring occasionally, until wilted, about 8 minutes.

2. Place the cooked fresh or the thawed frozen spinach in a colander and, with your hands or the back of a spoon, press out as much liquid as possible. It should be rather dry. Chop the spinach fine.

3. In a large skillet, melt the butter. Add the shallots or onion and sauté until softened, 5–7 minutes. Add the spinach and cook, stirring, until the spinach is tender and the butter is absorbed, 3–5 minutes. Stir in the parsley and dill and season with salt and pepper. Set aside to cool.

4. Preheat the oven to 350°F.

5. Force the cottage cheese through a sieve, rubbing with the back of a spoon, or push through a food mill into a large bowl. Beat in the cream cheese, and then the eggs, one at a time. Add the spinach mixture, cheddar, and Parmesan, and combine thoroughly.

6. Grease a 13-by-9-inch baking pan and sprinkle the bottom and sides with the matzoh meal. Pour the spinach batter into the pan and smooth the top. Scatter the pine nuts over evenly, if using, and bake for about 40 minutes, or until light golden and edges are starting to pull away from the sides of the pan. It should feel slightly firm, but it will not set until it has cooled for at least 20 minutes. Serve warm (reheat if necessary) or room temperature, cut into squares.

YIELD: 6–8 servings

COOK'S NOTE: Beautifully fresh Swiss chard is increasingly available in markets these days. It is much easier to clean than spinach, and I find its sweet yet distinctively earthy, green leaves make an excellent substitute in this recipe.

I also vary the cheeses; experiment with some of your favorites. Or try this: Replace the cheddar with ⅓ pound grated Jarlsberg and substitute about 2½ ounces of crumbled feta (break it up well using your fingers) for the cottage cheese; omit the Parmesan and add 1 teaspoon grated lemon zest and an additional ¼ cup chopped dill. The feta is salty, so remember to adjust the seasoning accordingly.

One-quarter cup chopped fresh mint is a lovely addition.

POTATO-ONION KREPLACH,
POT STICKER STYLE

DAIRY

Without the potato, the Jewish Lithuanian household could not have existed. Mother was in her element with it. It was as if all her creative force bore down on that lowly tuber to transform it into one tempting magical form after another.

—DON GUSSOW, *CHAIA SONIA*

Inspired by the unabashed charms of homey mashed potatoes, generations of Eastern European Jewish cooks recast them in infinite incarnations. They reappeared as *chremslach* (crispy fried balls) or mixed with golden onions as savory fillings for knishes, blintzes, and kreplach.

My kreplach, with a voluptuous stuffing of buttery potatoes and burnished onions, fall somewhere between boiled and fried—prepared, in other words, like Chinese pot sticker dumplings. They make a sensational appetizer, brunch treat, or dairy side dish.

About 1 pound potatoes (preferably russet or Yukon Gold), peeled and cut into large cubes (about 3 cups)	*2 tablespoons chopped fresh dill, plus additional for garnish*
1 large garlic clove, peeled	*Freshly ground black pepper*
Salt	*24 wonton wrappers (see page 30; it's a good idea to have some extra in case of tearing)*
½ pound onions, coarsely chopped (2 cups)	*Flour for dusting*
3 tablespoons unsalted butter	*Accompaniments: chopped scallions and sour cream or yogurt cream (page 30)*
1 tablespoon mild olive, avocado, or vegetable oil, plus additional for frying	

1. Put the potatoes, garlic, and 2 teaspoons salt in a medium-large saucepan. Add 2 quarts of cold water and bring to a boil. Cook, partially covered, until the potatoes are tender, 15–20 minutes. Drain the potatoes, reserving about ½ cup cooking liquid. Don't wash out the saucepan.

2. While the potatoes are cooking, in a heavy 9- to 10-inch skillet, sauté the onions in 2 tablespoons butter and 1 tablespoon oil over medium heat, lifting and tossing them, until they are speckled gold and brown, about 15 minutes.

3. Mash the potatoes until smooth (unlike knishes, kreplach are too small for a few homey little lumps), using your favorite tool—a food mill, ricer, potato masher, or electric mixer (just don't use a

blender or food processor, which would make a gluey mess). Return the potatoes to the saucepan. With the heat on very low, beat in the fried onions and all of the cooking fat, the remaining 1 tablespoon butter, and the dill. Season well with lots of salt and pepper. If necessary, whisk in enough reserved potato water to make the mixture creamy and fluffy. Let cool, then refrigerate until cold.

4. Have a small bowl of water at hand. Place a wonton wrapper on a lightly floured surface, leaving the remaining wonton wrappers covered with a damp dish towel. Mound 1 heaping tablespoon of filling in the center of the wrapper. Dip your finger in the water and lightly moisten the surface of the wrapper all around the filling. Now bring up the sides of the wrapper, pleating the edges as necessary, so that they completely surround the filling. The finished krepl should resemble a little open sack made of pasta, encasing the potato stuffing. The stuffing should be visible close to or at the top of the sack. Continue making more kreplach, using the remaining filling and wrappers.

5. Heat ¼ inch oil in a 10- to 12-inch heavy skillet until hot but not smoking. Add as many filled wonton sacks as will fit comfortably without crowding the pan. As you place each wonton in the skillet, lightly tamp down the bottom so that it sits flat. Cook over medium heat until the bottom surfaces of the wontons are crisp and golden, 4–5 minutes. Standing back to avoid being splattered, add ⅓ cup water to the pan, cover tightly, and let the wontons steam until they are fully cooked, about 2 minutes more. The sides should be springy to the touch. Remove the lid, increase the heat, and cook for another minute, until the water evaporates and the wontons are crispy again on the bottom. Cook the remaining wontons in the same way.

6. Serve immediately, sprinkled with chopped scallions and dill, and accompanied by sour cream or yogurt cream.

YIELD: 4–6 servings

GARLIC MASHED POTATO KNISHES

DAIRY

Fat, fragrant cloves of garlic, six or seven at a time, were often sautéed whole with foods in my mother's kitchen. No one bothered to fish them out before serving—whoever unearthed the little treasures from a pile of chicken was as much to be envied as the one who landed the wishbone.

As a teenager, I was smugly pleased to read that some food savant dubbed garlic "the ketchup of the intellectuals," gratified that I had been nurtured since babyhood to stand with Camus and Huysmans.

Readers who have noticed my lavish use of the "stinking rose" will note such love is not merely familial—it is ancestral. Stoked with Pharaoh's garlic when forced to build his pyramids, Jews loved it still when wandering in the desert and pined for it as much as for the winy, thirst-quenching pomegranates they had left behind.

In these knishes, where phyllo substitutes for the traditional pastry dough, light and fluffy garlic mashed potatoes stand in for the accustomed onion-potato filling. The garlic does not stop there, however. It is used to flavor the melted butter brushed so deliciously between each flaky phyllo layer.

10–12 sheets of frozen phyllo, plus several extra to allow for tearing	*3–4 heaping tablespoons finely minced fresh garlic (according to taste)*
3 large russet (baking) potatoes, or about 1½ pounds Yukon Gold, peeled and cubed	*About ¾ cup heavy cream, half-and-half, or whole milk*
1½ sticks (12 tablespoons) unsalted butter (you may need up to 4 tablespoons more, depending on how generously you butter the phyllo)	*Salt and freshly ground black pepper*
	1 large egg, beaten
	Oil for greasing the pan

1. Thaw the frozen phyllo sheets slowly in the refrigerator for 8 hours or overnight. Remove the unopened package from the refrigerator about 2 hours before you begin the recipe to allow the sheets to come to room temperature.

2. In a saucepan, cover the potatoes with cold, salted water and bring to a boil. Cook, partially covered, until the potatoes are tender, about 15 minutes.

3. While the potatoes are cooking, slowly melt the butter with the garlic over low heat, stirring, until the garlic just begins to color, 5–7 minutes. Don't allow it to cook beyond the palest blond color—it should be tender, not crunchy. Cover the pan, turn off the heat, and let the garlic sit in the warm butter so the flavors continue to mingle until the potatoes are ready.

4. Mash the potatoes until smooth, using your favorite tool—a food mill, ricer, potato masher, or electric mixer (but not a blender or food processor). Whisk in about 4 tablespoons of the garlic butter (use a slotted spoon to retrieve most of the minced garlic and add that too). Beat in the cream, half-and-half, or milk and season to taste with salt and pepper. The potatoes should be very smooth and light, like very thick whipped cream (punctuated with bits of garlic), not dense and pasty like potato fillings you could slice with a knife. It will stiffen somewhat more when chilled. If necessary, add a bit more half-and-half, cream, or milk. Beat in the egg, let cool to room temperature, and refrigerate until cold.

5. Preheat the oven to 350°F. Lightly grease 2 baking sheets.

6. Remove the phyllo sheets from the package and carefully unroll them on a damp kitchen towel. Using kitchen scissors or a sharp knife, cut the stack of sheets in half, then cut these two stacks in half again, forming 4 equal stacks of rectangles (exact size will depend on brand of phyllo used). Immediately cover the cut phyllo sheets with a large piece of plastic wrap and another damp towel to prevent them from drying out.

7. Work with one phyllo sheet at a time, keeping the rest covered with the plastic wrap and towel. Remove 1 sheet from the stack and brush it lightly and quickly with the melted garlic butter so it doesn't dry out. Carefully lay another sheet evenly on top of the first, and brush with the melted butter. Lay a third sheet on top, brushing lightly again with butter. Spoon about 1½–2 tablespoons of filling along the short bottom edge, leaving a 1-inch border at the sides. Fold the bottom edge toward the center so that it partially covers the filling, then fold the sides in. Roll up the knish, jelly-roll fashion, into a neat, cylindrical package. Brush the knish lightly with more melted butter over all surfaces and place seam side down on the prepared baking sheet. Keep the baking sheet lightly covered with plastic wrap as you continue making knishes with the remaining phyllo and filling, using the second baking sheet as you fill up the first. If necessary, melt some more butter and add it to the garlic butter. (You can refrigerate the knishes at this point, well wrapped, up to 1 day before baking.)

8. Bake the knishes for 20–25 minutes, or until golden brown. Serve hot or warm.

YIELD: About 14 knishes

COOK'S NOTE: Prepare these in miniature for a divine cocktail nibble. Or use the filling in blintzes or kreplach.

You can store leftover phyllo sheets in the refrigerator, airtight, for about 5 days. Do not refreeze them.

SAUTÉED CHIVE MAMALIGA WITH FETA-YOGURT CREAM

There are those who would deny mamaliga's place in the culinary pantheon, where it is exalted right up there with pastrami and *carnatzlach* in Aaron Lebedoff's nostalgic song from the Yiddish stage, "Rumania, Rumania." True, its illustrious *landsmen* (compatriots) resonate with more jazz—and garlic—but peasant-bred mamaliga is so deeply comforting to eat. Like its Italian cousin polenta, this velvety cornmeal porridge will happily accommodate your flavor mood of the moment, cradling savory braises, stews, and grilled meats or rich cheeses. And mamaliga, like polenta, can be served immediately after it is boiled, or baked with melting cheese, or, my favorite method, cooled, sliced, and lightly fried, as in this recipe.

I like to accentuate the corn taste by lightly toasting the meal first and by using unrefined corn oil to sauté the firm, cooked slices. For dairy meals (Romanian and Italian Jews often make it from white cornmeal on the dairy extravaganza of Shavuot), mamaliga is usually prepared with milk and butter and seasoned with a sharp cheese like feta or a milder Balkan sheep's milk cheese, *bryndza*. I mellow the saltiness of the feta with spicy scallions and the sour tang of yogurt, a cool complement to the crunchy fried crust.

---

2 cups yellow or white cornmeal, preferably stone-ground

3½ cups milk

Salt

4 tablespoons unsalted butter, plus additional for greasing the pan and as needed for sautéing

¼ cup chopped fresh chives or ½ cup finely chopped scallions (use white and green parts)

Freshly ground black pepper

2–3 tablespoons oil, preferably unrefined corn oil, plus additional as needed

FETA-YOGURT CREAM (SEE COOK'S NOTE)

⅔ cup coarsely grated feta cheese

⅓ cup yogurt cream (page 29) or sour cream

¼ cup finely minced scallions

Chopped fresh fragrant herbs, like mint or dill (optional)

Freshly ground black pepper

---

1. In a large, wide, heavy-bottomed saucepan (enameled cast iron is ideal), toast the cornmeal slowly, stirring with a wooden spoon, until the kitchen is filled with the fragrant aroma of grilled corn and the golden color begins to deepen slightly. Watch carefully so the cornmeal doesn't burn.

2. Remove the pan from the heat, and let the cornmeal cool to room temperature. Add the milk, 3½ cups of water, and 1 tablespoon salt to the cornmeal and whisk until thoroughly combined. Simmer

over moderately low heat, stirring frequently to prevent lumps from forming, until the mamaliga is very thick and pulls away from the sides of the pan, about 30 minutes. It should no longer taste raw or grainy. If necessary, cook 5–10 minutes longer. Stir in 3 tablespoons of the butter and the chives or scallions, and season with pepper to taste and more salt if needed.

3. Transfer the mamaliga to a 13-by-9-inch, lightly buttered or oiled baking dish or a baking sheet with sides. Smooth the top, let it cool, and refrigerate it, covered loosely with wax paper, until firm, about 2 hours. (It will keep in the refrigerator, tightly covered, for up to 3 days.)

4. Make the feta-yogurt cream. Stir all the ingredients together and adjust the seasonings. Allow the flavors to marry for at least 30 minutes.

5. Cut the mamaliga into thin slices or triangles in the baking pan. In a large cast-iron or nonstick skillet, heat the remaining 1 tablespoon butter and 2 tablespoons of the oil over moderately high heat until hot but not smoking. Fry the mamaliga slices in batches, carefully turning once with 2 spatulas, until golden and crisp, 2–3 minutes per side. If necessary, add more oil and butter to the pan, but make sure the pan is hot before adding additional mamaliga. Serve the mamaliga topped with the feta-yogurt cream.

YIELD: 6–8 servings

COOK'S NOTE: It's easiest to prepare mamaliga in a large batch, so I often wind up with more than I need at one time. You may want to serve half, and reserve the remainder for another meal (it will keep for about 3 days). I have therefore given proportions for feta-yogurt cream by the cup, so you can prepare as much you need.

Prolonged heat softens firm mamaliga, as it does polenta. To avoid transforming fried slices into a runny, molten mass, keep mamaliga well chilled until you are about to fry it. The oil and butter should be hot enough to form a light crust on the mamaliga as soon as it hits the pan. Finish frying quickly; slow cooking might melt the slices.

For a delicious breakfast or brunch, fry leftover slices as directed, top with very thin slices of cheddar, and cover the pan just until the cheese melts. Or omit the chives when initially preparing mamaliga, and serve fried leftover slices with maple syrup or honey butter. You can also bake leftover mamaliga: Place in a well-buttered or oiled baking dish and drizzle with melted butter; scatter the grated or shredded cheese of your choice over the top; and bake until the mamaliga is heated through and the cheese is melted and bubbly.

NONDAIRY AND PAREVE GRAINS AND VEGETABLES

When the darkest blues hit, of course I can eat nothing at all. But with the mid-light varieties, say, cornflower to royal on the blue misery scale, I turn to starches and heavy vegetables.

Not for me a pint of ice cream or chunk of cake. I can't drown my bitters with a sweet.

I'd rather play Billie Holiday. Or music that aches tenderly in a minor key: some klezmer by the Klezmatics. There is a huge bowl of kasha, moistened with melting cubes of eggplant and soft-fried onions or rich potato kugel with dark wild mushrooms. And a small spoon. Jewish foods like these were meant to nourish fragile souls as well as hungry bodies.

The grain and vegetable dishes featured here are either pareve or easily made so, with the substitution of vegetable for chicken stock. Other grain and vegetable recipes scattered throughout the book are listed below.

OTHER NONDAIRY AND PAREVE GRAIN AND VEGETABLE SUGGESTIONS

KASHA VARNISHKES WITH FRIED EGGPLANT, MUSHROOMS, AND ONION MARMALADE

PAREVE, MEAT,
OR DAIRY

> But Ephraim and Izzy, given their secret horde of Jewish soul food, were not as
> infected as the rest of the company....[T]he ever-resourceful Izzy...was able to
> leaven their intake of poisonous meat with delicacies that Izzy had shrewdly held
> back. So one Friday night they might gorge themselves on kasha fried in chicken fat
> and the next on rice prepared in a similar fashion.
>
> —MORDECAI RICHLER, *SOLOMON GURSKY WAS HERE*

Properly cooked so it remains dry and fluffy, kasha, when mixed with noodles, could swallow up butter or chicken fat by the cupful. I remove the temptation to slather on lots of fat by moistening this hearty grain with plenty of caramelized onions and mushrooms. I also add sautéed eggplant for the same reason: fried cubes of it, like mushrooms, bring a melting butteriness to foods.

Though most American recipes for kasha varnishkes call for bow tie noodles, I find them too thick and starchy here, requiring, like the kasha, a lot of additional moisture. I break wide noodles in half to resemble the square noodles originally used—and best suited—for this dish.

The eggplant, mushrooms, and onions enrich and lighten the kasha varnishkes at the same time. You don't really *need* all three (and if pressed for time, you could eliminate either the mushrooms or the eggplant—or the noodles), but cooked together, this is a very satisfying dish, substantial enough to serve as centerpiece for a delicious vegetarian meal (or near-vegetarian, if using chicken broth). To simplify preparations, make it in advance, up to the point of heating the ingredients in the oven. And actually, you need use only one skillet for all the vegetables.

---

1 large eggplant (about 1–1¼ pounds), peeled
  and cut into 1-inch cubes

Coarse kosher salt

About ½ cup olive oil

1½ pounds onions, coarsely chopped (6 cups)

Freshly ground black pepper

1–2 tablespoons fresh thyme or marjoram,
  according to taste

2 cups mushrooms (about ½ pound), wiped
  clean, trimmed, and sliced

1 tablespoon chopped garlic

1 large egg

1 cup kasha, preferably coarse grind

2 cups vegetable or chicken broth, homemade
  (page 80 or 63), or good-quality
  low-sodium canned

4 ounces broad (wide) egg noodles (broken in
  half, if desired)

Olive Oil Schmaltz (page 28), margarine, or,
 if vegetable broth is used, unsalted butter, if
 needed

¼ cup finely minced scallions, or 3–4
 tablespoons chopped fresh chives, for garnish
2 tablespoons chopped fresh parsley, for garnish

---

1. Put the eggplant in a colander and sprinkle evenly with 2 teaspoons salt. Weight the eggplant down (I use a plate or bowl with a large-size can of plum tomatoes on top), and let drain for about 1 hour, stirring the pieces after 30 minutes. Rinse the eggplant and press it very dry with paper towels.

2. While the eggplant is draining, heat 3 tablespoons oil in a 10- to 12-inch heavy skillet over medium heat. Add the onions, and salt and pepper them lightly. Cook for 2 minutes, stirring so they are thoroughly coated with oil. Cover, turn the heat down to the lowest simmer, and cook slowly until the onions are meltingly tender, 35–40 minutes. Stir from time to time to make sure the onions don't burn. When they are very soft, remove the lid, raise the heat to high, and brown them to a rich caramel gold. Stir frequently with a wooden spoon to redistribute the syrupy juices. If necessary, turn the heat down a bit to prevent the onions from sticking and burning. When the onions are thick and jamlike, stir in the thyme or marjoram. Adjust the seasoning and transfer the mixture to a very large bowl.

3. Lightly rinse out the skillet and dry it, add 2 tablespoons fresh oil, and turn the heat to high. Add the mushrooms and cook, stirring frequently, until they release some juice, about 5 minutes. Sprinkle with salt and pepper, add the garlic, and continue sautéing, lifting and turning often until all the liquid has evaporated and the mushrooms are golden brown, about 7 minutes. Add the mushrooms to the onions.

4. Wipe out the skillet and in it heat the remaining 3 tablespoons oil over medium-high heat until hot but not smoking. Add the eggplant, in batches if necessary, and fry until tender and lightly browned on both sides. Add more oil to the skillet if needed, but always make sure the oil is very hot before adding the eggplant—this will prevent the eggplant from absorbing too much oil. Transfer the eggplant to the onions and mushrooms in the bowl.

5. Preheat the oven to 350°F.

6. Prepare the kasha. In a medium bowl, beat the egg with a fork. Stir in the kasha and mix until each grain is thoroughly coated with egg. Heat the broth to simmering. In a heavy skillet with high sides or a wide, heavy saucepan, toast the kasha over medium heat, turning and breaking up the kasha constantly until the egg begins to dry and the grains separate, about 3 minutes. Add the hot broth and salt and pepper to taste, then cover and simmer over very low heat until tender and all the liquid is absorbed, 10–15 minutes.

7. Meanwhile, bring 2 quarts of water and 1½ teaspoons salt to a rolling boil. Add the noodles and cook until tender but still firm to the bite. Drain and stir into the vegetables.

8. In a lightly greased 3-quart shallow casserole, combine the kasha with the other ingredients. Adjust the seasoning to taste. If the mixture seems dry, add schmaltz or dot with butter or margarine as needed. Bake just until heated through. Sprinkle with the scallions or chives and the parsley, and serve hot.

YIELD: 6–8 servings

DECONSTRUCTED KASHA VARNISHKES (KASHA AND ORZO WITH GRILLED PORTOBELLO MUSHROOMS)

MEAT, PAREVE, OR DAIRY

The bewitching aroma of sizzling, meaty mushrooms has been a powerful enchanter since ancient times. In the Babylonian Talmud, a rabbi recounts that he became so intoxicated by the captivating fragrance of a mushroom dish that his health would have been in grave danger had he not quickly been given some of the mushrooms to nibble.

These deconstructed kasha varnishkes feature sliced portobellos, marinated and grilled to enhance their resemblance to meat. Instead of noodles, the pasta is orzo, cooked in broth so it is flavorful and very moist when combined with the dry, fluffy kasha.

The meat will never be missed if you serve this at a vegetarian or dairy meal, substituting vegetable stock for the chicken broth.

---

6 large portobello mushrooms

1 tablespoon minced fresh garlic

1 tablespoon plus ½ teaspoon soy sauce

1 tablespoon fresh lemon juice

2 teaspoons plus 3 tablespoons olive oil

1 tablespoon chopped fresh rosemary (to make the mushrooms even more meatlike) (optional)

1 cup orzo

4 cups rich chicken or vegetable broth (page 63 or 80) or good-quality low-sodium canned

1 large egg

1 cup kasha, preferably coarse-grind

Salt and freshly ground black pepper

¾ pound onions, chopped (3 cups)

Olive Oil Schmaltz (page 28), unsalted butter, or margarine, if needed

2–3 tablespoons chopped fresh parsley, for garnish (optional)

---

1. Clean the mushroom caps and stems with a damp paper towel. Carefully cut the stems off flush with the caps. Trim off the woody bottom section of the stems and discard. Chop the stems coarsely and set aside. In a large resealable plastic bag, combine 2 teaspoons garlic, 1 tablespoon soy sauce, the lemon juice, 2 teaspoons oil, and the rosemary, if using. Add the mushroom caps, press out the air, and seal the bag. Let the caps marinate at room temperature, turning the bag over occasionally, until you are ready to broil them.

2. Soak the orzo in a bowl of fresh cold water for about 5 minutes to remove some of the starch. Empty into a strainer, rinse, and then drain. Bring 2 cups broth to a boil, stir in the orzo, and cook, covered, over low heat for 15 minutes until the orzo is tender and all the liquid is absorbed. Keep warm and covered until ready to combine ingredients.

3. Preheat the broiler.

4. In a medium bowl, beat the egg with a fork. Stir in the kasha and mix until each grain is thoroughly coated. Heat the remaining 2 cups broth to simmering. In a heavy skillet with high sides or a wide, heavy saucepan, toast the kasha over medium heat, turning and breaking up the kasha constantly until the egg begins to dry and the grains separate, about 3 minutes. Add the hot broth and salt and pepper to taste, cover, and simmer over very low heat until tender and all the liquid is absorbed, 10–15 minutes. Keep covered and warm.

5. In a heavy 10-inch skillet, heat 2 tablespoons oil over medium-high heat and sauté the onions, stirring, until they are deep golden brown. Season well with salt and pepper. Transfer the onions to a large bowl. In the same skillet, sauté the reserved chopped mushroom stems and remaining 1 teaspoon garlic in the remaining 1 tablespoon oil over high heat. Cook until the mushroom edges are tinged with bronze. Sprinkle with the remaining ½ teaspoon soy sauce and pepper to taste and cook, stirring, for 1–2 minutes to marry the ingredients. Transfer to the bowl, keeping it covered and warm.

6. Arrange the mushroom caps on a foil-lined broiler rack, and broil them, gill side down, about 4 inches from the heat, for about 5 minutes. Turn, baste with any juices (or spilled bits of garlic), and broil for 5–6 minutes, or until tender and cooked through. Transfer the mushrooms to a cutting board.

7. Add the cooked orzo and kasha to the onions and mushroom stems in the bowl. Combine the ingredients well and season with salt and pepper, if needed. If dry, add a little schmaltz, butter, or margarine.

8. To serve, spoon some of the kasha-orzo mixture onto each plate. Slice the mushrooms on an angle and season to taste. Arrange the mushroom slices decoratively over the kasha mixture and nap with any accumulated mushroom juices. If desired, sprinkle with chopped parsley.

YIELD: 6 servings

SAUTÉED CABBAGE AND
GARLIC NOODLE KUGEL

Like potatoes, beets, and carrots, protean cabbage turned up on Ashkenazi tables in many forms, from tart sauerkraut to a sugared filling for delicate strudel dough, not to mention lusty cabbage soup and meat-stuffed cabbage rolls. A favorite among Central European Jews was an irresistible tangle of sautéed cabbage ribbons and golden egg noodles, lavishly sprinkled with poppy or caraway seeds.

First parboiled, the cabbage is then lightly browned, intensifying its flavors to a nutty sweetness, which is heightened by the poppy seeds. Garlic cloves—lots of them—are my addition. They're very slowly sautéed until the olive oil is deeply flavored and the garlic is soft and mellow.

I've also added eggs and broth, and made the recipe a kugel, or baked pudding. Sturdy, economical dishes that can be cooked ahead and reheated for holiday meals, kugels were originally starchy puddings baked along with the Sabbath cholent. Eventually, they became very popular and Jewish cooks began baking them in separate pans, binding the ingredients—savory or sweet—with eggs, and thickening them with various starches. They remain well-liked today, especially potato and noodle puddings, for preparing a kugel is an excellent way to avoid last-minute preparation and give "staying power" to a side dish or vegetable.

This kugel complements any grilled or roasted meat or chicken.

2 tablespoons toasted matzoh meal (see page 26) or toasted bread crumbs	6 large garlic cloves, roughly chopped (3–4 tablespoons)
One 1½ to 2-pound head of green cabbage	3 tablespoons poppy seeds
Salt	Freshly ground black pepper
8 ounces medium egg noodles (preferably flat, not the twisted spiral kind, which won't absorb as much of the flavoring)	6 large eggs
	2 cups homemade chicken or vegetable broth (page 63 or 80) or good-quality low-sodium canned
5 tablespoons extra-virgin olive oil, plus additional oil for greasing the pan	

1. Prepare a 13- by 9-inch baking pan: Grease it well and sprinkle the bottom with the matzoh meal or bread crumbs, shaking out any excess.

2. Start the cabbage. Discard any bruised or tough outer leaves, then cut the head into six wedges. Trim away the hard core portions. In a large pot or Dutch oven, bring 4–5 quarts of cold water and

1 tablespoon salt to a rolling boil. Add the cabbage and cook, uncovered, for 8–10 minutes, or until the cabbage is just tender. Reserving the cooking water in the pot, scoop out the cabbage with a slotted spoon and transfer it to a colander to drain.

3. Bring the reserved cabbage cooking water back to a boil in the pot and in it cook the noodles until just tender. Drain them well, then transfer to a large bowl and toss with 1 tablespoon of the oil.

4. In a 10- to 12-inch heavy skillet, warm the remaining 4 tablespoons oil over very gentle heat. Add the garlic and cook slowly, stirring occasionally, until the garlic turns palest blond, 8–10 minutes. Scoop out the garlic with a slotted spoon and set it aside in a small bowl. Reserve the oil, now deliciously infused with garlic, in the skillet.

5. Preheat the oven to 350°F.

6. Using your hands, squeeze out as much liquid as possible from the cabbage in the colander. (Alternatively, you can press down on the cabbage with the back of a spoon if you are reluctant to use your hands, although I find this method less efficient.) Lay the squeezed cabbage between layers of paper towels and press to remove surface moisture. Slice the cabbage into coarse shreds, then cut the shreds into bite-size pieces.

7. Heat the reserved garlic oil in the skillet over moderately high heat. Toss in the cabbage and sauté, lifting and turning over high heat, until it is flecked here and there with a nutty brown, about 10 minutes. Add the reserved garlic and the poppy seeds, season generously with salt and pepper, and cook, stirring, for 2–3 minutes to marry the flavors. Remove the pan from the heat and let cool slightly.

8. Assemble the kugel. In a large bowl, whisk together the eggs and the broth until smooth. Stir in the noodles and the cabbage and combine thoroughly. Spoon the mixture evenly into the prepared baking dish and bake for 50 minutes, or until the kugel feels firm, its lightly browned edges are pulling away from the sides, and a knife inserted in the center comes out clean.

9. Allow the kugel to set for at least 25 minutes before cutting into squares to serve. Reheat if necessary.

YIELD: 6–8 servings

WILD MUSHROOM–POTATO KUGEL

PAREVE

The Irish potato. For most of us, the starchy tuber, like leprechauns and shamrocks, is inextricably linked to the Emerald Isle. But the potato had a profound effect as well on the Jews of Poland and Russia, where it became a staple from the mid-nineteenth century on. Without the potato, in fact, the phenomenal Jewish population explosion in Eastern Europe would never have occurred, according to the noted Jewish food historian John Cooper.

As they decreased their reliance on bread, these Jews began eating the cheap, nutritious potato two and three times a day, breakfasting on potatoes in their jackets, eating spuds with onions or cabbage for dinner.

Potato kugel was always a treat. Although I have not found old kugel recipes calling for wild mushrooms mixed with the potatoes, the pairing makes perfect geographic, as well as gustatory, sense: Boletus mushrooms (also known as porcini or cèpes) grow wild all over Poland and Russia—and Israel too.

Here I sandwich woodsy dried mushrooms between layers of grated raw potatoes that have been combined with savory fried onions and seasoned liberally with freshly ground pepper. Baked in a hot oven, the elegant kugel emerges gloriously crusty, and full of deep, earthy perfumes.

Rinsing then squeezing the grated potatoes dry before adding them to the other ingredients concentrates the potato flavor and eliminates that watery, muddy taste that mars some kugels.

---

1 ounce dried wild mushrooms (preferably boletus, i.e., porcini, or cèpes; shiitakes don't work well here)

4 tablespoons olive or vegetable oil, plus additional for greasing the pan

¾ pound onions, thinly sliced (3 cups)

Salt and freshly ground black pepper

2 teaspoons chopped garlic

6 large or 8 medium russet (baking) potatoes, peeled

4 large eggs, beaten

Excellent-quality extra-virgin olive oil for drizzling (optional)

---

1. Soak the mushrooms in 2 cups of hot water for 1 hour, or until soft. Drain the mushrooms through a strainer lined with paper towels or a coffee filter, reserving the soaking liquid. Wash the mushrooms under cold running water to remove any remaining grit, then chop them coarsely.

2. Heat the oil in a 10-inch heavy skillet over medium heat. Add the onions and sauté until crisp and light brown, about 15 minutes. Transfer to a bowl and season with salt and pepper. In the same skillet (no need to wash it out), place the chopped mushrooms, garlic, and reserved mushroom soaking liquid.

Boil the mixture over high heat, stirring occasionally, until all the liquid is evaporated. Add salt and pepper to taste and remove the skillet from the heat.

3. Preheat the oven to 400°F.

4. Grate the potatoes in a food processor or over the large holes of a hand grater. Transfer them to a colander, rinse well, then drain, using your hands to squeeze out as much liquid as possible. In a large bowl, combine the potatoes, eggs, fried onion, and plenty of salt and pepper.

5. Grease the bottom and sides of a large (13-by-9-inch, or similar), shallow, heavy baking pan (preferably enameled cast iron or metal, not glass), and place the pan in the oven until the oil is sizzling hot (this will produce a deliciously crisp crust).

6. Turn half the potato mixture into the pan, spread the mushrooms over it, cover with the remaining potato mixture, and smooth the top. If desired, drizzle a little extra-virgin olive oil over the top. Bake uncovered for about 50 minutes, or until the top is golden and crisp. Let the kugel cool until set. If necessary, reheat before serving.

YIELD: 8–10 servings

ONION-CRUSTED LIGHT POTATO KUGEL

Some people tear off long ribbons of crisp skin from freshly roasted birds. Others will pick off the nuts or steal the chocolate curls from picture perfect cakes.

This kugel is made for the onion snatchers: a lavish meltingly tender layer of sweet, bronze-edged onions, aromatic with rosemary, beckons from atop the crisp crust. I add mashed potatoes to the grated raw ones for an especially light and creamy interior.

1½ pounds onions, very thinly sliced (6 cups)	6 large or 8 medium russet (baking) potatoes,
Salt	peeled
6 tablespoons olive oil, plus additional for	4 large eggs
drizzling (use the finest-quality extra-virgin	1 teaspoon baking powder
oil for drizzling)	1–2 tablespoons chopped fresh rosemary
1 teaspoon minced fresh garlic	(according to taste)
Freshly ground black pepper	

1. Separate the onions into rings. To extract moisture, toss in a large bowl with 2 teaspoons salt and set aside for about 20 minutes. Turn the onions around from time to time. Dry the onions between sheets of paper towels or cotton kitchen towels, pressing down to soak up as much of the exuded liquid as you can.

2. In a 10- to 12-inch heavy skillet, heat 3 tablespoons oil over medium-high heat. Add the onions and garlic and cook, lifting and tossing with a spatula as they soften and become golden brown, 15–20 minutes. The mixture should be well salted and peppery, so season to taste accordingly. Set aside to cool.

3. Dice 2 (if large) or 3 (if medium) of the potatoes and place in a saucepan of salted water. Bring to a boil, then simmer until the potatoes are tender. Mash the potatoes, using a ricer, food mill, or masher, until smooth, and place in a very large bowl. Stir in about half of the fried onions, setting the rest aside.

4. Preheat the oven to 400°F.

5. Grate the remaining potatoes in a food processor or over the large holes of a hand grater. Place the grated potatoes in a colander or large strainer and rinse well under cold water to remove most of the

starch. Squeeze out as much liquid as possible, then add them to the mashed potatoes. Beat the eggs in another bowl until thick and light. Whisk in the baking powder. Combine the eggs with the potatoes and season generously with salt and pepper.

6. Pour 3 tablespoons oil into a large, shallow, heavy baking pan (9-by-13-inch or similar size, preferably enameled cast iron or metal, not glass). Thoroughly rub oil around the bottom and sides of the pan and place in the oven until sizzling hot. Transfer the potatoes to the pan and spread with a spatula; top with the remaining fried onions. Sprinkle with the rosemary. Drizzle everything with a few drops of oil. If you love salty crusts, you may want to sprinkle a bit more coarse salt and some pepper over the top.

7. Bake for about 30 minutes on the uppermost shelf of the oven, then turn the temperature down to 350°F. Continue baking for 25–40 minutes longer, or until the kugel is firm, the top is golden, and the onions are crispy.

8. Let the kugel cool until set. If necessary, reheat before serving.

YIELD: 8–10 servings

MOROCCAN-FLAVORED CARROT KUGEL

PAREVE

The feast of Sukkoth or the feast of Simhat Torah.

They looked for him everywhere.

Where is he, where is he?

    It turned out that, because of the fine weather, Grandfather had climbed up on the roof, had sat down on one of the chimney pipes, and was regaling himself with carrots.

—MARC CHAGALL, *MY LIFE*

Sweet, golden carrots are an Ashkenazi favorite not only around the fall holidays, but throughout the year as well. This light, airy pareve kugel is not at all dense and sodden like many vegetable puddings. Mint provides refreshing grace notes (I used dried here because an equivalent amount of fresh mint would compromise the delicate mousselike texture of this kugel). And fresh carrot juice, either home-juiced or purchased from a greengrocer or health food store, adds a subtle sweetness to the kugel. If it is unavailable, use a light vegetable stock.

---

1 whole matzoh (egg matzoh works particularly well here)

1 ½ teaspoons dried mint

¾ teaspoon ground cumin

½ teaspoon ground cinnamon

Freshly ground black pepper

Pinch of cayenne, or to taste

2 teaspoons fresh lemon juice

1 cup fresh carrot juice or vegetable broth

1 teaspoon finely minced fresh garlic

3 large eggs, separated

Salt

1 tablespoon olive or vegetable oil, plus additional for greasing the pan

2 cups peeled and finely grated carrots (12–14 ounces)

Fresh mint or parsley sprigs, for garnish (optional)

---

1. Preheat the oven to 325°F.

2. In a large bowl, crumble the matzoh into small pieces. Sprinkle with the mint, cumin, cinnamon, black pepper and cayenne to taste, and the lemon juice. Combine the carrot juice or broth and garlic in a small saucepan and heat slowly until very hot. Don't let the juice boil—it may turn bitter. Pour over the matzoh mixture, stir, and set aside to cool.

3. Beat the egg whites with a pinch of salt in a large bowl until stiff but not dry. In another bowl, using the same beaters (no need to wash them), beat the egg yolks and 1 tablespoon oil until thick and foamy. Add the yolks, grated carrots, and 1 teaspoon salt (or to taste) to the matzoh mixture and combine well. Use a spatula to fold the whites gently into the carrot mixture. Work quickly and lightly, until thoroughly combined and no white is visible. Transfer to an oiled shallow baking dish (8-inch square).

4. Bake for 40–50 minutes, or until firm and golden brown around the edges. Let the kugel cool until set, then cut into serving pieces. Garnish with mint or parsley, if desired. Serve warm or room temperature. This reheats well, and is excellent the next day.

YIELD: About 6 servings

Matzoh and matzoh meal are frequently used to thicken kugels. (Matzoh tool.)

NONDAIRY AND PAREVE GRAINS AND VEGETABLES

FRESH CORN KUGEL

Thickened only by creamy pureed corn kernels and scented with flowery dill, this summery kugel depends for sweetness on truly fresh corn, whose sugars have not yet begun the descent into starch. Pale white corn will produce an exquisitely delicate kugel; more robust yellow kernels make for a richer pudding with a decidedly corny taste.

½ cup chopped onions

1 tablespoon mild olive or vegetable oil, plus
  additional for greasing the pan

3½ cups fresh corn kernels (cut from 3–7 ears of
  sweet corn; the number of ears will depend on
  whether you use slim, silvery white-kernel
  corn or thicker, butter-yellow varieties)

1 cup chicken broth, preferably homemade (page
  63), or good-quality low-sodium canned

Salt and freshly ground black pepper

4 large eggs

2 tablespoons chopped fresh dill

2 tablespoons toasted matzoh crumbs (egg
  matzohs are especially nice) or toasted
  matzoh meal (see page 26)

Boiling or scalding-hot tap water, for hot-water
  bath

---

1. Preheat the oven to 325°F.

2. In a 7- or 8-inch skillet, sauté the onions in the oil over moderate heat, stirring, until very soft, 7–8 minutes. The onions should remain tender and sweet, so don't allow them to color past gold. Set aside to cool.

3. Put 2 cups of the corn (setting aside remaining corn kernels for later use) in a food processor or blender. Add ½ cup of the broth and puree the mixture until smooth, scraping down the bowl when necessary. Add the remaining ½ cup broth, and salt and pepper to taste, and pulse to combine well.

4. Lightly grease the bottom and sides of a 12-inch gratin dish.

5. In a large bowl, beat the eggs until smooth and light. Stir in the dill, the cooled sautéed onion, the pureed corn, and the reserved 1½ cups corn kernels. Transfer the mixture to the prepared dish.

6. Season the toasted matzoh crumbs or matzoh meal with salt and pepper, and sprinkle over the top of the kugel.

7. Place the gratin dish inside a larger baking pan and pour in enough boiling (or scalding-hot tap) water to come two-thirds of the way up the sides of the gratin dish. Bake the kugel for about 1 hour and 10 minutes, or until the golden brown top is puffed slightly and a toothpick inserted in the middle comes out clean.

8. Let the kugel cool for at least 25 minutes, or until set, before cutting into wedges to serve. Reheat if necessary.

YIELD: 6–8 servings

FRUIT SAUCES

Simple fruit sauces are the traditional embellishment for myriad Jewish dishes, including latkes, blintzes, and matzoh brie, and a superb accompaniment to brisket and pot roast. They are equally good on their own as dessert, with perhaps a few good cookies, or as a low-calorie lift for plain yogurt or cottage cheese. And don't forget waffles, pancakes, pound cakes, and such.

Sweetened with reduced fruit juice, not sugar, these fresh-tasting sauces have an intense fruit flavor. After you've become familiar with these recipes, create your own favorites, capturing the season's bounty and flattering it with well-chosen spices and dried fruits.

And for another delicious fruit sauce, try the Fresh Persimmon Sauce on page 282.

INTENSE APRICOT APPLESAUCE

When my father came home from his Saturday night gin game on Sunday morning, he would often bring lox, bagels, and bialys from The Delicacy Shop, the Jewish appetizing store in our Long Island community. When the triple "schnides" (from "schneiders"—gin rummy shutouts) were in his favor, we'd awaken to a breakfast of salmon in its many other guises—baked, pickled, and smoked Nova Scotia–style—as well as sable, whitefish, herring in sour cream sauce, scallion cream cheese, and beefsteak tomatoes.

But always there would be the Middle Eastern confection we knew as shoe leather—a sheet of dried apricot, rolled as thin as onion skin, as mouth-puckering as lemonade.

Is it me or the shoe leather? Today's leather, or its many unflattering imitations, is too sweet, or too thick, or too bland. I'd never make it, though—it is the kind of craving, like pistachio nuts, that demands instant gratification. When I hunger for the taste, I tuck into the tartest dried apricots I can find (in Middle Eastern or Jewish appetizing stores, these are usually the ones from California, not Turkey). If I have enough left over, I make this applesauce, which is wonderful with latkes or pot roast—or just a spoon.

About ½ cup (2½–3 ounces) tart dried apricots (approximately 15), cut into quarters

1⅓–1½ cups apple juice

1 vanilla bean, split

½ teaspoon minced peeled fresh ginger

Salt

About 2 pounds apples, unpeeled, cored, and cut into chunks (6 cups)—if you want to puree the sauce in a food processor instead of a food mill, peel the apples (choose the freshest local apples available—a mixture of sweet, spicy varieties, like Gravenstein, Gala, Braeburn, Stayman Winesap, and Grimes Golden, rather than tart Granny Smith or Rhode Island Greening, will work best in this tangy sauce)

---

1. Simmer the apricots, 1⅓ cups apple juice, the vanilla bean, ginger, and a pinch of salt in a 6-quart Dutch oven or very wide, heavy saucepan, covered, until the apricots are very tender, about 25 minutes (but it may take longer if the fruit is particularly dry). Add the apples, and continue cooking, covered, until very soft, another 25 minutes or so. Stir occasionally, and add additional juice, if required, to prevent sticking. When ready, the mixture should be thick and pulpy, with no liquid visible. If necessary, boil it a few minutes, uncovered, to evaporate any remaining liquid.

2. Remove the vanilla bean (if desired, rinse and dry it, so it can be reused or added to granulated sugar to flavor it). Put the fruit through a food mill. Or, if you used peeled apples, you can puree it in a food processor to a smooth or slightly chunky consistency, as you prefer.

3. Cover and refrigerate until chilled. It is also lovely—and more assertive—served warm or room temperature.

YIELD: About 2½ cups

Fruit sauces are a traditional accompaniment to Hanukkah latkes. (Bronze Hanukkah lamp [menorah]. Eastern Europe, 19th century.)

FRESH RASPBERRY APPLESAUCE

PAREVE

"Is there a blessing for a sewing machine?" Tzeitel, Tevye's daughter, asks the rabbi in *Fiddler on the Roof*. "There is a blessing for everything," she is assured.

In addition to the well-known prayers Jews recite when eating bread or drinking wine, there are many blessings to be uttered when relishing the beauty of the universe: seeing a rainbow, inhaling aromatic spices, and a charming one reserved for enjoying especially fragrant fruits.

That is the one for this raspberry applesauce, perfumed with the scent of fresh berries, vanilla—and a splash, perhaps, of rose water. Like exotic Indian desserts, the fragrant taste of rose water is not to everyone's liking, but my daughter and I are very fond of it, in gentle doses. *Potchkehing* with this sauce on a warm September day, we found that a small amount of rose water enhances the raspberry flavor and aroma. Not surprising. With shared attributes like a protective armor of thorns and sensuous perfume, the raspberry and the rose, after all, are cousins.

About 2 cups raspberry- or other berry-flavored fruit juice, such as raspberry-cranberry, apple-raspberry, or apple-strawberry (use pure, unsweetened juice, not juice cocktail, if possible)

1 vanilla bean, split

Salt

About 2 pounds flavorful apples, unpeeled, seeded, and cut into chunks (6 cups) (sweet varieties with lots of character, like Gravenstein, Gala, Braeburn, Jonathan, Stayman Winesap, and the heirloom Golden Russet, work best here; if possible, search out local, seasonal varieties)

1 cup fresh raspberries (about 6 ounces)

Light floral honey (orange blossom would be perfect) or sugar to taste (optional)

A few drops of rose water (optional)

---

1. You'll be reducing the juice quite a bit, so choose a 6-quart Dutch oven or a very wide, heavy saucepan large enough to accommodate all of the fruit. Put in 2 cups of juice, along with the vanilla bean and a pinch of salt. Cook, uncovered, over high heat, until reduced to about ½ cup of thick, syrupy liquid.

2. Add the apples and mix well to coat with the juice. Cover the pan and simmer over low heat for 20 minutes. Stir from time to time, and add a little more juice if needed to prevent sticking.

3. Stir in the raspberries and cook for 5–10 minutes, until all of the fruit is very soft. When ready, the mixture should be thick and pulpy, with almost no liquid visible. If necessary, boil it a few minutes, uncovered, to evaporate any remaining liquid.

4. Remove the vanilla bean (if desired, rinse and dry it, so it can be reused or added to granulated sugar to flavor it). Put the sauce through the fine disk of a food mill or push the solids through a fine-mesh strainer to trap the apple skins and at least some of the raspberry seeds.

5. Vibrant with raspberries, this sauce may be a bit tart for some palates, especially if the apples are somewhat tangy. If so, add a little honey or sugar to taste while the sauce is still warm. And, if desired, stir in the rose water.

6. Cover and refrigerate until thoroughly chilled.

YIELD: About 3 cups

SPICED POMEGRANATE MOLASSES APPLESAUCE

PAREVE

I didn't want to fall in love. I resisted the total embrace. After all, what food writer who lived through sun-dried tomatoes would not see it as a fling?

Nevertheless, pomegranate molasses (also known as grenadine molasses and pomegranate syrup, the pomegranate essence created by slowly simmering the juice, usually with sugar and lemon, until it forms a luscious, tangy syrup) shows up in several recipes in this book, making as regular appearances as wine. Which it resembles, only fruitier. Or raspberry liqueur, only tarter, and nonalcoholic.

But in the end, it has a taste all its own, a heavenly, perfectly balanced act of sweet and sour, floral and berry—a flavor combination particularly prized by Jews.

That is why I was not surprised when a grocer in Brooklyn's Syrian-Jewish neighborhood suggested it as a substitute for the rather difficult-to-find *temerhindi,* or *ourt,* a tangy sweet-and-sour sauce made from tamarind pulp, that I needed to prepare the Syrian meat rolls, Kibbe Gheraz. "Syrian Jews from Aleppo use *ourt,* and the ones from Damascus cook the same dishes with pomegranate molasses."

Whether he was right or not (it is slightly tarter and more berry-tasting than *ourt*), it worked well in the kibbe, and I have been adding it ever since—to meat and chicken marinades, hummus, and even applesauce. Today it is stocked by many specialty stores, as well as Middle Eastern markets. (See page 31 for more on pomegranate molasses.)

Cardamom and cinnamon play up the spicy notes in the pomegranate molasses here, making this a delicious complement to poultry and meats, especially briskets and pot roasts (see Aromatic Marinated Brisket with Chestnuts on page 115). It's also tempting plain, or just topped with a touch of yogurt cream (page 30) or *labneh.*

About 1 ½ cups pure, unsweetened apple juice

1–2 cardamom pods, lightly crushed with the side of a knife or a kitchen mallet (use the larger amount for a more pronounced aromatic spiciness—1 pod will make a difference)

1 cinnamon stick

Salt

About 2 pounds flavorful apples, unpeeled, cored, and cut into chunks (6 cups)—if you are going to puree the sauce in a food processor

instead of using a food mill or strainer, peel the apples (choose a mixture of apples with sweet but complex flavors to echo the character of the sauce, such as Braeburn, Gala, Gravenstein, Grimes Golden, Northern Spy, and Stayman Winesap, rather than tart varieties; look for fresh, local apples if possible)

About 2 tablespoons pomegranate molasses or ourt, *or to taste*

1. In a 6-quart Dutch oven or wide, heavy saucepan large enough to accommodate all of the apples, combine the juice, cardamom, cinnamon, and a generous pinch of salt. Boil uncovered, over high heat, until the liquid is reduced by about half. Add the apples, mix well to coat with juice, and simmer, covered, until very tender, about 25 minutes or so, depending on the variety of apples. Stir them from time to time and, if necessary, add a bit more juice to prevent sticking.

2. The sauce should be thick and pulpy with little liquid visible. If necessary, boil it down for a few minutes, uncovered. Pick out and discard the cardamom and cinnamon. Put the sauce through a food mill or force it through a colander or strainer to remove the skins. Or, if you used peeled apples, process in a food processor until smooth or leave somewhat chunky, according to preference.

3. Transfer the sauce to a bowl. Stir in 2 tablespoons pomegranate molasses or *ourt* and taste. Add a little more if you want the sauce tarter. (If this is your first time using pomegranate molasses or *ourt*, you may want to start with less.)

4. You can serve the sauce chilled, but it is also excellent at room temperature or warm from the pot with briskets, pot roasts, or latkes.

YIELD: About 2 cups

COOK'S NOTE: You can use this recipe as a guide, omitting or supplementing the pomegranate molasses and spices with your own aromatic additions, like a strip of lemon, orange, or tangerine peel, a few prunes, or even peppercorns. Combine these seasonings with the juice—or try a fruitier, unsweetened juice, such as cranberry- or raspberry-apple. Taste the finished sauce and adjust for sweetness.

GINGER-PEAR SAUCE

PAREVE

The secret ingredient in this intense fresh pear sauce is a few pureed prunes, which round out the sweet and tangy notes, adding body and a buttery finish.

It's fabulous on matzoh brie, sweet latkes and blintzes, pancakes, and French toast. Or try it swirled into plain yogurt. Sweeter tooths than mine might enjoy it served alongside brisket and pot roast, or topping savory latkes.

About 1 ½ cups pineapple juice
1 vanilla bean, split
1 tablespoon minced candied ginger
Pinch of salt
About 3 pounds ripe, juicy pears, such as
  Bartlett or Comice, peeled, cored, and cut
  into chunks (6 cups)

3 pitted prunes, quartered
Light floral honey or sugar to taste (optional)

---

1. We start here again with a reduced fruit juice, so use a very wide, large, heavy saucepan, like a 5- or 6-quart Dutch oven. Put 1 ½ cups pineapple juice, the vanilla bean, ginger, and salt in the saucepan and boil, uncovered, over high heat, until reduced to ½ cup, about 15 minutes.

2. Stir in the pears and prunes, cover the pan, and simmer over low heat for 25–35 minutes, or until the pears are very tender. Time will vary depending on the variety of pears you use. Stir from time to time, and add a little more pineapple juice if needed to prevent sticking.

3. When ready, the mixture should be thick and pulpy, with very little liquid visible. Most pears are juicier than apples, so to avoid a watery sauce, evaporate almost all of the remaining liquid by boiling for a few minutes over high heat, uncovered.

4. Remove the vanilla bean (if desired, rinse and dry it, so it can be reused or added to granulated sugar to flavor it). Put the fruit through a food mill or puree in a food processor until smooth. It should not need any sweetening, but add a bit of honey or sugar if your pears are not as sweet and ripe as they might be.

5. The sauce is delicious served still warm, or cover and refrigerate until chilled. Store tightly covered in the refrigerator for 4–5 days.

YIELD: About 3 cups

COOK'S NOTE: This combination also makes a first-rate blintz filling. Reduce the juice, vanilla, ginger, and salt to about ⅓ cup of syrupy liquid. Sauté the pears in butter over medium-high heat. Chop the prunes fine and add to the pears, along with the reduced juice. Cook until the pears are tender. Boil down any remaining pear liquid. Chill before filling the blintzes.

SWEET KUGELS AND DESSERTS

After a perfect meal, I prefer a simple dessert: a gentle conclusion to the evening's tastes, not a lavish, sugary departure from them.

The old Yiddish favorite, *rozinkes and mandlen* (winy raisins and warmed almonds), or juicy pear slices with toasted walnuts, thinly cut oranges dotted with pomegranate rubies, a bowl of berries, some dead-ripe peaches. I love fruit compotes poached and sweetened just enough to heighten their flavors and soften their textures. Treats that speak of the seasons and taste of themselves best complement the big-flavored dishes I've presented in this book.

I don't like complicated desserts. Dishes that do require a bit more fuss must still retain their innocence—which is why many of these desserts are as likely to show up on the breakfast table as at dinner's end. You'll find softly rich but unadorned cheesecakes, milky puddings, decadent prune kreplach, and more, featured for the holidays.

In this chapter there are several recipes for one of my favorite desserts, noodle pudding or kugel, whose lush, melting texture is forgiving enough for even the most pastry-shy and invites lots of homey experimentation. Quantities are deliberately large, because leftovers make such wonderful breakfasts.

And there is a new take on an old love: rugelach with a buttery caramel filling.

OTHER DESSERT
SUGGESTIONS

RICH NOODLE KUGEL BAKED WITH
FRESH PLUMS AND NECTARINES

> ...not only the obviously trashy, but also the falsely important, the falsely
> beautiful, the falsely clever, the falsely attractive....[L]iterary characters
> personifying [it] will include Polonius and the royal pair in *Hamlet*,...Joyce's Mar-
> ion Bloom,...Anna Karenina's husband, Berg, in *War and Peace*.
> —VLADIMIR NABOKOV, *NIKOLAI GOGOL*

Nabokov, in his brilliant literary study *Nikolai Gogol,* was describing the Russian notion of *poshlust,* but he could just as easily have been writing about the Yiddish *ongepotchkeh.* Often translated as "overdone," "gaudy," or "excessively fussy" (possibly from *potchkeh,* "to fuss with"), *ongepotchkeh* is what happens when those desperately seeking elegance collide with their own innate bad taste.

My all-time favorite Yiddish word—just pronouncing it forces you to take a deep, round swig of life—*ongepotchkeh* is manifested frequently in Jewish foods. There are, of course, the extravagantly sculpted gelatin molds embedded with canned mandarin oranges and other faux gourmet fruits. Or gefilte fish studded with sun-dried tomatoes.

But the paradigm of *ongepotchkeh* is taking noodle kugel—a luxurious confection of pasta, eggs, butter, and milk or cheese or both—and then slathering it with some sweet stickiness that may have been a fruit in another life. The very lushness of a noodle pudding demands an innocent topping—not processed pie gunk filling, but the clean flavors of simple, lightly cooked fresh fruits, like the subtly sweetened seasonal fruits found in American fresh fruit crisps or crumbles.

In this version, the gentle acidity of fresh summer plums and nectarines emphasizes the sweet sumptuousness of the cheesecakelike pudding.

The trick to creating lighter, less dense noodle puddings—more pudding than noodle—is using just enough pasta for the pudding to hold its shape. And I let the kugel rest before baking for at least four hours or overnight: The noodles, bathed in the rich, sweet dairy ingredients, emerge meltingly tender and beautifully flavored.

Salt

8 ounces medium flat egg noodles (not the twisted spiral kind, which won't absorb as much of the liquids and flavoring)

1 stick (8 tablespoons) unsalted butter, cut into pieces, plus additional butter or oil for greasing the pan

1 cup (8 ounces) cottage cheese

8 ounces cream cheese, softened and cut into bits

2 cups milk

¼ cup sour cream

3 large eggs

½ cup pure maple syrup or granulated white sugar

2 teaspoons vanilla extract

5–7 tablespoons light brown sugar, preferably the granulated variety

About 2 pounds plums and nectarines, unpeeled (unless the skins are very thick or damaged) and cut into quarters or, if large, into eighths

1–1 ½ teaspoons ground cinnamon, according to taste

1. In a large pot, bring 3 quarts of cold water and 1 teaspoon salt to a vigorous boil. Add the noodles and cook until just tender. Drain, stir in the butter, and let cool.

2. Force the cottage cheese through a sieve into a large bowl (if you don't break down the curds suffi-ciently, the kugel will have an unpleasant chewy or grainy texture). Beat on low speed until smooth and fluffy. Add the cream cheese bit by bit, beating until totally incorporated. Beat in each of the fol-lowing, one by one, until thoroughly combined: the milk, sour cream, eggs, maple syrup or white sugar, vanilla, and a pinch of salt. (I don't recommend a food processor here: it liquefies the cottage cheese too much.)

3. Add the noodles to the bowl and stir in thoroughly. Butter the bottom and sides of a 13-by-9-inch baking pan and sprinkle with 2–3 tablespoons brown sugar. Pour the noodle-cheese mixture into the prepared pan. Cover the pan with foil and refrigerate for at least 4 hours or, preferably, overnight.

4. Preheat the oven to 350°F. Uncover and bake the pudding for 45 minutes. Remove the pan from the oven and arrange the fruit decoratively on top, peel side down. Sprinkle the fruit with about 3–4 table-spoons brown sugar (this will depend on the sweetness of the fruit—plums, especially, vary widely in sweetness—as well as your personal preference) and the cinnamon. Return the pudding to the oven and bake for about 30 minutes, or until the fruit is bubbling and the kugel is golden. All the luscious, syrupy juices exuded by the fruit may make the top appear somewhat wet, but these juices will disap-pear into the kugel as it cools. It will need to cool for at least 30 minutes to set before it can be cut.

5. Serve warm (reheat if necessary), at room temperature, or chilled (not icy cold). Excellent for dessert, brunch, or an instant breakfast.

YIELD: About 10 servings

COOK'S NOTE: Vary the kugel with your choice of other fruits according to the season or your own favorite combinations. Some ideas: fresh figs and raspberries; cherries and apricots; strawberries and peaches. If the fruit is particularly juicy, drain before adding, and, in addition to sweetening to taste, sprinkle with one of the following toppings, as needed, to absorb some of the juice.

Cookie Crumbs: Crumble shortbread or gingerbread cookies. If desired, add brown sugar (light or dark) to taste.

Streusel: Combine ¼ cup sliced almonds or ¼ cup finely chopped toasted walnuts, pecans, or skinned hazelnuts; 3 tablespoons packed light brown sugar; 2 tablespoons cold unsalted butter, cut into small pieces; 2 tablespoons all-purpose unbleached flour; generous pinch of salt. If using almonds, put them in a bowl first and crush them with your fingers, then add the rest of the ingredients and rub between your fingers until the mixture resembles coarse crumbs.

Graham Cracker Crumbs: Combine ⅓ cup crushed graham crackers; 2 tablespoons packed brown sugar or white sugar; 2–3 tablespoons cold, unsalted butter, cut into small pieces. Rub the ingredients between your fingers until the mixture resembles coarse crumbs.

ROASTED APPLE–WALNUT NOODLE KUGEL

Beauty diffuses itself in the world as an apple.

—THE ZOHAR

Here apples combine with walnuts and prunes to work an alchemy of golden autumn tastes. For a luscious dairy version, see Cook's Note.

---

6 large or 8–10 medium (about 3 pounds) sweet, flavorful apples (such as Royal Gala, Golden Delicious, or Braeburn), peeled, cored, and quartered or, if large, cut into sixths

⅓ cup packed brown sugar

2 tablespoons fresh lemon juice

2 cups apple juice

½ cup granulated sugar

⅓ cup pitted prunes, quartered

1½ teaspoons vanilla extract

Salt

4 ounces medium flat egg noodles (not the twisted kind, which won't absorb as much of the liquids and flavoring)

½ cup walnuts, lightly toasted and coarsely chopped

1 teaspoon ground cinnamon

⅛ teaspoon nutmeg, preferably freshly grated, or mace

4 large eggs, separated

Oil (walnut, avocado, canola, or your favorite) or margarine for greasing the pan

⅓ cup graham cracker crumbs (optional)

---

1. Preheat the oven to 400°F. Line a large baking sheet or very shallow roasting pan with foil and on it spread out the apples in a single layer, rounded sides down (so that most of the sugar will be trapped and melted in the curve, rather than sliding off onto the pan). Sprinkle with the brown sugar and lemon juice and roast in the middle of the oven until lightly browned and just tender, 25–35 minutes, depending on the variety of apples. Turn the apples halfway through the cooking process, and spoon the accumulated syrupy juices over them. Remove the apples from the oven and reduce the oven temperature to 350°F. When the apples are cool enough to handle, cut into large chunks.

2. In a medium-size, wide, heavy saucepan, combine the apple juice, granulated sugar, prunes, vanilla, and a pinch of salt. Bring to a boil and continue cooking over high heat, stirring occasionally, until reduced by about half. Remove from the heat and let cool slightly.

3. Bring 2 quarts of cold water and 1 teaspoon salt to a rapid boil in a large saucepan. Add the noodles and cook until tender. Drain well. In a large bowl, combine the noodles, prune mixture, roasted

apples, walnuts, cinnamon, and nutmeg or mace. Beat the egg yolks well until thick and light, and stir into the mixture. Beat the whites until stiff but not dry. Gently fold in about one-third of the whites, then fold in the rest.

4. Grease an 8- or 9-inch square baking pan (or one of similar capacity) thoroughly. Turn the batter into the pan and smooth the top. If desired, sprinkle with graham cracker crumbs.

5. Bake the kugel for about 45 minutes, or until it feels firm, the sides pull away from the pan slightly, and the top is lightly browned. Let cool completely to set. You can eat it at room temperature, but to really savor the toasty apple flavors, warm the kugel until heated through. It may not cut neatly, and perhaps it will appear somewhat messy on the plate, but it will taste divine.

YIELD: 6–8 servings

COOK'S NOTE: This is also lovely flavored with a little crystallized ginger.

For a dairy version, follow the above recipe up to the point of adding the egg yolks. In a separate bowl, use an electric mixer on low speed to beat 8 ounces cream cheese (softened and cut into bits) with 1 cup evaporated milk until smooth and fluffy. Beat in the yolks. Combine this with the noodle-prune-apple mixture, then fold in the beaten whites, as above. Pour into a slightly larger pan (at least 9 inches square) that has been well greased. Sprinkle the top with ½ cup graham cracker crumbs mixed with 3 tablespoons melted butter. Bake for 45–50 minutes at 350°F, following the directions for cooking and serving above.

PEACH-BUTTERMILK KUGEL

With their gilded blush and sweet perfume, showy peaches dazzled the Talmudists. For decorating a sukkah, they deemed the sumptuous fruit was fit to hang beside treasures like "hand-made carpets and tapestries,…nuts, almonds,…pomegranates and bunches of grapes, vines, oils, and fine meal…." (Bez. :157)

Peaches—juicy, fresh fruit in the topping and tangy dried ones dispersed throughout—bring unexpected luxury to this sleek buttermilk custard noodle pudding. A slightly more indulgent variation—creamier and sweeter—follows in the Cook's Note. Either makes an enticing breakfast, brunch, dessert, or even a simple entrée in a summer dairy dinner.

Salt

8 ounces medium or wide flat egg noodles (not the twisted, spiral kind, which won't absorb as much of the liquids and flavoring)

4 tablespoons unsalted butter, cut into pieces, plus additional butter or oil for greasing the pan

4 large eggs

⅓–½ cup pure maple syrup (use the larger amount for a dessert kugel; you may prefer to use the smaller amount if you plan to serve the kugel for breakfast or during a meal)

1 teaspoon vanilla extract

3 cups well-shaken buttermilk

6–7 ounces dried peaches, snipped with kitchen scissors into small pieces (1 cup)

TOPPING

5–6 medium, ripe peaches (about 3–4 cups when cut into wedges), peeled only if the peel is thick or bitter

1 teaspoon almond extract, or 2 tablespoons amaretto or cassis (optional)

About ¼ cup granulated or packed regular brown sugar (depending on sweetness of fruit and personal preference)

¼ cup unbleached all-purpose flour

2 tablespoons unsalted butter, cut into bits

¼ teaspoon ground cinnamon

⅛ teaspoon salt

---

1. Bring 3 quarts of cold water and 1 teaspoon of salt to a rapid boil in a large saucepan. Add the noodles and cook until just tender. Drain well, toss with the butter, and set aside to cool.

2. In a large bowl, beat together the eggs, maple syrup, vanilla, and a pinch of salt. Add the buttermilk and continue beating until the ingredients are smooth and thoroughly incorporated. Stir the dried peaches into the noodles (or use your fingers to toss them together and break up any clumps of dried

fruit) and turn into a greased 13-by-9-inch baking dish. Pour the buttermilk mixture evenly over the noodles. Cover the pan with foil and refrigerate for at least 4 hours or, better still, overnight.

3. Preheat the oven to 325°F. Uncover and bake the pudding for 50 minutes. Meanwhile, prepare the topping. Cut each peach into about 8 wedges (you should have 3–4 cups peach wedges) and if desired, toss with the almond extract, amaretto, or cassis. In a small bowl, crumble together the brown sugar, flour, butter, cinnamon, and salt with your fingers until the mixture resembles coarse meal. After the kugel has cooked for 50 minutes, remove it from the oven and arrange the peaches decoratively on top (if the peaches have thrown off a lot of liquid, drain it all out first). Strew the crumble mixture over the fruit and return the pan to the oven for an additional 40–50 minutes, or until the fruit is bubbling and the kugel is golden, just pulling away from the edges of the pan, and slightly firm. (If the fruit you are using is somewhat firm and not particularly juicy, it will not, of course, bubble, so check that it is meltingly tender and completely cooked through.)

4. Let the kugel cool for at least 30 minutes until set before cutting. Serve warm (reheat if necessary), room temperature, or slightly chilled (not icy cold).

YIELD: About 10 servings

COOK'S NOTE: For a lighter kugel, you can omit the crumble mixture from the topping, but make sure the peaches are well drained. After arranging the peaches over the kugel, just sprinkle them with brown sugar to taste.

For a creamier, less custardy pudding, use 3 eggs, 2 cups of buttermilk, and add 4 ounces of softened cream cheese. Beat the cream cheese with the eggs first, then add the maple syrup (use only ⅓ cup—you're using less of the tangy buttermilk, and the cream cheese is somewhat sweet-tasting), vanilla, salt, and buttermilk as above. Make sure to beat all the ingredients well until thoroughly blended.

In the fall, replace the peaches with an equal amount of juicy apples with lots of character: Cortland, Grimes Golden, Idared, Northern Spy, Winesap. Select a mixture of three different kinds for more depth of flavor. Juicy Barlett or Bosc pears would also be delicious. Peel and cube the fruit. Instead of the dried peaches in the filling, substitute ½ cup raisins and ½ cup stemmed dried figs, cut into small pieces (or substitute 1 cup of either). I use my hands to toss the dried fruit with the noodles: it's easier that way to break up any clumps the figs might form. Reduce the syrup to ⅓ cup (this dried fruit is sweeter)—or use honey instead. For the topping, change the flavorings to lend a whiff of the Middle East. Melt 3 tablespoons unsalted butter in a heavy, 10- to 12-inch skillet. Stir in 4–6 tablespoons honey or 5–6 tablespoons packed light or dark brown sugar (according to sweetness of fruit and personal preference), ¼ teaspoon ground cardamom, ¼ teaspoon ground cinnamon, 1 teaspoon peeled and grated fresh ginger (optional), ⅛ teaspoon salt, and 1 tablespoon fresh lemon juice. Or omit the cardamom and ginger and replace with ½ teaspoon vanilla extract and ⅛ teaspoon nutmeg, preferably freshly grated, or ground cloves. Cook for 3 minutes. Add the apples (or pears), stir well to coat them with the pan syrup, and cook, stirring, for 4 minutes to meld the flavors.

Denser than peaches, the apples (or pears) will take longer to cook, so arrange the fruit decoratively over the kugel at the beginning, when first placing the kugel in the oven. Bake the kugel for 1½ hours–1¾ hours, until the fruit is tender and the kugel is golden, just pulling away from the pan's edges, and feels slightly firm.

Follow the cutting and serving directions above.

Wood carved cookie form for hamantaschen with Austrian double-headed eagle (the Hapsburg coat of arms). (Austria, Nemirov, Podolla, 1870.)

CARAMEL RUGELACH

DAIRY

I am a vanilla person: one of the few food lovers completely unseduced by chocolate's charms. Perhaps that explains why I made the match—buttery caramels with tender rugelach. It was *bashert*, or meant to be; two delicious unchocolate sweets just waiting to be introduced.

And using store-bought caramels makes these rugelach as easy to prepare as, well, the chocolate chip kind. But the sweet molten filling does tend to seep out somewhat during baking. I find that adding chopped pecans and shaping the rugelach as rolled rectangles rather than crescents helps cut down on leakage. And when needed, I just trim away the caramel that has found its way out of the baked cookies.

PASTRY

2 ⅓ cups unbleached all-purpose flour

¼ teaspoon salt

3 tablespoons granulated brown sugar

8 ounces cream cheese, chilled and cut into bits

2 sticks (½ pound) unsalted butter, chilled and
  cut into bits

¼ cup sour cream

1 teaspoon vanilla extract

FILLING

½ cup granulated or packed light brown sugar

1 ¾–2 cups (about 12 ounces) packaged
  caramels, such as Kraft's, cut into small bits

About 1 cup pecans, coarsely chopped

1. Make the pastry. In a food processor, mix the flour, salt, and brown sugar. Add the cream cheese, butter, sour cream, and vanilla and pulse just until the mixture begins to form a ball around the blades. Do not overprocess. Transfer the dough to a work surface and knead lightly and quickly into a smooth, compact roll. (Or prepare manually: In a large bowl, quickly mix together the cream cheese, butter, sour cream, and vanilla until well blended. Gradually add the flour, salt, and sugar. Knead the mixture lightly until thoroughly combined and smooth.)

2. Divide the dough into 4 equal parts. Put each piece between two sheets of wax paper and flatten into a large oblong using the palm of your hand. If necessary, refrigerate briefly until the dough is firm enough to roll.

3. Work with one oblong at a time, keeping the others refrigerated. Roll the oblong between the wax paper into a 12-by-7-inch rectangle, about ⅛ inch thick. Leaving the dough in the wax paper, refrigerate for at least 4 hours or up to 2 days. Repeat with the other 3 rectangles.

4. Loosen the wax paper from both sides of the dough. (The paper becomes pressed into the dough with rolling and will be difficult to remove after you cut the dough unless it has been loosened first.) Place the dough rectangle back down on a sheet of the wax paper, and sprinkle it all over with 2 tablespoons brown sugar. Now cut the rectangle in half. You should have two 6-by-7-inch sections. Cut each section into 4 equal strips, giving you 8 in all. Leaving a ½-inch border, place some caramel pieces and pecans over each dough strip (be generous—the more caramels, the more luscious the taste; see Cook's Note). Roll each strip up tightly, jelly-roll fashion, and place seam side down, about 1 inch apart, on a baking sheet lined with parchment. (If the dough becomes too soft to work with during the rolling or filling, place it on a lined cookie sheet in the freezer until firm again.) Refrigerate the prepared rugelach while you make rugelach with the rest of the dough. The prepared rugelach should be refrigerated for at least 30 minutes before you bake them.

5. Preheat the oven to 375°F. Bake in the middle of the oven for about 20 minutes, or until pale golden. If necessary, adjust the pans during baking so the rugelach cook evenly. Transfer the pan to a rack and let the rugelach cool completely. Remove the rugelach carefully with a thin-bladed spatula. Store the rugelach in airtight containers for up to 4 days.

YIELD: 32 cookies

COOK'S NOTE: Rugelach may be frozen, unbaked. You need not defrost before baking, but increase baking time by 5–7 minutes.

If your caramels are soft enough, press the pieces with your fingertips to flatten them. You'll get a smoother, tighter roll.

My good friend Dr. Mary McLarnon, who helped me perfect these little treats, prefers them warm. She recommends gently heating them in a microwave or toaster oven. But never eat them hot: caramels, like all sugar when heated, can badly burn your mouth. She also suggests these would be delicious made with English toffee or homemade caramels.

THE HOLIDAYS

SABBATH

❦❧❦❧❦❧❦❧❦❧❦❧❦❧❦❧❦❧❦❧❦❧❧

The Sabbath is the choicest fruit and flower of the week,
the Queen whose coming changes the humblest home into a palace.
—JUDAH HA-LEVI, *KUZARI*

It was the darkness and emptiness of the streets I liked most about Friday
evening, as if in preparation for that day of rest and worship which the Jews greet
"as a bride."...I waited for the streets to go dark on Friday evening as other
children waited for Christmas lights.
—ALFRED KAZIN, *A WALKER IN THE CITY*

No wonder the Sabbath is frequently personified as a beautiful queen, princess, or bride: traditional Jewish families eagerly begin feverish preparations for its arrival as if for a royal visit.

Cooks seek out the best foods and wines in the markets, and often put aside especially choice or exotic fruits found during the week to be savored when the Sabbath comes. Most of the finest Jewish recipes derive from the Sabbath kitchen: for many poor Jews it was the one day of the week that they would taste meat, chicken, or wine.

The freshly scrubbed house percolates with the sounds and smells of Sabbath cooking. Latkes suffused with garlic and rosemary sizzle in hot olive oil. A sniff of our tsimmes, puckery-sweet with rhubarb and prunes, tantalizes the nose. And the crisp skin of lemon-roasted chicken and puffy little matzoh balls, waiting for soup, invite filching by hungry children just home from school.

For the most observant, everything must be readied before the Queen's arrival, not only the Friday evening meal but Saturday's hot lunch as well. Kindling fires and cooking are among the thirty-nine activities classified as work, and therefore prohibited while the Sabbath is in progress. In addition to the festive foods like challah, chicken soup, chopped chicken livers, and gefilte fish, Jews have created a whole set of special dishes to accommodate the special Sabbath restrictions: cholents, hamins, and *dafinas*, lusty one-pot meals made beforehand, then left to cook overnight in the slowest ovens; savory kugels and *fritadas* (frittatas) warmed up on hot trays; and spicy fresh fish dishes from Jewish kitchens all over the globe, prepared ahead and served cold.

As night falls on Friday, the hustle and bustle cease and a hush falls over the house. The table, cleared of mail, keys, and other weekday detritus, has been transformed: now it is an elegant altar of spotless linen, gleaming silver, and china set to honor the Sabbath.

As Jews light the candles and recite the Kiddush blessing over the wine to usher in the Sabbath, the father blesses the children. The joyous family meal is especially delicious and savored leisurely.

The following day, the Queen's presence is still felt, as the family continues to move in step with her unique rhythm. Since the most ancient times (it is the only holiday mentioned in the Ten Commandments), even those whose six-day work week revolved around mindless drudgery and endless toil could look forward to an evening, then an entire day—the Sabbath—devoted to resting their bodies, renewing their spirits, and strengthening the bonds with those they loved.

> A Jew without hot food on the Sabbath is like a king without a state.
>
> —JEWISH PROVERB

In Talmudic times (70–500 A.D.) a hot meal was not an everyday occurrence. To honor the Sabbath, it became a mitzvah, good deed, to serve hot food at the Saturday midday meal. Here we dish up robust, slow-cooked Duck and White Bean Cholent or a *dafina* combining falling-off-the-bone lamb with little boats of stuffed eggplant in wide soup bowls, accompanied by tart, crisp green salads. In warm weather, we might serve *desayuno,* a Sephardi-style brunch, featuring Spinach-Cheese Squares, roasted eggs, and perhaps an Ashkenazi Sorrel-Onion Noodle Kugel.

Saturday night, when it is time to bid farewell to the Sabbath, she is escorted off in the enchanting Havdalah ceremony. Jews burn a braided candle, pour a full cup of wine, and breathe in fragrant spices, reminding them of the special Sabbath sweetness they have tasted. This sweetness will fortify them as they return to the routine world. Just until Wednesday, when they began anticipating the beautiful Sabbath to come.

Many American Jews, even if they are not Orthodox, still find some way to mark the Sabbath as sacred and separate it from the workaday week. For some, this is the special Friday night dinner or the quiet Saturday spent with loved ones.

For me, as a child, it was the Kiddush, the blessing chanted before the Friday evening meal to usher in the Sabbath. Never bound by custom, my father always let me, his daughter, "make" the Kiddush, though traditionally the benediction is recited by men, because I, a passionate eight-year-old who had just begun Hebrew school lessons, was burning to take over the ceremony.

And so it became my job as much as setting the table every evening. I chanted the prayers and sipped the sweet, syrupy wine from my father's worn Kiddush cup, shined so often and so hard that no inscriptions were any longer visible. Then I'd pass the cup around so everyone could drink in the Sabbath's sweetness—mother, father, sister, brother, grandfather, and usually a guest or two—and back to me. A circle that was warm embrace and inviolate family nexus.

There were times, of course, that I absented myself, when I was a guest at a friend's, or later a boyfriend's home. And I can still hear the note of disappointment—and chastening—in my father's voice when I told him I wouldn't be home for dinner: "Do you know it's Friday night?" he'd ask.

But next Friday, I'd be back. No Kiddush wine ever tasted so sweet as at my father's table.

OTHER SUGGESTIONS FOR SABBATH

For Friday Night Dinner

Chopped Chicken Liver from the Rue des Rosiers (page 47) or
Chopped Chicken Liver with Caramelized Onions (page 51)
Chicken Gefilte Balls and Green Olive Sauce (page 58)
Classic Chicken Soup (page 63) with one of the kreplach or
matzoh ball recipes (see Index)
Golden Gefilte Fish with Golden Horseradish (page 85)
Gefilte Fish Quickly Steamed Between Cabbage Leaves (page 90)
Salmon Gefilte Fish Poached in Fennel-Wine Broth with
Ginger-Beet Horseradish (page 93)
Flanken with Tart Greens (page 108)

A S A B B A T H   D I N N E R

"Let us, O Lord, have a glimpse of this Paradise that awaits the righteous in the Next World," the Jews entreated God.

And so, according to tradition, God gave them the Sabbath Day, so they could taste the pleasures of Paradise here on earth.

In Talmudic times, Jews scattered aromatic herbs around the Sabbath-clean floors and placed sweet-smelling herbs and flowers on the table during Sabbath meals. The lovely fragrance emitted not only glorified Queen Sabbath, but also gave Sabbath observers a sense of Paradise to come.

This Sabbath dinner is infused with the heady scents of lemon, cinnamon, rosemary, and, of course, garlic, traditionally eaten at Sabbath dinners when its reputed aphrodisiac qualities would ensure fulfillment of the Friday night marital obligations.

LEMON-ROASTED CHICKEN

For maximum flavor, I rub the marinade right into the chicken flesh beneath the skin and then I roast it on a layer of lemons. Butterflying the chicken enables you to spread the marinade on more of the meat under the skin and to remove more of the fat trapped there, especially between the joints. Because so much fat is removed with this method, the skin never becomes soggy and a final sizzle under the broiler crisps it up delectably.

One 3½- to 4½-pound frying or roasting
chicken (preferably fresh, not previously
frozen), butterflied down the backbone and
pounded gently so it lies flat easily
1½ tablespoons coarsely chopped garlic
(4–5 large cloves)
2 tablespoons chopped fresh thyme, or
4 teaspoons dried thyme

3 tablespoons fresh lemon juice
Salt and freshly ground black pepper
Olive oil for the pan
2 lemons
½ teaspoon packed light brown sugar

---

1. Rinse the chicken and pat dry. Remove all visible fat. Starting at the neck end, gently loosen the skin by sliding your hand underneath the breast and carefully working your way back to the legs. Remove as much fat as possible beneath the skin, paying particular attention to the fat deposits around the thighs.

2. In a food processor or blender, puree the garlic, 1 tablespoon fresh or 2 teaspoons dried thyme, the lemon juice, ½ teaspoon salt, and ¼ teaspoon pepper. Lift up the skin and spread about half the mixture all over the breast and down to the drumsticks. Rub the remaining mixture all over the outside of the chicken. Cover loosely with plastic wrap and refrigerate for at least 4 hours, but preferably overnight.

3. About 30 minutes before you are ready to begin cooking the chicken, remove it from the refrigerator to bring it to room temperature. Preheat the oven to 350°F.

4. Choose a heavy, ovenproof skillet (12-inch cast iron is ideal) large enough to accommodate the chicken. Rub it lightly with oil. Thinly slice the lemons, discarding the pits, and arrange them evenly over the bottom of the skillet. Sprinkle the lemons with the brown sugar. Turn the heat to moderately

high and cook for 5 minutes. Add the chicken, skin side down, and continue cooking for about 10 minutes. Occasionally slide a wooden spoon under the chicken to prevent the skin from sticking to the lemons. Peek underneath—the skin should be coloring a rich gold in spots.

5. Sprinkle the top with the remaining 1 tablespoon fresh or 2 teaspoons dried thyme and salt and pepper to taste, and place the skillet, chicken still skin side down, in the oven. Roast for 30 minutes. Leaving the layer of lemons on the bottom of the pan, turn the chicken on its other side, skin side up. Season it all over with salt and pepper and continue roasting for 30–55 minutes longer, or until the juices run clear when the thigh is pierced with a skewer or a thermometer inserted into the thickest part of the leg or thigh reads 170°F.

6. Give the chicken skin a final crisping by running the chicken under the broiler for a few minutes, moving the pan as necessary so both the front and back are evenly browned and crackly.

7. Let the chicken rest for about 10 minutes before carving.

YIELD: About 4 servings

RHUBARB-PRUNE TSIMMES

When it comes to combining foods, I'm not one for hard and fast rules. I've been seduced by cheesecake made supernal with a zap of ground chiles, and I adore savory meats, poultry, and even fish perfumed and mellowed by fruits. But unmitigated sugariness makes my mouth say dessert; fruits must have a spicy or tart accompaniment to segue gracefully into a main course. To me, a tsimmes (a sweetened, festive fruit and vegetable stew, with or without meat) of sweet fruits is one-dimensional without some tang or heat.

To provide well-nuanced character here, I add the sprightly acidic bloom of fresh rhubarb to sweet-and-sour prunes and fragrant honey for a meatless tsimmes irresistible as a side dish or condiment for poultry or meat. Make this tsimmes in spring or early summer with big-flavored field rhubarb or year-round with the milder lipstick pink hothouse variety.

---

1 large onion, chopped (about 2 cups)
2 tablespoons vegetable oil
2 garlic cloves, finely chopped (about 2 teaspoons)
Salt and freshly ground black pepper
¼ cup fragrant honey (floral, like lime or
* orange blossom, or herbal, like lavender or*
* thyme, would be perfect)*
¼ teaspoon ground cinnamon

3 medium carrots, scrubbed (and peeled, if
* desired) and cut into 1-inch chunks (1½ cups)*
1 cup prune juice
1 pound rhubarb, ends trimmed, tough strings re-
* moved with a vegetable peeler, and stalks cut into*
* 1-inch pieces (discard leaves; they can be toxic)*
1½ cups pitted prunes, halved (or quartered,
* if large)*

---

1. In a 10-inch heavy skillet, sauté the onion in the oil over medium heat until wilted, about 5 minutes. Stir in the garlic and cook for a minute or two. Season generously with salt and pepper to taste, turn the heat down to medium-low, cover, and sweat the mixture slowly, stirring occasionally, until the onions are quite soft but still pale-colored, 10–15 minutes.

2. Add the honey and cinnamon, and mix until well distributed. Add the carrots and cook, stirring, for about 5 minutes.

3. Add the prune juice and bring the mixture to a boil. Add the rhubarb and the prunes and simmer over moderate heat, stirring every once in a while, until the rhubarb is soft and the carrots are tender but not falling apart, 12–18 minutes.

4. Turn the heat up to high and boil the mixture, uncovered, until the liquid in the pan is thick and syrupy. Taste and adjust seasonings.

YIELD: About 4 servings

GARLIC-ROSEMARY POTATO LATKES

PAREVE

These exceptionally fragrant potato pancakes require no topping or sauce as adornment. They are perfect as is, ready to accompany any roasted or grilled chicken or meat.

About 1 ½ pounds Yukon Gold, or 3 large russet (baking) potatoes, peeled
2 tablespoons chopped garlic
1 tablespoon fresh rosemary leaves
1 large egg, beaten
1 tablespoon matzoh meal or unbleached all-purpose flour

¾ teaspoon salt, or to taste
¼ teaspoon freshly ground black pepper, or to taste
½ teaspoon baking powder
Olive oil, for frying

1. Coarsely shred the potatoes, using the grating disk in a food processor. (Don't wash out the food processor—you'll be using it again right away.) Transfer the potatoes to a colander or strainer and use your hands or a wooden spoon to press out as much moisture as possible.

2. Remove the grating disk from the processor and replace with the steel blade. Return about one-third of the shredded potatoes to the food processor. Add the garlic and rosemary and process, using the pulse motion, until roughly pureed. Transfer the mixture to a large bowl. Add the remaining shredded potatoes, the egg, matzoh meal, salt, pepper, and baking powder to the bowl. Mix until thoroughly combined. Refrigerate for about 15 minutes to mingle the flavors.

3. In a heavy, 10- to 12-inch skillet (cast iron is ideal), heat about ¼ inch of oil over high heat until hot but not smoking. Drop ¼ cup of the potato latke batter into the pan and flatten with a spatula. Repeat with more batter, cooking no more than 4 or 5 latkes at a time; crowding the pan will give you soggy latkes.

4. Regulate the heat carefully, reducing it to medium as the latkes fry until golden and crisp on the bottom, about 4 minutes. To prevent oil from splattering, use two spatulas (or a spatula and a large spoon) to turn the latkes carefully. Fry until crisp and golden on the other side.

5. It's best to flip the latkes only once, so that they don't absorb too much oil. So, before turning, lift the latkes slightly with the spatula to make sure the underside is crisp and brown.

6. As the latkes are done, transfer them to paper towels or untreated brown paper bags to drain.

7. Continue making latkes in the same manner until all the batter is used. If necessary, add more oil to the pan, but always allow the oil to get hot before frying a new batch.

8. Serve straightaway. Or keep the latkes warm in a 200°F oven (place in a single layer on an oven-proof platter lined with paper towels) and serve when they are all ready to be brought to the table.

YIELD: About 4 servings

Kiddush cup for the blessing made over wine that ushers in the Sabbath and holidays. (Silver, engraved. Augsburg, 1749–1751.)

DRIED FRUIT COMPOTE WITH FRESH
PINEAPPLE, PISTACHIOS, AND MINT

❧❧❧❧❧❧❧❧❧❧❧❧❧❧❧

PAREVE

When the chill weather comes, old-fashioned dried fruit compotes are the classic finish to simple Sabbath dinners. Light and wholesome, they taste of deep flavors and contain no milk products to compromise the dietary laws.

But there's the rub. Without the tart dairy tang of sour cream, crème fraîche, or yogurt as complement, the meltingly silky fruit turns cloyingly sweet after just a few bites. Compote needs a bright acidic sparkle to pull its flavors into balance.

Fresh, ripe pineapple is the answer. Its brash tart-sweetness is not overwhelmed by the dark-winy dried fruit. Simmered in tea that's been infused with orange and spices, the dried fruit matures in the refrigerator for a day or two—three or four is even better (the compote will keep for up to two weeks in the refrigerator). Just before serving, I stir in chunks of sassy-sweet, beautifully perfumed pineapple, a crunch of pistachios or almonds, and chopped fresh mint.

If avoiding dairy is not a concern, serve the compote—with or without the pineapple—with sour cream, crème fraîche, yogurt cream, or *labneh,* for dessert or a delightful breakfast. The compote also makes a wonderful companion to cheese blintzes.

---

2 bags fragrant black tea, such as Earl Grey,
English Breakfast, Assam, or Darjeeling
A 2-inch piece of vanilla bean, split
1 cinnamon stick
2–3 cardamom seeds, crushed
3 cloves
½ cup sugar minus 1 tablespoon
(if not using dates, use ½ cup sugar)
Pinch of salt
½ fresh orange

1 pound prunes, pitted
½ cup dried apricots, halved, or if large, quartered
¼ cup dates, pitted and chopped (optional)
1 tablespoon fresh lemon juice
1 perfectly ripe fresh pineapple, peeled, cored and cut into bite-size chunks (see Cook's Note)
Chopped, toasted pistachios or sliced, blanched almonds, for garnish
Chopped fresh mint, for garnish

---

1. In a 4- to 5-quart heavy saucepan, combine 3 cups of water, the tea bags, vanilla bean, cinnamon, cardamom, cloves, sugar, salt and a wide strip of zest (with no white pith) cut from the orange (reserve the rest of the orange). Bring to a boil, then reduce the heat and simmer, stirring occasionally, for 10 minutes. Remove the tea bags, cinnamon, cardamom, and cloves, and discard them, leaving the vanilla bean and orange zest in the pan.

2. Add the dried fruit to the pan, stir well, cover, and simmer gently for 30–35 minutes, or until the fruit is very tender. Lift out the orange zest and discard it. Find the vanilla bean and either discard it or rinse it so it can be reused. Stir in the juice from the reserved ½ orange and the lemon juice.

3. Cool the compote to room temperature then cover it tightly. Refrigerate at least 6 hours. But the fruit tastes best if prepared a day or two before you serve it, so the flavors can fully unfold, mingle, and mature.

4. Just before serving, gently toss the pineapple with the compote and spoon the mixture into pretty glass bowls or large stemmed glasses. (If you don't plan to serve all of the compote at one meal, toss only part of the pineapple with the compote in the serving bowls, reserving the remaining pineapple to be added just before serving the rest of the compote.) Top with the pistachios or almonds and a sprinkle of the fresh mint.

YIELD: 8–10 generous servings

COOK'S NOTE: Other spice combinations work well here: Try vanilla with black peppercorns or a bay leaf, or experiment with some of your own favorites. Or eliminate the spices and add amaretto or Frangelico. Replace the sugar with orange blossom honey or with half sugar and half raspberry preserves.

Both the new, supersweet variety of fresh pineapple and canned pineapple lack the requisite tang essential for this recipe. If you can't find a fresh, tart-sweet pineapple, substitute navel oranges, peeled and sliced.

CHOLENT

Call it cholent, *shalet, dafina,* hamin, *s'keena, tabit:* Nearly every Jewish community in the Diaspora has come up with a version, or several, of this quintessential Jewish dish. It is a one-pot hot meal—meats, vegetables, legumes, and/or grains are all cooked together in a casserole—traditionally prepared on Friday afternoon and left to simmer very slowly in the oven until the Saturday midday meal.

These casseroles were created to solve a singularly Jewish problem: how to honor the Sabbath lunch with hot foods when no fires may be kindled—or ovens lit—after sundown on Friday. (The Jewish Sabbath, like all Jewish days, begins with sunset and ends the following evening. "And there was evening and there was morning: the first day," says Genesis 1:5.)

Because the Sabbath laws prohibit the act of cooking as well as lighting fires, observant Jews do not stir the dish, add additional ingredients or seasonings, or degrease the cholent while the Sabbath is in progress. Cooks trim as much fat as possible before cooking, or they can prepare the cholent well in advance, refrigerate it, and remove the fat before reheating. (Warming up cooked food on a previously lit fire—a stove burner or oven kept on overnight—is permissible.) Guests may season the food at the table.

But you need not restrict the cholent of Sabbath to the traditional Saturday lunch. Robust and aromatic, it is ideal cold-weather comfort food. Prepare it on a blustery January or February morning when rattling winds make you long for richly caramelized, slow-cooked flavors, and let it stew all day in a gentle oven or crockpot, steaming up the windows. You'll come home to an ineffably tantalizing fragrance and a deeply soul-satisfying meal.

Ah, the aroma. Too often it is more glorious than the taste. Because the ingredients can be rather heavy (when meats were scarce, cooks often took the kitchen sink approach, tossing in virtually everything but to fill out their cholents) and are cooked so long, traditional cholents, especially to the uninitiated, can be unpleasantly thick and tired-tasting.

SOME GUIDELINES—DELICIOUS CHOLENTS FOR CONTEMPORARY TASTES

- Today there is no reason not to limit the amount and number of starches used. Beans with rice, perhaps, or a dumpling, along with some white potatoes, is usually the most I include in a Sabbath stew.
- Barley, simmered for very long periods, tends to swell up enormously, drinking up a great deal of the cooking liquid, and can become rather mushy. If you include it, go easy, adding just enough to lend a creaminess to the cholent. Or try soaking it overnight in cold water (½ cup barley to 2 cups water) when you soak the beans, for fluffier barley.

- If you are cutting down on meat, include more sturdy vegetables along with the beans. Carrots, celery root, fennel, parsley root, parsnips, and rutabagas are all good choices. They will impart their earthy, herbal flavor and, in turn, beautifully absorb the aromatic cooking juices. Roasted shallots make a wonderful addition.

- Because the lengthy cooking flattens out the flavors, eliminating the complex high notes, before serving, introduce some fresh, vivacious tastes. Shower the cholent lavishly with fresh herbs or wake it up with a jolt of freshly ground black pepper or finely minced fresh garlic. Something citrusy—the finely grated peel or a splash of juice—will also enliven the cholent and pull the flavors into balance, while mitigating its richness.

- Yes, it is a *rich* dish. If health reasons do not permit you to indulge in a regular portion, enjoy it as an appetizer. Round out the rest of the meal with a big, tart salad and whole grain bread like sour rye. Chilled Crenshaw melon, or other seasonal fresh fruit, makes the best finish.

- Cholents freeze beautifully and reheat well. Leftovers become perfect make-ahead meals. And it's easy to remove the fat from cholents prepared in advance. Remember to add a dash of fresh flavoring just before serving.

DUCK AND WHITE BEAN CHOLENT

This meltingly spoon-tender duck and creamy bean casserole is reminiscent of a fine cassoulet, to which it is no doubt related. European Jews wealthy enough to enrich their cholent—the stew that for many was the taste of Sabbath itself—with duck and goose found their lush flesh would remain succulent and tender even after the prolonged cooking from Friday afternoon to midday Saturday. Today, kosher *confit d'oie* (long-simmered preserved goose) is still sold in Jewish delicatessens in France for creating lavish Alsatian-style cholents.

But the lengthy, gentle braising that renders such incomparably supple meat and enchants the house with a heavenly perfume will also fade the pungent seasonings. They will need some brightening up. So just before serving, I send in a fresh infusion of flavors: brisk minced garlic, rosemary, and snappy lemon zest.

---

1 ½ cups (about 12 ounces) dried white beans, such as cannellini or Great Northern, washed, picked over, soaked overnight in cold water to cover by at least 2 inches, and drained

One 4½- to 5½-pound fresh duck (or thawed frozen), wingtips, tailbone, and neck removed

1 tablespoon olive oil

Salt and freshly ground black pepper

1 cup chopped shallots

8 large garlic cloves, peeled and coarsely chopped

1 cup dry red wine

10–12 pitted prunes, quartered

4 large waxy potatoes, peeled and cut into quarters, or 6 medium, halved (2–2½ pounds)

2 tablespoons chopped fresh rosemary

1 tablespoon chopped fresh sage

2 teaspoons grated orange zest

About 6 cups homemade chicken broth (page 63), or good-quality low-sodium canned

LEMON-GARLIC GARNISH

2–3 teaspoons grated lemon zest, or to taste

2 teaspoons minced or pressed fresh garlic

1 tablespoon finely chopped fresh rosemary

2 tablespoons finely chopped fresh parsley, preferably flat-leaf

½ teaspoon salt

---

1. Place the beans in a very large (7- to 8-quart) Dutch oven or heavy, flameproof casserole in which you will be cooking the cholent.

2. Cut the duck into eighths (or have the butcher do it). Reserve the liver and any giblets for another use. Pull off and discard as much excess fat as possible. Rinse the duck inside and out and thoroughly dry with paper towels.

3. Heat the oil in a 10- to 12-inch heavy skillet (cast iron is ideal) until very hot but not smoking. Working in batches, add the duck and brown on both sides over medium-high heat, beginning skin side down. Transfer the duck as it is cooked to the Dutch oven or casserole. Let the cooked duck rest until cool enough to handle, then remove the skin from each piece. If your cholesterol count permits, return the skin to the skillet and fry over moderately high heat until crisp on both sides, to render as much fat as possible (it will be a delicious flavoring for the cholent). Cut the skin into small bits and add to the Dutch oven or casserole. Sprinkle the skin and the duck pieces all over with salt and pepper. (Alternatively, if you choose not to crisp the skin, simply discard it.)

4. Discard all but 1 tablespoon of the fat remaining in the skillet. Add the shallots and sauté over medium heat until softened, about 5 minutes. Add the garlic and continue cooking for 3 minutes, or until golden. Transfer the mixture to the Dutch oven.

5. Add the wine and prunes to the skillet and turn the heat up to high, scraping up all the browned bits with a wooden spoon. Cook until the liquid is reduced by half, then transfer the mixture to the Dutch oven.

6. Preheat the oven to 200°F. Add the potatoes to the Dutch oven, sprinkle the herbs, orange zest, and salt and pepper to taste over all, and combine well. Add 6 cups broth—it should just cover all of the ingredients, so if necessary, add a bit more. Bring to a gentle boil and then simmer for 10 minutes. Cover very tightly with foil and the lid. Transfer to the oven and bake undisturbed for 8 hours, or overnight.

7. Prepare the lemon-garlic garnish. Combine all the ingredients in a small bowl, cover, and refrigerate until ready to serve.

8. Just before serving the cholent, stir in the lemon-garlic garnish.

YIELD: 4–6 servings

HERBED BEEF CHOLENT WITH ONION GONIFS

"Gonif," she called, trailing me into the kitchen. Other children stole from the cookie jar. But what cookie could compare with my grandmother's huge cold matzoh balls, satin-sleek with fat, gleaming like golden goose eggs in the moonlight?

"Stop! There won't be any left for tomorrow. You little gonif, you thief."

But she was laughing. She always made extra. It was the one food she knew I'd always eat and she was engaged in a constant struggle to put more weight on me, which would no doubt cure me of the twin maladies, anemia and straight hair.

Reading through a pile of Jewish cookbooks in a secondhand store years later, I was intrigued to learn about a matzoh-ball-type dumpling cooked in a cholent, ironically called a gonif. It seems the dumpling, placed on top of all the savory ingredients, steals their flavors and becomes enriched by them.

In the following cholent, the slow-cooking herbed flanken or short ribs make these oniony gonifs quite rich indeed. I also usually include poultry, so those who want to cut down on some of the red meat in this very filling dish can do so.

ONION GONIFS

4 tablespoons olive oil

¼ pound onions, finely chopped (1 cup)

Salt and freshly ground black pepper

5 large eggs

1 cup matzoh meal

3 tablespoons finely chopped fresh parsley, preferably flat-leaf

2 teaspoons grated lemon zest

1 ½ teaspoons baking powder

⅓ cup chicken broth, preferably homemade (page 63), or good-quality low-sodium canned

BEANS

2 cups (1 pound) cannellini or Great Northern beans, or a combination of either of these white beans and cranberry or kidney beans, washed, picked over, soaked overnight in cold water to cover by at least 2 inches, and drained

3 large carrots, scraped and quartered

1 bay leaf

1 fresh thyme sprig

1 fresh rosemary branch

½ small onion, peeled

2 large garlic cloves, peeled and smashed

MEAT

2 tablespoons coarsely chopped onions

1 tablespoon coarsely chopped garlic

1 tablespoon minced lemon zest

2 tablespoons fresh lemon juice

1 tablespoon chopped fresh rosemary

2 teaspoons minced fresh thyme

2 teaspoons salt

5 peppercorns, crushed

Olive oil to film the pan

3 ½–4 ½ pounds flanken or short ribs, cut in
pieces

1 ½–2 ½ pounds turkey thighs or legs (optional)

FOR THE REST OF THE CHOLENT

2 tablespoons olive oil

About ½ pound onions, chopped (1 ½ cups)

2 parsnips, peeled and quartered

3 tablespoons coarsely chopped garlic

½ cup dry red wine

One 16-ounce can Italian plum tomatoes,
chopped, and their juice

2 tablespoons chopped fresh rosemary

1 tablespoon chopped fresh thyme

Salt and freshly ground black pepper

6–8 small waxy or all-purpose potatoes (about
2 pounds), such as red new potatoes or Yukon
Gold (if you have access to heirloom varieties,
Caribe, Russian Banana, or Yellow Finn
would be particularly delicious), scrubbed,
unpeeled (unless the peel is thick or
unpleasant), and halved

4 cups beef or chicken broth, preferably homemade (page 78 or 63) or use good-quality low-
sodium canned

Chopped fresh flat-leaf parsley and minced
fresh chives, for garnish

---

1. Start the gonifs. Heat 1 tablespoon of the oil in a 7- to 8-inch skillet, add the onions, and sauté over moderate heat until softened and pale gold, about 5 minutes. Add salt and pepper to taste and set aside to cool.

2. In a large bowl, beat the eggs until light and foamy. Add the remaining 3 tablespoons oil and beat until smooth. Fold in the matzoh meal, parsley, lemon zest, baking powder, about 1 ½ teaspoons salt (or to taste), and a generous amount of pepper. When the onions have cooled to room temperature, stir them in, along with the broth. Mix very well, cover the bowl, and refrigerate for at least 1 hour or up to 12 hours.

3. Prepare the beans. Put them in a large saucepan together with the carrots, bay leaf, thyme, rosemary, onion, and garlic. Add enough cold water to cover the ingredients by 2 inches. Bring to a gentle boil over medium heat, skimming off all the froth as it rises to the top. As soon as it begins to boil, reduce the heat to a simmer, partially cover the saucepan, and cook for about 40 minutes, or until the beans are almost tender. Drain the beans. Pick out and discard the herbs, onion, and garlic, but reserve the carrots. Transfer the beans and carrots to a 7- to 8-quart Dutch oven or flameproof casserole.

4. While the beans are cooking, start the meat. Prepare an herb paste: In a blender or a mini food processor, combine the onions, garlic, lemon zest and juice, rosemary, thyme, salt, and peppercorns.

Puree, stopping to scrape down the container as necessary, until the mixture is well combined and fairly smooth. Scrape the mixture into a 13-by-9-inch glass baking dish.

5. Trim as much fat as possible from the meat and pat it dry. (You really can't skim the fat from the cooked cholent unless it is prepared well in advance and refrigerated.) Lightly grease a heavy 10- to 12-inch skillet and heat it over medium-high heat until hot but not smoking. Add the flanken or short ribs, in batches if necessary so you don't overcrowd the pan, and brown lightly on all sides over medium-high heat. Transfer the meat to the prepared baking dish and smear the herb paste all over. Heat the skillet again (if needed, grease it lightly with oil again) over moderately high heat. Add the turkey, if using, and lightly brown it on all sides, then transfer it to the baking dish and rub all over with the herb paste.

6. Preheat the oven to 200°F.

7. Now assemble the cholent ingredients. Discard any fat in the skillet and heat the 2 tablespoons oil. Add the onions and sauté over moderately high heat until softened and lightly speckled with brown, about 5 minutes. Add the parsnips and garlic, and continue sautéing until dotted bronze around the edges. Add the wine, bring to a boil, and cook, scraping up all the browned bits, for 2 minutes. Stir in the tomatoes and their juice, the rosemary, thyme, and salt and pepper to taste, and bring to a simmer. Cook, stirring, for 2–3 minutes, to mingle the flavors. Stir the mixture into the beans in the Dutch oven.

8. Salt and pepper the bean mixture to taste, taking into account the saltiness of the broth you are using in the recipe. Add the beef, turkey, and potatoes, burying them in the beans. Add the broth and bring to a slow boil.

9. Lightly form the gonif batter into dumplings the size of golf balls. (Don't compress the batter too much or the gonifs will be dense and hard. If you prefer, you can make the gonifs small—about the size of walnuts.) When the broth is gently boiling, slide in the gonifs, one at a time. Cover the pot tightly with foil and the lid and transfer it to the oven. Let the cholent cook undisturbed for 8 hours, or overnight.

10. To serve, place 2 gonifs, 2 potato halves, beans, and meat and/or poultry in each shallow soup bowl. Ladle in some broth. Sprinkle generously with the parsley and chives to freshen the flavors.

YIELD: 6–8 servings

GARLICKY LAMB AND LIMA HAMIN
WITH LITTLE EGGPLANT BOATS

This Sabbath stew celebrates timeless Sephardi tastes. Nestled on top of limas and rice, garlic-suffused lamb simmers slowly overnight to melt-in-the-mouth tenderness. For added dimension, I cook little meat-stuffed eggplants along with the stew. Sephardim frequently include stuffed zucchinis or other vegetables in their hamins; they are analogues of the gonif, the starchy dumplings Ashkenazim add to their cholents. Like a gonif, these eggplant boats seem to pilfer the fragrant aromas from the stew as they cook to creamy succulence.

The idea for these eggplant boats came from Oded Schwartz's *In Search of Plenty*. For a simpler, but still memorable, preparation, make the hamin without them.

---

3 small-medium eggplants (6–8 ounces each)
Coarse salt
2 cups dried large lima beans (about 1 pound), washed, picked over, soaked overnight in cold water to cover by at least 2 inches, and drained
1 ½ cups long-grain rice, rinsed
6–8 small lamb shanks (5–6 pounds)
6 tablespoons olive oil
¾ pound onions, chopped (3 cups), plus ½ cup chopped shallots, or 1 pound onions, chopped (4 cups)
Freshly ground black pepper

1 whole head of garlic, separated into cloves and peeled
1 ½ cups chopped plum tomatoes (about three-quarters of a 28-ounce can, drained, or 1 pound fresh)
Grated zest and juice of 1 lemon
2 teaspoons fresh thyme leaves, or ¾ teaspoon dried thyme, crumbled
½ pound lean ground beef
6 cups beef or chicken broth, homemade (page 78 or 63), or good-quality low-sodium canned

---

1. Cut a large, thin lengthwise slice from each eggplant. These will be the lids for the eggplant gonifs, so reserve them. Scoop out as much eggplant flesh as possible without damaging the peel. (Many people use spoons, melon ballers, or apple corers, but I find they are not sharp enough. A small paring knife is easier to manipulate without tearing the peel.) Put the eggplant flesh in a colander, toss with 2 teaspoons coarse salt, and weight it down with a plate or bowl topped with a heavy object, like a can of tomatoes. Let the eggplant drain for about 30 minutes while you prepare everything else.

2. Place the drained limas and rice on the bottom of a very large, heavy flameproof casserole or Dutch oven (about 7- to 8-quart capacity).

3. Trim the lamb of as much visible fat as possible. Wipe with damp paper towels and pat thoroughly dry. In a 10- to 12-inch heavy skillet, heat 2 tablespoons oil until hot but not smoking. Sear the lamb over medium-high heat, in batches if necessary to avoid crowding the pan, until evenly browned on all sides. Transfer the meat to a platter and set aside.

4. Wipe out the fat from the skillet and in it heat 2 tablespoons of fresh oil. Add the onions and sauté over medium-high heat, lifting and turning them until golden-brown, about 15 minutes. Salt and pepper well and stir into the raw limas and rice. (Don't wash out the skillet yet.) Salt and pepper the browned lamb all over and arrange on top of the limas and rice. Strew the garlic cloves over the lamb.

5. In a small bowl, stir together 1 cup of the tomatoes, the lemon zest and juice, thyme, and salt and pepper to taste, and pour over the garlic layer.

6. Preheat the oven to 200°F.

7. Rinse the eggplant flesh under cool, running water and then squeeze it dry with your hands, extracting as much of the bitter juices as possible. Pat dry with paper towels. Heat the remaining 2 tablespoons oil in the skillet, add the shallots (or alternative onions), and sauté until softened, about 5 minutes. Add the eggplant flesh and cook over medium-high heat, stirring, until tender, about 2–3 minutes per side. Stir in the ground beef and sauté until the meat loses its red color. Stir in the remaining ½ cup tomatoes and salt and pepper to taste. Cook, stirring, for 2 minutes. Stuff the eggplant shells with the meat mixture and cover with the reserved eggplant lids. Arrange these eggplant gonifs on top of everything in the casserole. Pour in the broth.

8. Bring to a gentle boil on top of the stove and simmer for 10 minutes. Cover the casserole tightly with foil and the lid, place in the oven, and cook for 8 hours, or overnight.

9. To serve, cut the eggplants in half or thirds. The lamb will be meltingly tender and falling off the bone, so you need not serve each guest an entire shank. Instead, dish out some lamb pieces, accompanied by limas, rice, and a piece of the velvet-soft stuffed eggplant.

YIELD: 6–7 servings

ROSH HASHANAH

1 and 2 Tishri (September or October)

The pineapple groans under her sharp knife like a live fish. Its juice, like white
blood, trickles onto my fingers. I lick them. It is a tart-sweet taste.
Is this the taste of the New Year?
—BELLA CHAGALL, *BURNING LIGHTS*

Some of the townspeople stood on the wooden bridge reciting the "tashlikh"; others
lined the river banks. Young women took out their handkerchiefs and shook out their
sins. Boys playfully emptied their pockets to be sure no transgressions remained.
—ISAAC BASHEVIS SINGER, "TASHLIKH"

Rosh Hashanah celebrates both the New Year and a birthday—humankind's. But in place of revelry, there is reflection; instead of joyful music, the shrill wail of the shofar summons us to cleanse our souls and our hearts.

For Rosh Hashanah is the Day of Judgment, when God inscribes our fate for the coming year in the Book of Life. The decree, however, is not final. We can change our destiny during the next ten days, the Days of Awe, with prayer, charity, and reparation of the wrongdoings we committed against others. Then on Yom Kippur the book is shut, the judgment sealed.

The holiday is at once solemn and festive: Joy comes from trust in God's compassion, as well as the anticipation of renewal and fresh starts. Nearly 2,500 years ago, the prophet Nehemiah proclaimed, "Eat the rich and drink the sweet."

That sweet, rich Rosh Hashanah meal becomes more than mere rejoicing—it too is a form of prayer. The table is transformed into an altar to supplicate God, as we partake of symbolic foods embodying our wishes: honeyed and sugared treats for a sweet year, round foods for a fulfilled year, unbroken by tragedy, foods that grow in profusion at this season and those eaten in abundance, like rice, signifying hopes for fecundity, prosperity, and a wealth of merits.

Rosh Hashanah is also known as the Day of Remembrance, and eating these special dishes reminds us how we must behave. Whole or part of an animal's head (sweetbreads, tongue, etc.), an entire fish, including the head, or even a head of roasted garlic might be served, urging us to be a model of righteousness, at the head of our peers. The sweets tell us to act in a way that would cause no sadness.

We begin dinner with a prayer for a sweet year, dipping challah, or other sweet bread, and apples into fragrant honey. Other families start with sugared pomegranates, dates, figs, or quince in rose petal syrup. Fish, symbolizing fertility and God's blessings, is the customary first course on most menus. Rapid-growing seasonal vegetables, like leeks, Swiss chard, black-eyed peas, and pumpkins, to name just a few, appear throughout the meal in major roles and supporting parts: Here you will find delicate Greek leek croquettes and black-eyed peas with cilantro and tomato from Egypt. Sumptuous main dishes follow: Brisket Braised in Pomegranate Juice with Onion Confit and Pomegranate Seeds and a Syrian specialty, Apricot-Stuffed Meat Rolls with Tart-Sweet Cherry Sauce. From Iran comes a glorious low-fat chicken, scented with cumin and turmeric, and eaten wrapped in fresh green herb leaves. And usually, two (or more) desserts, like the simple, fresh Hungarian Plum Tart, incorporating the "new fruit," a fruit eaten for the first time this season, and a noodle kugel lush with coconut milk and caramelized pineapple conclude the meal.

Sweetness and abundance are not confined to foods. Conversation is joyous—it is, in fact, forbidden to display anger. And it is a mitzvah, a good deed, to invite guests, especially strangers and poor people, those, as Nehemiah said, "for whom nothing is prepared" to share the meal.

A few foods, however, are unwelcome at the Rosh Hashanah table. Nuts are not eaten by some Ashkenazi Jews because the numerical value of the Hebrew word for nuts is equal to the value of the word for sin. And nuts can cause an excess of saliva, impairing one's ability to recite prayers. Others do not eat pickles, horseradish, or other sour foods, while Moroccans avoid foods that are black, like olives and grapes—all are considered bad omens.

During the afternoon it is traditional to go to the nearest body of free-flowing water—ocean, lake, river, or in arid areas like Israel, a well—to cast away sins, a cathartic ceremony known as tashlikh. Penitents, as in I. B. Singer's story above, watch their sins of the past year float away into the water, tangibly expressed as the lint and crumbs shaken from pockets and handkerchiefs.

As children, we wanted to put as much distance as possible between ourselves and our iniquities. The little beach town we grew up in was an island, with both ocean and bay. For my sister and me, though, there was really no choice about where to take our transgressions. We had seen bottles, shreds of clothes, and dead horseshoe crabs tossed up by the ocean and left like offerings on the beach. We did not want our sins riding in on the waves, returned to us—or to anybody else, for that matter. In the warm slant of the Indian summer sun, we stood above the cool waters of Reynolds Channel. Our black velvet dresses had no pockets and we never carried handkerchiefs, so we peeled off our little white kid gloves, shaking out the fingers into the currents below.

Once, one of us dropped a glove. And from the dock, we watched it swim away in the roiling black waters, our accidental scapegoat, like our sins, never to return.

OTHER SUGGESTIONS FOR ROSH HASHANAH

Golden Gefilte Fish with Golden Horseradish (page 85)
Gefilte Fish Quickly Steamed Between Cabbage Leaves (page 90)
Egyptian Ground Fish Balls with Tomato and Cumin (page 96)
Aromatic Marinated Brisket with Chestnuts (page 115)
Classic Chicken Soup (page 63) with Fried Onion and Chicken Kreplach (page 130)
Moroccan-Flavored Carrot Kugel (page 171)
Dried Fruit Compote with Fresh Pineapple, Pistachios, and Mint (page 208)
(omit nuts, if desired)
Pumpkin and Sweet Potato Soup with Sweet Potato Knaidlach (page 259)
Caramelized Onion and Carrot Tsimmes with Candied Ginger (page 268)
Maple-Roasted Pears with Passion Fruit and/or Fresh Raspberry Sauce (page 269)

HONEY FOR DIPPING CHALLAH AND APPLES

May it be Your will, our God and God of our forebears,

to renew for us a good and sweet year.

—ROSH HASHANAH PRAYER

Traditions create the "we"-ness of families. There are traditions each family observes as Americans (we eat turkey on Thanksgiving, we watch fireworks on the Fourth of July), and there are practices followed as members of an ethnic group (as Ashkenazi Jews, we eat latkes on Hanukkah). But it is the unique traditions that each family invents for itself that make the family a "we" unlike any other.

On Rosh Hashanah many Jews dip apples and chunks of challah into honey, embodying their prayers for a sweet new year. So from her earliest days, my daughter always looked forward to the holiday, when she was actually told to indulge her Pooh-like honey-love, dunking slice upon slice of fruit and eggy bread into unmitigated sweetness.

As she grew older and the difference became greater and greater between carefree summer days and the more regulated ones spent in school, she no longer eagerly awaited the falling leaves or the holidays. We sought ways to ease the transition. For students, as well as for Jews, autumn is a time for beginning anew, for fresh starts. So to kindle an anticipation for school, we searched during summer vacations in France for a new notebook, in Maine for another backpack, and in Quebec for special pencils Québecois. And to make Rosh Hashanah an even sweeter holiday, we began scouring the markets on every trip for a different honey. Jews traditionally save a new fruit from the autumn harvest to eat on Rosh Hashanah. We had a new honey as well: creamed lavender honey one year from Provence, wild blueberry honey from Maine, chestnut honey from Italy, honey fragrant with hibiscus and frangipane from Bermuda.

Now we always bring a fragrant honey back from every trip. And that has become our own Rosh Hashanah tradition: Every year we open a lovely new honey.

There is a world of difference between ordinary supermarket honey and an artisanal product. If you absolutely can't track down a special honey for Rosh Hashanah, make your plain honey more distinctive by beating into it a few drops of a flavoring extract (like strawberry, lemon, or even almond) or a spoonful of very reduced aromatic fruit juice (apple-raspberry, for example).

LEEK CROQUETTES FROM RHODES

PAREVE

Nicknamed the People of the Book, Jews since ancient times have thrived on inventive word play, coaxing enough meaning from words and numbers to poach old Humpty Dumpty with envy.

Rosh Hashanah, for instance, celebrates the pun in the prayers recited at the evening meal over many of the symbolic foods. On this solemn holiday, blessings in Hebrew and the many languages of the Diaspora reflect a rather humorous tickling of words. Who cannot see the twinkling in the eyes of the sages as we, in a modern English adaptation, eat beets to "beat back our foes" and dates to "date this year as one of happiness and peace"? Leek in Hebrew is *kartee,* which sounds like the word *yihartu,* to cut off. So Sephardim eat leek patties to "cut off their enemies."

The late Rachel Almeleh, a superlative New York home cook, gave me this heirloom recipe for leek-potato croquettes from her native Rhodes, Greece. The croquettes are dipped in egg just before frying, so they absorb very little oil. Unusually light and delicate, they make lovely appetizers and cocktail nibbles.

---

4 medium leeks (about 1½ pounds), trimmed, washed free of sand, white and pale green parts coarsely chopped (about 3 cups)

1 medium-large russet (baking) potato or about ½ pound other nonwaxy potatoes, like Yukon Gold, scrubbed but left unpeeled

1 slice seedless rye, semolina, light sourdough, challah, or other flavorful bread, crust discarded, bread torn into pieces (about ¾ cup)

2 tablespoons chopped fresh dill

Salt and freshly ground black pepper

2 large eggs, beaten

Olive or vegetable oil, for frying

Lemon quarters

---

1. Put the leeks and potato in a medium saucepan with enough cold, salted water to cover by 1 inch. Bring the water to a boil and simmer for about 40 minutes, or until the potato is tender. Drain the vegetables well. When the potato is cool enough to handle, peel it and force it through a ricer or a food mill fitted with the medium disk into a large bowl. Squeeze the leeks with your hands to extract all excess moisture. Place the leeks and the bread in a food processor, puree, and add it to the potato. Stir in the dill, salt and pepper to taste, and just enough of the beaten eggs (about 2 tablespoons) to form the mixture into 2-inch croquettes. Reserve the remaining eggs, covered and refrigerated. Cover the croquettes with plastic wrap and refrigerate for about 25 minutes.

2. Place the reserved beaten eggs in a shallow bowl near the stove. In a 10- to 12-inch heavy skillet, heat ¼ inch oil until hot but not smoking. Dip each croquette into the egg, letting the excess drip back into the bowl, then slip it gently into the hot oil. Fry the croquettes in batches, turning carefully once, until golden brown on both sides. Drain on paper towels.

3. Serve with the lemon quarters.

YIELD: 6–8 servings

COOK'S NOTE: These are also excellent on Passover, when leeks, symbolic of springtime as well as of the food eaten by the Pharaoh's pyramid-builders, are often served. Just replace the bread with an equal amount of plain or egg matzoh soaked in chicken or beef broth or water and squeezed dry.

Penitents cast their sins into the water in the New Year's ceremony, tashlikh. (Jewish New Year postcard. Publisher unknown.)

BRISKET BRAISED IN POMEGRANATE JUICE WITH ONION CONFIT AND POMEGRANATE SEEDS

MEAT

Cut open a pomegranate. Hundreds of juice sacs form a nearly perfect star, red as blood. Little wonder it is celebrated in myth and ritual by all ancient peoples—Chinese, Greeks, as well as Jews—as a symbol of fertility and abundance.

On Rosh Hashanah, Jews often eat the pomegranate, one of the *miperi ha-eretz*, seven choice fruits of ancient Israel, in fulfillment of the commandment to eat a fruit not yet sampled this season. For, according to Kabbalistic tradition, the pomegranate contains exactly 613 seeds, the precise number of commandments a pious Jew must follow; eating this perfect fruit on Rosh Hashanah embodies the hope that we may perform as many good deeds and righteous acts as the pomegranate has seeds.

The pomegranate's virtues are not merely symbolic. Latest scientific research suggests it may slow the aging process and fight diseases like cancer. For the cook, it adds a tart, complex fruitiness to foods, tenderizes tough cuts, and even reduces the amount of salt needed in meat dishes. In this recipe, the juice tenderizes the brisket and invests the amethyst gravy with a haunting depth. More beautifully layered autumn colors and flavors unfold slowly: a cushion of bronze caramelized onions cooked to a jammy confit, or "onion marmalade," giving way to a shower of tart-sweet pomegranate seeds. It's a glamorous showstopper, worth every minute in the kitchen. For a discussion of pomegranate substitutions, see Cook's Note.

BRISKET

3 tablespoons olive or vegetable oil

A first-cut beef brisket (about 5 pounds), trimmed of excess fat, wiped with a damp paper towel, and patted dry

2 medium onions, coarsely chopped (about 2 cups)

2 leeks, washed well and coarsely chopped (include both white and pale green parts)

6 large garlic cloves, peeled and crushed

2 large carrots, coarsely chopped

1 celery stalk with leaves, coarsely chopped

2 cups pomegranate juice (see Cook's Note)

2 cups chicken broth, preferably homemade (page 63), or good-quality low-sodium canned

3 fresh thyme sprigs or 2 teaspoons dried thyme

2 fresh rosemary branches

2 bay leaves

Salt and freshly ground black pepper

CONFIT

3 tablespoons olive oil

4 large onions (about 2½ pounds), very thinly sliced

Salt and freshly ground black pepper

¼ cup chicken broth

½ cup dry red wine

½ cup pomegranate seeds (see Cook's Note)

1. Prepare the brisket. Heat the oil over medium-high heat in a large, heavy-bottomed roasting pan, using two burners, if necessary, or in a wide 6-quart Dutch oven or flameproof casserole. Add the brisket and brown well on both sides, about 10 minutes. Transfer the brisket to a platter and set aside. (Alternatively, you might find it easier to sear the meat under the broiler. Just cover the broiler pan well with foil to minimize cleanup. Preheat the broiler. Place the brisket under the broiler, fat side up, and broil for 5–6 minutes on each side, or until nicely browned. Move the meat around as necessary, so it sears evenly on the back and front portions. Transfer the brisket to a platter and set aside.) Preheat the oven to 325°F.

2. Pour off all but about 1 tablespoon of fat remaining in the pan and add the onions and leeks. Cook, stirring occasionally, over medium-high heat, until the vegetables are softened, 5–7 minutes. Add the garlic, carrots, and celery and continue cooking until the onions are golden, 7–10 minutes, stirring and scraping the pan to prevent scorching or sticking.

3. Add 1 cup pomegranate juice and bring the mixture to a boil, scraping up the browned bits from the bottom of the pan with a wooden spoon, until the liquid is reduced by about half. Add the remaining 1 cup juice, the broth, thyme, rosemary, and bay leaves and bring the mixture to a simmer. Season to taste with salt and pepper.

4. Lightly salt and pepper the brisket on both sides, and add it to the pan, fat side up, spooning the vegetable mixture all over the meat. Cover the pan tightly, and braise the brisket in the oven, basting every half hour, until the meat is very tender, 2½–3½ hours. (Turn the oven down to 300°F if the braising liquid begins to bubble rapidly.)

5. While the brisket is cooking, make the confit. In a 10- to 12-inch heavy skillet, warm the oil. Add the onions, season lightly with salt and pepper, and toss to coat with the oil. Cook, tightly covered, over the lowest heat, stirring occasionally so the mixture does not burn, for 1 hour, or until the onions are very soft and pale gold in color. Add additional salt and pepper to taste, the broth, and wine. Raise the heat and boil the mixture, uncovered, stirring, until all the liquid is evaporated and the onions turn golden. Taste and adjust the seasoning (it may take quite a bit of salt), then turn off the heat. Cover the mixture and keep it warm. Stir in the pomegranate seeds just before serving.

6. Transfer the brisket to a cutting board and cover it loosely with foil. Prepare the gravy. Strain the braising mixture, reserving the vegetables. Skim and discard as much fat as possible from the liquid. Puree the reserved vegetables and 1 cup of the defatted braising liquid in a food processor or a

blender. Transfer the pureed mixture and the remaining braising liquid to a skillet and reduce the gravy over high heat to the desired consistency. Taste for seasoning.

7. Cut the brisket into thin slices across the grain at a slight diagonal. Spread the onion confit over a serving platter and arrange the sliced brisket on top. Ladle the hot gravy over the meat and serve immediately.

YIELD: 8 generous servings

COOK'S NOTE: This dish owes its distinctive character to both winy pomegranate juice and fresh, tart-sweet pomegranate seeds. Do try to get fresh pomegranates. They are usually available from the end of August through December. Look for large fruits, bulging with seeds, heavy for their size. The leathery rind should be smooth, with some sheen, not dull and dried out. Store them in the refrigerator. Once cut open, remove the seeds and freeze them in an airtight container for an instant burst of color and flavor in a multitude of sweet and savory dishes. You will get 2 cups pomegranate juice by squeezing 4–6 pomegranates (see Pomegranate-Orange Sunsets, page 245). Or you can buy bottled pure pomegranate juice at health food and Middle Eastern stores. Do *not* substitute pomegranate molasses for the juice. One large pomegranate will give you about 1 cup of seeds.

Although the dish is not the same without fresh pomegranates, I can suggest alternatives for a very good, if different, taste:

For the pomegranate juice, try *unsweetened* pure apple-cranberry juice, given complexity with either a couple of tablespoons of pomegranate molasses or about ¼ cup prune juice and 1 tablespoon fresh lemon juice. Taste and make adjustments according to the sweetness of the juice, until you have a good balance of tart and sweet.

And if absolutely necessary, substitute ½ cup (about 2½ ounces) dried cranberries for the pomegranate seeds.

SYRIAN APRICOT-STUFFED MEAT ROLLS WITH TART-SWEET CHERRY SAUCE (KIBBE GHERAZ)

> Beckoning from the fruit baskets on the wooden stands were meaty plums and honey-sweet yellow apricots—it seemed as if onto those wooden stands and into the woven baskets of the poor women peddlers had rolled countless small suns, a treasure of golden ducats.
>
> —CHAIM GRADE, "LAYBE-LAYZAR'S COURTYARD"

Syrian Jews frequently spark their festive dishes, like stuffed grape leaves and zesty kibbe, with dried apricots, especially on Rosh Hashanah, when their deep golden color is symbolic of coins and therefore of good fortune.

A labor of love, kibbe are prepared by grinding rice or bulgur with lean lamb or beef to form an outer shell (a chore made infinitely easier with a food processor), which is then stuffed with a savory meat filling. This version creates a little universe of flavors. Sliced and sauced, it makes an exquisite presentation: rich brown meat punctuated by orange-gold apricots and toasted pine nuts, a harmony of tangy pomegranate molasses or tamarind and dark, sweet purple cherries.

I prefer the tart taste of California apricots here. Rolled up with the meat filling, they provide a welcome counterpoint to the opulent flavors. If your family refrains from eating nuts on Rosh Hashanah, omit them.

I have gently adapted this from the family recipe originally given to me by Lisa Matalon, an excellent Syrian-American home cook.

SHELL
¾ pound (about 2 cups) long-grain white rice
1 pound extra-lean ground beef or lean lamb
Salt

FILLING
½ pound ground beef or lamb
2 tablespoons finely chopped celery (include
    some leaves)

1 tablespoon fruity olive oil
1 ½ teaspoons salt
1 teaspoon ground allspice
½ teaspoon ground cinnamon
3–5 tablespoons pine nuts, toasted lightly
    (optional)

About 6 ounces dried apricots (28–32),
preferably tart, covered with hot water and
allowed to plump until soft, then drained
and patted dry

2–4 tablespoons olive oil

CHERRY SAUCE
1 large onion, diced (about 2 cups)
Salt and freshly ground black pepper to taste

1 cup unsweetened prune juice
One 16-ounce can pitted dark sweet cherries, in
syrup, drained and liquid reserved
About 3 tablespoons pomegranate molasses
(or even better, if you can find it, ourt
or temerhindi, page 31)
2–3 tablespoons fresh lemon juice
1 ½ teaspoons sugar, or to taste
Accompaniment: Syrian Pilaf (page 231) or
steamed white rice

1. Make the kibbe shell. Soak the rice in several changes of warm water, drain it, and pat it dry with paper towels. Grind the rice in a food processor until it resembles meal. Add the extra-lean beef or lamb and about 1 ½ teaspoons salt and puree the mixture, using the pulse motion, until very well combined. (Alternatively, have your butcher grind the meat once, then add the rice and grind again twice.)

2. Make the kibbe filling. In a large bowl, mix the ground meat, celery, oil, salt, allspice, and cinnamon until they are thoroughly blended.

3. Now prepare the rolls. Divide the rice-and-meat shell mixture into 4 equal parts. Repeat with the filling mixture. Place one portion of the shell mixture between two sheets of plastic wrap, and using a rolling pin (if you keep kosher and do not have a separate rolling pin for meat dishes, a wine or other smooth glass bottle will do in a pinch), roll it out into a rectangle, approximately 5 by 7 inches. Remove the top layer of plastic wrap. Cover the shell with one portion of filling. Pat the filling over the shell (or replace the plastic wrap and roll it out), leaving a small border along the sides. Sprinkle the pine nuts, if using, over the filling, then follow with a flat layer of 7 or 8 apricots (the sides of the apricots should not be overlapping, or the kibbe will be lumpy when rolled). As you would a jelly roll, carefully roll up the kibbe, widthwise, using the plastic wrap. Pinch both ends together and gently press around the seam area to make sure the roll is well sealed. Keeping the roll between the plastic wrap, gently pat it smooth. Make three more rolls in the same fashion.

4. Refrigerate the kibbe for at least 15 minutes to firm them up (they will be rather soft after all that handling).

5. In a 6-quart Dutch oven or heavy-bottomed deep sauté pan large enough to hold the rolls in a single layer, heat 2 tablespoons oil until hot but not smoking. Add two of the rolls, seam side down, and fry over medium-high heat until golden. Using two spatulas or a spatula and a wooden spoon, carefully turn the rolls until they are lightly browned and gently crusted on all sides. (Don't allow a hard, dark crust to form.) Transfer them to a platter and repeat with the remaining rolls, transferring them to the platter when they are ready.

6. Make the cherry sauce. If the oil in the pan is very dark, wipe it out and add 2 tablespoons fresh oil. Otherwise, just add the onions to the oil remaining in the pan, salt and pepper lightly, and cook, stirring, over medium-high heat until soft and rich golden, 10–12 minutes. Stir in the prune juice, reserved cherry liquid, pomegranate molasses or *ourt*, 2 tablespoons of the lemon juice, sugar, and salt and pepper to taste.

7. Bring the sauce to a boil, then lower the heat to a simmer and place all the rolls back in the pan. Spoon the pan sauce over the meat, cover the pan, and cook over low heat, basting occasionally, for 35 minutes. Add the reserved cherries and simmer for 15 minutes longer.

8. Transfer the kibbe to a platter, and if desired, reduce the sauce a bit by boiling it, uncovered, over high heat for a few minutes. Taste and adjust the seasoning, adding more sugar, pomegranate molasses or *ourt*, or lemon juice until you reach a graceful balance of tart and sweet flavors.

9. To serve the kibbe, slice the rolls on a diagonal, so that each slice encloses some of the filling. Nap with the sauce. Accompany with Syrian pilaf or plain steamed rice.

YIELD: 6–8 servings

SYRIAN PILAF

To prepare this simple pilaf, Syrian Jews briefly sauté fine, dried egg noodles with rice before adding the liquid. Use subtly perfumed basmati rice to heighten the distinctive nutty flavor.

---

3 tablespoons olive oil

⅔ cup fine egg noodles

1½ cups (about 9 ounces) long-grain rice, preferably basmati, rinsed in a colander in

several changes of cool water, drained, and patted dry

About 1 teaspoon salt, or to taste

Heat the oil in a heavy saucepan. Crush the noodles with your hands, and add them to the oil. Cook, stirring, until lightly browned. Watch carefully so they don't burn. Add the rice, stir the mixture until the rice is coated with the oil, and add 3 cups of water and 1 teaspoon salt, or to taste. Bring the liquid to a boil, then cover and cook over very low heat for 18–20 minutes, or until the liquid is absorbed. Turn off the heat. Fold two paper towels or a small kitchen towel and place on top of the rice. Replace the cover, and let the rice sit for at least 5 minutes, or until ready to serve (the rice will remain warm for about 30 minutes). Fluff the rice with a fork before serving.

YIELD: About 4 servings

COOK'S NOTE: When not serving the rice with a sauce or a saucy accompaniment, such as the kibbe or the recipe for black-eyed peas, *lubia* (page 236), make it more flavorful by substituting broth for the water. And after browning the noodles, sauté 1–2 cups of chopped onion over moderate heat until deep gold, 10–15 minutes. Then stir in the rice.

IRANIAN STUFFED CHICKEN WITH FRESH GREEN HERBS AND GOLDEN SOUP

You pick up strips of silky, moist poached chicken glistening with amber broth and wrap them in an array of fresh green herbs—mint, scallion slivers, basil, tarragon, cilantro—then pop the scented packet in your mouth. Between bites there is the stuffing—cumin-scented rice and dal-like split peas, tinted sunshine yellow with turmeric—that has been cooked to melt-in-the-mouth tenderness inside the gently simmered chicken.

Only much later do you realize that this sensory feast—unlike most from the Rosh Hashanah repertoire—is nearly fat free, rich only in its extravagance of aromatic fragrances and brilliant gold colors.

An added bonus is the wonderful broth that comes with poaching the chicken, to be served at this meal or saved for the second Rosh Hashanah dinner tomorrow.

For Yassmine Hakim, the Jewish New Year has been almost as festive as Passover, ever since she was a child growing up in Teheran, where her huge extended family—replete with lots of mischievous, giggling cousins—gathered around her grandmother's table to eat this family favorite, along with countless *khoreshes* (Iranian stews) and elegant rices.

Today in her New York apartment, Yassmine keeps up the celebratory level of excitement at her own Rosh Hashanah table by investing the symbolic foods, like tongue, black-eyed peas, and pomegranates, with the same degree of importance as those on the seder plate. "I scatter them around the table and offer them as hors d'oeuvre, but first, all of us, especially the children, have fun unlocking the mysteries, discussing the ritual significances of the different foods." After these are eaten and cleared away, a panoply of main courses and rices are brought out, just as in Teheran.

The original Iranian recipe, while utterly delicious, is somewhat tricky to do, but I have come up with an easy and foolproof, though somewhat unconventional, cooking method. I precook all of the stuffing and wrap it up in a thin piece of cotton. Then I split the bird open, slip the stuffing package inside it, and roughly truss the bird closed around it. No need to sew up the chicken and no fear that stray stuffing will seep into the broth and cloud it up. The stuffing drinks in the chicken's lovely juices, and removing it and serving it is a breeze.

Beautifully fresh herbs are essential here; some herb blossoms, if you can get them, added to the mix make for a stunning presentation.

STUFFING

2 tablespoons extra-virgin olive oil

1 ½ cups finely chopped onions

1 ½ tablespoons cumin seeds, crushed with a
mortar and pestle or coarsely ground in a spice
mill (for extra flavor, lightly toast the seeds
until fragrant before crushing)

½ teaspoon turmeric

1 cup basmati rice, rinsed well

½ cup yellow split peas, picked over and rinsed
well

Salt and freshly ground black pepper

CHICKEN

A large roasting chicken, 4–7 pounds (neck,
liver, and giblets removed and reserved for
another use)

Enough fresh, cold water to cover the bird
(if you use bottled water for coffee or tea,
use it here)

Salt

1 large onion, peeled and cut in half

2 medium celery stalks, preferably with leaves

1 cup chickpeas, picked over, rinsed, and soaked
overnight (optional)

Freshly ground black pepper

1 to 1 ½ teaspoons turmeric

TO SERVE WITH THE CHICKEN

An assortment of fresh herbs, including at least
three of these: basil, mint, tarragon, cilantro,
scallions

Small red radishes

Herb blossoms or other edible flowers (optional)

---

1. Start the stuffing. In a wide, 3-quart saucepan, warm the olive oil. Add the onions and sauté them over moderate heat, stirring occasionally, for about 10 minutes, or until they are softened and just beginning to turn pale gold. Don't brown them. Add the cumin and turmeric and stir for 2 to 3 minutes, until they become very fragrant. Add the rice and split peas, and stir to coat them with the onions and oil. Add 3 cups cold water, about 1 ¾ teaspoons salt, and pepper to taste. Bring to a boil, then simmer, covered, over very low heat for 20 minutes. Taste and adjust the salt and pepper. Remove the pot from the heat.

2. You'll need a thin cotton cloth to enclose the stuffing. I prefer an inexpensive, large white cotton men's handkerchief (unlike other cloths, it never unravels), but a piece of clean cotton sheeting (that has been washed in unscented laundry detergent), premade muslin soup bag (sold in some kitchenware supply stores), or a double thickness of good-quality cheesecloth will also work well. Spoon the stuffing onto the center of the cloth and mold it into a rough oblong shape about 8 by 5 inches. Pull the cloth over the stuffing to enclose it completely. Twist the ends and tie them and the middle closed with kitchen string, allowing a little extra room for the stuffing to expand.

3. Using kitchen shears, cut through the chicken along the backbone as if butterflying it, or have the butcher do it. Remove as much loose fat as possible and rinse the chicken well with cold water. Spread the chicken open and place the bag of stuffing inside it. Fold the chicken over the stuffing to enclose it, then tie the chicken closed with a light truss. That will make it easier to turn the chicken if needed, and to remove it from the pot. Place the chicken on the bottom of a stockpot (about an 8-quart for a small bird; 10- to 12-quart for an extra-large chicken). Add water to cover it and about 1 teaspoon salt. Bring to a strong simmer, but don't allow the water to boil.

4. As the chicken cooks, skim off all the froth and scum that rises to the surface. After the water begins to simmer gently, continue skimming for 15–20 minutes, until very few impurities come to the surface, then add the onion, celery, optional chickpeas, a few grinds of pepper, and about 1 teaspoon turmeric. The water now should be a light, golden yellow (it will turn burnished gold later from the chicken juices). You may need to add up to ½ teaspoon more turmeric, especially if your chicken is large and required a lot of water to cover it. Bring the water back to a strong simmer, skimming occasionally, then partially cover the pot and reduce the heat to very low. The bubbles should be breaking slowly and silently along the surface; do not let the soup boil or the chicken will be tough. Check occasionally to make sure the chicken is completely covered with liquid. If there is not enough liquid to cover it, don't add more water—that will dilute the soup too much. Instead, turn the chicken carefully from time to time, so all sides are gently bathed in liquid during most of the cooking.

5. Poach the chicken for 1 to 2 hours (depending on the size of the bird), until its juices run clear when the thigh is pierced with a thin metal skewer or long-pronged fork.

6. While the chicken is cooking, prepare the herb accompaniment. If the basil leaves are large or the stems thick, pull off the leaves and discard the stems. Trim off any hard or woody stems from the mint, and trim the cilantro and tarragon. Cut off the bearded roots and about 2–3 inches of the dark green ends from the scallions, then sliver the scallions lengthwise. Trim the radishes and thinly slice them. Set out the herbs and the radishes decoratively in a basket lined with a pretty napkin or on a platter. If you have any herb blossoms or other edible flowers, like nasturtiums, violets, Johnny jump-ups, or borage flowers, intersperse them among the green herbs for a striking presentation.

7. To serve the chicken, carefully transfer the chicken to a warm serving platter. I find it easiest to do this by grabbing on to the trussing string with tongs, and holding a plate or very wide, sturdy spatula directly under the chicken with the other hand, while a second set of hands stands at the ready with the platter. Discard the trussing string and remove and discard the chicken skin, leaving the meat on the bones. Arrange the chicken attractively on the platter. Untie the bag and scoop out the stuffing,

mounding it in the middle of the chicken. Spoon a little hot broth over everything to moisten it, and tuck a few clusters of herbs around the chicken and stuffing as garnish.

Or slice the chicken off the bone (after discarding the skin), and place in warmed, shallow soup bowls. Spoon some of the stuffing around the chicken and arrange a few sprigs of herbs artfully on top. Ladle about a half cup of steaming broth over everything.

To eat the chicken, take some herbs in hand: a strip of scallion and a couple of tarragon leaves, for instance. Then, still using your hands, pull off a small piece of chicken and roll the herbs around it. If you'd like, sprinkle with a few grains of coarse salt before popping the little packet in the mouth.

8. If you have added chickpeas, taste one for tenderness after removing the chicken, and if needed, simmer the broth a little longer until the peas are done. Discard the onion and the celery.

If you are serving the broth and chickpeas as a prelude to or alongside the chicken: Tent the chicken and stuffing with aluminum foil to keep them warm as you defat the broth. Use an inexpensive gravy separator to remove the fat. Or scoop out the chickpeas, using a perforated ladle, and place them in a large bowl. Line a fine mesh sieve with two to three layers of dampened paper toweling or with coffee filters and fit the sieve over the bowl. Slowly pour the broth through the sieve into the bowl, trapping the fat in the paper towels or filters. If the broth is still fatty, repeat with clean paper towels. Wash out the pot before reheating the soup.

Because the bag of stuffing adds quite a bit of volume to the contents of the pot, necessitating more water than usual to cover the ingredients, you may need to reduce the broth somewhat to concentrate the flavors. Boil uncovered over high heat to the desired strength. Adjust the salt and pepper. Serve the broth with the chickpeas in warmed shallow serving bowls garnished with chopped fresh herbs and some of the poached chicken, shredded.

If you are serving the broth at another meal: Allow it to cool, uncovered, to room temperature, then chill in the refrigerator until the fat congeals in a layer on top. When ready to serve, spoon off the fat and discard it. Reheat the broth until piping hot. Reduce if needed and adjust the seasoning.

YIELD: 4–8 servings, depending on the size of the chicken and other dishes served

EGYPTIAN BLACK-EYED PEAS
WITH CILANTRO (LUBIA)

PAREVE

Black-eyed peas probably arrived in ancient Judea from China via the Silk Route, and consuming them on Rosh Hashanah is a Middle Eastern tradition dating back to the Talmud.

For Egyptian Jews like Rachel Abboudi, who shared her family recipe with me several years ago, eating black-eyed peas embodies their wishes for prosperity and good fortune in the coming year. In this easy-to-prepare dish, Mrs. Abboudi spikes the beans (they are related not to peas, but to the mung bean family) with tomatoes, cilantro, and garlic. I like to simmer a little of the cilantro root (or when not available, the stems) along with the beans for a different dimension and more intensified flavor of the fragrant herb.

The long-grain rice here is no afterthought but integral to the dish: in one of those culinary mysteries, the rice's fluffy, nutty quality is needed to unlock the butteriness of the beans.

Enjoy this too as a fine, meat-free meal, with lavish quantities of cilantro added for a wild herbal freshness.

---

2 large garlic cloves, chopped
3 tablespoons olive oil
Two 10-ounce packages (4 cups) frozen black-eyed peas, or 1½ cups dried black-eyed peas, picked over, drained, and rinsed (try frozen black-eyed peas, if available; they are usually more flavorful than the dried variety)
One 8-ounce can tomato sauce

2 teaspoons chopped fresh cilantro root (or, if unavailable, chopped cilantro stems) and
3 tablespoons chopped fresh cilantro leaves, plus additional whole leaves for garnish
Salt and freshly ground black pepper
Accompaniment: Syrian Pilaf (page 231) or steamed white rice

In a large saucepan, cook the garlic in the olive oil over gentle heat until softened and just tinged with gold, 2–3 minutes. Add the peas, tomato sauce, cilantro root (or stems), and enough fresh cold water to cover the peas by about 1 inch. Bring the mixture to a boil and simmer, covered, over low heat. If using frozen peas, add salt and pepper to taste after cooking for 10 minutes; if using dried peas, add salt and pepper to taste after 20 minutes. Add more water if necessary to keep the peas quite soupy: there should be enough water to form some sauce. Cook frozen peas for a total of 20–30 minutes; dried for 35–45 minutes, or until the peas are tender (exact time will depend on the age of the peas). Stir in the chopped cilantro and serve the *lubia* over the pilaf or rice, garnished with additional cilantro leaves.

YIELD: 6–8 servings

HUNGARIAN PLUM TART

In the course of the two days of Rosh Hashanah, she also eats a plum and a pear—fruits she has not tasted earlier in the season. As a child I always marveled: where did she find the strength and patience to keep herself all summer long from sampling the fresh fruits in her own baskets, so as to be able to recite the Sheheheyonu over them on the New Year.

—CHAIM GRADE, *MY MOTHER'S SABBATH DAYS*

Jews save a special fruit for the Rosh Hashanah Sheheheyonu: a blessing made over fruit savored for the first time that season. For many, the taste of Rosh Hashanah is the midnight blue prune plum that begins arriving in markets at the tail end of the summer. Carole Goldberg's mother brought the recipe for this simple but sublimely fresh prune plum tart from her native Transylvania, where her family prepared it to greet the holiday at the beginning of this century.

Explosive with deep ripe fruit flavor and a dusting of cinnamon, it is more a cross between cobbler and crunch than a traditional tart. I have modified the original recipe slightly. Carole uses pareve margarine so she can serve the tart at a meat meal; I prefer it with the clean, sweet taste of pure butter, perfect as a teatime treat for company with a generous dollop of ice cream. Either way, it is delicious and a snap to prepare.

20–24 fresh prune plums, pitted and quartered, or 6–8 pitted black plums, cut into sixths or eighths (depending on size of plums)
¼ cup firmly packed dark brown sugar
3 tablespoons plus 1 cup unbleached all-purpose flour
1 teaspoon ground cinnamon
About 1 cup granulated sugar, according to taste

1 teaspoon baking powder
¼ teaspoon salt (omit if using margarine)
1 large egg, beaten
½ teaspoon almond extract
1 stick (8 tablespoons) unsalted butter or pareve margarine, melted, plus additional for greasing the pan
Optional accompaniment: *vanilla or coffee ice cream or freshly whipped heavy cream*

---

1. Preheat the oven to 350°F. In a 13- by 9-inch greased baking dish, arrange the plums cut side up in a single layer. Stir together the brown sugar, 3 tablespoons flour, and the cinnamon in a small bowl, and sprinkle the mixture over the plums. In a large bowl, using a fork, blend together the granulated sugar (use up to 2 tablespoons less than 1 cup if you prefer, as I do, a less sweet dessert or if the plums are particularly sweet), remaining 1 cup flour, baking powder, salt, egg, and almond extract until the mix-

ture resembles coarse meal. Crumble it over the plums. Drizzle the melted butter or margarine over all and bake the tart in the middle of the oven for 35–45 minutes or until the plums are tender and the topping is golden.

2. Serve the tart at room temperature, accompanied by ice cream or whipped cream, if desired. It is also wonderful warm from the oven, especially with the cool contrast of the ice cream.

YIELD: 6–8 servings

BOMBAY PINEAPPLE–COCONUT MILK KUGEL

Leaving their shoes at the portals, the Bene Israel of Bombay—Indian Jews who once numbered 24,000—entered barefoot into beautiful synagogues illumined and perfumed by coconut oil burning in the hanging lamps.

Coconuts also provided the milk used extensively in their kosher cuisine. As a pareve substitute for dairy milk, it could be cooked with meat and employed in desserts served at meat meals without contravening the dietary injunction that prohibits mixing meat with dairy.

The community—now mostly dispersed to Britain, Canada, America, and largely to Israel—is one I have visited only in my armchair or in exhibits at local museums. One day I will get there. Meanwhile, in homage to their exotic cuisine, I devised this celestial pareve pudding.

It is a playful culinary pun on traditional Ashkenazi noodle kugels: coconut milk replaces the dairy variety; orzo, a pasta in rice clothing, becomes the noodles; and the pineapple and spices provide the evocative scent of the tropics.

Soft, creamy custard on the tongue, it tastes sweetly spicy and fruity, and makes a lush, graceful finish to the lavish Rosh Hashanah dinner.

One 20-ounce can of pineapple rings in
  natural, unsweetened juices
3 tablespoons maple sugar or brown sugar
Mild oil, such as avocado, sunflower, or
  almond, for greasing the pan
Salt
½ cup orzo
2 cups unsweetened coconut milk

1 cinnamon stick
½ teaspoon peeled and finely chopped fresh
  ginger
1 vanilla bean, split
3 large eggs
½ cup granulated sugar
Boiling or scalding-hot tap water, for hot-water
  bath

---

1. Preheat the broiler. Drain the pineapple and arrange in a single layer on a foil-lined broiler pan. Sprinkle evenly with the maple or brown sugar. Broil the pineapple on one side only until it is a rich, golden brown and the sugar has melted, 5–8 minutes.

2. Lightly grease an 8-inch square baking dish with the oil. Spread the pineapple pieces (with any sugar drippings), sugared side down, in a single layer on the bottom of the pan. (If there is an extra ring or two, cut it in quarters and use it to fill in the spaces between the rings.) Set aside. Turn the oven temperature down to 350°F.

3. Bring 2 quarts of water and 1 teaspoon salt to a rapid boil. Add the orzo and cook, stirring occasionally, until tender. Drain well, rinse a few seconds under cool water, and drain again.

4. While the orzo is cooking, combine the coconut milk, cinnamon, and ginger in a medium saucepan. Scrape the seeds from the vanilla bean and add to the pan. Turn the heat to low and simmer gently for 10–15 minutes to infuse the milk with the fragrance of the spices. Don't allow the mixture to boil. Remove from the heat and let cool slightly.

5. In a large bowl, beat the eggs, granulated sugar, and a pinch of salt until thick and light. Add the coconut milk mixture, pouring it through a strainer into the bowl. Discard the spices. Add the cooked, drained orzo and combine well.

6. Distribute the mixture evenly over the pineapple in the prepared pan. Place the pan in a larger baking pan and add enough boiling or scalding-hot tap water to the larger pan to come halfway up the sides of the kugel pan.

7. Bake for 60–75 minutes, or until a knife inserted in the center comes out clean. The kugel must cool to set. You can serve it right from the pan, or invert it when cool: run a knife along the edges of the pan, turn the pan upside down on a serving plate, and unmold.

8. Serve the kugel chilled, but not icy cold. Or for a more exotic finale, try it slightly warm (reheat gently).

YIELD: About 8 servings

BREAKING THE YOM KIPPUR FAST

The fast begins before sundown on 10 Tishri (September or October)
and lasts until the first stars appear the following night

❧❧❧❧❧❧❧❧❧❧❧❧❧❧

At the close of Yom Kippur a voice issues from heaven and says, "Go and eat your
bread joyfully, drink your wine in good spirit, for God has accepted your efforts."
—ECCLESIASTES RABBAH 9:7

Then my father came back to life, and in the evening he broke his fast
after the Ne'ilah service.
—YEHUDA AMICHAI, "THE TIMES MY FATHER DIED"

When the first stars twinkle in the autumn sky, the piercing blast of the shofar, the ram's horn trumpet ancient as Israel, is sounded at last. Spiritually refreshed now and confident of God's compassionate judgment, Jews will break the long fast in the company of family or perhaps surrounded by friends at a potluck get-together.

On Yom Kippur, the holiest day of the calendar, Jews refrain from all food and drink, including water, denying our purely physical, animal needs to approach a resemblance to angels.

It is no coincidence that this solemn day occurs in the midst of the autumn bounty, just before the most exuberant of the harvest festivals, Sukkot, the Jewish thanksgiving. In Temple times, Yom Kippur was the day the priests purified the Temple and expiated the sins of all the Israelites in anticipation of the Sukkot festivities. As Philo, the Greek Jewish historian (c. 20 B.C.–A.D.50), explained: Before Jews enjoy God's generosity when eating a meal, they always pause to utter a blessing. So on Yom Kippur, as they are about to partake of the lavish harvest they will consume in the coming year, they must stop eating entirely, to offer not just a single benediction, but an entire day devoted to prayer.

The fast cleanses not only the body but the soul as well. It is not merely an act of contrition, an affirmation of sincerity; it focuses our concentration on the spiritual. And by experiencing hunger, we know suffering, and are moved to compassion for others.

This is a time of intense self-examination, settling accounts, both financial and spiritual, and making amends. In the synagogue, we confess and ask forgiveness for sins committed against God. But equally important is seeking pardon from our fellow human beings: we must make peace with enemies and personally ask for forgiveness from friends and loved ones whom we have wronged, even unwittingly, throughout the year.

As the fast draws to a close, excitement builds with the cathartic release that comes from starting over. At my parents' house, it was as if we had each returned from a different, faraway place, or that, for the past twenty-seven hours, we had been forbidden to use our mouths to speak as well as to eat. The solemnity of the holiday gave way before the mounting crescendo of our voices. The meal served was dairy, because it was thought to be gentle for our tender tummies, but it was anything but. The wild cacophony of our chatter was matched at the table by the loud tastes of salt and sweet—smoked and pickled fish and rich, sweet noodle puddings—to restock the bodily supplies lost during the fast.

In the recipes that follow we begin with something fresh and fruity to cleanse the palate and rev the blood sugar: winy pomegranate swizzled with orange juice or a simple instant apple ice from Iran. Following the American tradition of zesty and sweet flavors, there are a smoked whitefish salad crunchy with fennel and home-cured salmon spiced like pastrami, mellowed by a fragrant almond challah and luscious blintzes filled with autumn quinces and apples. For dessert, serve an exquisite caramelized pear noodle kugel scented with two gingers. Or choose any of the sweet noodle kugels or other dishes ideal for breaking the fast listed below. And don't forget a huge pot of good, strong coffee to assuage those caffeine-withdrawal headaches.

OTHER SUGGESTIONS
FOR BREAKING THE
YOM KIPPUR FAST

Lentils "Hummus Style," with Pomegranate and Mint
and Toasted Za'atar Matzohs (page 53)
Apricot Blintzes with Toasted Pistachios and Yogurt Cream (page 142)
Apple-Cranberry Blintzes with Maple-Ricotta Cream and Sugared Walnuts (page 144)
Sorrel-Onion Noodle Kugel (page 148)
Spinach-Cheese Squares (page 150)
Rich Noodle Kugel Baked with Fresh Plums and Nectarines (page 186)
Peach-Buttermilk Kugel (page 191)
Hungarian Plum Tart (page 237)
Turkish Silken Rice Pudding with Fresh Raspberry Sauce (page 357)

IRANIAN ROSE-APPLE ICE (POLUDEH)

PAREVE

"Refresh me with apples," Solomon wrote in the "Song of Songs." Iranian Jews, too, recognize the revivifying talents of the universal fruit: they cleanse palates murky from the long fast with a light, very simple apple ice.

The added rose water provides more than mere refreshment: In some Middle Eastern temples, the *shammash* (sexton of the synagogue) sprinkled drops of fragrant rose water onto the congregants' hands to lift their spirits during Yom Kippur services.

Cool, clean, and delicately perfumed, Malka Anavian's Iranian family recipe makes a suave prelude to the salty, rich fish dishes at the break-the-fast table.

3 medium sweet, fragrant apples (about 1½ pounds), such as Braeburn, Gala, Jonagold, or York	*1 cup water (quality is important here, so if you use bottled water for coffee or tea, use it here)*
5–6 tablespoons sugar, or to taste	*1 tablespoon rose water*
	Finely crushed ice

1. Peel the apples and grate them over the large holes of a grater or in a food processor. Transfer the mixture to a bowl. Sprinkle with the sugar and let stand for about 30 minutes. Stir in the water and the rose water.

2. Arrange a scoop of crushed ice in each of six stemmed glasses or shallow glass bowls. Top each with a portion of the apple mixture.

YIELD: 6 servings

COOK'S NOTE: For an especially festive presentation, serve the *poludeh* over crushed ice in hollowed-out large lemon or other citrus halves, garnished with unsprayed edible rose petals. And you can substitute apple juice for the water; reduce the sugar to taste.

POMEGRANATE-ORANGE SUNSETS

PAREVE

Make haste, give me a cup,

Before the dawn starts to rise,

Of spiced pomegranate juice

From the perfumed hand of a girl

—SAMUEL HA-NAGID (993–1056), "AN INVITATION"

(TRANSLATED BY DAVID GOLDSTEIN)

Sephardim break the fast with several refreshing beverages: sweet "milks" made from almonds or pumpkin seeds; juices of pomegranates, apricots, watermelon, or apples. American Ashkenazi Jews traditionally drink fresh orange juice, befitting a meal at which they typically serve breakfast foods. This gorgeous juice—a mixture of pomegranate and orange—combines the best of both cultures.

Pour your guests these break-the-fast beverages in fine, clear crystal to capture the swirl of colors. Serve regular sunsets in tall tumblers or water goblets; offer frozen sunsets in stemmed cocktail glasses, like frozen margaritas.

Chilled orange juice—about 4 ounces for each serving
Ice cubes
Fresh or bottled pomegranate juice (see Cook's Note, page 246)—3–4 ounces for each serving

Mint leaves and/or thin slices of fresh orange, for garnish

---

1. For regular sunsets. Pour the orange juice into tall glass tumblers or large water goblets filled with ice cubes. Gently pour in the pomegranate juice to taste (I usually combine approximately half and half proportions, but exact amounts will depend on the sweetness of the juices as well as personal preference). Colors should be marbled like a vibrant sunset; if necessary, lightly mix by swirling pomegranate juice through orange juice with a cocktail stirrer or chopstick. Garnish each glass with a mint leaf and/or orange slice. Serve right away.

2. For frozen sunsets. Fill an ice cube tray with pomegranate juice and freeze until completely solid. Put about 8 frozen pomegranate cubes in a blender. Add 1 cup of orange juice and process until smooth. Divide between two large stemmed glasses, serve with a straw, and garnish with mint leaves and a slice of fresh orange. Serve straightaway. (If the liquid begins to separate from the frozen froth, just stir it up with a cocktail stirrer.)

COOK'S NOTE: To make fresh pomegranate juice, score just the rind of a pomegranate, as you would an orange, in quarters lengthwise. Then peel off the rind in sections carefully—it stains seriously! Scoop out the seeds and juice sacs surrounding them, breaking apart and discarding all the bitter white pith. Put the seeds and the juice sacs through a food mill, or whirl in a blender—not a food processor, which would crush the seeds—for 30 seconds, and then strain. Or rub the seeds and sacs against a strainer or colander. You can also put them through an electric juicer.

Just be sure to remove all of the acrid, mouth-puckering white pith. When I was pregnant with my daughter, the only thing that would settle my stomach was the terrific pomegranate punch served at Brownie's, an old vegetarian restaurant near me (now the site of the Union Square Café). One day, my insides in dire turmoil, I attempted to re-create the drink, throwing the entire peeled fruit, pith and all, in my juicer. I could have dyed a rug with it, but I couldn't drink it.

Three medium pomegranates will yield approximately 1–1½ cups of juice. Fresh juice will keep for about 1 week in the refrigerator, 3 months in the freezer.

Pure, bottled juice is available at Middle Eastern shops and many specialty and health food stores. Don't use pomegranate molasses for this recipe.

ALMOND CHALLAH

DAIRY

When you bake your own hallahs for the Sabbath, they have a different taste entirely. Your heart rises as you watch the loaves rise in the pan.
—CHAIM GRADE, *MY MOTHER'S SABBATH DAYS*

Bread has always been the heart of the Jewish meal. When the benediction over the bread is made, it is unnecessary to recite prayers over any of the other foods eaten.

The exception is the Kiddush, the blessing chanted over wine that introduces every Sabbath and important holiday. At these times the challah is covered with a white cloth, some say to protect it from embarrassment at seeing the wine blessed first.

This sumptuous, fragrant challah, a gift from my friend, artist and playwright Linda Rathkopf, is extra-luscious with sweet ground almonds, which stand in for some of the flour. A delectable accompaniment to dairy meals, it is easily made in a food processor. If you have the very large capacity machine (eleven cups), make the full-size loaf, a stunning bread of truly impressive proportions. The equally delicious three-quarter loaf can be prepared in the smaller seven-cup food processor. Or fashion either batter into two loaves.

I give instructions for both sizes here.

WHOLE LOAF (1 LARGE CHALLAH)

½ cup (about 2¾ ounces) blanched almonds

½ cup sugar

2 teaspoons salt

1 cup whole milk, warmed to 100°–110°F, plus
  a few additional drops as needed

2 envelopes (¼ ounce each) active dry yeast

4 large egg yolks

5 cups bread flour

2 sticks (16 tablespoons) unsalted butter, melted

THREE-QUARTER LOAF (1 MEDIUM CHALLAH)

Scant ½ cup (about 2½ ounces) blanched
  almonds

6 tablespoons sugar

1½ teaspoons salt

¾ cup whole milk, warmed to 100°–110°F, plus
  a few additional drops as needed

1½ envelopes (⅜ ounce total) active dry yeast

3 large egg yolks

3¾ cups bread flour

1½ sticks (12 tablespoons) unsalted butter,
  melted

Unsalted butter or oil for greasing the bowl

TOPPING FOR EITHER CHALLAH

1 large egg yolk beaten with 1 teaspoon milk,
  for glaze

About 2 tablespoons sesame seeds, or 3–4
  tablespoons chopped almonds

1. In an 11-cup (for whole loaf) or 7-cup (for medium loaf) food processor, process the almonds with the sugar and salt until finely ground. Pour the warmed milk on top but do *not* mix. Sprinkle the yeast over the milk and allow it to dissolve and proof, 5–10 minutes.

2. Add the egg yolks and pulse briefly. Add the flour, 1 cup at a time, pulsing briefly after each addition. With the machine on, add the melted butter, pouring it very slowly toward the end, until most of the dough forms a ball around the blade. If necessary, add a few additional drops of milk. Continue processing a few minutes more to knead the dough.

3. Shape the dough into a ball and place it in a greased bowl. Cover with greased plastic wrap. Allow the dough to rise in a warm draft-free place until double in bulk, 3–4 hours.

4. Punch the dough down and divide it into two pieces, one piece containing about two-thirds of the dough, the other, the remaining one-third. Now divide the larger piece into three, and, using your palms, roll these pieces into three long identical ropes. Braid the ropes. An easy way to do this evenly is to start the braid in the middle, then turn it upside down and braid the other side. Turn the ends under and press down to keep them joined together. Divide the smaller piece of dough in three and braid in the same fashion.

5. Place the smaller braid on top of the first braid. Transfer to a greased baking sheet, then cover with plastic wrap. Let the loaf rise until double in bulk, 1–1½ hours.

6. Preheat the oven to 350°F. Glaze the dough all over with the egg wash. Sprinkle generously all over with sesame seeds or chopped almonds. Bake 45 minutes for the large loaf, 35 minutes for the medium one, until golden brown and the loaf sounds hollow when tapped on the bottom. Transfer to a rack and let cool.

YIELD: 1 large or 1 medium challah

SMOKED WHITEFISH AND FENNEL SALAD

DAIRY

From a list of some long lines people endure in New York City (*The New York Times*, August 4, 1996):

Zabar's [the legendary New York culinary emporium that began as a humble Jewish appetizing store]: As preparations to break the Yom Kippur fast begin, the line at the lox counter has been known to wend its way out the door onto Broadway, around the block, and along West End Avenue.

Smoked and pickled fish are among the most popular break-the-fast foods for American Jews, who feel it helps the body replenish some of the essential salts lost during fasting.

The saltiness of the fish can be overbearing though, especially for stomachs reeling and tongues still furry from fasting. To temper the salt in this whitefish salad, I substitute the clean fresh taste of fennel for the traditional celery and replace the lemon juice with slightly sweet-yet-still-acidic grapefruit juice.

About 6 tablespoons sour cream

About 2 tablespoons mayonnaise

About 3 tablespoons fresh grapefruit juice

¼ teaspoon fennel seeds, finely crushed with a mortar and pestle or ground in a spice mill

1 small fennel bulb, stalks removed and reserved for another use, some of the feathery fronds chopped and set aside for garnish, if desired

1½–2 pounds smoked whitefish, carefully removed from the bones (about 2 cups)

2 tablespoons chopped fresh dill, plus additional for garnish

Freshly ground black pepper

Accompaniments: attractively cut fresh raw vegetables (carrots, celery, endive leaves, etc.), bagels, bialys, or matzohs

---

In a large bowl, combine the sour cream, mayonnaise, grapefruit juice, and fennel seeds. Use a vegetable peeler to trim any strings from the fennel, if necessary, then cut the bulb into small dice and add it to the bowl. Stir in the whitefish, dill, and pepper to taste. Taste and adjust the seasoning, adding more sour cream, mayonnaise, or grapefruit juice as needed. Garnish with additional chopped dill and fennel fronds, and serve with raw vegetables or toasted bagels, bialys, or matzohs.

YIELD: About 6 servings

COOK'S NOTE: When spooned over hot latkes, this salad makes a wonderful first course in a fish meal. It is especially good on the Celery Root–Potato Latkes (page 276).

PASTRAMI-STYLE SALMON

PAREVE

He was in the oxygen tent when I walked in.

"Did you bring them, *dollek*?"

"Yes, Gramp." The sick-sweet hospital smell receded before the warm, heady scents of garlic and pepper mixed with rich tobacco as I unwrapped the hot pastrami sandwich, sour pickle, and expensive cigar.

We both knew it was going to be his last meal. He was now ninety-four, and cancer of the lymphatic system coursed rapidly through his body.

Though well-lubricated with fat (why bother removing it now?), the pastrami was difficult for him to swallow at this point. So he chewed slowly and deliberately, letting the aromatic meat juices trickle down his throat. Then he pulled off the oxygen tube for a few quick puffs before the nurse came in. I tamped out the cigar and put it away "for later." I kissed his bristly cheek stubble and caressed his bald pink head. "I love you, *dollek*."

Years later, pregnant with the daughter I named for him, I ordered one of those mile-high deli hot pastrami sandwiches, likewise moistened with quantities of the same garlic-suffused fat.

Unfortunately, I lacked his fortitude. It's been fourteen years, and I haven't had pastrami since.

I don't miss the meat, but the seasoning is something else. I've tried a number of pastrami-flavored salmons, and though delicious, they wanted the heat and punch of the requisite Romanian garlic-pepper coat.

Here is my version, which avoids the need for a smoker. Simple to prepare, it costs a fraction of the commercially cured kinds. You just need to allow three or four days to cure the fish. For a break-the-fast meal, you might serve it with cream cheese and assorted breads, like matzoh, bagels and bialys, and thin pumpernickel. It also makes a sophisticated starter, in skinny slices garnished with lemon, capers, and chopped onions.

2–2½ pounds fresh center-cut salmon fillet (not salmon steak), in one piece, cleaned but skin left on

About 6 large, fat garlic cloves, coarsely chopped

2½ tablespoons coarse kosher salt

2 tablespoons paprika

2 tablespoons packed brown sugar

3 tablespoons whole black peppercorns

2 tablespoons pickling spice

Accompaniments: matzoh, pumpernickel bread, bagels, or bialys; cream cheese, lemons, capers, chopped onions

---

1. Cut the salmon in half, down the backbone. If desired, cut the backbone away. Try to remove as many bones as possible—a tweezer is ideal for this. Put both pieces of fish on a platter, skin-side down.

2. In a food processor or blender, place the garlic, salt, paprika, and brown sugar and pulse to combine well, stopping to scrape down the bowl as necessary. Scrape out the mixture and massage it well into the flesh of both pieces of salmon.

3. Lightly crush the peppercorns and pickling spice, either with a mortar and pestle or by placing them in a small plastic bag and hammering a couple of times with a mallet or rolling pin. Rub this seasoning onto the fish. Place one piece of fish evenly on top of the other, flesh-to-flesh, skin side up. Place this re-formed fish in a resealable plastic bag or wrap tightly with plastic wrap. Set the wrapped fish on a platter or in a pan large enough to hold it flat, and top with a large plate. Weight the plate down with a few cans or heavy bottles and refrigerate.

4. Let the salmon cure in the refrigerator for 3–4 days, removing the weights and turning the fish, still in the plastic bag or wrapper, twice a day. Remember to replace the weights after you have turned the fish.

5. When ready to serve, scrape off and discard the marinade and spices. Pat the salmon dry, then cut it on the diagonal into very thin slices. The salmon is easiest to slice when it is very cold.

6. Serve the salmon with plain or egg matzoh or black pumpernickel bread spread with a thin layer of cream cheese. Or accompany with traditional bagels and bialys. For a pareve (neither meat nor dairy) presentation, garnish with lemons, capers, chopped onions, and thinly sliced dark bread.

YIELD: 10–12 servings

HONEYED QUINCE–APPLE BLINTZES
WITH SOUR CREAM–DATE SAUCE

DAIRY

Fragrant quinces studded with cloves were carried to synagogue on Yom Kippur by children in Bulgaria to keep them from fainting during the long service, recalls Suzy David, in her delightful book, *From the Sephardic Kosher Kitchen.*

Throughout the Sephardi world, these aromatic fruits are dished up in many ways during the High Holy Days: paired with meat or poultry in stews, served in luscious compotes, or, most often, as the sugary confection known as *bimbriyo* in Ladino.

Once popular in the United States for making marmalade (that word derives, in fact, from the Portuguese for quince, *marmelo*), quinces are not always easy to find in markets today. And the hard, bitter white flesh must be coaxed with long, slow cooking, flattered with honey or sugar. Then dry and dense give way to rich and yielding, turning beautiful rose-gold along the way.

I've partnered the quinces here with apples, a frequently made match. To enjoy the blintzes at break-the-fast, prepare them a day or two ahead, or freeze them. Fry or bake just before serving.

BLINTZES

2 ripe quinces (1–1½ pounds or 1¾ cups or so, when diced) (see **Cook's Note**)

1 cup apple juice

About 2½ tablespoons fragrant honey

Pinch of salt

2 whole cloves

1 teaspoon vanilla extract

2 medium-large apples (1–1½ pounds, or 2 cups when cut into large dice; choose juicy, sweet varieties such as Braeburn, Cortland, Golden Delicious, Jonagold, Melrose, or Mutsu, to complement the tart quinces)

½ teaspoon ground cinnamon

1 recipe blintz leaves (page 136)

Unsalted butter, oil, or a combination, for frying or baking

SOUR CREAM–DATE SAUCE

Boiling water, for soaking

¼ cup finely chopped dates (snip them with kitchen scissors, dipping the blades into hot water)

1 cup sour cream

¼ cup sliced almonds, lightly toasted (optional)

---

1. Prepare the quinces. Rinse them well, washing off any downy fuzz. Quarter and peel them. Then, using a very sharp knife, carefully cut out the core, seeds, and any other hard bits. Cut the quinces into large dice.

2. In a nonreactive saucepan, combine the apple juice, 2½ tablespoons honey, the salt, cloves, and vanilla and bring to a boil. Add the quinces, reduce the heat, and simmer, covered, until tender. Timing will vary: begin checking after 10 minutes; it may take up to 25 minutes.

3. Meanwhile, peel, core, and cut the apples into large dice. When the quince is tender, stir in the apples, cover, and simmer for about 5 minutes. Turn off the heat, and let the fruit cool in the pan liquid for 15–20 minutes.

4. Make the sauce. Pour the boiling water over the dates to soften them. Drain well and place in a bowl with the sour cream. Beat well with a fork until thoroughly combined.

5. Remove the cloves from the fruit and discard. Using a slotted spoon, transfer the fruit to a bowl, leaving the cooking liquid in the pan. Boil this reserved liquid over high heat, uncovered, until reduced to about 1 tablespoon of thick, syrupy glaze. Stir the glaze into the fruit mixture. Taste, and if needed, add a bit more honey. Stir in the cinnamon. Let the mixture cool completely before filling the blintzes, using a heaping tablespoon of filling for each of the blintz leaves. Fry or bake them (see page 138) and serve right away, or prepare in advance (refrigerate them for up to 2 days or freeze them) and fry or bake them just before serving.

6. Serve the blintzes with a dollop of the sour cream–date sauce. The toasted almond slices may seem like gliding the lily, but they add a wonderful crackle when sprinkled over the sauce.

YIELD: 16–18 blintzes

COOK'S NOTE: Make sure the quinces are ripe. Unlike most fruits, which sweeten up nicely when stewed unripe, quinces may retain an unpleasant tannic taste, similar to unripe persimmons. Don't worry about bruises: if they are very fragrant and give slightly when pressed, they will be luscious.

　　If you cannot find quinces, replace them with an equal amount of tart green apples, like Granny Smith, or even better, Rhode Island Greening. You'll need a little lemon juice to bring up the flavors.

DOUBLE GINGER–CARAMELIZED
PEAR NOODLE KUGEL

Many of my Polish grandmother's recipes date from the time she was sent to Germany to live with an aunt and uncle after her parents died.

The German relatives forced her into a servitude out of the Brothers Grimm. Because of the extraordinary physical demands put on her body, Grandma Rebecca did not reach puberty until she arrived in America in 1911 at age 17, her passage paid for by older sister Anna.

But in Germany, she did learn to cook, and there developed an abiding passion for sweet-and-sour foods, often using gingersnaps as flavoring for dishes like carp, stuffed cabbage, and simple fruit desserts.

In this variation of one of her kugels, I combine tangy crystallized ginger with caramelized pears to mirror the sweet-and-sour gingersnap topping.

---

3 cups whole milk	*2 medium-large ripe Bartlett or Bosc pears*
1 thin strip of lemon zest	*(about 1 pound), peeled and sliced about*
1 cinnamon stick	*¼ inch thick*
1 cup thin dried egg noodles	*8 ounces sour cream*
Salt	*4 ounces cream cheese, softened and cut into bits*
½ cup granulated sugar	*3 large eggs, beaten*
4 tablespoons unsalted butter, plus additional	*½ teaspoon vanilla extract*
2 tablespoons, softened, for topping	*About 1 cup gingersnaps, crumbled*
⅓ cup firmly packed brown sugar	
1–2 tablespoons finely chopped crystallized	
ginger, according to taste	

---

1. In a 3- to 4-quart, heavy-bottomed saucepan, combine the milk, lemon zest, and cinnamon and bring to a boil over medium heat. Continue cooking over lively heat, stirring occasionally and adjusting the heat if the milk threatens to bubble over, until the mixture is reduced to a little over 2 cups. Stir in the noodles and a pinch of salt, and cook for 4–5 minutes. Add the granulated sugar and stir until it melts. Remove the pan from the heat and let cool to room temperature.

2. Preheat the oven to 375°F. Melt the 4 tablespoons butter in an 8- or 9-inch square baking pan in the oven (or if the pan is flameproof, on top of the stove), swirling the butter around to cover the bottom

and sides of the pan. Sprinkle the butter with the brown sugar and ginger, and arrange the pears evenly on top.

3. In a large bowl, beat together the sour cream, cream cheese, and ¼ teaspoon salt until smooth. Whisk in the eggs and the vanilla. Remove and discard the lemon zest and cinnamon stick from the noodle mixture, then add it to the cream cheese mixture. Combine everything well. Pour the contents of the bowl over the pears in the prepared pan. Combine the gingersnap crumbs and remaining 2 tablespoons butter and sprinkle over the top of the kugel.

4. Bake the kugel for about 50 minutes or until a knife inserted in the center comes out clean. (The kugel should be slightly firm.) Let cool until set. To serve, run a knife along the edges of the pan, invert the pan onto a serving plate, and unmold. Or cut and serve the kugel from the baking dish.

Best eaten warm (reheat if necessary) or slightly chilled (not icy cold).

YIELD: 6–8 servings

The shofar's blast announces the end of the Yom Kippur fast. (Ram's horn with engraved inscription. Europe, 18th century.)

SUKKOT

15 Tishri (September or October)

a nine-day festival, including Shemini Azeret and Simchat Torah

꧁꧁꧁꧁꧁꧁꧁꧁꧁꧁

To me it is the finest time of the year.... The sun no longer bakes like an oven, but caresses with a heavenly softness. The woods are still green, the pines give out a pungent smell. In my yard stands the succah—the booth I have built for the holiday, covered with branches, and around me the forest looks like a huge succah designed for God himself. Here, I think, God celebrates his Succos.

—SHOLOM ALEICHEM, "HODEL"

Eating a rich harvest dinner in a starry sukkah, surrounded by the smells of winy autumn fruits and fresh vegetables commingled with fragrant sprays of foliage, it is easy to feel a part of God's natural world. I well remember the sukkah we had when I was twelve: between crisp brown pears and ruby pomegranates we tied wild bayberry branches and scattered warty clusters of the powder gray berries on the floor, suffusing the open room with their spicy scent as we scurried in and out. My brother, my sister, and I hacked tall, feather-headed reeds from sandy lots and sea dunes, spread them out on the trellised roof, and slouched them in the corners—beachy stand-ins for sheaves of corn. In the blaze of candlelight at the evening meal, I could taste the salt in the air on my sweet stuffed cabbage. The best of camping out and eating home, it was cold but magical. And it turned out to be our last sukkah—the following year we moved a few blocks away from our house to an apartment overlooking the ocean.

The sukkah, a temporary booth made of wood, canvas, even aluminum, with a roof of leafy branches, that Jewish families construct out-of-doors to eat meals in during the holidays, is symbolic on many counts, linking the festival to both its ancient agricultural origins and a deeper religious significance. Jews who have no sukkah of their own often take their meals in the sukkot (plural of sukkah) of friends or relatives, or in the large community sukkah of their synagogue.

The holiday began as an exuberant feast of thanksgiving, one of the three pilgrimage festivals (the others are Passover and Shavuot) when the ancient Jews traveled to the Temple to offer gratitude for the seasonal crops. Not only the most important harvest of the year, it was also the final one: After the fine grapes and gold-green olives were reaped and ready for pressing, the wheat, figs, dates, and pomegranates gathered and stored, everyone was free to rejoice and give thanks, as well as to pray for the arrival of badly needed autumn rains and a plentiful harvest in the coming year.

Roofed with twisted vines and carob and olive branches, sukkot in earliest times were purely functional: makeshift little structures the vintners and farmers slept in during the harvest to protect their bounty from predators, both animal and human. When Sukkot was established as a Temple Festival, the travelers erected similar temporary booths for their sojourn in Jerusalem. Later when the holiday was linked to the Israelites' period of wandering in the wilderness, the temporary booths were given a ritual significance as well. They came to symbolize the portable shelters of the Israelites in the desert.

By the time of the Second Temple, more Jews journeyed to Jerusalem at Sukkot than at any other festival, coming to offer gratitude not just for a bountiful harvest, but for God's providential care throughout history as well. Before the Second Temple was destroyed in A.D. 70, they came from as far away as the western shores of the Mediterranean, from Rome and Babylon, from all the foreign lands in the ancient world that Jews had settled. Welcoming them, the city was festooned with sweet-smelling myrtles and palms, beautiful flowers and fruits. Outside the Temple, four huge golden lamps blazed, and according to the Talmud, "the illumination, like a sea of fire, lit up every courtyard of the Holy City." Priests provided music with an array of flutes, lutes, lyres, and cymbals, men paraded with glowing torches, and there was joyous singing and dancing throughout the week-long festivities. Worshipers carried floral wands, and according to Plutarch, slept beneath roofs of plaited ivy and vines.

Today, when most Jews live in urban areas and the agricultural cycle of Israel is less relevant in the Diaspora, the sukkot they construct remain evocative reminders of divine protection. At Sukkot Jews around the world recapture the jubilation of the farmer at the close of an abundant harvest, and at the same time, relive the fragile, precarious life of the Israelites in the desert. For me, these bittersweet sensations are heightened as they echo in the natural world: amidst the season's bounty, the falling leaves reflect the evanescence of existence all around us.

Not surprisingly, vegetables and fruits, often appearing in concert together, take centerstage in our menus for Sukkot: Prunes enrich the caramelized onion and carrot tsimmes, and brilliant pomegranate seeds add sparkle to a pumpkin soup already lush with sweet potato matzoh balls. The traditional stuffed vegetable is well represented, including a fall-scented meat-and-mushroom-stuffed cabbage. In keeping with the calendar, maple-caramelized pears sauced with passion fruit or fresh raspberries conclude the rich meal.

Many Sukkot recipes are sweet. Ripe, flame-gold carrots, pumpkins, and apricots are naturally sugary. Such tastes continue the wish expressed just two weeks before at Rosh Hashanah for a good and sweet year.

OTHER SUGGESTIONS
FOR SUKKOT

PUMPKIN AND SWEET POTATO SOUP WITH SWEET POTATO KNAIDLACH (MATZOH BALLS)

"Let the sky rain potatoes," Shakespeare's Falstaff cries out in quest of aphrodisiac aids. The old lecher was calling for sweet potatoes, the more common and accepted potato of the time (the word "potato" did not refer to the white tuber until around 1775, according to the *Oxford English Dictionary*).

To the Jews around the globe who readily embraced the sweet potato and the other imports from the New World, pumpkins and squashes, the rapidly growing vegetables evoked not *amour* exactly, but abundance and fertility.

In Jewish communities from Morocco to Melbourne, these vegetables are especially prized during the fall holidays, Rosh Hashanah and Sukkot, when their sugary flesh, reflecting the many colors of the sun, symbolizes the sweetness and the seasonal plenty of an abundant harvest.

The sweet potatoes I've added to my Polish grandmother's recipe for matzoh balls (knaidlach) softly echo the pureed golden vegetables that give this soup its delicately sweet edge and velvety smoothness.

Scarlet seeds from a pomegranate hanging in your sukkah or some diced red onions add crunch, tang, and a burst of color.

KNAIDLACH (MATZOH BALLS)

1 large sweet potato (about 1 pound)
2 tablespoons sautéed onions (reserved from
  preparing the soup)
1 large egg, beaten
Nutmeg, preferably freshly grated, to taste
Salt and freshly ground black pepper
½–¾ cup matzoh meal

SOUP

About ½ pound onions, chopped (2½ cups)
3 tablespoons mild olive or vegetable oil

1½ pounds sweet pumpkin or butternut,
  kabocha, hubbard, or other sweet winter
  squash, halved and peeled, seeds and strings
  discarded, flesh cut into 1-inch pieces
1 large sweet potato (about 1 pound), peeled
  and cut into 1-inch pieces
7–8 cups chicken broth, preferably homemade
  (page 63), or good-quality low-sodium canned
Salt and freshly ground black pepper

Pomegranate seeds or minced red onion, for
  garnish (optional)

---

1. Start the matzoh balls. Preheat the oven to 375°F. Prick the sweet potato with a fork and bake it for 1–1½ hours, or until tender.

2. Meanwhile, make the soup. In a large saucepan or Dutch oven, cook the onions in the oil over moderate heat, stirring, until pale golden. Reserve 2 tablespoons for the matzoh balls. Add the pumpkin or

other squash and sweet potato to the onions in the saucepan and cook, stirring, for about 5 minutes. Stir in 7 cups of the broth and simmer over moderately low heat, partially covered, for 30 minutes, or until the vegetables are very tender. In a food processor or a blender, puree the soup in batches until smooth. (If you have an immersion blender, you can puree the soup right in the pot.) Return the soup to the saucepan and add salt if needed and plenty of black pepper. Thin the soup if you wish with some of the remaining 1 cup broth, and set it aside.

3. Make the matzoh balls. When the baked sweet potato is cool enough to handle, peel it. Force the sweet potato and the reserved 2 tablespoons cooked onions through a ricer or food mill fitted with the medium disk into a bowl. Stir in the egg, nutmeg, and salt and pepper to taste. Add ½ cup of the matzoh meal, or enough to make a soft dough, and refrigerate the dough, covered, for at least 1 hour or overnight. Shape the mixture into 16 walnut-size balls, transferring them as they are formed to a wax paper–lined plate.

4. In a large, wide pot, bring 4 quarts of water and 1 tablespoon of salt to a rapid boil. Slide in the balls, one at a time. Reduce the heat to moderately low, cover the pot, and simmer the balls for about 20 minutes, until light, fluffy, and cooked through. Don't lift the lid to peek—they need all that steam to puff up.

5. When the matzoh balls are ready, warm shallow soup bowls and heat the soup until hot. Using a skimmer or slotted spoon, transfer 2 matzoh balls to each heated bowl. Ladle the hot soup over them, and garnish each serving with a scattering of pomegranate seeds or minced onion, if desired.

YIELD: About 8 servings

STUFFED VEGETABLES

Eating stuffed vegetables on Sukkot is common among Jews of many culinary traditions. Reflecting the agricultural roots of the holiday, the colorful, fat vegetables, plump to bursting with lush, savory fillings, celebrate the glorious abundance of the harvest. And on a spiritual level, the rounded, seamless parcels embody the continuity of the Torah, the reading of which is both finished and recommenced each year on Simchat Torah, the last day of Sukkot.

What follows is a medley for a variety of tastes: stuffed cabbage, autumn-scented with wild mushrooms and meat; roasted red peppers filled with mujadderah, a mix of well-seasoned fried onions, lentils, rice, and pine nuts, in a garlic-tomato sauce; and substituting for grape leaves, fresh chard, packed with rice and artichokes.

CABBAGE STUFFED WITH
MUSHROOMS AND MEAT

Prepared with soaked matzoh instead of rice, these delicious cabbage rolls also make an elegant and filling main course at Passover. Green cabbage will work well—but I find the frilly savoy prettier and tastier.

CABBAGE ROLLS

½–¾ cup (about 1 ounce) flavorful dried
  mushrooms, preferably porcini (avoid dried
  shiitake here)

1 whole matzoh

1 cup chicken broth, preferably homemade
  (see page 63), or good-quality low-sodium
  canned

1 head savoy or green cabbage (about
  2 pounds)

½ pound onions, chopped (2 cups)

3 tablespoons olive oil

1 tablespoon plus 1 teaspoon minced fresh garlic

Salt and freshly ground black pepper

1 pound lean ground beef

¼ cup chopped fresh dill

3 tablespoons chopped fresh parsley

1 large egg, beaten

SAUCE

2 tablespoons olive oil

4–5 large garlic cloves, peeled and lightly crushed

2–3 medium carrots, chopped (1 cup)

Salt and freshly ground black pepper

2 cups good-quality canned Italian plum
  tomatoes, coarsely chopped, with their juice

2 cups chicken broth, preferably homemade, or
  good-quality low-sodium canned

Juice of 1 lemon

---

1. Put the mushrooms in a bowl, cover with very hot tap water, and let soak, covered, for 45 minutes.

2. In another bowl, crumble the matzoh into small pieces and cover with the broth. Let the matzoh steep for at least 20 minutes to drink in as much of the liquid as possible.

3. Using a sharp knife, carefully cut away the large outer leaves of the cabbage from the core end. Rinse, then blanch them in a large pot of boiling salted water, about 4 or 5 at a time, until just soft enough to bend and fold without breaking. Drain and pat dry as they are done, and set them aside to cool. Coarsely chop the inner leaves too small to roll and set aside no more than 2 cups of them for the sauce (any remainder should be discarded or saved for another purpose).

4. In a skillet, sauté the onions in 2 tablespoons of the oil over medium heat until softened and pale gold, about 10 minutes. Add 1 tablespoon of the garlic and cook for 5–10 minutes until its color deep-

ens to a rich, bronze-tinged gold. Season with salt and pepper and transfer to a large bowl. Wipe out the skillet with a paper towel.

5. Drain the mushrooms through a colander lined with a paper towel or coffee filter, reserving the mushroom liquid for stock or gravy. Rinse the mushrooms briefly under cold water to remove any grit, dry, and chop them. In the wiped out skillet, heat the remaining 1 tablespoon oil and add the remaining 1 teaspoon garlic. Sauté for 1–2 minutes, then add the mushrooms and salt and pepper to taste. Cook, tossing frequently, for 2–3 minutes to mingle the flavors. Then add the mushrooms to the onions, together with the beef, dill, parsley, and egg. Stir in the matzoh and its soaking liquid, a little at a time so it is completely absorbed. Season with salt and pepper to taste and mix everything together well (your hands are best for this).

6. Preheat the oven to 325°F.

7. Stuff the cabbage leaves. Place them on a work surface, curled ends up, like an open palm. Cut out the hard little triangle at the base of each stem. Put about ⅓ cup of filling (depending on the size of the leaf) in the center. Fold the stem end of the leaf over the filling, then tuck in the two sides. Pull the top tightly over these folds to enclose. The cabbage rolls should be compact and rounded. Place the finished rolls seam side down as you work.

8. Prepare the sauce. In a 6-quart Dutch oven or large, heavy ovenproof casserole, heat the oil until hot, then add the garlic and carrots. Sauté, stirring, over moderately high heat for about 5 minutes, until the vegetables begin to turn pale gold at the edges. Add the reserved chopped cabbage leaves, sprinkle with salt and pepper, and sauté, lifting and turning the vegetables so they don't scorch, over moderately high heat, until the cabbage is softened and very lightly browned in parts. While the vegetables are cooking, combine the tomatoes, broth, and lemon juice in a bowl and season to taste.

9. Place the cabbage rolls on top of the sautéed vegetables, keeping them seam side down. Pack them together closely, and if necessary, make a second layer. Pour the tomato sauce evenly over the cabbage rolls, cover the pot tightly, and bring to a boil. Transfer to the oven and bake for 2 hours. Uncover and bake for an additional 30 minutes to 1 hour, or until the cabbage is very tender.

10. You'll want to sop up every drop of the lusty, deep-flavored sauce, so serve the cabbage rolls with lots of challah or other good bread or mashed potatoes.

Excellent reheated and even better the second day.

YIELD: 4–6 servings

MUJADDERAH-FILLED ROASTED RED PEPPERS IN TOMATO-GARLIC SAUCE

Roasting removes the callow edge from crisp red peppers, turning their flavor sophisticated—at once hauntingly smoky and sweet—and their texture soft and voluptuous. If I'm going to the trouble of stuffing peppers, it's roasted red ones I'm after.

For a Sukkot dinner, I wanted a vegetarian filling to equal the flavor of these peppers, one that would not make you feel there was something missing where the meat should be. Popular all over the Middle East among Jews and Arabs, mujadderah, a rice and lentil combination made scrumptious with a shower of golden fried onions, was the perfect fit. It needed only sweet, toasted pine nuts for textural contrast and leafy cilantro to lend an herby freshness.

At dairy meals, present the peppers with dollops of thick yogurt cream or *labneh*.

PEPPERS

1 cup (about ½ pound) brown lentils

Salt

1 ¼ pounds onions, thinly sliced (5 cups)

4 tablespoons well-flavored extra-virgin olive oil (the rich taste of the oil should shine through here)

1 tablespoon finely chopped garlic

1 cup long-grain white rice

½ teaspoon ground cumin

Freshly ground black pepper

8 large red bell peppers (choose peppers that are unblemished, sturdy, and thick-walled)

4–5 tablespoons pine nuts, lightly toasted

3–4 tablespoons chopped fresh cilantro, plus additional, for garnish (optional)

TOMATO-GARLIC SAUCE
(SEE COOK'S NOTE)

2 teaspoons chopped garlic

1 tablespoon olive oil

1 pound fresh plum tomatoes, peeled and coarsely chopped, or fine-quality Italian canned tomatoes, drained and coarsely chopped

Salt and freshly ground black pepper

Optional accompaniments for dairy meals:

yogurt cream (page 30) or labneh, *seasoned perhaps with minced scallions, chives, or other fresh herbs*

---

1. Pick over the lentils carefully, discarding any stray objects or discolored beans, and rinse well in cold water. Drain, combine them in a large saucepan with 1 quart of fresh cold water, and bring to a boil. Reduce the heat and simmer for 20 minutes. Add salt to taste about 5 minutes before the end of cooking. Turn off the heat, and leave the lentils in the saucepan, covered, until you are ready to add the rest of the mujadderah ingredients.

2. While the lentils are cooking, in a 10- to 12-inch heavy skillet, sauté the onions in 3 tablespoons of the oil over medium-high heat, lifting and turning them occasionally, for about 15 minutes, or until softened. Add the garlic and cook another 15 minutes, or until the onions are a rich caramel color.

3. Add about one-third of the sautéed onion mixture to the cooked lentils, leaving the remaining onion mixture in the skillet. Stir the rice, cumin, and plenty of salt and pepper to taste into the lentils. If necessary, add more water so that everything is completely covered by about ½ inch of water. Mix the ingredients well, cover, and bring to a boil. Simmer for about 30 minutes, or until the rice is tender and all the liquid is absorbed. Peek every now and then to see if more water is needed, and give the mixture a stir.

4. While the mujadderah cooks, roast the bell peppers. It's best to do this over a gas flame, since you need to char the outsides quickly, without overcooking the tender flesh.

If cooking over a gas flame, use a long-handled fork and spear the pepper through the stem only, making sure not to pierce through the pepper anywhere else. Roast them, like marshmallows, over the open flame. Keep turning the peppers until the skins are lightly charred on all sides.

You can also roast them under the broiler. Place the peppers on a foil-lined broiler rack under a preheated broiler, as close as possible to the heat. Turn the peppers as the skins blister and blacken.

5. Put the charred peppers in a paper bag and twist the bag closed. Or put them in a covered bowl. Let them steam just until cool enough to handle so that they will be easier to peel. Rub the peel off with your fingers. Because these peppers are thick-walled, you can also rub off the peel with a dry paper towel, replacing the towel as it becomes saturated with the charred peel. Don't worry if you don't remove every piece of blackened skin—a few bits here and there will add to the smoky flavor. (Don't peel the peppers under water, because they will get too waterlogged.)

6. Using a small, sharp knife, cut out the peppers' stems and discard. Carefully pull out the seeds and membranes and discard. (See Cook's Note.)

7. Prepare the tomato-garlic sauce. The success of this quickly made sauce depends on cooking the ingredients in a skillet, rather than a saucepan, so the watery juices evaporate before the fresh taste is lost. In a heavy 9-inch skillet, sauté the garlic in the oil over medium heat until fragrant and softened—don't let it color more than pale yellow. Add the tomatoes and salt and pepper to taste, and turn the heat up to high. Cook, stirring, for 6–10 minutes, until nicely thickened, with a still-vivid tomato taste. Adjust the seasoning to taste.

8. Preheat the oven to 350°F.

9. Generously salt and pepper the remaining sautéed onions in the skillet and cook over medium-high heat, lifting and turning, until slightly crisp in places and tinged a toasty brown. When the rice and lentils are cooked, stir these onions into them. Then stir in 3 tablespoons of the pine nuts and the cilantro, if using.

10. Spoon some of the sauce on the bottom of a shallow baking dish just large enough to accommodate the peppers when standing upright. (Alternatively, if peppers tore and you are stuffing the pepper halves, choose a dish in which all the peppers will fit comfortably when lying flat.) Fill the peppers with the mujadderah (see Cook's Note) and sprinkle the tops with the remaining 1–2 tablespoons pine nuts and garnish with some additional cilantro, if desired. Arrange the peppers in the pan and spoon the remaining sauce over them. Bake for about 20 minutes, or until heated through.

For dairy meals, accompany the peppers with rich yogurt cream or *labneh* spiked with fresh herbs.

YIELD: 8 servings

COOK'S NOTE: When handling the roasted bell peppers, be especially gentle to avoid tearing their tender flesh. A small hole or two won't really matter with thick-walled bell peppers—the filling is rather dense and not likely to pour out of a little puncture. If you do rip the peppers, simply cut them all in half and lie them flat on their backs, like an open palm facing you, and mound the stuffing carefully inside. You will need a larger baking pan and more sauce, though, since peppers lying flat will take up more space. Double the sauce recipe, and save any extra for another use.

The sauce is very versatile: delicious on pasta, fish, chicken, or vegetables. You can double it if you use a very large skillet. Adjust cooking time as needed to evaporate the juices and thicken the sauce. Feel free to add your favorite fresh herbs, spices, grated lemon zest, or sliced fresh mushrooms to the sauce. Or stir in lemon or orange juice and cook over high heat until absorbed. Mellow overly acidic tomatoes with a pinch or two of sugar, if necessary, or for dairy meals, stir in a bit of sweet butter.

CHARD STUFFED WITH ARTICHOKES AND RICE

PAREVE

Fresh grape leaves rarely come my way, and the preserved variety can be tough and tired tasting. Taking my cue from Middle Eastern cooks, I often substitute more readily available, fresh green Swiss chard for the vine leaves. Served cold, traditional Sephardi recipes for meatless stuffed leaves are particularly flavorful, packed with an abundance of fresh herbs and evocative spices. I've added chips of artichoke for their velvety texture and buttery depth.

You might serve these grouped on a platter with other appetizers, such as lentil hummus (page 53), strips of marinated roasted red peppers, Chickpeas with Garlic and Barbecue Spices (page 296), or an array of crudités or composed vegetable salads. These Swiss chard rolls also make excellent finger food for holiday buffets and parties.

CHARD ROLLS

About 1 ½ pounds green Swiss chard,
   including stems (look for unblemished leaves,
   without holes or tears)
Salt
1 ¼ cups long-grain white rice
1 tablespoon finely minced garlic
2 tablespoons olive oil
1 ½ cups (about 4 ½ ounces) cooked fresh artichoke hearts or thawed, frozen artichoke hearts
   patted dry with paper towels and diced
Freshly ground black pepper
⅓ cup finely chopped fresh dill

⅓ cup finely chopped fresh mint or 2 teaspoons
   dried mint
2 teaspoons grated lemon zest
½ teaspoon ground allspice

SAUCE (SEE COOK'S NOTE)

Salt and freshly ground black pepper
2 tablespoons coarsely chopped garlic
⅓ cup extra-virgin olive oil
¼ cup fresh lemon juice
1 tablespoon dried mint

Lemon wedges

---

1. Prepare the chard rolls. Rinse the chard well, then cut the stems flush with the leaves. Set the stems aside for the sauce. In a large stockpot, bring 6 quarts of water and 1 tablespoon salt to a rolling boil. Add the chard leaves and blanch until they are just pliable enough to bend and fold without breaking, 2–4 minutes, depending on the size of the leaves. Scoop the leaves out with a strainer or kitchen tongs and briefly shake off the cooking water or drain in a colander, then let them cool and dry more thoroughly on kitchen towels or place them on a platter and pat dry with paper towels.

2. Rinse the rice in a sieve under cold water. Shake briefly to drain and transfer to a large bowl. In a medium skillet, sauté the garlic in the oil over medium heat until just pale gold, about 2 minutes. Add the artichokes and cook, stirring, for 3 minutes to marry the flavors. Season with salt and pepper, then

transfer the contents of the skillet to the rice, along with the dill, mint, lemon zest, allspice, and additional salt and pepper to taste. Mix the ingredients well.

3. Stuff the chard. Place the leaves on a work surface, shiny side up. They should be easy to roll, but with very mature leaves, you may find it necessary to cut out a hard little wedge of stem at the base. Spoon some filling (from 1–2 heaping teaspoons up to ¼ cup depending on the size of the leaf) in the center of each leaf, near the stem end. Fold the stem end of the leaf over the filling, then fold in the two sides. Now roll up the leaf, jelly-roll fashion, to form a neat little roll. The rolls should be compact, but don't roll them too tightly: You must allow a little space for the rice to expand.

4. Prepare the sauce. Slice the reserved chard stems into approximately 3-inch lengths, and line a 6-quart Dutch oven or large, heavy saucepan with them. Place the chard rolls close together on top of the stems, seam side down, in layers. Season each layer well with salt, pepper, and some of the chopped garlic. In a small bowl, stir together 1 ½ cups of water, the olive oil, lemon juice, and dried mint and pour evenly over the rolls. Place a heatproof plate just smaller than the diameter of the pan on top of the rolls and weight the plate down with several more heatproof plates.

5. Bring the liquid to a boil, cover the pan, and simmer the chard rolls over very low heat, checking every once in a while to see if more liquid is needed, for 2–2 ½ hours, or until the rice tastes cooked through, the rolls are very tender, and most of the liquid is absorbed.

6. Remove the pan from the heat. The stuffed leaves will seem close to falling apart, but don't worry. They will firm up nicely as they cool, still weighted down and covered. When they are room temperature, remove the plates, pour off any remaining liquid, and arrange the rolls on a platter. Discard the chard stems (or nibble them for a delicious cook's perk). Cover and refrigerate the stuffed chard rolls until cold so they will firm up further.

7. Sephardi Jews serve meatless stuffed leaves (chard, grape, and spinach) chilled or at room temperature, but not icy cold, which would obscure the delicate herbal flavor. (Meat-filled leaves, however, are served hot.) Arrange the rolls on individual appetizer plates with lemon wedges or present them as part of a platter of appetizers. Like stuffed cabbage, they are even better the next day after the flavors mingle and unfold.

YIELD: About 6 servings

COOK'S NOTE: For a tart-sweet variation, substitute prune juice for the 1 ½ cups water in the sauce. And instead of mint, flavor it with 1 tablespoon plus 2 teaspoons pomegranate molasses and 1 tablespoon brown sugar.

CARAMELIZED ONION AND CARROT TSIMMES WITH CANDIED GINGER

Aunt Celia had red hair the color of carrot tsimmes cooked in
honey and darkened with cinnamon.

—FAYE MOSKOWITZ, *AND THE BRIDGE IS LOVE*

Spicy, sweet, and tangy-sour notes harmonize beautifully in this meatless vegetable-fruit mélange. Serve it as a side dish or offer it as a condiment with chicken, turkey, or brisket.

3 tablespoons mild olive or vegetable oil	*1 tablespoon minced candied ginger*
1½ pounds onions (preferably red), thinly sliced (6 cups)	*1 cup fresh orange juice*
	1 tablespoon grated orange zest
Salt and freshly ground black pepper	*1 tablespoon fragrant honey*
4–5 medium carrots, scraped or peeled and sliced (2 cups)	*¼ teaspoon ground cinnamon*
	1 cup pitted prunes, quartered

In a 10- to 12-inch heavy skillet, heat the oil and add the onions. Salt and pepper lightly, and stir well. Cook, covered, over very low heat, stirring occasionally so the mixture does not burn, for 30–40 minutes, or until the onions are meltingly tender and almost transparent. Add the carrots, ginger, orange juice and zest, honey, cinnamon, and additional salt and pepper to taste. Raise the heat to medium-high and bring the mixture to a boil. Let it bubble for a few minutes, then reduce the heat and continue cooking, uncovered, stirring occasionally, until the carrots are tender and the onions are golden and syrupy, about 15 minutes. Add the prunes and simmer for 5–10 minutes longer, or until the prunes are quite soft. If necessary, boil for a few minutes over high heat to evaporate any liquid remaining in the pan. Adjust the seasoning. Keep the mixture warm, covered, until ready to serve. The tsimmes tastes best if allowed to stand for at least 10 minutes to allow the flavors to meld (or prepare in advance and just reheat before serving.)

YIELD: About 6 servings

MAPLE-ROASTED PEARS WITH PASSION FRUIT AND/OR FRESH RASPBERRY SAUCE

PAREVE

Fresh autumn-fruit desserts—from sumptuous apple cakes to svelte compotes—are traditional on Sukkot. For me, a light fruit dessert that is festive and satisfying without being rich makes a wonderfully renewing finale to the multi-course meal.

In this recipe I roast maple-glazed pears to give them a buttery depth and luxurious mouth feel with no added fat. More, perhaps, than any other fruit, passion fruit—evoking puckery citrus, berries, and lush tropical fruits with unknown names—tastes of faraway places. I like to add a few spoonfuls of the exotically perfumed juice to dress up the homey pears. If you cannot find passion fruit, set the pears on a garnet ribbon of fresh tart raspberry sauce.

Or do what I do—serve both.

Avocado, canola, or other flavorless oil, for filming the pan	*¼ teaspoon salt*
	1 tablespoon fresh lemon juice
3 large, firm-ripe Bosc pears (about 1½ pounds), peeled, halved, and cored	*2 ripe passion fruits (2½–3 ounces) (see Cook's Note) and/or 1 cup (about 6 ounces) fresh raspberries plus ¼ cup fresh orange juice and 3 tablespoons packed light brown sugar*
⅓ cup pure maple syrup	
½ teaspoon vanilla extract	

1. Preheat the oven to 500°F.

2. Very lightly film a 10- to 12-inch heavy, ovenproof skillet with oil and set it over medium-high heat until the oil is hot and shimmery but not smoking. Add the pears, cored side down, and cook for 2–3 minutes. Lift the pears with a spatula: The bottoms should be speckled or rimmed light bronze. (If not, cook for another minute or two.)

3. Turn the pears, then transfer the pan to the oven. Roast the pears, turning them 2 or 3 times (with a spatula, not tongs), for 7–8 minutes, until both sides are deeply bronzed in places, and they are beginning to caramelize. Stir together the maple syrup, vanilla, and ⅛ teaspoon salt and spoon half of the mixture over the pears. Continue roasting for 2–3 minutes longer, then turn the pears and coat the other side with the remaining syrup. Roast for another 2–3 minutes, or until both sides are a rich butterscotch color, caramelized, and tender enough to pierce easily with a thin knife or skewer.

4. Transfer the pears with a slotted spoon to a glass or enamel pie plate or baking dish just large enough to hold them in a single layer. Add the lemon juice and remaining ⅛ teaspoon salt to the syrupy juices in the pan. Cook over medium heat, stirring constantly, for a minute or two, to marry the ingredients. Spoon the mixture evenly over the pears.

5. If you are using the passion fruits: Set a small sieve over a bowl and cut the fruit in half. Working over the bowl to catch any drips of the precious juice, scrape all the yellow-green pulp and the seeds into the sieve. Rub the fruit through the sieve with the back of a spoon or a fork to extract every bit of the juice. Spoon the juice over the caramelized pears, tossing them gently so they are evenly coated. Cover the dish with plastic wrap and refrigerate for at least 3 hours or overnight to mingle the flavors.

If you are using the raspberries: Put them in a blender or food processor with the orange juice and brown sugar and puree until smooth. Strain the puree through a fine sieve to remove the seeds and store, covered, in the refrigerator until serving time. (It will keep for up to 3 days, refrigerated.)

6. To serve: If you prepared the raspberry sauce, spoon it in an attractive ribbon across each of six dessert plates. Arrange a pear half over the ribbon (or in the center of the plate if you did not make the sauce), and spoon some of the syrupy juices over the pears.

YIELD: 6 servings

COOK'S NOTE: The leathery rind on ripe passion fruits will be deeply wrinkled. Keep unripe fruits at room temperature for a few days, until the skin is wrinkled.

If you are not serving the raspberry sauce, a garnish of pomegranate seeds makes a lovely, seasonal, tart-sweet finish.

HANUKKAH

An eight-day festival beginning 25 Kislev

(late November or December)

❧❧❧❧❧❧❧❧❧❧❧❧❧

> The wicks in the potatoes, our Hanukkah candles, smoked and sputtered and
> finally extinguished. My mother said to me, "Go wash up and we'll eat potatoes
> with goose fat. In honor of Hanukkah, I splurged and bought a jar of goose fat—
> fresh, delicious goose fat."
> —SHOLOM ALEICHEM, "BENNY'S LUCK"

This black and nearly moonless night will be long and chilled with winter's breath.

Against this darkness, Jews will light a candle. And at sunset every evening, they will add yet another candle, until eight days later, at Hanukkah's end, their ritual lamps, or menorahs, are ablaze with orange-gold flames.

Hanukkah, the Festival of Lights, celebrates deliverance from the darkness of religious persecution. The Syrian king from the Seleucid dynasty, Antiochus IV Epiphanes, attempting to impose Hellenistic culture over the various ethnic minorities in his empire, had outlawed all other religions. Those who practiced Judaism risked torture, even death. On 25 Kislev, 167 B.C., Antiochus defiled the Temple, polluting the altar with pagan sacrifices, and desecrating the ritual objects.

The Maccabees rose in revolt. At last, they were able to recover Jerusalem. On 25 Kislev three years later, they cleansed and purified the Temple, rededicating it to God. But the single cruse of untouched oil they found was only enough to burn for one day. Instead, miraculously, the tiny amount lasted for eight days, time enough for them to sanctify a fresh supply.

Remembering these events, Jewish families kindle at least one set of lights, illumining them with a shammash, or an extra "helper" candle. Lights are placed from right to left, like the Hebrew script; the candle furthest left, representing the current night, is always lit first.

Hanukkah is a home-centered celebration and children are encouraged to participate by lighting their own menorahs. The unique menorahs of nineteenth-century Alsace featured places for up to thirty-two lights, so many family members could light candles at the same time.

The burning menorah is a transcendent image that resonates powerfully in the dead of winter, reflecting the triumph of faith over faithlessness and hope over despair. Poignant menorahs have been fashioned from wicks of tattered clothes lit in egg shells, scooped out potato halves, and even, in a concentration camp, a shoe polish tin with a bit of machine oil.

The original oil, of course, was pure, fragrant olive oil, and that is commemorated on the table. There are crisply fried treats, both sweet and savory, especially latkes, or pancakes, made from potatoes (dished up hot and glossed with sour cream, fresh fruit sauce, or a sprinkle of sugar) or luscious cheese latkes. The meats too are rich and fat: crackly-skinned goose or tender brisket with luscious gravy. Unlike many other Jewish dishes, these traditional foods were not designed to be prepared in advance, for although Hanukkah is widely celebrated among Jews, it is a "minor festival"—meaning that Jews are not prohibited from cooking or other forms of work.

After dinner the joyous mood continues with songs, games, and presents, accompanied by fresh-baked cookies and pastries, like rugelach brimming with golden caramels.

CHILDREN'S LATKES

Children adore latkes: a platterful means a party, whether eaten at home or served as part of a school multicultural holiday presentation. To make them extra-special, buy several plastic squeeze bottles—the kind used for ketchup and mustard. Fill with sour cream and different kinds of applesauce, and let the kids use them to design their own garnish on the latkes.

OTHER SUGGESTIONS
FOR HANUKKAH

My Mother's Fried Cauliflower (page 56)

Tangy Russian Cabbage Soup with Pot Roast—Beet Kreplach (page 71)

Oven-Fried Smoked Salmon Croquettes (page 101)

Braised Brisket with Thirty-six Cloves of Garlic (page 113)

Aromatic Marinated Brisket with Chestnuts (page 115)

Fried Chicken Cutlets, Italian-Jewish Style (page 132)

Kasha Varnishkes with Fried Eggplant, Mushrooms, and Onion Marmalade (page 160)

Caramel Rugelach (page 194)

Garlic-Rosemary Potato Latkes (page 206)

Lemon-Fried Chicken with Tart Salad Topping (page 340)

CREAMY POTATO-ONION LATKES

PAREVE OR DAIRY

They had a silver Hanukkah menorah full of the finest oil with a large shamash
candle ready to kindle the other wicks. Nothing but the best. From the kitchen one
could smell the heavenly aroma of freshly rendered goose fat.
"We're having latkes tonight," Benny told me as we stood at the door, and my
stomach rumbled with hunger!
—SHOLOM ALEICHEM, "BENNY'S LUCK"

It comes as no surprise that, as with other Jewish foods, there is no definitive way to make a potato latke. Most cooks use raw potatoes, but some grate boiled potatoes. And a few use a combination of both.

When made entirely of cooked potatoes, latkes, to my palate, are not latkes at all, but croquettes: they lack the requisite crunch and the deeply satisfying fried potato taste that are the hallmarks of the genus. But adding a little cooked potato to grated raw ones makes for lighter latkes, with real potato crust and soft centers (a trick I employed for the Onion-Crusted Light Potato Kugel, page 169, and that Irish cooks use in their potato pancake, boxty). While this combination latke is wonderful on its own with the traditional accompaniments, its lightness makes it an excellent candidate as well for a side dish served with substantial meats and poultry.

In this recipe, I swirl savory frizzled onions into the cooked potato before combining it with the grated raw potato. The latke fries up with a thin, crackly potato crust enclosing an airy, onion-luscious mashed potato center.

About 1¾–2 pounds russet (baking) or Yukon Gold potatoes, peeled	1 large egg
½ pound onions, chopped (2 cups)	1 teaspoon baking powder
2 tablespoons olive oil, plus additional for frying	Accompaniments: sour cream, yogurt cream (page 30), or labneh; a fruit sauce (pages 176–82); or plain applesauce
Salt and freshly ground black pepper	

---

1. Cut about one-third of the potatoes into small chunks and boil them in a saucepan of salted water until tender. Drain and mash until very smooth (no lumps wanted here) by forcing through a food mill, ricer, or colander into a large bowl.

2. While the potatoes are cooking, sauté the onions in 2 tablespoons oil over medium-high heat, stirring, until golden and just speckled with brown, 10–12 minutes. Season the still-hot onions generously with salt and pepper and stir them into the mashed potatoes. Let the mixture cool.

3. Coarsely grate the remaining potatoes in a food processor fitted with the grating disk, or grate by hand. Put the grated potatoes in a colander, rinse under cool water, then use your hands or a wooden spoon to extract as much moisture as possible.

4. Add the grated potatoes to the mashed ones. Whisk in the egg, baking powder, and additional salt and pepper to taste. Mix well until thoroughly combined.

5. Using about ¼ cup for each latke, form the batter into small, flat patties about ½ inch thick and 3–3½ inches wide. Heat about ¼ inch of oil in a 10- to 12-inch heavy skillet until hot but not smoking. Fry the latkes a few at a time; crowding the pan will make the latkes soggy.

6. Watch the heat carefully, reducing it if necessary when the latkes are golden and crisp on the bottom. To prevent the oil from splattering, use two spatulas (or a spatula and a large spoon), to turn the latkes gently. Fry until crisp and golden on the other side. If necessary, add more oil to the pan, but wait until it is hot before adding the latkes.

7. It's best to flip the latkes only once, so that they don't absorb too much oil during cooking. So, before turning, lift the latkes slightly with the spatula to make sure the underside is crisp and brown.

8. Drain the latkes as they are done on paper towels or untreated brown paper bags. If necessary, keep the latkes warm in a single layer on an ovenproof platter or baking sheet lined with paper towels in a 200°F oven while you prepare the rest. But they are at their best served as soon as possible.

YIELD: About 4 servings

COOK'S NOTE: These are also delicious prepared with about 2 ounces of skinny smoked salmon slivers and 2 tablespoons minced fresh dill stirred into the batter, and fried as above. Or serve smoked salmon or Smoked Whitefish and Fennel Salad (page 249) on top of the latkes.

CELERY ROOT–POTATO LATKES

PAREVE

Early in the afternoon, she would begin grating the potatoes on a vicious four-sided grater, the invention of some fiendish anti-Semite who must have seen the opportunity to maim half the Jewish population each December.

—FAYE MOSKOWITZ, *AND THE BRIDGE IS LOVE*

The food processor ended the grater Reign of Terror that marked the Festival of Latkes.

But the four-sided grater offered one advantage (aside from the bits of torn knuckles so many grandmothers swore made their latkes that much more delicious): Part of the potatoes could be shredded on the coarse side, to make a crispy crust, and the rest grated rather fine, to ensure a little creamy layer within. All coarse would mean all crunch—texture without an intense potato taste—while completely fine produced latkes with too much mush beneath their thin crisp coat, causing them to absorb huge amounts of oil.

The solution is simple: Grate the potatoes, using the coarse shredding disk, then process about one-third of them to a coarse puree. Result: crisp, crunchy, and creamy, all at once.

To impart an earthy, vegetal depth to the latkes, combine the potato batter with other grated root vegetables, like beets, Jerusalem artichokes, parsley root, or parsnips. For this recipe, I add celery root, underscoring its herbaceous, nutty flavor with crushed celery seeds.

Celery root–potato latkes are excellent with most meats and poultry, and particularly good with brisket. Or serve them with sour cream, yogurt cream, or crème fraîche at a dairy meal. For a delicious appetizer or brunch dish, top these latkes with Smoked Whitefish and Fennel Salad (page 249), or some sliced smoked fish, sour cream, and dill.

---

1 medium-large celery root (1–1½ pounds, without leaves), trimmed and peeled

About 1 pound Yukon Gold or russet (baking) potatoes, peeled

1 large egg, beaten

1 teaspoon salt, or to taste

¼ teaspoon freshly ground black pepper, or to taste

½ teaspoon baking powder

1 large garlic clove, minced

½ teaspoon celery seeds, crushed

2 tablespoons matzoh meal or all-purpose flour

Olive oil, for frying

Accompaniments: sour cream, yogurt cream (page 30), labneh, or crème fraîche; or brisket or smoked fish

---

1. Shred the celery root, using the grating disk in a food processor. You should have about 2 cups. Transfer to a colander.

2. With the same disk, grate the potatoes. Transfer about half the potatoes to the celery root in the colander and use your hands or a wooden spoon to press out as much moisture as possible from the vegetables in the colander.

3. Remove the grating disk from the processor and replace with the steel blade. Process the remaining grated potatoes, using a pulse motion, until roughly pureed. Transfer to a large bowl, add the coarsely grated vegetables, the egg, salt, pepper, baking powder, garlic, celery seeds, and matzoh meal or flour. Mix well until thoroughly combined.

4. In a 10- to 12-inch heavy skillet (cast iron is ideal), heat about ¼ inch of oil over high heat until hot but not smoking. Using a ¼-cup measure, drop the batter into the pan, then flatten the latkes with a spatula. Cook no more than 4 or 5 latkes at a time; crowding the pan will make the latkes soggy.

5. Regulate the heat carefully, reducing it to medium as the latkes fry until golden and crisp on the bottom, about 4 minutes. To prevent the oil from splattering, use two spatulas (or a spatula and a large spoon) to turn the latkes carefully. Fry until crisp and golden on the other side. (It's best to flip the latkes only once, so that they don't absorb too much oil. So, before turning, lift the latkes slightly with the spatula to make sure the underside is crisp and brown.) As the latkes are done, transfer them to paper towels or untreated brown paper bags to drain.

6. Continue making latkes in the same manner until all the batter is used. If necessary, add more oil to the pan, but always allow the oil to get hot before frying a new batch.

7. When needed, keep the latkes warm in a single layer on an ovenproof platter lined with paper towels in a 200°F oven. But they are at their best served as soon as possible.

YIELD: 4–5 servings

CRISPY SHALLOT LATKES
WITH SUGAR DUSTING

PAREVE OR DAIRY

Not Mallomars, S'Mores, or Rice Krispie Treats. My secret childhood sweet was crispy, hot potato latkes sprinkled with sugar, the way my grandmother made them. She knew that a latke's beauty is fleeting: irresistible hot, they turn charmless and sodden cold. Why rush along the process with cool toppings, like sour cream and applesauce? Besides, the unlikely alliance of flavors still delights, even after all these years when former loves, like sweet-and-sour stuffed cabbage and red-hot cinnamon candies, no longer give me a tickle.

Instead of decreasing the onion—or eliminating it altogether—as do many Jewish cooks who serve their latkes with sugar, my grandmother laced her latkes lavishly with it. The spicy onion contrasts with the sugar, creating layers of flavor that somehow heighten the potato taste. I use shallots here because they are more deeply flavored than onions, and you need fewer to achieve an intense onion taste. Also, adding a lot of onion, which contains so much moisture, might make the latkes soggy or absorb too much oil. With shallots, the potatoes remain crispy.

Don't go overboard with the sugar—a little goes a long way. Use superfine or regular granulated sugar, not confectioners', and sprinkle it on when the latkes are very hot so it doesn't form a powdery cloak, but really melts in. Or serve the latkes unadorned, and offer guests pretty little salt shakers filled with sugar.

You can, of course, have the latkes with the more traditional sour cream or yogurt cream and a fresh fruit sauce, but do try the sugar once.

---

1 ½ cups peeled and thinly sliced shallots

2 tablespoons unsalted butter or fine-quality olive oil

About 1 ½ pounds russet (baking) or Yukon Gold potatoes, peeled

1 large egg, beaten

About ¾ teaspoon salt, or to taste

¼ teaspoon freshly ground black pepper, or to taste

½ teaspoon baking powder

1 tablespoon matzoh meal or all-purpose flour

Olive oil, for frying

Sugar, preferably superfine, for dusting

---

1. In a heavy, medium saucepan, cook the shallots in the butter or olive oil over moderate heat, stirring occasionally, until golden and crispy, about 15 minutes. Drain on paper towels and let cool.

2. Coarsely shred the potatoes, using the grating disk in a food processor. Transfer the potatoes to a colander or strainer and use your hands or a wooden spoon to press out as much moisture as possible. (Don't bother washing out the food processor.)

3. Remove the grating disk from the processor and replace with the steel blade. Return about one-third of the shredded potatoes to the food processor and roughly puree, using the pulse motion. Transfer the mixture to a large bowl, add the remaining shredded potatoes and the egg, salt, pepper, baking powder, and matzoh meal or flour. Stir in the shallots. Mix until thoroughly combined.

4. In a 10- to 12-inch heavy skillet (cast iron is ideal), heat about ¼ inch of oil over high heat until hot but not smoking. Using a ¼-cup measure, drop the batter into the pan; then flatten the latkes with a spatula. Cook no more than 4 or 5 latkes at a time; crowding the pan will make the latkes soggy.

5. Regulate the heat carefully as the latkes fry until golden and crisp on the bottom, about 4 minutes. To prevent the oil from splattering, use two spatulas (or a spatula and a large spoon) to turn the latkes carefully. Fry until crisp and golden on the other side. (Avoid turning the latkes more than once or they will absorb too much oil. Before turning, lift the latkes slightly with the spatula to make sure the underside is crisp and brown.)

6. Transfer the cooked latkes to paper towels or untreated brown paper bags to drain and sprinkle them lightly with sugar (I use a scant ½ teaspoon for each). Continue frying latkes in the same way until all the batter is used. If necessary, add more oil to the pan, but always allow the oil to get hot before frying a new batch.

7. If you must, keep the latkes warm in a single layer on an ovenproof platter lined with paper towels in a 200°F oven, but they are best eaten straightaway.

8. Pass additional sugar when serving (little salt shakers filled with sugar are attractive and make it less likely that a guest will dump an inedible amount of sugar on a latke), and if desired, accompany the latkes with sour cream or yogurt cream (page 30) and a fresh fruit sauce (pages 176–82).

YIELD: 4 servings

SCALLION LATKES WITH
SCALLION DIPPING BRUSHES

◆◆◆◆◆◆◆◆◆◆◆◆◆◆◆◆◆◆◆◆◆◆◆◆

Hot, plump, they glisten, the latkes, with pearls of fat, and they jump
on the fire like newborn little babies when they are slapped with the hand.
We watch the cook as though she were a magician.
"Havah, the thick latke is for me, isn't it?"
—BELLA CHAGALL, *BURNING LIGHTS*

Not even Merlin, though, could make the magic of a potato pancake last the full eight days of the holiday, and after a while, my search for something different turns into an obsession.

These scallion latkes, reminiscent of those savory little pancakes served as *dim sum*, make use of ancient Chinese wisdom. The bracing, clean flavors of ginger, vinegar, and soy provide a sparkling antidote to the oily richness, as well as welcome respite from the ubiquitous sour cream. Of course, if you prefer, you can still serve the latkes with sour cream or yogurt cream (page 29).

SCALLION BRUSHES

10–12 thin scallions

Ice water

DIPPING SAUCE

2 tablespoons soy sauce

2 tablespoons orange juice

1 tablespoon rice, Chinese black, or cider
  vinegar

2 teaspoons Asian toasted sesame oil

1 teaspoon peeled and grated fresh ginger

Chili oil to taste (optional)

LATKES

2–2½ bunches of scallions, white and light
  green parts, trimmed and thinly sliced
  (2½ cups)

2 tablespoons mild olive or vegetable oil, plus
  additional oil for frying

1 teaspoon peeled and minced fresh ginger

1½ teaspoons minced fresh garlic

1½ teaspoons soy sauce

About 1½ pounds Yukon Gold or russet
  (baking) potatoes, peeled

½ teaspoon baking powder

1 large egg

Salt and freshly ground black pepper to taste

2 tablespoons matzoh meal or all-purpose flour

1. Make the scallion brushes. Cut off and discard the roots and all but 3 inches of the green part of the scallions. Using scissors or a small paring knife, cut slits about ½ inch deep into both sections of each scallion stalk, creating a fringe. Carefully fan out the fringed edges. Place the scallions in a bowl of ice water, and refrigerate for 2 hours or until the fringed edges curl up.

2. Prepare the dipping sauce. Stir together all the ingredients and let the flavors mingle for at least 30 minutes.

3. Start the latkes. In a large skillet, sauté the scallions over moderately high heat in the oil until tender and just beginning to brown at the edges. Stir in the ginger, garlic, and soy sauce, and cook, lifting and turning, for 2–3 minutes. Remove with a slotted spoon and set aside to cool briefly. Make the latkes following the directions for Crispy Shallot Latkes with Sugar Dusting on page 278, stirring in the sautéed scallions instead of the shallots. (You will need salt here—the soy sauce merely flavors the scallions. Putting in enough soy sauce would make the latkes too wet. Figure about 1 teaspoon of salt.)

4. When ready to serve, pat the scallion brushes dry. Guests should use the brushes to coat each latke with dipping sauce, then top the latke with the brush.

YIELD: 4 servings

CHEESE LATKES WITH FRESH PERSIMMON SAUCE

DAIRY

Crisp potato latkes are the taste of Hanukkah for most Ashkenazi Jews. But the first latkes, according to many food historians, were probably made of cheese. Today, latkes based on sweet curd cheeses—farmer, pot, and cottage—are still popular for Hanukkah and Passover as well, for they are usually thickened with a touch of matzoh meal, not flour.

Delicate and dairy-clean tasting, this version begs for a fresh complement of bright-tasting fruit. Instead of the traditional syrup or preserves, which would overpower the natural milky sweetness, I prepare this seasonal persimmon sauce. Colored the glowing orange of menorah flames, it couldn't be fresher—or simpler. Just puree the raw pulp and season it lightly with lime and maple.

If you can't get persimmons, serve these latkes with the equally orange Intense Apricot Applesauce (page 176). Or serve both.

The latkes make a marvelous breakfast, brunch, light lunch, or snack. Or serve them as a starter or finish to a more elaborate dairy meal.

PERSIMMON SAUCE

3 medium, dead-ripe persimmons, preferably
  the jelly-soft, acorn-shaped Hachiya type
  (see Cook's Note)
1–2 pinches of salt
2–3 teaspoons fresh lime or lemon juice
1–2 tablespoons pure maple syrup

LATKES

½ pound farmer cheese (a 7.5-ounce package is
  fine)

2 tablespoons cream cheese
4 large eggs, separated
½ teaspoon vanilla extract
½ cup matzoh meal
¼ teaspoon salt
½ teaspoon ground cinnamon

Unsalted butter and mild vegetable oil, like
  avocado or canola, for frying

---

1. Prepare the sauce. Cut off and discard the leaf end of the persimmons and slice the fruits in half. To puree the fruit, scoop out the flesh and press it through a food mill or sieve. For less mess—with just a bit more elbow grease—puree the washed fruit unpeeled; the peels will remain trapped by the mill or sieve. Add the salt, lime or lemon juice, and maple syrup to taste. Refrigerate the sauce to marry the flavors.

2. Make the latkes. In a food processor, combine the farmer and cream cheeses, egg yolks, and vanilla and process until well-blended and smooth. Add the matzoh meal, salt, and cinnamon, and process until thoroughly incorporated. Transfer the batter to a bowl. In a separate bowl, whip the egg whites until they form firm peaks. Gently fold the egg whites into the batter.

3. Heat 2 tablespoons each of butter and oil in a heavy 10- to 12-inch skillet over medium heat until hot but not smoking. Drop the batter by heaping tablespoonfuls and fry until the bottoms are golden brown, 2–3 minutes. Using two spatulas, turn and cook until lightly browned on the other side, 1–3 minutes. Remove and keep warm on a heated platter or baking sheet in a 200°F oven. Continue making latkes with the remaining batter. Add more butter and oil only if necessary, always allowing the fat to get hot before frying more latkes. Keep an eye on the heat to make sure that the butter does not burn.

4. Serve the latkes hot and pass the persimmon sauce.

YIELD: 3–4 servings

COOK'S NOTE: With Hachiya persimmons, ripeness is all: the difference between mouth-puckeringly astringent and voluptuously sweet. The rounded, squat Fuyu persimmon contains no harsh tannins and is never astringent; though excellent sliced, it will not make as luscious a puree. Choose meltingly soft Hachiyas with deeply colored, unbroken skin.

GREEK-INSPIRED CHEESE LATKES

DAIRY

On Hanukkah we remember not just the courageous military exploits of the Maccabees: Since the Middle Ages, it has also been the custom to commemorate the derring-do of a fearless woman.

When the ruthless Assyrian general Holofernes laid siege to the city of Bethulia, a beautiful, devout widow, Judith, devised a scheme based on what she knew best—food. Seduced by her loveliness, Holofernes invited her into his tent, where he lay under a canopy woven with purple silk, gold, and emeralds. There she fed him the salty cheese she had brought. A morsel of cheese, then a quaff of wine to slake his salty throat. And with each bite of cheese, his thirst grew ever more demanding. At last the wicked general fell into a drunken sleep, whereupon the resourceful widow grabbed a saber and beheaded him. She put the head in a bag and quietly stole out of camp.

Early the next day, the head was impaled on the city walls. Holofernes' frightened soldiers fled, leaving behind their vast plundered riches, and the siege of Bethulia was broken.

Dairy products, like cheese latkes, are frequently eaten on Hanukkah in memory of Judith's deed. Here the feta, an echo of her salty cheese, is offset not by wine, but the fresh tastes of green herbs and lemon.

½ pound feta cheese (a solid, unbroken chunk)
½ pound farmer cheese (a 7.5-ounce package is fine)
½ cup chopped fresh herbs, such as dill, scallions, mint, flat-leaf parsley (choose at least two kinds)
1 large egg beaten with 1 tablespoon fresh lemon juice (you may need an additional egg, so have more on hand)

1 cup matzoh crumbs (page 25—egg matzohs work particularly well here) or matzoh meal, seasoned with freshly ground pepper to taste and ½ teaspoon crushed dried oregano
Olive oil, for frying
Lemon quarters and additional chopped herbs, for garnish

---

1. Keep each cheese refrigerated until you are ready to start preparing the latkes, so it will be as firm as possible. Pat the cheese dry with paper towels. Using a sharp knife, cut each cheese into 8 thin slices. If a slice crumbles as you are cutting, pat or mold it back into shape with your hands.

2. Take a slice of feta, sprinkle it with 1 tablespoon of the herbs, and cover with a slice of farmer cheese. Use your hands to form the latke into a smooth, flat patty.

3. Dip the latke first into the egg and then the matzoh crumbs or matzoh meal. Continue making the latkes with the remaining cheese and herbs. Refrigerate the latkes for at least 30 minutes.

4. Heat ¼ inch of oil in a 10- to 12-inch heavy skillet over high heat until hot but not smoking. Fry the latkes, in batches if necessary, turning once (using two spatulas if needed to prevent splattering), until golden on both sides. These latkes must be fried quickly over high heat (medium-high heat, if recommended by the skillet manufacturer) so the cheese does not melt.

5. Drain briefly on paper towels or other absorbent paper. Serve immediately, garnished with lemon and sprinkled with herbs.

YIELD: About 4 servings

On Hanukkah, wealthy Jews dined on roast goose, and others savored latkes sizzled in rich goose fat. (*Jewish Man with Goose,* by Ilya Schor. Woodcut, c. 1950.)

BLACK GRAPE, GOAT CHEESE, AND NOODLE LATKES WITH FRAGRANT HONEY

DAIRY

I had wandered several blocks from our Philadelphia hotel. The December sky was already purple and my toes frozen numb when I found the tiny bakery and hobbled in. Enveloped by the smells of strong coffee and a dazzling array of freshly baked focaccia, I immediately felt that all was right with the world.

The focaccia I chose was an unusual interplay of exuberant Mediterranean tastes—rosemary, goat cheese, midnight blue-black grapes and walnuts—all held in delicate balance by a final drizzle of fragrant honey.

I was so intrigued by the combination of flavors, I wanted to repeat them in another dish. I was thinking of a noodle pudding, but since it was so close to Hanukkah, I decided to update a traditional noodle latke recipe.

Honey is used here as a seasoning, not merely a sweetener. For superior results, select a honey with complex, highly aromatic notes: an herbal one, like Greek thyme or rosemary or musky, slightly bitter chestnut honey.

Delicious and not at all difficult to prepare, the latkes do require a bit of special attention. Since heat can make cheese soft and runny, work quickly shaping and frying the latkes to ensure that the cheese does not ooze out in the pan. Or try shaping the latkes, then chilling them again before frying.

Excellent for brunch, lunch, or as part of a dairy meal, these latkes also make a fine conclusion to a light supper.

Salt

4 ounces medium egg noodles (these should be flat; it is difficult to form these latkes with twisted, corkscrew-type noodles)

2 large eggs

¼ cup walnuts, lightly toasted and coarsely chopped

1 tablespoon plus 2 teaspoons finely chopped fresh rosemary

Freshly ground black pepper

4 ounces fresh (not aged) goat cheese, chilled

1 cup (about 7 ounces) black grapes, such as Muscat, seeded and cut into quarters

Unsalted butter and mild vegetable oil, such as avocado or canola, for frying

Fragrant honey (see recipe headnote)

---

1. Bring 2–3 quarts of water and 1 teaspoon salt to a rapid boil in a large pot. Add the noodles and cook until just tender but still firm. Meanwhile, in a large bowl, whisk together the eggs, walnuts, rosemary, and salt and pepper to taste. Drain the cooked noodles thoroughly, let them cool slightly, then combine them well with the egg mixture. Cover the bowl and refrigerate the mixture until cold and firm, about 1 hour. The noodles will have absorbed all the egg. Cut the cold goat cheese into bits and add it to the bowl, together with the grape quarters. Mix well.

2. Take about ⅓ cup of the mixture, making sure it includes some cheese and grape pieces, and shape it into a patty. Place it on a platter and continue forming patties until you have used up all the batter. Handle the patties carefully—they will be somewhat fragile—and always be sure each contains some of the cheese and grapes. If time permits, refrigerate the patties to firm them up before frying.

3. In a 10- to 12-inch heavy skillet, heat 2 tablespoons each of butter and oil over high heat until hot but not smoking. Working in batches, if necessary, add the latkes. Flatten each slightly with a spatula and fry quickly until golden brown, about 3 minutes. Turn carefully, using 2 spatulas if necessary, and brown on the other side. Avoid turning more than once. Add more butter and oil if needed to fry the rest, but be sure to let the fat get hot before adding the patties.

4. Drizzle some honey on the hot latkes and serve immediately.

YIELD: 4 servings

FISH IN POTATO LATKE CRUST
WITH HORSERADISH CREAM

PAREVE/DAIRY

It's not the potato latke (pancake)—or even a latke at all—that is required eating on Hanukkah. It is food fried in oil.

Each year, however, brings a new slew of picture books on Tante something-or-other's latkes, and for many Jews, especially the children, it's hard to sever the Hanukkah-latke connection.

But crisp, fried latkes do not a meal make, though many nights they consume all my family's appetite and my kitchen time as well.

At such times, I dip fish fillets into the latke batter and serve forth a one-pan fish-and-chips, Jewish style.

About 1 ½ pounds russet (baking) or Yukon
  Gold potatoes, scrubbed or peeled and cut into
  chunks
1 medium onion, peeled and quartered
2 large eggs
2 large garlic cloves, coarsely chopped
1 tablespoon chopped fresh dill
1 teaspoon cider vinegar
1 teaspoon salt, or to taste
¼ teaspoon black pepper, or to taste

2 tablespoons matzoh meal or all-purpose flour
Olive or vegetable oil, for frying
Flour for dredging
2 pounds flounder, lemon sole, or similar white-
  fleshed fish fillets, wiped with a damp paper
  towel and patted dry (if the fillets are not
  small, cut them into long strips, so they will be
  easier to batter)
Accompaniments: Horseradish Cream
  (page 289); lemon wedges

---

1. In a food processor, using the grating disk, coarsely grate the potatoes together with the onion. Transfer the mixture to a strainer and drain it well, using your hands to squeeze out all the excess moisture. (Don't wash out the processor.) Replace the grating disk with the steel blade. Return the grated mixture to the processor and add the eggs, garlic, dill, vinegar, salt, pepper, and matzoh meal or flour. Process to a smooth batter. Put the batter in a large bowl.

2. Heat ¼ inch of oil in a 10- to 12-inch heavy skillet until hot but not smoking. Spread some flour on a large sheet of wax paper or a plate. Dredge a fillet in the flour, covering it completely and shaking off the excess, then dip it into the latke batter, coating well on both sides. Quickly slide it into the hot oil. Repeat, frying a few pieces at a time, and making sure you do not crowd the pan. Fry until browned on both sides and cooked through (exact time will vary, depending on the thickness of the

fish). Drain on paper towels or untreated brown paper bags. Serve with horseradish cream and lemon wedges.

YIELD: 6–8 servings

HORSERADISH CREAM   DAIRY

½ cup peeled, finely diced cucumber
Salt
1 cup yogurt cream (page 29) or sour cream
  (plain yogurt will be too watery)
1 large garlic clove, minced and mashed to a
  paste with ¼ teaspoon salt

2 tablespoons chopped fresh dill
1 tablespoon drained bottled white horseradish,
  or to taste
Freshly ground black pepper

Start the horseradish cream at least 30 minutes before serving to develop the flavors. Sprinkle the cucumber with ¼ teaspoon salt. Let stand for 10 minutes. Wrap in paper towels or a kitchen towel and squeeze out as much liquid as possible. In a small bowl, combine the cucumber with the other ingredients. Adjust the seasoning to taste. You can refrigerate the horseradish cream, but let it come to room temperature before serving.

YIELD: About 1 cup

APRICOT- AND ORANGE-SCENTED
GOOSE WITH ROASTED GARLIC

Dickens's Tiny Tim wasn't the only one clamoring for a fat, juicy roast goose on his holiday table. Alsatian as well as Central and Eastern European Jews who could afford a dinner of poultry to celebrate winter Sabbaths were particularly fond of goose, especially for the festive Friday night meal that fell during Hanukkah.

No golden eggs did these geese supply, but something better: streams of molten ivory schmaltz, rendered fat. Enough for delectably crisp Hanukkah potato pancakes, with plenty left over to be sealed in ritually cleansed jars for use at Passover.

Like most Sabbath foods, the succulent bird was chockablock with garlic, the ancient aromatic love potion enlisted to make sure the Friday night connubial duties would be performed.

The passion for garlic still smolders, but today a fatty bird bespeaks a déclassé cook.

There are several methods for removing most of the fat from a goose. The so-called Peking Duck technique—immersing the bird in boiling water to open its pores and then drying the skin, sometimes with a hair-dryer—reduces much of the thick fat layer. But it entails finding a pot huge enough to submerge a 10-pound bird, and worse, washing it clean of goose fat afterward. Not to mention the dryer.

I use a simpler method. First work your hands under the skin to pull out all the loose fat. Then douse the skin with boiling water, vinegar, and honey to melt some of the subcutaneous fat, and pierce all over so the fat will exude. Piquant orange and apricot flavoring rubbed under the skin permeates the flesh and parries the richness.

One 10- to 12-pound goose

1 cup cider vinegar

1 tablespoon honey

1 head of garlic

3–4 tablespoons finely julienned orange or
  tangerine zest

6–8 dried apricots (preferably tart), quartered,
  plumped in boiling water for 15 minutes, and
  drained

2 tablespoons chopped fresh rosemary

1 tablespoon juniper berries, crushed

1 tablespoon olive oil

Salt and freshly ground black pepper

2 cinnamon sticks

GRAVY

1 tablespoon olive oil

The reserved neck, wingtips, and giblets from
  the goose

½ cup chopped shallots

½ cup scraped or peeled and chopped carrots

1½ teaspoons chopped garlic, plus 4 large garlic
  cloves, peeled

½ cup cider vinegar or apple brandy

1 tablespoon honey

3 cups chicken broth, preferably homemade
  (page 63), or good-quality, low-sodium
  canned

1 teaspoon juniper berries, crushed

½ teaspoon peppercorns, crushed
¼ cup diced apricots (preferably tart), plumped
  in 1 cup boiling water until soft
  (this will take about 30 minutes, depending
  on dryness of fruit) drained, and soaking
  liquid reserved

½ cup fresh orange juice
1 teaspoon grated orange or tangerine zest
1 teaspoon chopped fresh rosemary
Salt and freshly ground black pepper

---

1. Remove the goose neck, wingtips, and giblets and reserve for the gravy. Cut off and discard the tail-bone. Remove all visible fat and loose skin, inside and out. Then separate the skin from the body: starting at the neck end, gently loosen the skin by sliding your hand underneath the breast and carefully working your way back to the legs. Pull out as much fat as possible from beneath the skin, paying particular attention to the fat deposits around the thighs. Discard the fat or reserve it for rendering, as you choose. Pull out any quills left on the goose skin with tweezers. Using a sharp skewer, embroidery needle, or the pointed tip of a paring knife, prick the goose all over, especially where the subcutaneous fat is thickest, like around the thighs. To avoid jabbing the flesh, hold the pricking instrument almost parallel to the goose, rather than upright.

2. Preheat the oven to 325°F.

3. Put the goose on a rack in a deep roasting pan and set the pan in the sink. Combine 6 cups of water, the vinegar, and honey in a saucepan and bring to a rolling boil. Pour half of the mixture evenly over the goose. Reheat the remaining mixture to boiling, then turn over the goose and pour the remaining mixture over it. Little droplets of melted fat will begin to appear on the skin. Prick the goose again all over to encourage more of the fat to find its way out. Discard all the water in the pan and wipe the goose thoroughly inside and out with paper towels. Let it drain on the rack, uncovered, to exude more fat and air dry, as you prepare the seasonings.

4. Separate the garlic head into cloves and discard the roughest, outer, papery husk, leaving the thin layer of peel intact. In a small baking dish just large enough to accommodate all the ingredients snugly, add the garlic cloves and scatter the orange or tangerine zest, apricots, rosemary, juniper, and oil. Sprinkle lightly with salt and pepper. Cover the dish tightly with foil and bake for 30 minutes, or until the garlic cloves are very soft. Let cool until you can handle the garlic. Leave the oven on.

5. Squeeze the garlic from the husks (discard the husks), and combine the garlic pulp and other ingredients from the baking dish in a food processor or blender. Puree until smooth.

6. Dry the goose again with paper towels; it should have released more of the melted fat. Spoon the roasted garlic mixture under the goose skin, pushing it all over the breast and down the drumsticks.

Generously salt and pepper the goose inside and out, rubbing the seasoning into the skin. Lightly crush the cinnamon sticks with a mallet or rolling pin and place them in the cavity. Truss if desired. (If my goose is extra-large—12 or more pounds—and its limbs, when extended, sidle over the edge of my largest roasting pan, I usually do a simple truss to make it fit more compactly.)

7. Roast the goose breast side down on the rack for 1½ hours, pouring out the fat occasionally as it accumulates in the pan. Remove the goose from the oven, turn it breast side up, and prick the skin again several times. Roast, pouring out the fat occasionally, for another 1–1½ hours, or until the juices of the thigh run clear when pierced with a knife and the leg meat feels soft when pressed. (These are more accurate indicators than the internal temperature; a goose will often measure 170°F—well-done—well before the meat is tender yet still moist.)

8. Remove from the oven and increase the oven temperature to 400°F. Prick the goose again all over. Transfer the goose to a large rimmed baking sheet or pan with shallow sides to trap the fat. When the oven reaches 400°F, roast the goose for 15 minutes longer to turn the skin beautifully crisp and brown. Remove from the oven and let stand for about 20 minutes before carving.

9. While the goose is cooking, prepare the gravy. In a 10- to 12-inch heavy skillet, heat the oil until hot but not smoking. Add the reserved neck, wingtips, and giblets (save the liver for broiling—the cook's perk) and sauté for about 10 minutes over medium heat until golden brown. Transfer to a heavy, wide saucepan. Pour out all but 1 tablespoon of oil remaining in the skillet, and add the shallots, carrots, and chopped garlic. Sauté, stirring, until the vegetables are tinged with brown, 8–10 minutes, then transfer them to the saucepan. Combine the vinegar or apple brandy with the honey, and use to deglaze the skillet over moderately high heat, scraping up all the browned bits with a wooden spoon. Transfer the contents of the skillet to the saucepan. Add the chicken broth, juniper, and peppercorns, and bring the mixture to a boil. Lower the heat and simmer slowly for about 1 hour. Strain through a sieve into a bowl, pressing down on the solids to extract all of their flavorful juices. Skim off any fat. Wash and dry the saucepan and return the strained stock to it. Add the whole garlic cloves, apricots and their soaking liquid, and cook the mixture over high heat until reduced by about half. Add the orange juice, zest, and rosemary and cook for 3–4 minutes. Season with salt and pepper to taste. Transfer to a blender (in batches, if necessary), and emulsify until smooth. Taste for seasoning, and keep warm or reheat gently before serving.

10. Carve the goose. Serve each guest a portion of the meat, topped with some of the irresistible skin. Pass the gravy.

YIELD: 6–8 servings

PURIM

Purim, the most joyous holiday of all, is a wild carnival of food, wine, and laughter. A time to let go in life-affirming festivities, free as possible of inhibitions, enjoying the day to the fullest.

And why not? Purim marks the period Jews were barely snatched from the hangman's noose. We celebrate our physical life because we came so close to extermination.

The historical foundations of Purim as recounted in the Book of Esther have never been fully substantiated; the story itself is rife with inconsistencies. But to paraphrase Voltaire, if Purim did not exist, it would be necessary to invent it. Parallels to its central theme of genocide have been replayed throughout the Diaspora, culminating in the unspeakable: twentieth-century Germany replacing ancient Persia, a thwarted Haman recast as the demonically successful Hitler. Two thousand years later, the need for Purim became even more important.

The Persian King Ahasuerus ruled an empire stretching from India to Ethiopia. His proud chief vizier, Haman, grew incensed one day when Mordecai, a Jewish courtier, refused to bow down to him. In revenge, he determined to have all the Jews in the empire annihilated. Convincing the rather wimpish king was an easy matter—Haman told him the Jews were subversive and backed up his argument with a bribe of silver talents—and the date of the genocide was set for 13 Adar. But two startling events made the king change his mind. He found out that Esther, his beautiful queen, was actually a Jew (and none other than Mordecai's adoptive daughter) when she pleaded with him to save the lives of her people. And he suddenly discovered, in the middle of an insomniac night, that he had never rewarded Mordecai for saving his life by foiling an assassination plot some time ago. So Ahasuerus ordered Haman to be hanged instead and the Jews were saved. Mordecai and Esther declared that the next day should be celebrated evermore with feasting and merrymaking.

All the stops are giddily pulled out as life turns into a lusty, riotous party. There is boisterous revelry even in the synagogue. While the Book of Esther is read, children clang pots, pans, and groggers, ear-splitting noisemakers, blotting out the name of Haman; some Eastern Jews write "Haman" on the soles of their feet and "stamp" him out. Nor is the sacred literature exempt: hilarious parodies of the Torah and Talmud are presided over by comic Purim rabbis.

Wine flows freely, adding to the jubilant mood and ensuring unrestrained rejoicing.

Disguise too offers freedom to abandon oneself. Venetian Jews, dazzled by the wild exuberance of their Gentile neighbors during Carnival (which occurs around the same time), adopted the custom of masquerading in costumes and elegant masks at the end of the fifteenth century. The tradition spread to Jewish communities around the world. Today many children—and adults—dress up for glorious carnival processions and parties.

As befits a holiday of deliverance, charity is donated: money must be given to at least two impoverished people. And the culinary highlight of the holiday begins with another gift, *mishlo'ah manot*, "sending portions." These are platters of no less than two "portions" of baked goods, sweets, or fruits, traditionally exchanged among friends and relatives.

This is the time for homemade, bite-size hamantaschen, the traditional three-cornered cookie, prepared in generous quantity to use up all the flour before Passover. Fill them with fruits: fresh apples or a Middle East–inspired melange of dried apricots, dates, and pistachios. Or stuff buttery poppy seed hamantaschen with a raisin-walnut puree.

The Purim seudah—the festive meal eaten toward nightfall—is especially splendid: gefilte fish painted gold with saffron and savory prune-filled kreplach, napped with dreamy honeyed cream. In the midst of such lavish delicacies, we nibble on humble chickpeas, zesty, in this revisionist version, with garlic and barbecue spices. It is customary to serve grains and legumes because Queen Esther would not eat the nonkosher meat at her husband's palace, and she contented herself at the fabulous banquets with plain peas and beans that were said to keep her beautiful.

But there are plenty of pastries left over from *mishlo'ah manot*. And still more wine to be drunk.

OTHER SUGGESTIONS FOR PURIM

Lentils "Hummus Style," with Pomegranate and Mint and
Toasted Za'atar Matzohs (page 53)
Mishmash Kreplach (page 111)
Fried Onion and Chicken Kreplach (page 130)
Potato-Onion Kreplach, Pot Sticker Style (page 152)
Kasha Varnishkes with Fried Eggplant, Mushrooms, and Onion Marmalade (page 160)
Deconstructed Kasha Varnishkes (page 163)
Caramel Rugelach (page 194)
Mujadderah-Filled Roasted Red Peppers in Tomato-Garlic Sauce (page 263)
Toasted Almond–Coconut Macaroons (page 332)
Hazelnut Macaroons (page 334)

CHICKPEAS WITH GARLIC
AND BARBECUE SPICES

PAREVE

A herring tidbit in cream sauce, a stuffed grape leaf, a piece of sweet egg *kichel*—Jewish cuisine is rich in tantalizing noshes. Perhaps this is because a little snack calls for just a little brocha, or blessing, not the full ritual benediction required before and after eating a complete meal.

Jews have enjoyed chickpeas since biblical times. Known as *arbas* or *nahit* to Ashkenazi Jews and *garvansos* to Sephardim, they are a popular snack food, eaten like popcorn, especially on Purim when they are served to mimic Queen Esther, who ate legumes and grains instead of the king's nonkosher food.

In our house, we usually ate them boiled plain, with heaps of coarsely ground black pepper. In this recipe I sprinkle them with a seasoning similar to a more recently beloved nosh—barbecued potato chips.

And the spiciness of this little cocktail nibble encourages one to fulfill that pleasant Purim injunction: "Drink until you can no longer differentiate between the names Mordecai and Haman."

---

1 cup (about ½ pound) dried chickpeas (see Cook's Note)	*½ teaspoon paprika*
Salt and freshly ground black pepper	*½ teaspoon dry mustard*
1 teaspoon garlic powder	*½ teaspoon brown sugar*
½–¾ teaspoon chili powder, or to taste	*⅛ teaspoon ground cinnamon*

---

1. Pick over the chickpeas and rinse them well in several changes of cold water. Soak them overnight in enough cold water to cover by 2 inches. Or use the quick-soak method: put them in a large saucepan and add about 5 cups of cold water; bring the water to a boil and simmer for 2 minutes; remove pan from heat and let the chickpeas stand, covered, for 1 hour. Drain the peas.

2. In a large saucepan, bring the chickpeas to a boil with enough fresh cold water to cover by 2 inches. Lower the heat, cover, and simmer until very tender, 1–2 hours, depending on the age of the peas. They should be rather soft, not at all al dente, but don't overcook to mushiness (you'll be cooking them further with the spices, and you should be able to pick them up and munch them like popcorn, dissolving in your mouth, not in your hands). Drain well, place in a large, heavy skillet, preferably nonstick, and shake over low heat until very dry.

3. Add the remaining ingredients—use a generous hand with the salt and pepper—and toss well until the chickpeas are evenly coated. Taste and adjust the seasonings as needed. These are best served warm.

YIELD: About 3 cups

COOK'S NOTE: If you must, substitute drained, canned chickpeas for dried ones. Dry and season them in the skillet, as instructed above. But canned chickpeas tend to be rather mushy and bland (too much flavor leaches into the canning liquid) for this recipe.

While listening to the story of Purim unfold in the Book of Esther, children furiously clang groggers to drown out the name of the evil Haman every time it is mentioned. (Grogger [noisemaker]. Silver, filigree. Galicia, Eastern Europe, 18th century.)

POACHED PRUNE KREPLACH WITH
HONEYED CREAM AND PECANS

A joy at any time of year, kreplach in seventeenth-century Poland and Prague were made extra-special for Purim with a dough enriched with honey and spices. The opulence proliferated with luscious fillings of preserves, fruit, or raisins and nuts, according to John Cooper, author of *Eat and Be Satisfied*.

Made with wonton wrappers, these kreplach are very simple to prepare. But they are every bit as luxurious as their seventeenth-century forebears, each taste a rich amalgam of plump prunes, sweet cream, and crunchy pecans. They make a sensational dessert or snack or a resplendent addition to a brunch or dairy dinner.

PRUNE KREPLACH

About 24 plump pitted prunes (it is a good idea
  to prepare a few extra, though, for tasting)
Sweet red Jewish wine or red Concord grape
  juice to cover the prunes generously (2–3 cups)
1 cinnamon stick
2 whole cloves
Salt
About 48 wonton wrappers (allow a few extra in
  case of tearing)

Egg wash (1–2 large eggs, as needed, each
  beaten with 1 teaspoon of water)

HONEYED CREAM SAUCE

1½ cups heavy cream, preferably not ultrapas-
  teurized
1 teaspoon vanilla extract
2 tablespoons fragrant honey, or to taste

¼ cup pecans, toasted and coarsely chopped

---

1. Combine the prunes, wine or juice, cinnamon, cloves, and a pinch of salt in a medium saucepan and simmer over low heat, partially covered, until the prunes are very tender, about 20 minutes. Boil for a few minutes, uncovered, over high heat, stirring constantly, to evaporate any remaining liquid, watching carefully that the mixture does not burn.

2. Discard the cinnamon stick and cloves and let the prunes cool in the pan, then refrigerate them, covered, for at least 20–25 minutes before stuffing the kreplach.

3. Fill and trim the kreplach (see page 30), using 1 prune and 2 wonton wrappers for each krepl and sealing them with the egg wash. For a festive presentation, consider using cookie cutters to make attractive shapes.

4. Poach the kreplach. In a large, very wide pot, bring at least 5 quarts of lightly salted water to a boil. Slip in the kreplach, one by one, being careful not to overcrowd the pot (if necessary, cook them in batches or use two pots). Lower the temperature slightly (the kreplach might explode if the water is boiling furiously) and poach for 3–6 minutes, or until tender (exact time will depend on the brand of wonton wrapper used). Lift the kreplach out, a few at a time, with a large skimmer, gently shaking the skimmer to dry the kreplach (the kreplach are too fragile to pour into a colander).

5. Prepare the sauce. Put the cream, vanilla, and honey in a medium, heavy saucepan and boil over medium-high heat until reduced by about half. (If allowed to cool, reheat slowly until hot before serving.)

6. This rich dish is best enjoyed in small portions. Serve each person 3–4 kreplach topped with the honey sauce and sprinkled with the pecans.

YIELD: 6–8 servings

For Krochmalna, Purim was a grand carnival. The street was filled with maskers and
bearers of gifts. It smelled of cinnamon, saffron and chocolate, of freshly baked
cakes and all sorts of sweets and spices whose names I did not know.

—ISAAC BASHEVIS SINGER, *IN MY FATHER'S COURT*

As a child, I devoured butter-luscious hamantaschen by the bakery boxful. Tricornered sweet pastries enclosing open pools of jewel-toned jams—raspberry, apricot, and prune—or silver blue poppy seeds, they are named for the arch-evil Haman. Every Purim I delighted in consuming the wicked enemy.

My sweet tooth, I know, has grown smaller. But it seems to me that bakery hamantaschen, like bagels and muffins, have definitely grown larger. In fact, they are enormous: life-size replicas of Haman's pockets, or hats, or huge, pointy ears, not the symbolic little likenesses to which the pastries have been variously ascribed. Bigger here is not better: the crusts have become drier, the fillings duller. I am bored after just a few bites.

And so I've taken to making my own miniature version. Shaping small pieces of the buttery dough was tricky—as I molded it, the warmth of my fingertips made it too soft—until I began working the dough through a sheet of plastic wrap. I am partial now to fruit fillings, studded with nuts for texture and added flavor, and three simple fresh and dried fruit recipes follow.

PASTRY

*1¼ sticks (10 tablespoons) unsalted butter, plus
 butter for greasing the pan*

½ cup sugar

1 large egg

3 tablespoons apple or fresh orange juice

½ teaspoon vanilla extract

3 cups unbleached all-purpose flour

1½ teaspoons baking powder

¼ teaspoon salt

*1 recipe for filling (Fresh Apple, page 302;
 Apricot, Date, and Pistachio, page 303; or
 Raisin-Walnut, page 304) or a ready-made
 filling of lekvar or prune butter
 (available in the baking section of many
 supermarkets), plain or mixed with
 chopped, toasted walnuts*

---

1. Prepare the pastry. In a food processor, blend the butter with the sugar. Add the egg, juice, and vanilla and pulse until smooth. Stir together the flour, baking powder, and salt, then add to the food processor. Pulse until the ingredients are combined and form a ball around the blades.

Or make the dough using an electric mixer: In a large bowl, cream the butter with the sugar until it is light and fluffy. Beat in the egg, and then the juice and vanilla. Combine the remaining ingredients and mix in. Transfer to a lightly floured board and knead the mixture until all the flour is well-incorporated and the dough is smooth.

2. Divide the dough into 4 balls and wrap each well with plastic wrap. Refrigerate for at least 2 hours and up to 3 days. (The dough may also be frozen, wrapped airtight, for up to 1 month.)

3. Preheat the oven to 350°F.

4. Work with one ball of dough at a time, leaving the rest wrapped and refrigerated. (If you have frozen the dough, let it thaw until it is workable.) Divide the ball into 12 pieces of equal size; when rolled between your palms into balls, they should be slightly larger than walnuts. Flatten the balls between sheets of plastic wrap with the palm of your hand, and pat them into even rounds about 3 inches in diameter. I find this way there is less waste, the dough won't become tough from overhandling, and it is easy for those who lack experience or skill in handling dough. Pastry mavens may prefer to roll out the dough between sheets of plastic wrap or wax paper to about ⅛ inch thickness, then cut out rounds approximately 3 inches in diameter, using a cookie cutter or the rim of a glass. Reroll the scraps and cut them out.

5. I've found that hamantaschen edges sometimes open slightly during baking, if not very firmly sealed. But warm fingertips pinching the buttery dough can make it too soft to work with or result in overhandling the dough. Keeping the dough well-chilled until you are ready to use it does help, but working with such small pastry rounds also means the dough will warm up rather quickly. Here's the solution: Place a pastry round on a piece of plastic wrap. Spoon a heaping teaspoon of filling in the center. Then, working your fingers under the plastic wrap so that they don't touch the dough directly, fold one side of the pastry up, making a little rim along the filling. Then fold the two adjacent sides up and together, forming a triangle. Pinch and smooth the edges through the plastic wrap until the seams are just about invisible. The plastic wrap keeps the dough moist and pliable. You should have a little triangle of pastry, the filling exposed in the center like a tiny, open tart. Pinch the edges together tightly at all three corners so there is no gap for the filling to seep out.

6. Place the finished hamantaschen about 1 inch apart on lightly greased cookie sheets. (For easy cleanup, you may want to line the sheets with parchment or greased foil to catch spills.) Continue making hamantaschen until you have used up all the dough and filling. Keep the unbaked hamantaschen in the refrigerator until you are ready to put them into the oven.

7. Bake for 20–25 minutes, or until pale golden. Cool them on the baking sheets for about 5 minutes, then transfer them to racks to cool completely (wait until they have cooled before removing them or

they might crumble). Or, if you don't need the baking sheets for another batch, cool them on the sheets set on racks.

YIELD: About 48 hamantaschen

FRESH APPLE HAMANTASCHEN FILLING

DAIRY

This filling makes tiny, open-faced apple-walnut tarts, fragrant with the all-American spices of an old-fashioned pandowdy and glossed with a lick of syrupy molasses.

2 tablespoons unsalted butter
About 1 ½ pounds sweet, flavorful apples with
  lots of character, peeled, cored, and diced
  (4 cups)(use Gravenstein, Gala, Braeburn,
  Jonathan, and Stayman Winesap; if possible
  search out local, seasonal varieties)
About 3 tablespoons packed brown sugar
1 tablespoon molasses, plus additional for
  glazing the filling

¾ teaspoon ground cinnamon, plus additional
  for sprinkling
½ teaspoon fresh lemon juice
¼ teaspoon nutmeg, preferably freshly grated
2 pinches of ground cloves
⅛ teaspoon salt
½ cup walnuts, lightly toasted and coarsely
  chopped

1. In a 10- to 12-inch heavy skillet, melt the butter over medium-high heat until sizzling. Add the apples and sauté for about 3 minutes, lifting and turning them. Stir in the brown sugar and molasses and mix well to coat the apples evenly. Add the cinnamon, lemon juice, nutmeg, cloves, and salt and cook over moderately high heat for 5 minutes or until the apples are just tender. You should have no liquid left in the pan; if any remains, briefly boil rapidly over high heat to evaporate it. Taste and adjust the seasoning. You may need to add more sugar depending on your preference and the sweetness of the apples.

2. Transfer the apples to a medium-large bowl, and let cool to room temperature. Stir in the walnuts and refrigerate, covered, until cold.

3. When you make the hamantaschen, brush the exposed filling with a bit of molasses (or just dab it on with your fingertip) and sprinkle with cinnamon.

YIELD: Enough filling for 48 hamantaschen

APRICOT, DATE, AND PISTACHIO HAMANTASCHEN FILLING

Tart dried apricots mellowed with lush, sugary dates and crunchy toasted pistachios—this delicious remake of the sweet bakery apricot jam fillings I grew up with brings an aura of the Middle East.

---

1 ¼ cups (about 6 ounces) dried apricots, preferably tart, diced

⅔ cup (about 4 ounces) dried dates, preferably a
   soft variety such as Medjool or Barhi, pitted
   and diced

5 tablespoons packed brown sugar

About ⅔ cup apricot nectar or apple juice

½ teaspoon vanilla extract

Pinch of salt

1 ½ teaspoons fresh lemon juice

⅓ cup pistachio nuts, lightly toasted and
   coarsely chopped

In a heavy, nonreactive, 2½- to 3-quart saucepan, combine the apricots, dates, brown sugar, nectar or juice, vanilla extract, and salt. Simmer slowly, stirring occasionally, until all the fruit is very soft and the liquid is no longer visible, 10–15 minutes. (If the fruit is very dry, you may have to add more liquid and cook it a little longer.) Stir in the lemon juice and cook for 3 minutes to meld the flavors. Remove from the heat, transfer to a medium bowl, and let cool. Mix in the pistachios, cover, and refrigerate until cold.

YIELD: Enough filling for 48 hamantaschen

POPPY SEED HAMANTASCHEN
WITH RAISIN-WALNUT FILLING

I've taken the poppy seeds from the traditional hamantaschen filling and added them instead to the tender crust. The result, which reminds me of my grandmother's delicate *mohn kichel* (poppy seed butter cookies) makes a melt-in-the-mouth cushion for the rich, moist, raisin-walnut filling, my daughter's favorite.

FILLING

½ cup packed brown sugar

2 tablespoons ground cinnamon

Pinch of salt

2 cups (about 12 ounces) dark raisins

⅔ cup apple or fresh orange juice

1 tablespoon fresh lemon juice

1 cup walnuts, lightly toasted and coarsely
 chopped

1 recipe hamantaschen pastry (page 300), made
 with 3 tablespoons poppy seeds added to the
 flour and other dry ingredients

---

1. Make the filling. Combine the brown sugar, cinnamon, and salt in a food processor and pulse briefly to blend. Add the raisins. Pour in the juice through the feed tube, while pulsing just long enough to chop the raisins coarsely, 10–15 seconds.

2. Scrape the mixture into a heavy, nonreactive, 3-quart saucepan. Bring to a boil over moderately high heat, stirring to prevent burning, then lower the heat and simmer slowly, stirring occasionally, for 7–8 minutes, until the mixture has thickened and almost no liquid is visible. Stir in the lemon juice and cook for 2–3 minutes more to blend the flavors. Remove from the heat, transfer to a medium bowl, and let cool to room temperature. Stir in the walnuts and refrigerate, covered, until cold.

3. Fill, shape, and bake the hamantaschen, following the directions on page 301.

YIELD: 48 hamantaschen

PASSOVER

14–21 Nissan (March or April)

All people, in every generation, should see themselves as
having experienced the Exodus in Egypt.
—PASSOVER HAGGADAH

Marjorie felt the familiar old warmth enveloping her. The sweet grape taste of the
wine woke childhood recollections. She began to care less what Noel and his parents
were thinking, and she joined in the songs with abandon.
—HERMAN WOUK, *MARJORIE MORNINGSTAR*

A generous ransom paid for a much-sought-after piece of broken matzoh. Horrific plagues re-created out of wine drops, and bricks from a scrumptious fruit and nut paste. So many raucous cousins the dining table must be stretched with bridge tables until it snakes around the front door.

At every Passover seder, Jews revisit magical childhood memories.

A glorious ceremonial family dinner held on the first and second nights (Israelis and Reform Jews observe one night

305

only) of Passover, the seder brings to life the ancient Hebrews' liberation from slavery and their flight from Egypt. Nearly eighty percent of North American Jews—and many non-Jews as well—attend a seder every year, making Passover the most celebrated—and best loved—of all the Jewish holidays.

The story of the Exodus is a universal one, a struggle for political liberation and spiritual freedom relevant to all peoples. Moses, as God's emissary, pleaded with Pharaoh to free his people—the enslaved Hebrews who, smarting under the taskmasters' whips, were forced to build Egyptian cities. To convince the nefarious king to heed the request, God visited nine monstrous plagues on the Egyptians, ranging from boils on their skin to frogs in the water to total darkness. Still Pharaoh would not relent. Finally God sent the worst curse of all: the death of the first-born males, and Pharaoh at last conceded. That night the Hebrews ate a hurried meal of roasted lamb and unleavened bread and fled in haste, lest he change his mind.

And that he did. Now the Hebrews stood before the Red Sea, and behind them, they could feel the hot breath of the Egyptian pursuers mingled with the desert scorch. Moses lifted his arm and miraculously the waters parted so that they could pass through to safety. When the last Hebrew reached the shore, Moses returned the waters to their natural state, drowning the Egyptians and their chargers.

It is a stirring tale, meant to be felt, not merely told, and the injunction above, to relive the Exodus personally, is taken seriously. The symbolic seder foods are used to make the narrating vivid, and because most of these foods are consumed, we actually taste the experience and ensure it will become a part of us.

The matzoh recalls not only the flat, unleavened bread quickly prepared for the flight from Egypt, it also suggests the humility of the Hebrews first as slaves, and later as grateful worshipers before God. They had become acquainted with yeasted bread in Egypt, so leavened bread (and by extension, any form of leavening), puffed and swollen as with vanity and pride, symbolized their Egyptian oppressors. Jews are prohibited not just from eating leavening (*hametz* in Hebrew) during the eight days of Passover, they must fastidiously remove every crumb of it from their homes. This is a holiday of freedom and every trace of the tyrants must be cleared away.

After the meal, a piece of matzoh stealthily hidden by the leader of the seder becomes the object of a treasure hunt for all the children. Whoever finds this *afikomen* (the word means "dessert" in Greek) will demand a ransom (contemporary requests run from cash to charitable contributions to video games) for the meal cannot be concluded until it is eaten.

The focus of the table is the special seder plate filled with other ritual foods from the Passover saga. The highly symbolic egg, eaten extensively throughout the holiday, appears on the plate either roasted or *haminado*, Sephardi-style. It speaks of many things. Primarily, it recalls the festival offerings brought to the Temple in Jerusalem, and, as a symbol of mourning, reinforces our sense of loss at the Temple's destruction. But paradoxically, it also stands for the eternal and for new life, the hope and optimism that are evoked with every spring. A roasted lamb shank bone (sometimes replaced by a chicken wing or neck or even, for vegetarians, a roasted beet) brings to mind other sacrifices at the Temple.

Salt water gives us a taste of the tears and hard sweat of slavery, but it is tempered by the sweet vegetable we dip into it: parsley, celery, or soft lettuce, representing the renewal and growth of spring. Horseradish, arugula, romaine, or other bitter herbs sting our tongues with the harshness of slavery and oppression. And everybody's favorite is haroset, which mimics the brick and mortar the Hebrews used to build Pharaoh's cities. Variations on this fruit-and-nut theme reflect all the myriad foodstuffs available in the Diaspora. A simple but delicious take on an Ashkenazi-style haroset might include chopped apples and walnuts flavored with cinnamon and wine, then made pastelike with a bit of pureed bananas or dates; for a luscious Sephardi "mortar," blend pureed dates and wine with chopped walnuts. Coconut, pomegranate, lemon juice, and chestnuts are just a few possible additions.

The joy symbolized by the four cups of wine (or grape juice) each celebrant drinks during the seder is not complete: Recognizing that our enemies, too, suffered during the Exodus diminishes our gladness. So, with one finger we flick out a drop of wine for each plague visited on the Egyptians. The door is opened during the service so that the prophet Elijah, harbinger of peace and the Messianic Age, may come in to drink the cup of wine poured for him. Everyone watches this goblet closely to see if he has sipped, a sure sign of God's blessing.

Today some seders feature a special goblet, the *Kos Miryam*, or Miriam's cup, created by a group of women in the 1980s. The cup is filled with water and honors Moses' sister, who provided the Israelites with water from a well that followed her throughout the wandering and dried up when she died.

The ceremonies are spelled out in a special book called the Haggadah. To date, nearly 4,000 versions of it have been created, and new editions attempt to connect the ancient struggles of our ancestors to our modern lives in passionate and meaningful ways.

To some extent every family customizes the seder to reflect the needs and desires of the participants. When I was a girl, the children all whooped through the house madly searching for the afikomen, while cries of "cold," "warmer," and "hot-hot" guided us to find it, finally, crumbled perhaps in the paper sleeve of a 45 r.p.m. record like "The Witch Doctor." Then we launched into a little night music, riotously belting out songs from "Had Gadya" (a lovely Hebrew allegory in "The House That Jack Built" tradition) to "Swing Low, Sweet Chariot."

As we grew older, my father wove modern parallels of oppression and liberation into the traditional Passover narrative, sparking rousing political exchanges. Particularly poignant was our seder the night Rita, a friend from Papa Doc's Haiti, joined in.

Throughout the seder, intoxicating aromas emanate from the kitchen, tweaking appetites whetted by brief tastes of the ceremonial foods. At last it is time to eat. Reclining comfortably amid pillows and soft cushions to underscore the fact that we are a free people now, we set to the lavish feast, perhaps the most splendid of the Jewish calendar. Sweet wine, although traditional in many homes, is not mandated, and many Jews prefer to sip the excellent dry kosher-for-Passover wines available to complement the delicious food.

"Let all who are hungry come and eat," the Haggadah enjoins, and Jews make a point of inviting guests as well as extended family members to share the meal. Most families begin with eggs: Sephardim serve the roasted huevos haminados, while Ashkenazim customarily dip hard-boiled eggs in saltwater. Our family savored untraditional but wonderful chopped hard-boiled eggs and onions. There are rich, inventive dishes made of matzoh and the lively perfumes of early spring: fresh young fennel, asparagus, mushrooms, artichokes, and rhubarb. Slow-braised lamb, pot roast cooked with horseradish and beet juice, or gently simmered turkey remains moist and succulent, even when the pre-dinner service runs late. Sumptuous desserts relying on ground nuts and eggs instead of flour are intensely flavored yet remarkably light.

The holiday places prohibitions on many foodstuffs. Except for specially prepared matzoh, no products made from any grain (including derivatives like beer or grain-based vinegar) and no leavening, like yeast, may be consumed. In addition, Ashkenazi Jews also refrain from eating corn, legumes, and rice during Passover, and many Indian Jews give up sugar.

Yet Jewish cooks had to invent a unique cuisine that would provide delicious menus not only for the seders, but throughout the eight days of the joyous holiday. Matzoh, crumbled into pieces, crushed into meal, or finely ground into matzoh cake meal, as well as ground nuts and potato starch, replaced flour and bread crumbs in cooking and baking. Generous amounts of eggs, especially the beaten whites, ensured the Passover foods would be light and fluffy. So successful were the specialties originally created to conform with the stringent demands of the holiday that many have become the most beloved of all Jewish dishes, served up year-round: featherlight matzoh balls, eggy matzoh brie, honey-drenched fritters, and special latkes, to name just a few.

The distinctive Passover foods imbue the holiday with a unique rhythm all its own. Breakfast without the quick fixes of cold cereal and bagels, lunch with no sandwiches or pizza are more carefully planned and more leisurely eaten. The comfortable, relaxed mood that begins at the seder table with pillows and cushions remains with us through all the meals of the festival.

OTHER SUGGESTIONS FOR PASSOVER

Sweet and savory matzoh bries in "Breakfasts and Brunches" (pages 34–42)

Chopped Chicken Liver from the Rue des Rosiers (page 47) or Chopped Chicken Liver with Caramelized Onions (page 51)

My Mother's Fried Cauliflower (page 56)

Classic Chicken Soup (page 63) with Matzoh Balls (page 66), or Savory Herbed Matzoh Kleis (page 68)

Gefilte Fish Quickly Steamed Between Cabbage Leaves (page 90)

Salmon Gefilte Fish Poached in Fennel-Wine Broth with Ginger-Beet Horseradish (page 93)

Egyptian Ground Fish Balls with Tomato and Cumin (page 96)

Oven-Fried Smoked Salmon Croquettes (omit mustard) (page 101)

Flanken with Tart Greens (page 108)

Braised Brisket with Thirty-six Cloves of Garlic (page 113)

If rice is eaten during Passover: Roasted Garlic–Braised Breast of Veal with Springtime Stuffing (page 121)

Romanian Garlicky Ground Meat Sausages with Sour Pickle Vinaigrette and Roasted Red Peppers (page 125)

Fried Chicken Cutlets, Italian-Jewish Style (page 132)

Spinach-Cheese Squares (page 150)

Wild Mushroom–Potato Kugel (page 167)

Moroccan-Flavored Carrot Kugel (page 171)

Fresh fruit sauces (see pages 176–82)

Lemon-Roasted Chicken (page 203), with Rhubarb-Prune Tsimmes (page 205)

Dried Fruit Compote with Fresh Pineapple, Pistachios, and Mint (page 208)

Leek Croquettes from Rhodes (page 223)

If rice and legumes are eaten during Passover: Iranian Stuffed Chicken with Fresh Green Herbs and Golden Soup (page 232)

Cabbage Stuffed with Mushrooms and Meat (page 261)

Cheese Latkes with Fresh Persimmon Sauce (page 282)

Greek-Inspired Cheese Latkes (page 284)

MATZOHS

When the matza came out well, she held it up on the rolling pin
to show the rich lady how nice it looked.
—ABRAHAM REISEN, "MATZA FOR THE RICH"

I devoured pounds of the crisp crumbling matzohs with hunks of fresh butter
and streams of honey, leaving a trail of crumbs all over the house.
—EDNA FERBER, *A PECULIAR TREASURE*

One Passover spent in Paris, I ate thick matzoh, soft and crumbly as a cookie. In shops and restaurants in both the old ghetto area in the Marais and the newer North African–Jewish neighborhood surrounding the rue des Richers in the ninth arrondissement, I came across sweet varieties as well, prepared with wine, orange flower water, and sugar, tasting like exotic tea biscuits. They were, the boxes revealed, made from a secret family recipe from Oran, Algeria.

A sweltering August morning, strolling through Venice's *Gheto Novo* (New Ghetto, actually older than the *Gheto Vecchio,* Old Ghetto, but that's another story), my husband, daughter, and I snacked on what looked like quilted pillows of intricate ivory Venetian lace. They were *pane azimo,* pale matzoh, soft like the ones we'd had in Paris, baked at Panificio Giovanni Volpe, which also offers, even in summer, sugar cookies, delicate macaroons, and other *pane dolci,* sweets made with matzoh meal.

Eating these thick, puffy matzohs, I recalled the many Italian and French Passover recipes that specified thick or thin matzoh, and understood how Italian Jews who could not bear to go without their pasta might attempt to re-create lasagne with Venetian-style matzoh.

For Eastern European Jews, though, the best matzoh is the thinnest. In Abraham Reisen's story, "Matza for the Rich," the bakery workers expect a generous tip from the town's wealthy dowager for matzoh that is thin, crackly, and "comes out as if baked in the sun." Notwithstanding their plainness, when served hot and crisp, these familiar Ashkenazi matzohs can be quite tasty.

Hot is the operative word here, for hot matzoh—like hot bread—is an amalgam of wonderful toasty flavors and aromas. Watching *schmura* matzoh (the special matzoh handmade from wheat that is carefully watched over from the time it is harvested) being prepared by the Hasidic Lubavitcher community in Brooklyn, I was captivated by the tantalizing smells of the freshly baked matzoh. And straight from the scorching, wood-fired ovens, they were a marvel: gloriously toasty and crisp.

But when I brought the box home, the matzoh had dulled to a lackluster taste—they had more flavor than the packaged variety, but not much. I've learned to reheat matzohs to recrisp them as well as to recapture that fresh from the oven flavor.

TO HEAT MATZOH

Preheat the oven to 400°F. Wet the matzoh lightly on both sides with cold water (a few spritzes from a water spray bottle is perfect for this). Toast on an oven rack until dry and crisp, 3–5 minutes.

Matzoh, so central to Passover that it is often called *Hag ha-Matzot* or Festival of Matzohs, is served in place of bread or crackers during the full eight days of the holiday. The plain variety contains just flour and water—no fats, salt, sugars, additives, or preservatives—so you can use them to custom-design your own crackers, seasoning them with whatever you would try on flatbreads or crackers, and enjoy them not only on Passover, but throughout the year.

SEASONED MATZOH

Use these suggestions as a guide. I'm sure you'll have many ideas of your own.

1. Sprinkle the top of dampened matzoh with coarse salt, and if desired, freshly ground coarse pepper, and/or chopped fresh rosemary or other herbs. Bake until dry and crisp.
2. Gently rub the cut side of a garlic clove or onion over the matzoh until the matzoh is slightly damp. (A couple of vertical slashes in the cut side will make the garlic or onion juices flow more easily so the matzoh won't break apart in the process.) Sprinkle or spritz with a few drops of water, dust with salt, optional pepper and herbs, such as thyme, rosemary, or oregano, and bake until dry and crisp.
3. Sprinkle hot matzoh with grated Parmesan, cheddar, or other cheese, grated lemon rind, and cracked pepper. Or sprinkle the seasoning on unheated matzoh and run briefly under the broiler.
4. Brush matzoh with melted or softened butter or extra-virgin olive oil. Season with salt and optional pepper, grated garlic or onion, chopped fresh or dried herbs. Or steep minced garlic or onion in oil for a while, then brush the oil on the matzoh, using sprigs of rosemary or other herbs as a brush. Bake at 400°F until hot and just beginning to brown, or toast under the broiler.
5. For a sweet matzoh, brush egg matzoh with melted butter and sprinkle with brown sugar and cinnamon. Place under the broiler until the sugar melts.

For more on matzoh and matzoh meal, see page 25.

CHOPPED EGGS AND ONIONS

PAREVE

His own mother had spoiled him, her first-born son and the only child of her seven to go to college and then to law school. My maternal grandmother, Rebecca, loved to spoil my father too—her tall son-in-law, whose blue-black hair led strangers to mistake him for her own handsome son.

"Save that piece for your father," she would admonish us. "Go, put on lipstick," she'd urge my mother. "Max will be home soon."

Ignoring her, we would strip the crackling, garlicky skin from just-roasted turkey or chicken, greedily devouring it before he arrived home. And only once can I remember my mother applying lipstick just for my father in the candy shade of pink she wore to match the soft blush beneath her freckles. We knew when my father dished out the servings at the dinner table, the choicest morsels went first to the children, then to my mother, and he took what was left.

But if we wouldn't show him proper respect, Grandma Rebecca did. When she learned he loved chopped eggs and onions, she substituted it for the traditional Ashkenazi hard-boiled eggs dipped in salted water eaten at the beginning of the Passover meal.

I first ate eggs in salt water at a boyfriend's seder when I was seventeen. They tasted like a picnic ruined by high tide. Those who imagine I am impugning one of their favorite Passover foods might try the dish at any other time of year, without the spice of hunger to season it.

But chopped eggs and onions are delicious anytime. Spread on thin pumpernickel or egg matzoh, garnished with strips of roasted red pepper, black olives, or silky slivers of smoked salmon, it is light-years ahead of a traditional egg salad.

For Passover, serve it on soft lettuce leaves, or for a gussied-up presentation, in endive or radicchio leaves. Grated Black Radish and Endive Salad in Shallot Vinaigrette (page 50) is a superb complement.

My grandmother's version got its flavor boost from *grivenes,* the cracklings of fat and skin that are a by-product of making schmaltz, poultry fat. I add well-browned onions and their oil for the same effect.

3–4 tablespoons excellent-quality olive oil or avocado oil	*6 hard-boiled large eggs (see Cook's Note, page 49), peeled and cut into eighths*
½ cup thinly sliced onions, plus ½ cup finely chopped onions	*Olive Oil Schmaltz (page 28), as needed (optional)*
Salt and freshly ground black pepper to taste	*Accompaniments: see headnote above*

1. Heat 3 tablespoons of oil in a medium skillet, and add the sliced onions. (I use sliced onion here because chopped onion can be quite watery, so it doesn't fry as well and has a tendency to burn when made in small amounts.) Sauté over medium heat, stirring occasionally, until rich golden-brown. Salt and pepper lightly and remove from the heat to cool.

2. Scrape the sautéed onion and all the oil in the skillet into a wooden bowl and chop coarsely. Add the eggs and raw chopped onion and continue to chop until the mixture is well blended but not pasty. Mix in salt and lots of freshly ground pepper as you chop, or blend in the seasonings afterward with a fork (using a spoon will make the mixture too smooth). The mixture should hold together loosely; you will probably need to add some of the schmaltz or a bit more oil. Chill well, but remove from the refrigerator at least 15 minutes before serving.

YIELD: 4–6 servings

COOK'S NOTE: This should be rather coarse and crumbly, not at all paste-like. Using a food processor—even in pulsing motion— usually results in some overly large chunks and some paste. I find it much easier to chop this in an old-fashioned wooden chopping bowl with an inexpensive curved hand-chopper (like the half-moon-shaped Jewish *hockmeisser* or crescent-shaped Italian *mezzaluna*). It's much quicker to clean than the food processor too.

HUEVOS HAMINADOS

PAREVE

No less than twelve large brown paper bags spilled out of the kitchen for us to unpack when my father finished the Passover shopping. Every one, it seemed, contained at least one box of matzoh and a dozen eggs.

The matzoh lasted long after the eight-day holiday, when all our inventiveness had evaporated and we had thoroughly tired of eating it. But my father had to buy more eggs after just three or four days.

Eggs are indispensable for Passover cooking. Traditional favorites, like matzoh brie, knaidlach, and *bubelach*, little fritters, call for heaps of eggs to be mixed with matzoh or matzoh meal. And six to ten at a time, they are beaten into baked goods, replacing the forbidden leavening.

Symbol of life's mysteries and rebirth, they play a prominent role at the seder. There is the *beitzah,* or roasted egg, on the seder plate. Then most Ashkenazi Jews dip hard-boiled eggs into salt water, a practice that food historian John Cooper traces back to the hors d'oeuvre served at ancient Roman banquets.

The Sephardi seder favorite, huevos haminados, which are also served at life-cycle events and the Sabbath or holiday midday meal, were originally cooked on top of flavorful meats and legumes in hamins, the slowly braised Sabbath stews. But when hamin is not on the menu, or pareve eggs are desired, they are prepared as in this recipe, cradled in onion skins and gently simmered overnight in the oven or on top of the stove. Spent coffee grinds, or sometimes tea leaves, are added to the roasting materials for additional flavor. My friend Leyla Schick laughingly bemoaned the current paucity of cigarette smokers among her friends because some Turkish Jews claim a smidgin of cigarette ash enhances the roasted taste.

And what is the taste of a roasted egg? Huevos haminados are somewhat similar to the hard-boiled variety, but long hours of gentle cooking give them a softer texture, tender, never rubbery, and a rich, oniony fragrance.

Forget the discarded cigarette ashes. But do remember to save all your onion peels as they accumulate from cooking chores, storing them in a large perforated plastic bag in the refrigerator until needed.

4–5 packed cups outer skins of onions, rinsed if dirty	*2 tablespoons olive oil*
	2 teaspoons vinegar
12 large eggs, in the shell (make sure the shells have no cracks)	*1 teaspoon salt*
	½ teaspoon black pepper
2 tablespoons coffee grounds	

1. Preheat the oven to 200°F. Arrange half the onion skins on the bottom of a large ovenproof pot or casserole. Put the eggs on top. If the eggs are tightly packed, or if you must place the eggs in two layers, use additional onion skins to cradle them. Add the coffee grounds, oil, vinegar, salt, and pepper. Cover with the remaining onion skins. Pour in 2 quarts of cold water, adding a little more if necessary to cover the eggs. Cover the pot tightly and bake in the oven for at least 8 hours or overnight.

2. Remove the eggs and wipe them clean. Serve plain, hot, warm, or cold. Leftover eggs are easy to reheat. They are also wonderful sliced in salads (they make a terrific egg salad) or as a garnish for saucy stewed vegetables, like ratatouille.

YIELD: 12 eggs

וכבה ובעמך ובכל עבדיך יעלו הצפרדעים

Frogs, one of the ten plagues God sent to sway Pharaoh, appear all over the Egyptians' table. ("And the frogs clambered up. . . ." Passover Haggadah. Offenbach, Germany, 1722.)

CHICKEN SOUP WITH ASPARAGUS AND SHIITAKES, SERVED WITH ROASTED FENNEL MATZOH BALLS

Set in spring, when the earth is renewing and reassembling herself, Passover is celebrated as a sort of second New Year, reflecting the rebirth of the Jews as a free people after the Exodus from Egypt. Children start the season with new clothes, and houses are thoroughly cleaned and freshened up to make way for the new foods and special sets of dishes reserved just for Passover use.

And just as they delay until Rosh Hashanah their first tastes of the sweet new autumn fruits, so many Jews wait until Passover to savor the tender new vegetables of spring. In this delicious soup, woodsy shiitake mushrooms and early asparagus combine with delicate roasted fennel-flavored matzoh balls in a free-wheeling ode to spring.

MATZOH BALLS

2 small-medium fennel bulbs (about 1 pound, weighed with 2 inches of top stalks)

2 tablespoons olive oil

½ cup chicken broth, preferably homemade (page 63), or good-quality low-sodium canned

1 tablespoon coarsely chopped garlic

Salt and freshly ground black pepper

¾ teaspoon chopped fresh thyme

¼ teaspoon fennel seeds, ground in a spice grinder or with a mortar and pestle (optional)

2 large eggs

About ½ cup plus 2 tablespoons matzoh meal

SOUP

7 cups homemade chicken broth

¼ pound fresh shiitake mushrooms, stems removed and reserved for another use or discarded, caps wiped clean with a damp paper towel and thinly sliced

12–15 thin asparagus spears, trimmed and cut into 1-inch pieces

---

1. Prepare the matzoh balls. Preheat the oven to 400°F. Cut off the fennel stalks and reserve for another use (excellent for fish broths and stews). If there are some attractive feathery fronds, chop and set aside about 2 tablespoons of them to garnish the soup. Quarter the bulbs and trim away the stems, the bottom hard core, and any tough parts. Choose a shallow baking pan just large enough to fit the fennel in one layer and put in 1 tablespoon of the oil. Add the fennel and toss until well-coated. Roast the fennel until pale gold, about 20 minutes, then turn and roast for 10 minutes longer. Stir in the broth, garlic, salt and pepper to taste, and ½ teaspoon of the thyme. Cover the pan with foil and cook for 35–45 minutes longer, or until the fennel is very soft. Remove the foil, stir, and roast for a few more minutes to evaporate most of the liquid. Transfer the fennel and garlic to a food processor and

chop coarsely. Add the remaining ¼ teaspoon thyme, salt (it will need about 1 teaspoon), pepper to taste, and fennel seeds, if using. With the machine on, add the remaining 1 tablespoon olive oil through the feed tube.

2. Scrape the mixture into a large bowl. You should have about 1 cup of puree, so nosh on any extra. Whisk in the eggs, one at a time. Add the matzoh meal and stir well. If you can form a lump into a very soft walnut-size ball (the batter will become firmer when you chill it), don't add any more matzoh meal. If necessary, add just enough matzoh meal to enable you to do so. Refrigerate for at least 2 or up to 4 hours so the matzoh meal can drink in the liquid and seasoning.

3. When ready to cook, bring 4 quarts of water and 1 tablespoon of salt to a rapid boil in a large, wide pot. Dipping your hands into cold water if needed, roll the batter into walnut-size balls. When all the balls are rolled and the water is boiling furiously, turn the heat down to a gentle boil. Carefully slide in the balls one at a time and cover the pot tightly.

4. Turn the heat down to a simmer and cook over low heat for 30 minutes, without removing the cover. (They will cook by direct heat as well as by steam, which makes them puff and swell, and lifting the lid will allow some of that steam to escape.) Take out a dumpling and cut it in half. It should be light, fluffy, and completely cooked through. If it isn't, continue cooking a few more minutes. Remove the balls gently with a skimmer or large slotted spoon—they are too fragile to pour into a colander.

5. Make the soup. Put the broth in a large pot. Bring to a simmer. Add the matzoh balls, the mushrooms, and asparagus and simmer for about 5 minutes, or until the vegetables are tender.

6. To serve, warm shallow soup bowls. Using a slotted spoon, transfer the matzoh balls to the heated bowls and ladle the hot soup and the vegetables over them. Garnish with the reserved chopped fennel fronds.

YIELD: About 8 servings

COOK'S NOTE: You can cook the matzoh balls up to 2–3 hours in advance. Drain them and cover with some broth to keep them moist before setting them aside until you are ready to reheat them.

While you are roasting the fennel for this recipe, roast some garlic as well, if you are preparing the Toasted Matzoh Farfel with Wild Mushrooms and Roasted Garlic (page 330).

And experiment making matzoh balls with a puree of other vegetables, such as beets, carrots, leeks, mushrooms, or shallots. Roasted vegetables absorb less moisture than boiled or steamed ones (and therefore require less matzoh meal, making them lighter). They are also more flavorful.

FISH IN TOMATO, RHUBARB, AND BLOOD ORANGE SAUCE

PAREVE

Tomato's unexpected coupling with puckery rhubarb blossoms into a delightful marriage of flavors here. Worlds apart from the flat tomato-based sweet-and-sour foods I loathed growing up, this Sephardi fish classic sparkles with a cool, clean tang. I add just a bit of honey, relying more on caramelized onions, bright blood oranges, and the sweet heat of fresh ginger for the subtle but complex sweetening needed to tease the ingredients together seamlessly.

I steam or poach the fish separately, rather than cooking it directly in the sauce as many recipes suggest, because the liquid it exudes makes the sauce too watery.

Favored with early spring rhubarb, Greek and Turkish Jews often serve this as a fish entree at their seders. But it is equally fine as a refreshing main course, room temperature or chilled—especially when the weather grows warm, and delicious hot as well.

Because the flavors of the sauce demand time to develop fully, this is an excellent choice for make-ahead schedules. You can prepare the sauce up to three days ahead, and cook the fish just before serving (plan on extra time for cooling/chilling the fish if you are not serving it warm). Or make the fish when you prepare the sauce, and chill it, covered with sauce, until serving.

SAUCE

3 medium blood oranges (if not available, substitute 2 large, juicy navel oranges)

2 tablespoons olive oil

2 cups finely chopped onions

1 ½ teaspoons fresh ginger, peeled and finely minced

About 1 tablespoon orange blossom or other light floral honey

Salt and freshly ground black pepper

1 pound rhubarb, trimmed, fibrous strings removed with a vegetable peeler

1 cup fresh orange juice

Generous pinch of cinnamon

2 cups (about 1 pound) canned, peeled plum tomatoes, coarsely chopped, and ½ cup of their liquid

Juice of ½ lemon

FISH

3 pounds fish fillets or steaks (choose salmon or white-fleshed fish like red snapper, grouper, sea bass, halibut, cod, lemon or grey sole)

If steaming the fish, mild lettuce or cabbage leaves

Garnish: ⅓–½ cup finely minced fresh mint leaves

1. Start the sauce. With a vegetable peeler, remove a long strip of zest from one of the oranges. Put it in a small saucepan with water to cover, and bring to a boil. Drain, rinse, and pat it dry. Mince the

zest fine. Peel 2 of the blood oranges (or 1½ of the navel oranges), removing all of the bitter white pith and any seeds. Slice the oranges into chunks using a serrated knife. Set the orange zest and chunks aside. (You will be using the remaining blood orange, or half navel orange, to garnish the finished dish.)

2. In a 10-inch heavy skillet, warm the oil over moderate heat. Add the onions, and cook, stirring, for 5 minutes until they are shiny and lightly softened. Add the minced orange zest, ginger, and 1 teaspoon of the honey. Sprinkle lightly with salt and pepper. Continue cooking over low heat, stirring occasionally, until the onions are pale gold and very soft and sweet, 15–20 minutes.

3. While the onions are cooking, prepare the rhubarb. Cut it into 1-inch chunks and place it in a medium saucepan. Add ½ cup of the orange juice, the remaining 2 teaspoons of honey, the cinnamon, and a pinch of salt. Bring the mixture to a boil, then simmer, stirring occasionally, until the rhubarb is very tender, 6–8 minutes.

4. When the onions are ready, add the remaining ½ cup orange juice to the skillet and boil the mixture, stirring and scraping it so it does not burn, for 3–4 minutes, until the liquid evaporates and the onions are deep golden. Stir in the tomatoes and their liquid and cook over moderately high heat until they break up, about 10 minutes. Add the rhubarb mixture to the sauce, and cook over moderate heat for 5 minutes. Add the reserved orange chunks, and simmer for 5–7 minutes, until the sauce is thickened and the flavors well-blended. Season to taste with salt and pepper and some of the lemon juice. Taste again and, if needed, add additional honey or lemon juice until you reach your perfect sweet-and-sour balance.

5. Let the sauce cool to room temperature, then cover and refrigerate it for at least 12 hours or up to three days to blend the flavors.

6. Prepare the fish, either poaching or steaming it.

To poach the fish: In a deep, lidded skillet or sauté pan large enough to hold the fish in a single layer (if preparing several thin fillets, you will probably need to cook them in batches), bring 3 inches of water and salt and pepper to taste to a boil. Reduce the heat to a bare simmer, lower the fish into the water, and cover the pan. Poach until the fish is just cooked through, 6–12 minutes, depending on the variety and thickness of the fish.

To steam the fish: In a heavy, large, wide pot, like a 5- to 6-quart Dutch oven, add water to a depth of 1½ to 2 inches. Arrange a rack in the pan that stands at least 1 inch above the water. (If your rack's legs are not high enough, set it over 2 custard cups or empty tuna cans.) Bring the water to a boil. Line the rack with a layer of mild lettuce (iceberg or Boston, for example) or cabbage leaves, then place the fish on top in a single layer (if cooking thin fillets, you will probably have to steam the fish in batches). The leaf "bed" for the fish gentles the steam and prevents the cooked fish from falling through the rack as you try to lift it out. Reduce the heat to medium, cover the pot and steam until the fish is just cooked through, 6–12 minutes, depending on the variety and thickness of the fish.

To test the fish for doneness: Insert a thin-bladed knife in the thickest part. The fish should be opaque or show a slight bit of translucence, according to your preference.

7. Remove the fish to paper toweling or a clean kitchen towel (unscented by detergent) to drain, then carefully transfer it to a serving platter. Peel off any skin on the fish. You can serve the fish room temperature, chilled (but not icy cold), or warm. If not serving the fish warm, cool it to room temperature, and if desired, cover and chill it until cold. Blot up any liquid the fish may have thrown off. Spoon a generous amount of the sauce over the fish, reserving the rest.

Or prepare the fish ahead when you make the sauce. Follow the above directions for cooking, cooling, and saucing the fish. Cover and chill the fish for at least 12 hours and up to 2 days. Serve the fish room temperature, chilled (but not icy cold), or reheat it gently and serve it warm.

8. Just before serving, blot up any additional liquid exuded by the fish. Cut the remaining blood orange (or half navel orange) into very thin slices. Tuck the slices around the fish and sprinkle lavishly with the chopped mint. Pass a sauceboat with the remaining sauce (heated through, if serving the fish warm).

YIELD: 6–8 appetizer or main-course servings

COOK'S NOTE: The leftover sauce is also wonderful with poached or grilled chicken.

BRAISED LAMB WITH ARTICHOKES, LEMON, AND FRESH HERBS

Rubbed first with wild bitter herbs, tender young lamb was roasted, often over fragrant pomegranate wood, to mark each Passover in the Second Temple period. The Jewish historian Josephus estimated that 255,600 animals were sacrificed for the Passover celebratory feasts during the reign of Nero.

With the destruction of the Second Temple in A.D. 70, the custom lost favor as it evoked sorrowful memories of the Temple sacrifices that were no more. Eventually, Orthodox and Conservative Jews began to refrain from eating any roasted meat at the seder meals.

I have retained the ancient herb perfume in this braised lamb dish. Garlic, lemon, and artichoke build up more layers of flavor and texture—my attempt to compensate for the missing taste of roast pomegranate woodsmoke.

5–6 pounds bone-in lean lamb shoulder

3–4 tablespoons olive oil

2 large onions thinly sliced (about 5 cups)

10 large garlic cloves, peeled, plus
  2–3 tablespoons finely minced garlic

Salt and freshly ground black pepper

About ½ cup fresh lemon juice

2 tablespoons chopped fresh rosemary

2 teaspoons chopped fresh thyme

Shredded zest of 1 large lemon

1 cup chicken broth, preferably homemade (page 63), or good-quality low-sodium canned

8–10 medium artichokes(see Cook's Note), or two 9- or 10-ounce packages frozen artichokes, thawed and patted dry with paper towels

½ cup chopped fresh mint

---

1. Trim the lamb of as much fat as possible—very tedious, but careful trimming will eliminate the need to skim the fat from the pan later on. Cut the lamb into 1½- to 2-inch pieces, leaving the bones in (they'll add a lot of flavor). Do, however, cut the meat away from any large, unsightly bones. Pat the meat dry with paper towels.

2. Do the initial browning in a large, 10- to 12-inch heavy skillet (cast iron is ideal). Heat 2 tablespoons oil until hot but not smoking. Add the lamb in batches and sauté until nicely browned on all sides. Fry only a few pieces at a time; crowding the pan will steam the meat, rather than brown it. Add a little more oil to the pan only if necessary because you want to burn off as much fat as you can. Transfer the lamb as it is done to a platter.

3. If there is any rendered fat remaining in the pan, wipe it out. Add 1 tablespoon fresh oil and heat until hot. Add the onions and brown over medium-high heat, lifting and turning them as they become

deep gold, about 10 minutes, and scraping up any browned bits. Add the whole garlic cloves and cook for 2 minutes longer. Return the meat to the pan, season it with salt and pepper, and turn the meat over a few times to coat it well with the onions. Add ¼ cup lemon juice, 1 tablespoon rosemary, the thyme, and lemon zest and cook for 3 minutes.

4. Transfer the mixture and any scrapings from the bottom of the pan to a 6- to 8-quart Dutch oven or large, deep casserole and add the broth. Bring to a slow bubble, cover, and reduce the heat to the barest simmer. Cook for about 1½ hours, or until the meat is tender when pierced with a fork. Turn the meat frequently, basting it with the onions and pan sauce.

5. Add the artichokes, and cook, covered, until they are very tender, 15–20 minutes. I like to continue cooking until a few of the artichoke pieces break up and melt into the sauce, but follow your preference. The lamb too should be very tender. If there is a lot of liquid left in the pot, uncover and turn the heat up to high, evaporating enough so that the pan liquid is thick and syrupy. Stir in the mint, minced garlic, and remaining 1 tablespoon rosemary and ¼ cup lemon juice and cook for 3 minutes to blend the flavors. Taste and adjust the seasoning. There should be a pronounced lemon flavor, so add a bit more juice, if necessary. For easier and more attractive serving, remove the large bones that pull away from the meat easily. Serve hot.

YIELD: 8–10 servings

COOK'S NOTE: Follow this method to prepare fresh artichokes. To prevent the artichokes from discoloring, rub each surface you cut with fresh lemon. Or dip into a large bowl of cold water acidulated with the juice of a large lemon.

Slice off the artichoke stem and reserve. Pull off the tough outer leaves at the bottom of the artichoke and discard. Using a serrated knife or scissors, cut off the pointy top of the leaves just above the artichoke heart or choke and discard. With a very sharp knife, cut off and discard the remaining leaves, until you reach the palest soft leaves. Now cut the artichoke in half vertically and pull out and discard the purple-tipped leaves in the center. With a teaspoon, scrape out all of the fuzzy choke and discard. Trim the artichoke stem and peel it. Cut the stem into bite-size chunks. Halve the heart halves again, so you have quarters. The artichoke and the stem are ready to be used in the recipe. Prepare the remaining artichokes in the same way.

This dish tastes even better the next day. To prepare it in advance while retaining an herbal freshness, hold off on the herb and lemon finish. Remove from the heat and cool 1 hour, then refrigerate, covered, overnight. Scrape off any congealed fat from the surface. Reheat gently until heated through, and proceed with the final addition of herbs, garlic, and lemon juice.

VERONESE ROLLED TURKEY LOAF
(POLPETTONE)

Like its poor relation, the Ashkenazi *helzel,* a goose neck filled with fat, flour, and scraps of meat, this refined loaf of boned and rolled turkey (similar to a ballotine), favored by Italian Jews for holiday meals, relies on gentle cooking within a pouch sewn of poultry skin to keep the contents moist and succulent.

Variations of this polpettone are found throughout the Jewish communities of Italy, some calling for additions of ground veal or pistachios, some grinding the turkey instead of cubing it. This version comes from Ester Silvana Israel of Verona, who has gathered the recipes of the city's elderly Jews. It is often featured on Passover menus, surrounded by the Italian spring trio of purple artichokes, mushrooms, and baby peas.

A wonderful alternative to turkey roasted on the bone (many Orthodox and Conservative Jews refrain from eating roast meats at the seder meals), *polpettone,* bathed in broth and served at room temperature, remains moist and flavorful even during the longest seder.

To make the loaf, the turkey skin is removed, sewn into a neat pouch, and stuffed with cubes of the meat. Although it looks daunting, it is time-consuming, rather than difficult. The trickiest task is taking off the skin as nearly intact as possible. Turkey skin is much stronger and more elastic than chicken skin, but you must work carefully and patiently to avoid tearing it.

---

1 half turkey, skin intact (about 7–10 pounds)
3–4 eggs (use 3 if turkey is around 7 pounds,
* 4 if it weighs closer to 10), beaten*
3–4 large garlic cloves, finely minced
½ teaspoon ground allspice
Salt and freshly ground black pepper
2–2½ quarts chicken broth, preferably
* homemade (page 63), or good-quality*
* low-sodium canned*

1 large onion, quartered
3 large carrots, scraped and quartered
2 celery stalks, including leaves, coarsely
* chopped*
Optional accompaniment: *Green Olive Sauce*
* (page 60; substitute 2 teaspoons mayonnaise*
* for the mustard) or mayonnaise diluted with*
* some of the cooking broth*

---

1. Remove and discard the clumps of fat around the neck and tail openings of the turkey. Starting at the neck end, slowly work your hands under the skin, gently easing it away from the flesh. Move your hands all the way down the leg, then, using a small, sharp knife, cut the skin carefully away from the base of the leg. Now slip the skin off the leg, like pulling a sleeve over the turkey's wrist. It's very difficult to cut around the wingtip in the same way, so instead, cut a circle around the shoulder area, and

slip the skin down and off the wing. You'll have a big hole there, but you'll patch it up when sewing the pouch. When you have separated all the skin from the cavity, gently take off whatever excess fat can be removed easily without damaging the skin. Rinse the skin inside and out and pat it dry.

2. Thread a large embroidery needle with dental floss or strong white cotton thread and, using an overcast, or loop, stitch, sew a few stitches to close up the base of the leg, then patch up the hole made by the wing. Fold the skin in half to make a rectangle. Now sew the base and outer edge closed. You should have a neat pocket, open only at the top. The first time I made this, I was wondering where I would get more skin: surely this would never hold all that turkey flesh. But it stretches quite a bit and is very resilient, so you will be able to fit all the meat into it quite easily.

3. Set the skin aside while you cut all the meat—white and dark—from the turkey carcass and cube it. Cut away the tendons and discard. Include a small amount of turkey fat to help keep the loaf moist. Place the cubed meat in a bowl and stir in the eggs, garlic, allspice, and salt and pepper to taste.

4. Stuff the pouch with the meat mixture. Gently push the meat down into the pouch so you have enough room. Using the embroidery needle in an overcast stitch again, sew the top of the pouch closed. Rinse a clean thin kitchen towel (that has been washed in unscented laundry detergent) or double layer of cheesecloth in cold water and squeeze it out. Place the pouch in the towel and roll up very tightly. (I use inexpensive extra-large men's cotton handkerchiefs—they don't shred like cheesecloth and they can be washed and reused.) Tie the cloth securely closed in several places: at both ends, in the middle, and between the middle and the ends.

5. Put 2 quarts of broth in a heavy saucepan large enough to accommodate the filled pouch. Add the onion, carrots, and celery and simmer for 10 minutes. Reduce the heat to a slow simmer and add the turkey pouch. If necessary, add more broth so the pouch is covered. Simmer, covered, for 1½ hours.

6. Remove the pot from the heat. Leave the turkey loaf in the pot, and weight it down with several heatproof plates or one plate with a large weight placed on top. Let cool under the weights until it reaches room temperature. Remove the weights and the cloth covering and slice the loaf. (If it crumbles, it will still taste delicious.) Moisten each slice with several spoonfuls of the broth. Reduce some of the remaining broth over high heat and spoon over the turkey as a sauce before serving. The turkey will be very flavorful, but it will need the broth to stay moist. It's a good idea to keep any leftover loaf submerged under lots of broth.

7. If you want to serve the loaf warm, let it firm up at room temperature first, then reheat it slowly in the broth.

For a more elaborate sauce, serve the green olive sauce or some mayonnaise thinned with a little broth.

YIELD: 8–10 servings

COOK'S NOTE: This is my favorite way to eat this, especially leftovers. Simmer lots of chopped Swiss chard, spinach, or even broccoli rabe in some of the broth and spoon the mixture over slices of the turkey loaf arranged in a soup bowl. Then stir a little mayonnaise—or, if you have it on hand, a few spoons of pureed artichoke—into the broth to enrich the sauce. Scrumptious.

Artichoke puree is available jarred in many specialty stores or prepare your own by pureeing jarred artichoke hearts drained of oil (avoid those packed in strong marinade). Or puree cooked frozen artichoke hearts with a little extra-virgin olive oil and season to taste. Artichoke puree, also called artichoke paste, makes a superb substitute for cream or butter when you need to enrich or smooth out a meat or poultry sauce.

BEET-BRAISED POT ROAST WITH
HORSERADISH AND POTATO KNAIDLACH

MEAT

The last preparation was called pot roast, and I wanted to lick the dish after it.
—BABYLONIAN TALMUD: MEGILLAH

When the Purim revelries had passed, cooks in the Ukraine and northern Poland turned their attention to the long process of preparing *rosl*. They placed beets in earthenware crocks, covered them with fresh cold water, and let them slowly ferment, skimming the froth and foam weekly. A month later, a tangy, vegetal beet essence perfumed the shtetls, and the clear scarlet *rosl* was at last ready to be braised with pot roast or brisket and served as the popular Passover main course, *roslfleisch*.

With my cramped little kitchen and bulging closets, I've never had a place to secret a pot of fermenting beets for more than a day or two. So I substitute a delicious fresh beet soup or even jarred borscht as the braising liquid. To replace the tart, beautifully nuanced flavor of the traditional *rosl*, I add a bit of sour salt, then call upon beet's longtime partner, freshly grated horseradish, which throws off its clean bite when cooked and blooms with complex earthiness.

Tender, homey potato knaidlach, or dumplings, echoing the horseradish flavor, soak up the wonderful sauce the brisket provides. To make them I use prepared horseradish because the texture of freshly grated would be too coarse and woody for the dumplings, and the vinegar in the prepared kind preserves more of the kick, even after cooking.

POT ROAST

Salt and freshly ground black pepper

3–4 pounds boneless beef pot roast (choose chuck roast, beef shoulder roast, or brisket)

3 tablespoons olive oil

1 very large onion, chopped (2–3 cups)

4–5 large garlic cloves, peeled and crushed

2 flavorful, tart-sweet apples, peeled, cored, and cut into large dice (use McIntosh, Northern Spy, or Cortland)

4 cups beet borscht, preferably homemade (page 78), or good-quality bottled (if using bottled, strain out any pieces of cooked beet and discard or reserve for another use)

2 bay leaves

2–4 tablespoons freshly grated horseradish, plus more for garnish

Sour salt (available in Middle Eastern and European markets and specialty stores) (optional)

BEETS AND KNAIDLACH

1 pound fresh beets

6 large or 8 medium russet (baking) potatoes (about 3 pounds), scrubbed but not peeled

2 large eggs

Salt and freshly ground black pepper
About 1½ cups matzoh meal

About ⅓ cup prepared white horseradish,
drained

1. Make the pot roast. Rub salt and pepper to taste into the meat. Heat 2 tablespoons of the oil over medium-high heat in a 6-quart Dutch oven or wide, heavy pot. Add the meat and brown it well on all sides. Transfer it to a platter.

2. Wipe out the pot, add the remaining 1 tablespoon oil, and heat until hot. Add the onion and sauté over medium heat until softened and golden at the edges, about 10 minutes. Add the garlic and apples and sauté, tossing and turning the ingredients for 5 minutes longer. Add the borscht and bay leaves and bring to a boil over high heat. Continue boiling for about 5 minutes to reduce the mixture slightly and concentrate the flavors. Turn the heat down to the lowest setting, add the meat and spoon the vegetable-fruit mixture all over it. Cover the pot, leaving the lid slightly askew, and simmer the meat until it can be easily pierced with a fork and its juices are clear or palest rose. This could be anywhere from 2–3 hours or more, depending on the thickness of the meat. Turn the meat every 20 minutes or so, using spoons to avoid piercing it. Make sure the liquid is gently simmering, the bubbles just barely breaking—if needed, use a flame-tamer or *blech* or stack two burner grates together to maintain a very low flame.

3. Stir in the horseradish, season with salt and pepper and cook for 5 minutes. Transfer the meat to a platter and wrap loosely with foil. Strain the pan sauce, reserving the solids. Skim as much fat as possible from the liquid. Puree the reserved solids with as much of the defatted braising liquid as necessary in a blender or food processor, or use an immersion blender. Return the puree to the pot, add the rest of the defatted braising liquid, and reduce over high heat until you have reached the consistency you prefer. Taste for seasoning. I love the tangy undertone ¼–½ teaspoon sour salt imparts to the sauce. If you choose to add it, start with a small amount and keep tasting until you reach a beautifully subtle acid-sweet balance. And you can add a bit more horseradish if you'd like (freshly grated and heated briefly, it is more robust and earthy than pungent). Just cook for a few minutes after adding additional seasoning to marry the flavors.

4. While the pot roast is braising, prepare the beets and knaidlach. Preheat the oven to 350°F. Trim the greens (save and cook like spinach or chard) and the root ends from the beets. Scrub the beets well, but don't peel them. Tightly wrap each beet in foil and place on a baking sheet. Bake until tender, 1½–2 hours (if they are very large). Carefully remove the foil and set aside until cool enough to handle. Peel and cut the beets into quarters and set aside.

5. Make the knaidlach. Cover the potatoes with cold salted water, bring to a boil, and cook, partially covered, until fork-tender, 30–45 minutes, depending on the size and age of the potatoes. Drain the potatoes and set aside until cool enough to handle. Peel the potatoes and mash them well (no lumps wanted here), using a ricer or food mill or by pushing through a strainer. Spread them out on a sheet of wax paper to cool to room temperature. In a large bowl, combine the potatoes with the eggs, about 2½ teaspoons salt (or to taste), and several generous grinds of pepper. Add 1½ cups matzoh meal and knead with your hands for several minutes to combine the ingredients well. Transfer the dough to a work surface, lightly dusted, if necessary, with matzoh meal. If there is too much dough to handle easily, divide it in half and knead each separately. Add a bit more matzoh meal if the dough is sticky, but avoid adding too much, which would make the knaidlach heavy. Keep kneading until the dough is smooth. Shape the dough into four balls, then divide each into smaller balls about 2 tablespoonfuls each, a standard coffee measure. Flatten the balls slightly. Place a heaping ¼ teaspoon of horseradish in the center, then pinch the edges together to enclose the filling. Reshape each into a ball. Gently press the ball over the convex bowl of a teaspoon, flattening and indenting it slightly. (This will ensure that the knaidlach will cook through before the outside begins to disintegrate.) Continue stuffing and shaping the knaidlach until you have used up all the dough. (If you wish, you can refrigerate them at this point on a platter or in a baking dish, in a single layer, not touching, for 2–3 hours.)

6. Bring 4 quarts of water and about 1¾ tablespoons salt to a boil in a large wide pot. Cook the knaidlach in batches, so you don't crowd the pot, dropping them one at a time into the boiling water. Reduce the heat to moderate, and cook, uncovered, for about 10 minutes or until cooked through. The knaidlach will rise to the top, swell up, and become fluffy around the edges. To check for doneness, remove one from the pot and either taste or cut open. If knaidl is dark in the center, ascertain whether this is the horseradish filling or an uncooked part. Don't overcook the knaidlach or they will fall apart.

7. Remove the cooked knaidlach with a skimmer or large slotted spoon—they are too delicate to be poured into a colander. Place them on a platter and moisten them lightly with a little pot roast sauce or melted margarine, and tent with foil, as you prepare the remaining knaidlach. Or keep them warm in a 250°F oven.

8. To serve, slice the pot roast very thin, against the grain. Surround with cooked beets and potato knaidlach. Nap everything generously with sauce. If desired, sprinkle some freshly grated horseradish over all, or offer guests some to season their food instead of freshly ground pepper. Pass additional sauce separately.

YIELD: 8–10 servings

COOK'S NOTE: To grate horseradish, peel it, cut it into small chunks, and grind in a food processor. You'll avoid most of the eye-stinging volatile oils. And avert your face when opening the food processor lid for the same reason.

You may have knaidlach left over; it is difficult to decrease the recipe proportionally. They are delicious served as you would gnocchi, with tomato sauce, leftover gravy, or for non-Passover meals, melted margarine and toasted bread crumbs. To reheat, sauté them lightly and quickly.

It's more work, but the dumplings are even more flavorful with onions added to the stuffing. Sauté chopped onions or shallots in olive oil until rich gold, season well with salt and pepper, and let cool. When inserting the horseradish, add some of the onions as well.

As with most braised meats, the pot roast benefits from a day's rest. Preparing the meat ahead not only cuts down on last-minute seder cooking, but also makes it easier to remove any fat from the gravy. Just scrape off the congealed fat while refrigerator cold.

TOASTED MATZOH FARFEL WITH WILD MUSHROOMS AND ROASTED GARLIC

MEAT

...and the sun shone and the people went out into the fields and gathered for themselves mushrooms and truffles.
—BABYLONIAN TALMUD: TA'ANIT 23A

During the year, farfel is fashioned from noodle dough that is grated into barley-size bits, but on Passover, like everything else, a stand-in is made from matzoh.

Available packaged in supermarkets around Passover, matzoh farfel is essentially plain matzoh that has been broken into chips. Jewish cooks substitute it, often toasted first for extra flavor, for the many starches proscribed during Passover to prepare croutons, stuffings, and casseroles.

In this side dish suggestive of a turkey dressing, bland matzoh comes alive when toasted with roasted garlic, then simmered with fresh, savory wild mushrooms. (If you can only get cultivated white mushrooms, intensify their flavor by combining them with a small quantity of dried wild mushrooms soaked in warm water until softened. Strain the soaking liquid of any grit, then simmer the dried mushrooms in it until very tender. Season them with salt and pepper, and sauté them along with the cultivated mushrooms for a few moments to blend their flavors.)

Roasted garlic, while simple to prepare, can be time-consuming. It keeps well, though (up to five days in the refrigerator), so it is worthwhile making it in quantity. Called for in a few recipes in this book, it is wonderful for seasoning everything from poultry and meat to vinaigrettes. For a lush thickener, stir some into gravies and stews.

A cautionary note: resist the temptation to stir the farfel around a lot. As with turkey dressing, you'll wind up with mush.

---

1 head of garlic, unpeeled
2 teaspoons plus 4 tablespoons olive oil
2 teaspoons plus 1 tablespoon chopped fresh
rosemary
3 large eggs, beaten
12 ounces matzoh farfel (5½–6 cups)
Salt and freshly ground black pepper

About ½ pound (2–3 cups) fresh wild (or exotic cultivated) mushrooms, such as porcini, chanterelles, shiitake, oyster, etc., or a combination
About ¾ pound onions, chopped (2½ cups)
About 3½ cups chicken broth, preferably homemade (page 63), or good-quality low-sodium canned

---

1. Preheat the oven to 375°F. Roast the garlic. Break the head into single cloves and put them, unpeeled, into a baking dish just large enough to hold them snugly (I usually use a 4-inch square enameled casserole). Drizzle with 2 teaspoons of the oil and sprinkle 1 teaspoon of rosemary on top.

Cover tightly (use foil if you don't have a lid) and roast for 30–45 minutes, or until a soft puree is formed when you squeeze a clove. Avoid overcooking, which turns the garlic bitter. Leave the oven on. Squeeze the puree out by hand or run the unpeeled cloves through a food mill to trap the peels.

2. In a very large bowl, mash the garlic with the oil from the baking dish. Whisk in the eggs. Add the farfel and salt and pepper to taste and mix well.

3. Like a bread stuffing, matzoh farfel is usually toasted before cooking so it can absorb all the flavoring liquid without becoming soggy. Line a large cookie sheet with foil. Thinly spread the farfel mixture on it and toast it lightly in the oven, stirring occasionally so the pieces bake evenly, until golden and dry to the touch, 15–20 minutes. (If the farfel layer is not fairly thin, it will take excessively long to toast uniformly, so if your pan is not large enough, use two cookie sheets or toast in batches.)

4. Meanwhile, wipe the mushrooms clean with damp paper towels and trim them, discarding any tough stems. Slice the mushrooms thinly and set them aside. In a heavy, steep-sided skillet large enough to hold the farfel later (12-inch well-seasoned cast iron or enameled cast iron is ideal), heat 2 tablespoons of the oil until hot. Add the onions and sauté over medium-high heat, lifting and turning until the edges are a deep gold, about 15 minutes. Season lightly with salt and pepper, remove from skillet, and set aside. In the same skillet, heat the remaining 2 tablespoons oil over moderately high heat. Add the mushrooms, season lightly, and sauté, lifting and tossing, until tender, 5–8 minutes, depending on the type of mushroom. Return the onions to the skillet and sprinkle with 1 tablespoon of the rosemary. Add the farfel and stir briefly to combine the ingredients. Add 1 cup of broth and cook over medium heat, breaking up any lumps in the farfel with the back of a wooden spoon, until the broth is absorbed. Avoid stirring, but press down with the spoon to encourage the farfel to absorb the liquid and to separate the clumps . Lower the heat and continue adding broth, about 1 cup at a time, waiting until most of the liquid is absorbed before adding the next cup. After adding about 3½ cups broth in all, the farfel should be moist but not mushy. (If it is still slightly dry, add a few spoonfuls of broth as needed, simmering until it is absorbed. If it is too wet, evaporate the excess moisture over low heat.) The trick is adding the broth slowly while simmering the farfel over low heat. You eliminate the need to stir, and the broth is completely absorbed into the farfel. It is like preparing stuffing on the stovetop, and when finished, the farfel should have a pleasing, stuffinglike texture: moist and succulent, but neither spongy nor gummy.

5. Taste and adjust the seasoning. Sprinkle with the remaining 1 teaspoon rosemary before serving. Cover and let rest for 5 minutes.

YIELD: 8–10 servings

COOK'S NOTE: This recipe takes well to other big flavors. Try sautéed fennel or celery (cook until deep gold and enhance with crushed celery or fennel seeds); celery root, diced artichoke hearts, or a dose of crispy fried shallots. Artichoke farfel is especially delicious topped with toasted crushed hazelnuts.

TOASTED ALMOND–COCONUT MACAROONS

PAREVE

> The next day Moses entered the tent of the Pact, and there the staff of Aaron...had
> sprouted; it had brought forth sprouts, produced blossoms, and borne almonds.
> —NUMBERS 17:23

> Figs, grapes, and almonds are always beneficial, whether fresh or dried.
> One may eat of them as one needs.
> —MAIMONIDES, *RULES FOR PHYSICAL HEALTH*

Made of ground nuts so they are flour-free, easy-to-prepare macaroons are a Passover favorite of both Ashkenazim and Sephardim. The simple becomes seductive when the almonds are briefly toasted first, their skins left on, and drizzled with maple syrup or brown sugar.

To avoid disappointment, be sure to taste the almonds before you start the recipe to make sure they are fresh.

---

1 ¾ cups (about 9 ounces) whole natural almonds

1 tablespoon pure maple syrup or packed brown sugar, preferably dark

⅔ cup plus 1 tablespoon white or light brown granulated sugar

1 cup shredded unsweetened coconut

1 teaspoon amaretto, or ½ teaspoon kosher-for-Passover almond extract (optional)

4 large egg whites

Pinch of salt

---

1. Preheat the oven to 350°F. Line a baking sheet with foil. Toss the almonds with the maple syrup or brown sugar and spread them out in a single layer on the baking sheet. Toast until very fragrant, 10–12 minutes. Remove from the oven and let cool. Reduce the oven temperature to 325°F.

2. In a food processor, grind the cooled almonds with half of the sugar, using the pulse motion, until finely ground. Combine the ground nuts, coconut, and amaretto or almond extract, if you are using it, in a large bowl.

3. Beat the egg whites in another bowl with the salt until they form soft peaks. Gradually add the remaining sugar and continue beating until stiff but not dry. Gently fold the whites into the almond-coconut mixture.

4. Line a cookie sheet with parchment paper. (You will probably need either to use 2 cookie sheets or work in batches.) Drop heaping tablespoons of batter on the cookie sheet about 2 inches apart. Flatten the tops slightly. Bake for about 15 minutes, or until just dry to the touch and light golden with pale brown edges. Remove the sheet from the oven and transfer to a rack to cool or slide the parchment paper off.

5. Don't remove the macaroons until they have cooled completely, then carefully separate them. They store well in airtight containers for at least 5 days.

YIELD: 30–35 macaroons

COOK'S NOTE: This is also very good when pecans are substituted for the almonds. Be sure to use light brown granulated sugar.

HAZELNUT MACAROONS

PAREVE

These simply made macaroons are imbued with the vivid taste of hazelnuts—the toasty flavor of that transcendent Italian gelato, *nocciola*.

Nuts can turn rancid easily if not properly stored, so make sure yours are fresh and sweet-tasting.

---

*2⅓ cups (about 12 ounces) shelled hazelnuts
(also called filberts)*
*1 cup plus 2 tablespoons white or light brown
granulated sugar*
*½ teaspoon kosher-for-Passover pure almond
extract, or 1 teaspoon hazelnut-flavored*

*liqueur, such as Frangelico, or another nut-
flavored liqueur, such as amaretto (optional)*
3 large egg whites

---

1. Preheat the oven to 350°F. Toast the nuts: Spread them out in a single layer on a baking sheet, and roast in the oven, shaking occasionally, for about 15 minutes, or until they are fragrant and most of the skins have popped. Wrap the nuts in a dish towel and let them cool slightly. Rub them vigorously against each other in the towel to remove most of the loose skins. Don't bother about the remaining skins—they'll just add to the flavor. You can turn the oven off for now.

2. When the nuts are completely cool, grind them with the sugar in the food processor, using the pulse motion, until chopped fine. They won't be perfectly ground and they shouldn't be. With the machine on, add the extract or liqueur if you are using it, and the egg whites, a little at a time. Process just enough to combine the ingredients into a smooth paste. Scrape the mixture into a bowl and refrigerate, covered, for 15–20 minutes.

3. Preheat the oven to 325°F. Line a cookie sheet with parchment paper. (You will probably need either to use 2 cookie sheets or work in batches.) Drop rounded tablespoons of batter on the cookie sheet about 2 inches apart. Smooth and flatten the tops slightly with the back of a spoon or your fingertips (the batter will be quite sticky, so you may have to dip your finger occasionally in cold water). Bake for about 15 minutes, or until just dry to the touch, puffed, and beginning to color. Remove from the oven and transfer the sheet to a rack to cool or slide the parchment paper off. The macaroons will be very soft but will harden as they cool.

4. Don't remove the macaroons until they have cooled completely, then carefully separate them from the parchment. They store well in airtight containers for at least 5 days.

YIELD: 25–30 macaroons

COOK'S NOTE: For a magnificent variation, make Pistachio-Ginger Macaroons. Lightly toast 3 cups of shelled, blanched pistachios at 350°F for about 8 minutes, just until fragrant. Let them cool, then combine them in a food processor with 3 tablespoons (1½ ounces) candied ginger and 1¼ cups sugar, following the above directions. Add 3 large egg whites (omit the extract) and continue as above. Bake for 12–15 minutes at 325°F.

The flavor of these macaroons becomes bolder and more pronounced after a day or two.

The beautiful Hebrew allegorical song "Had Gadya" (in "The House That Jack Built" style) is traditionally sung at the close of the seder. (*One Only Kid*, by Eleazar Lissitzky, from the Had Gadya suite, 1919.)

SPRING COMPOTE

PAREVE

Tucked in among the horseradish, haroset, and other symbolic foods, there might be an orange on some of the newest seder plates. According to Alisa Solomon of the *Village Voice* (April 2, 1996), this addition has its roots in a wonderful story most attribute to theologian Susannah Heschel.

Solomon recounts that a man interrupted a talk Heschel was giving in Florida on women and Judaism some years ago, heckling, "A woman belongs in the rabbi's pulpit and other places of Jewish leadership like a loaf of bread belongs on a seder plate." Heschel retorted that "women were more like an orange on the seder plate—not a rebuke to tradition, but a fertile addition to it."

Bracing yet sweet, like the orange on a seder plate, this fresh compote features oranges, along with rhubarb, raspberries, and prunes. Accompanied by light, homemade macaroons, it makes a perfect coda to the rich seder meal.

¾ cup sugar

1 cinnamon stick

1 vanilla bean, split

1 pound rhubarb, washed, trimmed, tough strings removed with a vegetable peeler, and cut into 1-inch pieces (discard the leaves; they are toxic)

½ cup (about 4 ounces) pitted prunes, halved, or if large, quartered

3 blood or navel oranges, or a combination, peeled, white pith and any seeds removed

1 cup (about 5 ounces) fresh raspberries

Fresh mint leaves, for garnish (optional)

Optional accompaniment: *Toasted Almond–Coconut Macaroons (page 332) and/or Hazelnut Macaroons (page 334)*

---

1. Place 2 cups of water and the sugar, cinnamon, and vanilla bean in a medium, nonreactive saucepan and bring to a boil. Add the rhubarb and prunes and simmer over low heat until the rhubarb is just tender, 7–10 minutes. Don't allow it to get too soft—it will "cook" further while macerating. Using a slotted spoon, remove the rhubarb and prunes and transfer to a large attractive serving bowl. Slice the oranges into thin rounds (if they break apart into little sections after you slice them, that's perfectly fine), and add them, along with the raspberries, to the bowl.

2. Boil the syrup remaining in the saucepan over moderately high heat until reduced by about half. Remove the cinnamon and vanilla bean (you can dry the bean and save it for another use, like burying it in a bowl of sugar to prepare vanilla sugar) and pour the hot syrup over the fruit. Stir well. Let the fruit cool to room temperature, then cover and refrigerate for several hours.

3. Garnish the compote, if you'd like, with fresh mint leaves, and serve with the macaroons.

YIELD: 6–8 servings

HUNGARIAN CHOCOLATE-WALNUT TORTE

This is a taste of prewar Hungary, from the family repertoire of my dear friend Judy Abrams, gifted teacher and poet. Based on ground walnuts and leavened only with eggs, the light, fudge-luscious cake has not a jot of butter or flour, making it Passover-perfect for meat and dairy meals.

To conclude a meat meal, serve it plain or dusted fancifully with confectioners' sugar (a Passover recipe without cornstarch follows) or glazed with a simple chocolate icing.

As a dairy dish, the torte is exquisite covered in swirls of lightly sweetened whipped cream or with scoops of vanilla ice cream on the side, accompanied by a steaming cup of strong cappuccino.

Enjoy this beautifully moist and virtually no-fail torte not just on Passover but year-round. When well wrapped (without icing), it keeps very well, tasting even better a day or two after it is made.

As with all nut pastries, be sure the walnuts you are using are very fresh-tasting.

¾ cup sugar (if using half semisweet and half sweet chocolate) or ¾ cup plus 2 tablespoons sugar (if using all semisweet chocolate)

6 ounces fine-quality chocolate (preferably half dark sweet, sometimes labeled German Sweet Chocolate, and half semisweet, but all semisweet is also delicious), cut into small pieces

6 large eggs, separated

6 ounces (about 1¾–2 cups) shelled walnuts

3 tablespoons matzoh meal

Optional accompaniments: Passover Confectioners' Sugar (page 338) or Chocolate Icing (page 339); heavy cream, freshly whipped to soft drifts and barely or very lightly sweetened; or vanilla ice cream

Walnut halves, for garnish (optional)

---

1. Have all ingredients at room temperature.

2. Line the bottom of an 8-inch square cake pan or a 9-inch springform pan with parchment or wax paper.

3. Preheat the oven to 350°F. Set a rack in the lower third of the oven.

4. In a heavy-bottomed 2- or 3-quart saucepan, combine ½ cup of the sugar and ½ cup of water and bring to a boil, stirring constantly over medium heat. Continue boiling and stirring until all the grains of sugar have completely dissolved and the mixture forms a simple syrup. Remove the pan from the heat and stir in the chocolate until melted and smooth. Set aside to cool.

5. In a large bowl, beat the egg yolks until light and fluffy. Grind the walnuts with the remaining sugar and the matzoh meal in a food processor using the pulse motion and stir into the egg yolks. Add the cooled chocolate mixture and combine thoroughly.

6. Using clean beaters, beat the egg whites in another bowl until they hold stiff peaks. Gradually fold the whites into the chocolate-walnut mixture, incorporating them gently but thoroughly so that no whites are visible. Pour the batter into the prepared pan and bake for 35–40 minutes, or until puffed and almost set but still a little gooey in the center. A wooden toothpick inserted 1 inch from the edge should come out clean.

7. Remove the pan from the oven and let cool on a rack. When completely cool, unmold the cake by running a thin-bladed knife around the edges of the cake to release it from the pan (or release the springform); invert onto a platter. Peel off the parchment or wax paper. Serve the torte at room temperature.

8. If desired, lightly dust with Passover confectioners' sugar. For a lovely, simple presentation, place a doily or a stencil—handmade by you or, even better, your children—over the torte, then sprinkle with sugar. Carefully remove the doily or stencil.

Or glaze with chocolate icing. Lay long strips of wax paper or foil on a cake plate or serving platter and place the cake on top. Pour the glaze over the top of the cake, letting it drip down the sides. Using a spatula, evenly spread the glaze over the top and sides. Now pull out and discard the paper or foil strips—the plate will be clean and ready for serving. If you'd like, garnish with a few walnut halves attractively placed in the center of the cake. Refrigerate the cake for about an hour to set the glaze, but bring it to room temperature before serving.

The plain or frosted torte is heavenly with generous dollops of whipped cream or vanilla ice cream.

YIELD: About 10 servings

PASSOVER CONFECTIONERS' SUGAR   PAREVE

In a blender or food processor, whirl 1 cup minus ½ tablespoon regular granulated sugar until it is powdery. Place in a small bowl and stir in ½ teaspoon potato starch. Sift before using. (Recently commercial Passover confectioners' sugar, made without cornstarch, has appeared in some stores with large kosher-for-Passover sections. If available, by all means use it here.)

CHOCOLATE ICING

6 tablespoons unsalted butter or margarine
6 ounces fine-quality semisweet or bittersweet
  chocolate, cut into small pieces

Melt the butter or margarine slowly in a heavy saucepan over very low heat. When half is melted, gradually whisk in the chocolate, stirring well as it melts. After all the chocolate has been added, stir in 2 tablespoons of water and beat well until the glaze is completely smooth. Let the mixture cool for about 5 minutes to thicken slightly.

YIELD: Scant 1 cup

LEMON-FRIED CHICKEN WITH
TART SALAD TOPPING

"Why on this night do we dip twice, and on other nights, we dip only once?" asks the youngest child as part of the Four Questions at the seder, seeking an explanation of the mysteries encoded in the ritual Passover meal.

And the head of the family answers that on this night we dip bitter herbs into haroset to remind us of the mortar the Jews used to build Pharaoh's cities and the bitterness they suffered. We dip vegetables in salt water to commemorate both the joy of spring and the tears of the Jewish slaves.

But when did we dip once? In ancient times, when the diet of the Jews comprised mainly bread— and heavy bread at that, often made from barley or other coarse grains—they dipped the bread in vinegar, onions, or bitter herbs (the *maror* of the seder plate) to make the leaden starch more palatable and more digestible.

Arugula was then collected wild by the poor. Purslane, a lemony-flavored, small-leafed green currently gracing mesclun salads, and cress were gathered and later cultivated by Jewish farmers. Jews dipped rough bread into the sharp greens or combined them into a sandwich. (In some Haggadahs, Ashkenazi Jews, unfamiliar with this erstwhile Mediterranean custom of dunking, have changed the question to "…and on other nights, we dip not at all?")

"Lo, this is the bread of affliction," the Haggadah refers to the matzoh. And after a few days of the coarse, unleavened bread in every guise imaginable, we too, like the ancients, need spring's sharp greens coursing through systems now sluggish and logy.

In this adaptation of a popular Milanese dish, we reenact the dipping one more time: the crisp, matzoh meal–coated chicken is dipped into a salad of tart greens, tomato, and onion.

CUTLETS

2 large garlic cloves, peeled and crushed

3 tablespoons fresh lemon juice

1 teaspoon olive oil, plus ¼ cup for frying

1½ teaspoons salt, or to taste

¼ teaspoon freshly ground pepper, or to taste

1¾–2 pounds skinless, boneless chicken cutlets, trimmed of fat and gristle and pounded lightly to a uniform thickness

2 large eggs

1 cup matzoh meal, seasoned to taste with salt and pepper

1 tablespoon grated lemon zest

SALAD

½ pound ripe tomatoes, diced (1 cup)

¾ cup finely chopped onions

2 tablespoons fine-quality extra-virgin olive oil

1 tablespoon fresh lemon juice

1 teaspoon dried oregano

Salt and freshly ground black pepper to taste

2 cups sharp salad greens (such as arugula, watercress, endive, radicchio, sorrel, flat-leaf parsley, or purslane, or, preferably, a mixture of these), washed, dried, and torn into bite-size pieces

Accompaniment: Lemon wedges

---

1. Prepare the cutlets. In a large bowl, blend together the garlic, lemon juice, olive oil, salt, and pepper. Add the chicken, toss to coat thoroughly with the mixture, and refrigerate to marinate, covered, for 1–2 hours. Or marinate in a resealable plastic bag. Turn the chicken occasionally in the marinade to ensure even flavoring.

2. Beat the eggs well in a wide shallow bowl or pie pan. Stir together the matzoh meal and lemon zest and spread on a large sheet of wax paper or a plate. Taking one cutlet at a time, dip it into the beaten egg, coating well on both sides. Let the excess egg drip back into the bowl. Dredge the cutlets on both sides in the matzoh meal mixture. To prevent loose crumbs from falling off and burning in the hot oil, pat the cutlets firmly on each side so the matzoh meal adheres, then place them on a rack and let stand for about 15 minutes to set the coating.

3. Heat the ¼ cup olive oil in a 10- to 12-inch heavy sauté pan or skillet over medium-high heat until hot but not smoking. Add the cutlets (in batches, if necessary, to avoid crowding the pan) and sauté them for about 2 minutes on each side, or until golden and cooked through.

4. Transfer the cutlets as they are done to a paper towel–lined baking sheet to absorb excess oil, keeping them warm, if necessary, in a 200°F oven, until the rest are done.

5. Prepare the salad. In a bowl, combine the tomato, onions, olive oil, lemon juice, oregano, and salt and pepper to taste. Add the greens and toss well.

6. Serve the cutlets topped with the salad, accompanied by the lemon wedges.

YIELD: 4–5 servings

COOK'S NOTE: Divide the seasoned matzoh meal in half. When the first half becomes ragged with little clumps of egg from dredging the cutlets, replace with the reserved fresh half.

SNAPPER FILLETS IN PISTACHIO-MATZOH CRUST

❧❧❧❧❧❧❧❧❧❧❧❧❧❧❧

DAIRY

Take of the best fruits of the land in your vessels, and carry down the man a present,
a little balm, and a little honey, spices and myrrh, pistachios and almonds.

—GENESIS 43:11

Jacob never guessed that this gift for the "man," Pharaoh's governor, was in fact destined for none other than his own son Joseph, he of the technicolor-coat fame. But he was sure it—and a double measure of money—would please.

For pistachios always taste like a treat. I find them more addictive than potato chips when eaten out of hand, and I keep a supply of the pale green nuts in the freezer to glamorize savory foods and desserts. They give more than mere crunch—pistachios have an exotic, almost flowery-sweet taste, suggesting, as Waverly Root has pointed out, a spice more than a nut. Toasted pistachio nuts give a delightful buttery finish to this matzoh crumb crust and point up the richness of the sour cream topping, so that it need only be lightly slathered on the fish.

Simple but delicious, this comes together very quickly.

¼ cup shelled unsalted pistachios

2 tablespoons unsalted butter, plus additional butter or oil for greasing the pan

½ cup coarsely ground matzoh crumbs (egg matzohs are excellent for this if you use them during Passover) or matzoh meal (see page 25)

Salt and freshly ground black pepper

3 tablespoons sour cream

2 tablespoons grated onion

2 teaspoons grated lemon zest and/or— for a sassy seasoning with just a bit of heat— 1½ teaspoons of prepared white horseradish, drained

1¾–2 pounds red snapper fillets (or other nonoily white-fleshed fish fillets)

Lemon wedges

---

1. Preheat the oven to 375°F. Spread the pistachios on a foil-lined baking sheet and toast until fragrant, shaking the pan from time to time, 8–10 minutes. Toast the matzoh crumbs or matzoh meal at the same time: Melt the butter in a small baking dish in the oven; add the matzoh crumbs or meal, season with salt and pepper, and stir well. Bake, stirring occasionally, until golden, about 10 minutes.

2. Remove the pistachios from the oven and let cool slightly. Chop the nuts coarsely by hand or with a few pulses in a food processor. Combine the pistachios with the toasted matzoh crumbs or meal. Raise the oven temperature to 400°F.

3. In a small bowl, whisk together the sour cream, onion, lemon zest, and/or horseradish. Lightly grease a baking pan large enough to accommodate the fish fillets in one layer. Sprinkle the fish on both sides with salt and pepper and place in the prepared pan. Spread the sour cream mixture evenly over the fish and top with the pistachio-matzoh crumbs. Bake just until the fish is opaque throughout, 10–15 minutes, depending on the thickness of the fish. Serve with lemon wedges.

YIELD: 4–6 servings

MOZZARELLA IN MATZOH CARROZZA

DAIRY

This variation on the Neapolitan mozzarella in carrozza—a luscious golden-fried sandwich of molten mozzarella, sauced with a blend of garlic, lemon, and anchovies—may seem unusual, but softened matzoh works remarkably well as a substitute for the fluffy sliced white bread frequently used. The absorbent matzoh pairs beautifully with the assertive citrusy sauce.

I especially like the subtle way the slightly sweet egg matzohs soften the saline edge of anchovies, but plain matzohs are very good too.

The anchovies are essential here. They energize the flavors, bringing needed dimension to the dish, and when minced fine, will dissolve into the sauce virtually undetectable.

6–7 whole matzohs, egg or plain

About ½ pound mozzarella cheese, shredded or thinly sliced and then diced

6–12 fresh basil leaves, shredded (optional)

SAUCE

2 teaspoons finely minced garlic

2 teaspoons excellent-quality extra-virgin olive oil

3 anchovy fillets, finely chopped

Juice of 1 lemon (3–4 tablespoons)

Freshly ground black pepper

2 large eggs

Olive oil, for frying

Lemon quarters

Fresh parsley sprigs, for garnish

---

1. Make the matzoh carrozzas. Break each matzoh into 4 equal pieces. Fill a large shallow dish or pan with well-salted water. Dip 2 matzoh quarters into the water until just softened and pliant. Place some of the cheese, and basil, if using, on one of the matzoh quarters and top with the second piece of matzoh. Pat this mozzarella sandwich into a hamburger patty shape, molding it nicely with your hands and gently squeezing out any excess water. The cheese should be completely covered by the matzoh coating. Place the finished patty on a platter to dry slightly as you continue making more, using the rest of the matzoh.

2. Prepare the sauce. In a very small skillet or saucepan, cook the garlic in the oil over gentle heat until it is just tinged with gold, about 2 minutes. The garlic should remain quite soft—don't let it turn crisp or brown. Immediately add the anchovies, stirring and mashing until they have dissolved completely. Whisk in the lemon juice and pepper to taste. Cook, stirring, for 2–3 minutes, to blend all the flavors. Keep warm until ready to serve.

3. Beat the eggs in a shallow bowl with 1 tablespoon of water. Heat ¼ inch of oil in a 10- to 12-inch heavy skillet until hot but not smoking. Just before frying, slip each patty into the egg, immersing it completely, then letting the excess egg drip back into the bowl. Slip as many egg-coated patties into the hot oil as possible without crowding the pan and fry them until crisp and golden on both sides. Avoid turning the patties more than once. Fry the remaining patties, in batches if necessary. Drain lightly on paper towels.

4. Arrange two carrozzas on each plate and spoon some of the sauce over them. Serve with lemon quarters and fresh parsley sprigs, as garnish.

YIELD: 6–7 appetizer or light lunch servings

MANGO AND SOUR CHERRY
MACAROON CRUMBLE

DAIRY OR PAREVE

Around Passover at our house **macaroons** tend to proliferate like wire coat hangers from the dry cleaners. In addition to the ones I make, there are the cakey commercial variety I purchase from my nephews, who peddle Passover **sweets** as a fund-raiser for their school. A luscious fruit crumble is a fresh way to make use of the leftovers, and other suggestions follow this recipe (see Cook's Note).

1 cup amaretto

1 large, ripe mango, peeled, pitted, and cut into small chunks (1½–1¾ cups)

1 cup canned, pitted sour cherries packed in water (8 ounces), drained

2 tablespoons dried cherries or dried cranberries

¼ teaspoon nutmeg, preferably freshly grated

¼ teaspoon ground cinnamon

1½ cups macaroons (homemade or commercial variety), crumbled

½ cup almonds, lightly toasted and coarsely chopped

Pinch of salt

3 tablespoons unsalted butter or margarine, cut into bits, plus additional for greasing the pan

Optional accompaniment: vanilla ice cream

1. Preheat the oven to 375°F. In a small saucepan, reduce the amaretto to ½ cup over medium-high heat. Combine the mango, sour cherries, dried cherries or cranberries, nutmeg, and cinnamon in a bowl. Pour the hot amaretto over the fruit and stir with a wooden spoon to coat evenly. Set aside for about 30 minutes to macerate.

2. If the macaroons are very moist, toast them lightly on a baking sheet for 5–10 minutes, then let cool. Or leave them out overnight to dry until they are crumbly. Chop the macaroons by hand or in a food processor using the pulse motion. Transfer to a bowl and mix with the almonds and salt. Work in the butter with your fingers until the mixture resembles coarse crumbs.

3. Butter an 8- to 10-inch glass or ceramic pie pan or similar ovenproof dish. Spoon the fruit and accumulated juices into the prepared pan. Scatter the macaroon mixture evenly on top. Bake for 25–35 minutes, or until the fruit is bubbling and the topping is golden brown. Serve warm or cold, topped, if desired, with vanilla ice cream.

YIELD: About 6 servings

COOK'S NOTE: Here are some other ways to use macaroons:

Old-fashioned Biscuit Tortoni: Pack softened ice cream (some suggestions: vanilla, coffee, cherry vanilla) into paper cups. Sprinkle the tops generously with crushed macaroon crumbs and press in firmly. Or fold some crushed macaroons into the softened ice cream, then top with additional crushed macaroons. Wrap tightly with plastic wrap and freeze until solid, at least 2 hours.

Italian-style baked fruit: Lightly sweeten pear or peach halves. (If peaches are not flavorful—they are out of season in spring—slice them with equal amounts of mango.) Combine crumbled macaroons with some butter and stuff the fruit halves with the mixture (or flatten the mixture into disks and place over the sliced fruit). Place the fruit in a baking dish, and sprinkle with toasted almonds. Add a few tablespoons of white grape juice or other sweet fruit juice or wine to the pan to keep the fruit moist and prevent it from sticking, and bake until the fruit is tender and juicy, basting occasionally with the pan liquid.

Stir crushed macaroons into fruit compotes.

Bake finely crushed macaroons until dry and use for cookie crumb crusts—especially good for cheesecake or ice cream pies.

SHAVUOT

The beautiful holiday which commemorates the receiving of the Torah arrived, and with it spring came to the steppe. Zlochov was inundated by a sea of moist, green, velvety grass, which streamed from the steppe into the town.... Tall bunches of jessamine looked into every window of Zlochov, and the fragrance of white lilac filled the little rooms.

—SHOLOM ASCH, "WE WILL DO AND WE WILL OBEY"

The symbols of Shavuot's ancient agricultural origins are sweet with the perfumes of deep spring: soft-skinned fruits and sun-warm berries, decorative branches of fresh greens and fragrant flowers. One of the three pilgrimage festivals, the holiday began as a joyous harvest celebration. Seven weeks after Passover (Shavuot means weeks and the festival is sometimes known as the Feast of Weeks), the last of the barley harvest was ready to be gathered and the first fruits and new spring wheat was beginning to ripen.

The most beautiful fruits were set in baskets fashioned sometimes of silver and gold, and carried to the Temple in long processions accompanied by music and song.

Later Shavuot, like Passover and Sukkot, was linked to the Exodus, acquiring a more religious significance as it came to commemorate the anniversary of the covenant made between God and Israel on Mount Sinai, when Moses received the Ten Commandments and the Torah. If Passover celebrates the Israelites' release from slavery and their rebirth as a free people, their acceptance of God's Laws at Shavuot marks their spiritual liberation, the rebirth of their souls.

Iranian Jews know the holiday as Feast of the Flowers, Italians as Feast of the Roses. The sweet-smelling blossoms and leaves that adorn the synagogue and the home recall the beautiful processions through Jerusalem, as well as verdant, rose-covered Mount Sinai and the aroma of Paradise the Torah offers us. The fragrant new fruits appear in any—or every—part of the meal, from soup to dessert.

But it is with dairy dishes that Shavuot is most closely associated. It is difficult to believe that this custom is nowhere mandated, so strong is the tradition.

One explanation, of course, is found in nature: this is the season when animals, grazing on the fresh, new pasturage, produce an abundance of milk. But there are many spiritual interpretations too, relating the holiday to the revelation on Sinai. Because Moses brought them the laws of *kashrut* when he descended the mountain, the Israelites were permitted hereafter to eat only meat that was kosher. By the time he returned, however, they were famished and had no time to prepare a meat meal according to ritual. So they rejoiced with festive dairy foods—including, perhaps, cheese formed from milk that had soured during their long vigil. The Torah and Israel have both been compared to milk and honey, nourishing and sweet, while the whiteness of milk and of rice—another popular Shavuot food—evokes the purity of the Laws and the Commandments. And there are still a host of other exegeses based on the numerical equivalents of various words.

Whatever the reason, dairy is a highlight of the Jewish kitchen. This is the time to savor an array of lavish all-time Hall-of-Famers, presented here in sublime variations: from shav with salmon kreplach to a sensuous honey–ricotta cheese cake, from a richly textured cold fruit soup to luscious cheese blintzes coupled with a fresh berry compote.

O T H E R   S U G G E S T I O N S
F O R   S H A V U O T

WARM SHAV WITH SALMON KREPLACH

Sour pickles, tangy beets, and cabbage turned to kraut—Russian and Polish Jews have always had a taste for *ʒoiers*, or sours, the acidic vegetables that nudged along the sluggish digestion of their heavy starch diet.

After a winter of stodgy stored or pickled vegetables, tart and sassy sorrel was a spring treat. Like its cousin rhubarb, the spring *ʒoier* (sorrel is also known as sour grass) was considered a blood-cleansing tonic and used principally in two soups usually served cold. The more famous, shav, was a dairy soup often enriched with eggs; the other, *botvinya*, combined the sorrel with spinach and chunks of fish. The beautiful green that evokes Mount Sinai, where Moses received the Ten Commandments from God, and the lavish use of milk products, made shav a favorite for Shavuot meals.

Though I loved to munch on the refreshing, lemon-grassy sorrel leaves as a child, I couldn't abide shav. The green and cold viscosity of the egg-thick liquid put me in the mind of the lower depths of a frog pond and made me gag. Then one day my mother served it warm: the slime receded, in its place a princely soup.

Recently, reading about botvinya started me thinking about the exquisite combinations of salmon and creamy sorrel I've eaten in the Loire Valley. Rough chunks of salmon seemed too indelicate for the shav, however, so I encased them in thin kreplach. The result is this soup.

KREPLACH

2 scallions, thinly sliced

2 tablespoons unsalted butter

¾ pound salmon, skinned, boned, and cut into chunks

1 large egg yolk

2 tablespoons minced fresh chives

Salt and freshly ground black pepper

36–40 wonton wrappers (see page 30; it's a good idea to have a few extra in case of tearing)

Egg wash (1–2 large eggs, as needed, each beaten with 1 teaspoon of water)

SHAV

¼ pound onions, finely chopped (1 cup)

2 tablespoons unsalted butter

8½ tightly packed cups (about 14–16 ounces) sorrel, washed, stemmed, and cut into thin strips (try rolling a few leaves together at a time and snipping them into shreds with scissors; sorrel should be crisp and unwilted— avoid torn leaves or those with wet or soft spots; store in perforated bags in the refrigerator)

2 cups cold water (quality is important here, so if you use bottled water for coffee or tea, use it here)

2 cups milk, or 1 cup milk and 1 cup heavy or light cream

2 tablespoons chopped fresh dill

Salt and freshly ground black pepper

2 large egg yolks

1 cup sour cream

Accompaniments: Additional chopped scallions and/or dill; sour cream (optional)

1. Prepare the kreplach. Cook the scallions in the butter in a medium skillet over moderately low heat, stirring until softened. Add the salmon and continue cooking, gently tossing the mixture, until the fish is barely cooked through, 4–5 minutes (it will cook further in the kreplach). Let cool slightly, then stir in the egg yolk, chives, and salt and pepper to taste. Process the mixture in a food processor, pulsing until chopped fine. Transfer the filling to a bowl and refrigerate, covered, for 1 hour, or until cold.

2. Fill and trim the kreplach, as described on page 30, using 1 heaping teaspoon of filling for each wonton wrapper and the egg wash to seal.

3. Poach the kreplach. In a large, very wide pot, bring at least 5 quarts of lightly salted water to a boil. Slip in the kreplach, one by one, being careful not to overcrowd the pot (if necessary, cook them in batches, or use two pots). Lower the temperature slightly (the kreplach might explode if the water is boiling furiously) and poach until tender, 3–6 minutes (exact time will depend on the brand of wonton wrapper used). Remove the kreplach a few at a time with a large skimmer, shaking the skimmer gently a couple of times to dry the kreplach (they are too fragile to pour into a colander).

4. Prepare the shav. In a large nonreactive saucepan or 5- to 6-quart Dutch oven, cook the onions in the butter over moderately low heat, stirring, for about 10 minutes, until very soft. Stir in 8 cups of the sorrel, turn the heat up to medium, and cook for 5–7 minutes, or until it has melted into a puree.

5. Add the water, bring the mixture to a boil, and simmer for 10 minutes. Add the milk, and cream if you are using it, dill, and salt and pepper to taste, and heat slowly, stirring, until the soup is hot. Do not let it come to a boil.

6. In a bowl, whisk the egg yolks with the sour cream. Slowly pour a cup of the hot soup into the egg–sour cream mixture, stirring to prevent curdling. Then gradually stir this mixture into the soup, and cook, stirring, over low heat for 3–4 minutes, to blend the flavors. If you prefer a more refined texture, you can puree the soup to a smooth consistency in a food processor or a blender in batches. Or puree in the pot with an immersion blender. Stir in the reserved ½ cup sorrel strips.

7. To serve, place 5 or 6 kreplach in each warmed shallow soup plate and ladle the shav over them. Garnish with the chopped scallions and dill, and, if desired, a small dollop of sour cream.

YIELD: 6–8 servings

COOK'S NOTE: While 5–6 kreplach may seem like a lot for each portion, each krepl is made with a single wrapper, not two. My guests never have any trouble polishing them off.

GRANDMOTHER'S COLD FRUIT SOUP

To my grandmother, tiny, first-of-the-year strawberries were the luxury foods of her adopted country, meant to be savored slowly, open-faced on fresh corn-rye bread thickly spread with sweet butter and sprinkled with sugar. Not for her those seasonless behemoths whose hard white hearts you need an apple corer to remove.

Later on, as June warmed and local strawberries grew more plentiful and cheaper at her fruit market, Grandma would serve them with thick sour cream or heavy sweet cream, roll them in a blintz, and even, for special occasions like Shavuot, add them to an extravagant fruit soup.

This soup has several layers of flavor, derived from the tea, juice, and many kinds of fruit—fresh and dried—used in it. But it is the sweet melting strawberries that make it taste extraordinary.

---

2 cups freshly brewed black tea, such as orange pekoe, Darjeeling, Earl Grey, or English Breakfast

1 cup pitted prunes, quartered

½ cup dried apricots, peaches, pears, or apples, or a mixture, cut into small pieces

2 tablespoons honey, or more as needed

1 vanilla bean, split

1 cinnamon stick

1 strip of lemon zest

3–4 pounds mixed fresh, ripe, stone fruits, such as peaches, plums, nectarines, apricots, and cherries, peeled if tough-skinned, pitted, and cut into chunks (3–4 cups)

1 ½ cups (about 9–10 ounces) fresh, ripe strawberries, rinsed, hulled, and halved, or quartered if large, or a mixture of strawberries and raspberries, plus 6–8 strawberry halves or 6–8 raspberries for garnish

2 cups unsweetened apple-cranberry juice (or a similar, slightly tart fruit juice)

1 cup sour cream or yogurt cream (page 30), plus additional for garnish (plain yogurt is too watery here)

6–8 fresh mint leaves, for garnish (optional)

---

1. Combine the tea, prunes and other dried fruit, honey, vanilla, cinnamon, and lemon zest in a large, nonreactive saucepan and bring to a boil. Lower the heat and simmer for 15–20 minutes, or until the fruit is very soft.

2. Add the fresh fruits, berries, and apple-cranberry juice. Bring the mixture back to a boil, then simmer until all of the fresh fruit is quite soft, about 10 minutes.

3. Let the mixture cool somewhat, then taste, and if necessary, stir in more honey. Remove the vanilla bean and if desired rinse and dry it for another use. Discard the cinnamon and lemon zest.

4. Using a slotted spoon, remove about half the fruit from the saucepan, and puree it in a blender or food processor. Transfer the pureed fruit to a large bowl and whisk in the sour cream or yogurt cream. Stir in the remaining fruit and liquid from the saucepan. Cover and refrigerate until thoroughly chilled, at least 4 hours or overnight.

5. To serve, garnish each bowl with a dollop of sour cream or yogurt cream, a reserved berry, and, if using, a mint leaf.

YIELD: 6–8 servings

CHEESE BLINTZES WITH FRESH
BERRIED FRUIT COMPOTE

DAIRY

A perennial favorite, creamy cheese blintzes are often arranged on Shavuot plates to resemble the Jewish Law: placed side by side, they look like the Tablets given to Moses on Mount Sinai. Or like an unfurled scroll, the Torah.

The seasonal compote here, uncooked to retain the flowery freshness of the berry trio, partners perfectly with the rich, dairy blintzes.

If you want to serve the blintzes as Tablets, arrange them atop a puddle of the compote and sprinkle five tiny parallel lines of cinnamon over each, in imitation of the Ten Commandments.

BLINTZES

About 1 pound farmer cheese (two 7.5-ounce packages are fine)

⅓ cup cottage cheese, preferably dry-curd (pot cheese); if unavailable, use large-curd cottage cheese

2½ ounces (about 5 tablespoons) cream cheese, softened

1 teaspoon vanilla extract

3 tablespoons sugar, or to taste

2 large egg yolks

1 recipe blintz leaves (page 136)

Unsalted butter, oil, or a combination, for frying or baking

COMPOTE

1 cup (about 6 ounces) fresh ripe blueberries, picked over and rinsed

2 cups (about 12 ounces) fresh ripe strawberries, rinsed first, then hulled

About 4 tablespoons sugar

½ teaspoon ground cinnamon

1 cup (about 6 ounces) fresh ripe raspberries

Optional accompaniments: sour cream or yogurt cream (page 30); fresh mint leaves

1. You will have to eliminate some of the excess liquid from the cheese to avoid soggy blintzes or the need for fillers. I find a lot of liquid accumulates in the farmer cheese packaging, so after I unwrap it, I drain off the water and pat the cheese dry with paper towels. Put the drained farmer cheese in a large bowl.

2. If dry-curd cottage cheese is unavailable (it is increasingly hard to find, except at some deli counters in areas with large Jewish populations), drain the large-curd cottage cheese too. This is easiest done by draining it for 15–20 minutes through a strainer lined with a coffee filter or a layer of paper towels.

3. Meanwhile, use a fork to mash the farmer cheese very well. Add the cream cheese and vanilla and blend thoroughly. Add the drained cottage cheese and the sugar and mash until smooth. Taste and add more sugar if desired. Beat in the egg yolks, cover, and refrigerate thoroughly. The filling will be firmer and easier to work with when cold.

4. Prepare the compote. Put the blueberries and 1 cup of the strawberries in a bowl and smash them very roughly with a fork. Sprinkle with 2 tablespoons of the sugar and the cinnamon and stir well. Set aside to macerate for about 10 minutes. Puree the remaining 1 cup strawberries, 2 tablespoons sugar, and the raspberries in a blender or food processor. Force the pureed berries through a fine-mesh strainer (to trap most of the bitter seeds) into the bowl of smashed berries. Stir well, cover, and refrigerate for at least 30 minutes to meld the flavors. The flavors will continue to develop and strengthen, becoming sweeter as the sugar draws out the natural sweetness of the berry juices. Taste before serving and add more sugar if you prefer it sweeter.

5. Fill and fold the blintz leaves as directed on page 138, using 1 heaping tablespoon of filling per blintz. (I find these are best when filled and folded and then chilled again, wrapped, up to one or two days before the final baking or frying. The cold cheese filling is firmer and less likely to leak out when heated.) Bake or fry as directed on page 138.

6. Serve the blintzes with the fruit compote, accompanied, if you'd like, by sour cream or yogurt cream and garnished with mint leaves.

   The blintzes are also delicious served with a fruit sauce (see Index) or the Dried Fruit Compote with Fresh Pineapple, Pistachios, and Mint (page 208) instead of the berry compote.

YIELD: 16–18 blintzes

COOK'S NOTE: The compote keeps well for 3–4 days, refrigerated. Use leftover compote with pancakes, puddings (great with *sutlaj,* on page 357), or cheesecake.

   For a savory cheese blintz, omit the sugar and vanilla extract. Add salt and pepper to taste, 3 tablespoons finely chopped scallions or 2 tablespoons minced chives, and a handful perhaps of other fresh herbs, like 2 tablespoons parsley, 2–3 tablespoons mint or chervil, and ½–1 tablespoon grated lemon zest. Make the blintz leaves special by adding 2 to 3 tablespoons of minced fresh dill to the batter.

TURKISH SILKEN RICE PUDDING (SUTLAJ) WITH FRESH RASPBERRY SAUCE

DAIRY

Made without eggs, this velvety pudding is light and sleek, its dairy-pure sweetness nicely underscored by the sprightly raspberry sauce. I first prepared *sutlaj*—a standard at Turkish Shavuot, Sukkot, and *desayuno* meals—after hearing so many fond remembrances of it from the Turkish clients in my husband's law practice. My daughter adores puddings of every type; this rendition, my reworking of several recipes, is her all-time favorite.

Not only a smooth, refreshing summery dessert, cold *sutlaj,* made of cooked-down milk and ground rice, makes an excellent hot-weather breakfast, especially for finicky children. And you might try a Turkish mother's trick: Write each child's initial on top of the pudding in cinnamon.

Of course, the *sutlaj* is also delicious served unadorned, without a sauce.

PUDDING

⅓ cup rice flour (prepared by grinding white rice in a blender until it is powdery; you can also purchase it in many health food stores and Middle Eastern markets)

⅓ cup sugar

Pinch of salt

4 cups whole milk (not low-fat or skim)

1 teaspoon vanilla extract

½ teaspoon almond extract

Unsalted butter, for greasing the custard cups

2 tablespoons brown sugar

Boiling or scalding-hot tap water, for hot water bath

RASPBERRY SAUCE

½ cup unsweetened apple or apple-blend juice

2 tablespoons sugar

Pinch of salt

1 pint (6 ounces) fresh, ripe raspberries

½ teaspoon vanilla extract or rose water

1. Preheat the oven to 250°F.

2. In a large, heavy saucepan, combine the rice flour, sugar, and salt. Whisk in just enough milk to make a smooth paste. Turn the heat on low, and while stirring, gradually pour in the remaining milk. Although many Sephardi cookbooks advise stirring slowly in one direction to avoid lumps, I find it is more important to stir thoroughly and constantly. When all the milk has been added and the mixture is smooth, increase the heat to medium and bring to a boil, stirring all the while. Now reduce the heat to low and simmer, stirring, until the sutlaj begins to thicken, 15–20 minutes. Off the heat, whisk in the vanilla and almond extracts.

SHAVUOT

357

3. While the *sutlaj* is cooking, butter the bottom and sides of six 8-ounce custard cups or ramekins. Sprinkle each cup with 1 teaspoon brown sugar and press the sugar into the buttered bottom. Pour the sutlaj into the prepared cups. Arrange a kitchen towel in a baking dish so it lies flat and place the custard cups on the towel (this way the cups are easier to reach, they won't jostle about, and they will cook evenly). Pour enough boiling or scalding tap water into the pan to come halfway up the sides of the cups. Bake for 2–2½ hours, until the tops are golden brown. Remove the custard cups from the pan and let cool to room temperature. Cover and refrigerate for at least 2 hours before serving.

4. Make the sauce. In a small, nonreactive saucepan, combine the juice, sugar, and salt and boil over high heat until reduced by about half. Stir in the raspberries and vanilla or rose water. Remove from the heat, cover, and allow to steep until it reaches room temperature, stirring every once in a while. Refrigerate until cold.

5. To serve, gently slip a knife around the edges of each cup, place a serving plate on top of the cup, and invert. Surround the unmolded sutlaj with some of the sauce, and pass the remaining sauce separately.

YIELD: 6 servings

COOK'S NOTE: If you want to write your child's initial in cinnamon on top of the *sutlaj*, don't unmold. (It will not show up well against the brown sugar on the bottom.) Serve the *sutlaj* in the custard cup and pass the sauce separately.

OLD COUNTRY COTTAGE CHEESE CAKE

For a short while, I actually loved going to the dentist. Though we had left Manhattan for the suburbs when I was five, we didn't change dentists for a few years. So when my appointment to have a cavity filled coincided with my father's gin game night—often the case, since he played two or three times a week in those years—I usually spent the night alone with my parents in the city while my brother and sister remained home with my grandfather.

I always wore a party dress, because after my filling was securely in place, we'd go out to dinner. Then my mother and I took in a movie at one of the elegant Broadway cinema houses while my father played cards. If my hair needed cutting, we would visit Larry Matthews, an all-night beauty parlor.

Seated there on a couple of telephone books as my mousy brown hair was sheared in plain Buster Brown fashion, I watched the tall showgirls and ponies (shorter versions of the former) from the Copacabana and Latin Quarter, whose hair, in those pre-punk days, ranged from midnight blue to fuchsia.

Purple was for me, I swore. Yes, as soon as I turned sixteen.

Afterward, I'd nap in the bedroom of the apartment where the gin game was played late into the night. And I'd awake to slices of thick cream cheese cake, delivered fresh from Lindy's.

Of course, our idea of heaven changes as we get older. For one thing, I no longer want purple hair. And in cheesecakes, my tastes now run not to thick, creamy velvet, but to silk chiffon. My favorite is soft and feathery-light, less dense and less sweet. Like an old-fashioned Eastern European cheesecake, this unfussy cake is made of cottage cheese enriched with sweet butter and subtly scented with vanilla.

To truly savor this dreamy cake, present it at room temperature, never cold.

---

3 cups (24 ounces) large-curd cottage cheese	*⅔ cup sugar*
9 tablespoons unsalted butter, plus additional	*2 teaspoons vanilla extract*
butter for greasing the pan	*¼ teaspoon salt*
Enough plain, good-quality butter cookies	*4 large eggs, separated*
(e.g., Pepperidge Farm Bordeaux, or a buttery	*Boiling or scalding-hot tap water, for hot water*
shortbread variety) to make ½ cup crumbs	*bath (optional)*
when ground in a blender or food processor	

---

1. Spoon the cottage cheese into a fine-mesh strainer and let it drain over a large bowl for about 30 minutes. Meanwhile, melt the butter over low heat, then let it come to room temperature.

2. Making the cheesecake with a hot water bath offers some protection against cracked tops and over-cooked edges. If you decide to go this route, cover the bottom and sides of a 9- or 9½-inch springform pan well with heavy-duty foil to make it perfectly waterproof. Generously butter the bottom and sides of the pan. Sprinkle in the cookie crumbs and shake the pan to distribute them evenly over the bottom or sides.

3. Preheat the oven to 325°F.

4. Using paper towels, wipe out any liquid the cottage cheese threw off in the bowl and blot up any liquid dripping from the bottom of the strainer. With the back of a spoon, press the cheese through the strainer into the bowl. Scoop the cheese back into the strainer and sieve it again into the bowl. (Much easier the second time. All this sieving will break up the curds more thoroughly than a mixer or food processor, without liquefying the cheese, and ensures a smooth, non-grainy cake.) Beat the cheese on low speed until light and fluffy. Beat in ⅓ cup sugar, the vanilla, and salt. Beat in the egg yolks, one at a time, and the melted butter.

5. Using clean beaters, beat the egg whites in another large bowl until they form soft peaks. Continue beating, adding the remaining ⅓ cup sugar little by little, until the whites are stiff and shiny, but not dry. Gently fold one-quarter of the beaten whites into the cheese mixture, incorporating them completely. Add the remaining whites, lifting and folding until they are thoroughly incorporated.

6. Spoon the filling into the prepared pan. If using a hot water bath, set the pan inside a larger baking pan or ovenproof skillet and pour in enough boiling or scalding-hot tap water to come halfway up the sides of the springform pan. Place on a rack in the middle of the oven and bake the cheesecake for about 1 hour, or until puffed and lightly golden. Turn off the heat and let the cake cool in the oven with the door open for about an hour.

7. Remove from the water bath, if used. Transfer the cake in the springform pan to a rack to cool to room temperature. Cover the room temperature cake loosely with wax paper and refrigerate for at least 12 hours, preferably 24 hours.

8. For finest flavor and texture, serve the cheesecake at room temperature. Leave the sides on the springform pan until ready to serve.

YIELD: 10–12 servings

COOK'S NOTE: For a Passover version, omit the cookie crumbs and substitute blanched almonds or hazelnuts, chopped very fine with a little white or brown sugar to taste. Or use crushed Passover macaroons.

HONEY–RICOTTA CHEESE CAKE

DAIRY

How sweet are Thy words unto my palate.

Yea, sweeter than honey to my mouth!

—PSALM 119:103

The language of God was sweet indeed to the very young boys beginning *cheder,* religious elementary school. On their first day of classes, little students were presented with a slate on which the Hebrew alphabet was smeared with honey. After the teacher recited the letters, the child licked them off, tasting for the first time the sweetness of learning.

This lovely custom took place in many European communities on Shavuot, which marks the time when God gave the Torah, the written word, to the Jewish people. Dating back to at least as far as the twelfth century in France, the tradition spread to Eastern Europe, where it remained popular until the nineteenth century.

This Shavuot cheesecake, sweetened with a delicate orange blossom or acacia honey, evolved from improvisations on an ancient Roman-Jewish recipe for *cassola.* I sometimes perfume it lightly with a little rose water to heighten the floral notes.

The lush cake is exquisite as a solo turn with tea, or serve it as a rich finish to the Shavuot dairy lunch or dinner.

---

8 ounces cream cheese, softened

¼ cup sour cream

¾ cup light honey (look for a light floral one, like orange blossom or acacia)

2 teaspoons vanilla extract or rose water

¼ teaspoon salt

5 large eggs

24 ounces whole-milk ricotta cheese

Unsalted butter, for greasing the pan

Boiling or scalding-hot tap water, for hot-water bath

---

1. Have all ingredients at room temperature. Preheat the oven to 325°F.

2. In a large bowl, beat the cream cheese with the sour cream on low speed until soft and creamy. Stir in the honey, vanilla or rose water and salt. Beat in the eggs, one at a time. Don't overbeat the ingredients—the batter should not be foamy—and remember to scrape down the bowl after each addition.

3. Using a rubber spatula or the back of a spoon, push the ricotta through a sieve into a separate large bowl. Without washing the beaters, whip the ricotta until very light and fluffy. This double process—

sieving and whipping—will lighten the ricotta and rid it of its grainy texture. Then with the mixer still at low speed, slowly add the egg mixture to the ricotta, beating until just incorporated.

4. You can cook the cheesecake without a hot water bath, but I find the gentle heat of the bath offers some insurance against cracked tops and overcooked edges. Of course, you have to make the pan perfectly waterproof, so cover the bottom and sides of a 9- or 9½-inch springform pan well with heavy-duty foil. Generously butter the bottom and sides of the pan.

5. Pour the batter into the prepared pan, rotating the pan a few times to settle the batter and smooth out the bubbles. Set the pan inside a large baking pan or ovenproof skillet, and pour in enough boiling or scalding-hot tap water to come halfway up the sides of the springform pan. Place on a rack in the middle of the oven and bake for about 1 hour to 1 hour and 15 minutes, or until the cheesecake is set around the edges, but still slightly soft and quivering in the center. Turn off the heat, but leave the cheesecake in the oven for about an hour with the door open, where it will continue to cook.

6. Take the pan out of the waterbath and put it on a rack to cool to room temperature. Refrigerate the cheesecake, loosely covered with wax paper, for at least 8 hours, preferably 24 hours.

7. Serve the cheesecake at room temperature or cool, but not icy cold. Leave the sides on the springform pan until ready to serve.

YIELD: 10–12 servings

The author, age five, with her mother, at the Concord Hotel, Kiamesha Lake, New York.

ROSEBERRY-RHUBARB GELATO

The synagogue in Pitigliano, Italy, was bursting with roses and the sweet voices of the children's chorus filled the air. It was Shavuot, June 1938, and Edda Servi Machlin, author of the evocative cookbook-memoir *The Classic Cuisine of the Italian Jews,* was celebrating her bat mitzvah in a magnificent service employing the rich Pitigliano liturgy reserved for special occasions.

Persecution of Italy's Jews had already begun, yet here, as in America, ancient Hebrew traditions were still being updated for today's Jews: the bar mitzvah, once an exclusively male coming-of-age ceremony, was revised in Italy at least as far back as the 1920s to include girls.

In her book Ms. Machlin describes the simple but exquisite refreshments served at her bat mitzvah: a glass of sweet vermouth, a piece of delicate spongecake, and homemade gelato from the hand-cranked machine of the local ice cream maker.

Reading about that Shavuot celebration of long ago moved me to devise this beautiful deep pink gelato with intense fruit flavor and a faint fragrance of rose.

You can change the proportions of fruit here, or use all strawberries or all raspberries as you prefer. Adjust the sugar as necessary—raspberries usually require more sweetening.

About 4½ ounces rhubarb, fruit cut into 1-inch pieces (1 cup), tough strings removed with a vegetable peeler, leaves discarded (they are toxic)

¼ cup granulated light brown sugar and about ⅔ cup granulated white sugar, or all granulated white sugar

2 cups (about 12 ounces) fresh ripe strawberries, rinsed, hulled, and quartered

About 1 cup (about 6 ounces) fresh ripe raspberries

Generous pinch of salt

½ cup heavy cream (preferably not ultra-pasteurized), very cold

1 teaspoon rose water, or to taste

---

1. In a nonreactive bowl, toss the rhubarb with the brown sugar, if using, or ¼ cup white sugar, and set aside to macerate for about 20 minutes, stirring from time to time.

2. Transfer the rhubarb and all the accumulated juices to a small saucepan, and cook slowly over moderate heat, stirring occasionally, until very tender, 10–15 minutes. Force the rhubarb with its pan liquid through a food mill or a fine-mesh strainer into a bowl, cover, and refrigerate until cold.

3. Combine the strawberries, raspberries, and the remaining ⅔ cup sugar in a food processor or blender and pulse until the fruit is reduced to a smooth puree. Taste and adjust the sugar as needed. It should not be overly sugary, but remember that freezing will mute the sweetness somewhat. Pulse again if you add more sugar. Pass the puree through the finest disk of a food mill or a fine-mesh strainer (this will trap a good many of the raspberry seeds) into a large bowl.

4. Stir the chilled rhubarb and salt into the pureed berries. In a separate bowl, whip the cream until it holds soft peaks and fold it into the fruit. For an evocative floral hint, stir in the rose water. Add a little more for a deeper suggestion, tasting as you go and mentally adjusting for the slight muting of flavors that will occur with freezing.

5. Cover the bowl and refrigerate for at least 3 hours, until the mixture is very cold. Place in an ice cream maker and process according to the manufacturer's instructions. If the equipment offers a choice, select the slowest freezing process, which will produce a softer consistency.

YIELD: About 3½ cups

SUGGESTED MENUS

SABBATH

❧❧❧

SPRING AND SUMMER
Friday Evening Dinners
Fresh Challah

Salmon Gefilte Fish Poached in Fennel-Wine Broth with Ginger-Beet Horseradish (page 93)
or
Gefilte Fish Quickly Steamed Between Cabbage Leaves (page 90)

Classic Chicken Soup (page 63) with Savory Herbed Matzoh Kleis (page 68)

Lemon-Roasted Chicken (page 203)
Rhubarb-Prune Tsimmes (page 205)
Garlic-Rosemary Potato Latkes (page 206)
Tender Green Beans
Summer Tomato Platter: Red, Yellow, and Orange Tomatoes Sprinkled with Fresh Herbs

Fresh Peaches and Toasted Almonds
or
Bowl of Sweet Red and Yellow Cherries

Fresh Challah

Egyptian Ground Fish Balls with Tomato and Cumin (page 96)
or
Chopped Eggs and Onions (page 312) with
Black Olives, Garlic Dill Pickles, and Kosher Dill Pickled Tomatoes

*Roasted Garlic–Braised Breast of Veal with
Springtime Stuffing (page 121)
Moroccan-Flavored Carrot Kugel (page 171)*

*Fresh Seasonal Berries with Hazelnut or Pistachio-Ginger
Macaroons (page 334 or 335)*

Saturday Luncheons

*Chilled Fresh Borscht (page 75)
Yogurt Cream (page 30), Sour Cream, or Crème Fraîche*

or

Sorrel-Flavored Mushroom Barley Soup (served tepid) (page 73)

*Italian-Jewish Marinated Fried Fish (page 99)
Roasted Red Peppers (page 263) or Salad of Mixed Greens*

or

Fish in Tomato, Rhubarb, and Blood Orange Sauce (page 318)

Peach-Buttermilk Kugel (page 191)

or

Roseberry-Rhubarb Gelato (page 363)

Grandmother's Cold Fruit Soup (page 353)

Sorrel-Onion Noodle Kugel (page 148)

or

Spinach-Cheese Squares (page 150)

Salad of Boston or Bibb Lettuce, Light Vinaigrette

Fresh Nectarines or Melon Wedges with Caramel Rugelach (page 194)

or

Turkish Silken Rice Pudding with Fresh Raspberry Sauce (page 357)

FALL AND WINTER

Friday Evening Dinners

Fresh Challah

Chopped Chicken Liver from the Rue des Rosiers (page 47)
Grated Black Radish and Endive Salad in Shallot Vinaigrette (page 50)

or

Pastrami-Style Salmon (page 250)
Chopped Onion, Capers, Lemon Slices

Classic Chicken Soup (page 63) with Matzoh Balls (page 66)

Braised Brisket with Thirty-six Cloves of Garlic (page 113)

or

Eggplant-Stuffed Brisket Braised with Tomatoes, Saffron, and Honey
(page 118)

Fresh Steamed Spinach Dressed with Extra-Virgin Olive Oil and Lemon Juice

Sautéed Cabbage and Garlic Noodle Kugel (page 165)
or
Onion-Crusted Light Potato Kugel (page 169)

Ripe Comice or Bartlett Pears with Toasted Walnuts

Fresh Challah
Golden Gefilte Fish with Golden Horseradish (page 85)
Rich Beef Broth from Flanken (page 108) with Mishmash Kreplach (page 111)

Sephardi-Style Stuffed Meatballs with Celery Root and Carrots (page 128)
or
Cabbage Stuffed with Mushrooms and Meat (page 261)

Kasha Varnishkes with Fried Eggplant and Onion Marmalade (omit mushrooms) (page 160)
Salad of Fresh Tart Greens

Dried Fruit Compote with Fresh Pineapple, Pistachios, and Mint (page 208)
or
Fresh Citrus Platter: Clementines and Blood or Navel
Orange Slices Dusted with Cinnamon

Saturday Luncheons
Ruby Red Grapefruit Halves

Duck and White Bean Cholent (page 212)
or
Garlicky Lamb and Lima Hamin with Little Eggplant Boats (page 217)
or
Herbed Beef Cholent with Onion Gonifs (page 214)

Watercress and Orange Salad with Walnut Vinaigrette (page 76)

Seasonal Selection of Fresh and Dried Fruits: Red Grapes,
Apples, Medjool Dates, and Toasted Walnuts

Fresh Papaya Halves with Lime

Mujadderah-Filled Roasted Red Peppers in Tomato-Garlic Sauce (page 263)
Yogurt Cream (page 30) or Sour Cream
Arugula and Endive Salad

Hungarian Chocolate-Walnut Torte (page 337) with Fresh
Whipped Cream or Vanilla Ice Cream
or
Double Ginger–Caramelized Pear Noodle Kugel (page 254)
or
Turkish Silken Rice Pudding (page 357)
with Fresh Persimmon Sauce (page 282)

ROSH HASHANAH

❧❦❧❦❧

Challah
A Selection of Fresh Apples
Fragrant Honey
A Head of Roasted Garlic Cloves (page 290)

Leek Croquettes from Rhodes (page 223)
Egyptian Ground Fish Balls with Tomato and Cumin (page 96) with Tomato
and Sweet Pepper Sauce (page 97)

Brisket Braised in Pomegranate Juice with Onion Confit and Pomegranate Seeds (page 225)
Steamed Basmati Rice or Syrian Pilaf (page 231)
or
Iranian Stuffed Chicken with Fresh Green Herbs and Golden Soup (page 232)

Egyptian Black-eyed Peas with Cilantro (page 236)
Fresh Sautéed Swiss Chard or Spinach

Bombay Pineapple–Coconut Milk Kugel (page 239)
Autumn Fruit Platter: Comice Pears, Champagne or Concord Grapes
and Fresh Figs Drizzled with Honey and Mint

Challah
Pomegranate and Fresh Apple Quarters
Fragrant Honey

Golden Gefilte Fish with Golden Horseradish (page 85)
or
Gefilte Fish Quickly Steamed Between Cabbage Leaves (page 90)

Classic Chicken Soup (page 63) with Fried Onion and
Chicken Kreplach (page 130)
or
Golden Soup from previous night's Iranian Stuffed Chicken (page 235)

Syrian Apricot-Stuffed Meat Rolls with Tart-Sweet Cherry Sauce (page 228)

or

Eggplant-Stuffed Brisket Braised with Tomatoes, Saffron, and Honey (page 118)

Syrian Pilaf (page 231) or Steamed Couscous
Moroccan-Flavored Carrot Kugel (page 171)
Diced Zucchini Lightly Sautéed with Fresh Herbs
Salad of Boston or Bibb Lettuce, Chopped Fresh Dill, Mint, and Italian Parsley
Vinaigrette of Extra-Virgin Olive Oil and Fresh Orange and Lemon Juices

Hungarian Plum Tart (page 237)
Ripe Sweet Melon
Medjool Dates

BREAKING THE YOM KIPPUR FAST

Pomegranate-Orange Sunsets (page 245)

Almond Challah (page 247)   Fresh Bialys and Bagels
Smoked Whitefish and Fennel Salad (page 249)
Pastrami-Style Salmon (page 250)
Cream Cheese and Assorted Other Cheeses
Thin Slices of Mild Onion and Fresh Lemon
Platter of Rainbow Tomato Slices: Red, Yellow, and Orange
Raw Crisp Red Pepper Rings   Black Olives

Double Ginger-Caramelized Pear Noodle Kugel (page 254)
or
Peach-Buttermilk Kugel (page 191)
or
Turkish Silken Rice Pudding with Fresh Raspberry Sauce (page 357)
Iranian Rose-Apple Ice (page 244)

Honeyed Quince–Apple Blintzes with Sour Cream–Date Sauce (page 252)

or

Apricot Blintzes with Toasted Pistachios and Yogurt Cream (page 142)

or

*Apple-Cranberry Blintzes with Maple-Ricotta Cream and
Sugared Walnuts (page 144)*

Sorrel-Onion Noodle Kugel (page 148)

or

Spinach-Cheese Squares (page 150)

*Salad of Sliced Baked Beets, Boston Lettuce, and Fresh Chopped
Dill with Walnut Vinaigrette (page 76)*

Old Country Cottage Cheese Cake (page 359)

SUKKOT

Challah

Chopped Chicken Liver from the Rue des Rosiers (page 47)

or

Chopped Chicken Liver with Caramelized Onions (page 51)

Grated Black Radish and Endive Salad in Shallot Vinaigrette (page 50)

*Pumpkin and Sweet Potato Soup with Sweet Potato
Knaidlach (page 259)*

Cabbage Stuffed with Mushrooms and Meat (page 261)

Caramelized Onion and Carrot Tsimmes with Candied Ginger (page 268)

Salad of Fresh Tart Greens

*Maple-Roasted Pears with Passion Fruit and/or
Fresh Raspberry Sauce (page 269)*

or

Dried Fruit Compote with Fresh Pineapple, Pistachios, and Mint (page 208)
or
Fresh Seasonal Melon Splashed with a Late Harvest Moscato or Sauvignon Blanc

Chard Stuffed with Artichokes and Rice (page 266)

Tangy Russian Cabbage Soup with Pot Roast–Beet Kreplach (page 71)

Aromatic Marinated Brisket with Chestnuts (page 115)
Spiced Pomegranate Molasses Applesauce (page 180)
Roasted Potatoes
Mixed Green Salad

Roasted Apple–Walnut Noodle Kugel (page 189)
or
Maple-Roasted Pears with Passion Fruit and/or Fresh Raspberry Sauce (page 269)
or
Fresh Figs with Toasted Walnuts or Pecans

A Vegetarian Sukkot Dinner
Pomegranate-Orange Sunsets (page 245)
Chard Stuffed with Artichokes and Rice (page 266)

Sorrel-Flavored Mushroom Barley Soup (page 73)

Mujadderah-Filled Roasted Red Peppers in Tomato-Garlic Sauce (page 263)
Labneh, Yogurt Cream (page 30), or Sour Cream
Salad of Shredded Carrots and Beets with Butterhead
Lettuce, Walnut Vinaigrette (page 76)

Rich Noodle Kugel Baked with Fresh Plums (page 186)
and/or other Seasonal Fruit
or
Hungarian Plum Tart (page 237) with Vanilla Ice Cream or Fresh Whipped Cream

or

Sweet Orange-Fleshed Melon Garnished with Lime and Fresh Mint
Turkish Silken Rice Pudding (page 357)

HANUKKAH

Midweek Meals

Fresh Ruby Red Grapefruit Halves (sweeten if needed with Orange Blossom Honey)
or
Salad of Grapefruit, Avocado, and Romaine with Lemon-Vinaigrette Dressing

Fish in Potato Latke Crust with Horseradish Cream (page 288)
Steamed Broccoli with Butter

Double Ginger–Caramelized Pear Noodle Kugel (page 254)
or
Roasted Apple–Walnut Noodle Kugel (dairy version) (page 189)

Fresh Borscht with Dilled Onion-Butter Matzoh Balls (page 75)
Celery Root–Potato Latkes (page 276) with Paper-Thin
Slices of Pastrami-Style Salmon (page 250)
Sour Cream, Yogurt Cream (page 30), or Crème Fraîche
Sweet Onions and Lemon Quarters
Salad of Fennel and Orange Slices with Black Olives

Old Country Cottage Cheese Cake (page 359)

Mixed Green Salad

Fried Chicken Cutlets, Italian-Jewish Style (page 132)
Wild Mushroom–Potato Kugel (page 167) or Roasted Sweet Potatoes

Broccoli Rabe with Garlic (see recipe for Flunken with Tart Greens, page 108)

Fresh Seasonal Fruit Platter: Clementines, Red Grapes, Pears, and Apples
or
Maple-Roasted Pears with Passion Fruit and/or Fresh Raspberry Sauce (page 269)

Aromatic Marinated Brisket with Chestnuts (page 115)
Spiced Pomegranate Molasses Applesauce (page 180)
Creamy Potato-Onion Latkes (page 274)
Steamed Spinach Dressed with Sesame Oil, Toasted Sesame Seeds,
Soy Sauce, and Lemon Juice
Toasted Hazelnuts or Walnuts and a Selection of Apples (choose flavorful
varieties like Braeburn, Cortland, Gala, Golden Russet, Grimes Golden,
Macoun, Northern Spy, and Spartan)

Rich Beef Broth (from Flanken, page 108), served plain or with
Egg Noodles and Diced Carrots
Flanken with Tart Greens (page 108)

Crispy Shallot Latkes with Sugar Dusting (page 278)
or
Celery Root—Potato Latkes (page 276)
or
Creamy Potato-Onion Latkes (page 274)

Intense Apricot Applesauce (page 176)
or
Spiced Pomegranate Molasses Applesauce (page 180)

Mixed Green Salad

Fresh Pineapple or Papaya with Lime
or
Dried Fruit Compote with Fresh Pineapple, Pistachios, and Mint (page 208)

A Latke Party

*Lentils "Hummus Style," with Pomegranate and Mint
and Toasted Za'atar Matzohs (page 53)*
or
Chopped Eggs and Onions (page 312)
Thinly Sliced Pumpernickel
Black Olives, Scallions, Kosher Sour Pickles, and Pickled Dill Tomatoes

Crispy Shallot Latkes with Sugar Dusting (page 278), Creamy Potato-Onion Latkes (page 274)
*Sour Cream, Yogurt Cream (page 30), Ginger-Pear Sauce (page 182), Intense Apricot
Applesauce (page 176), Spiced Pomegranate Molasses Applesauce (page 180)*

Cheese Latkes with Fresh Persimmon Sauce (page 282)
or
Greek-Inspired Cheese Latkes (page 284)

*Salad of Sliced Blood or Navel Oranges, Watercress and Red Onions
Dressed with Extra-Virgin Olive Oil and Orange and Lemon Juices*
Caramel Rugelach (page 194)
Apple-Buttermilk Kugel (see Peach-Buttermilk Kugel variation) (page 192)
Old Country Cottage Cheese Cake (page 359)
Bowl of Toasted Almonds and Dark Raisins   Ripe Pears

Sabbath During Hanukkah

Challah
*Classic Chicken Soup (page 63) with Matzoh Balls (page 66) or
Fried Onion and Chicken Kreplach (page 130)*

Apricot- and Orange-Scented Goose with Roasted Garlic (page 290)
*Scallion Latkes with Scallion Dipping Brushes (page 280) or
Garlic-Rosemary Potato Latkes (page 206)*
Intense Apricot Applesauce (page 176)
or
Spiced Pomegranate Molasses Applesauce (page 180)
Sautéed Cabbage and Garlic Noodle Kugel (page 165)
Salad of Fresh Tart Greens

Fresh Mango with Lime Juice

PURIM

Almond Challah (page 247)

Poached Prune Kreplach with Honeyed Cream and Pecans (page 298)

Italian-Jewish Marinated Fried Fish (page 99) or
Oven-Fried Smoked Salmon Croquettes (page 101)
Roasted Red Peppers (page 263) or Salad of Mixed Greens
Kasha Varnishkes with Fried Eggplant, Mushrooms, and Onion
Marmalade (omit noodles) (page 160)
Broccoli with Browned Butter

Assorted Hamantaschen: Fresh Apple; Apricot, Date, and Pistachio; and Poppy Seed
Hamantaschen with Raisin-Walnut Filling (pages 300–304)

Chickpeas with Garlic and Barbecue Spices (page 296)

Golden Gefilte Fish with Golden Horseradish (page 85)

Tangy Russian Cabbage Soup with Pot Roast–Beet Kreplach (page 71)
or
Rich Beef Broth from Flanken (page 108) with Mishmash Kreplach (page 111)

Romanian Garlicky Ground Meat Sausages with Sour
Pickle Vinaigrette and Roasted Red Peppers (page 125)
or
Braised Brisket with Thirty-six Cloves of Garlic (page 113)
Mashed Potatoes
Salad of Tart Greens

Winter Fruit Platter: Toasted Almonds and Dark Raisins, Ripe
Pears and Peeled Kiwi Quarters

PASSOVER

꙳꙳꙳꙳꙳꙳

Seder Meals

Matzoh

Chopped Eggs and Onion (page 312) Garnished with Grated Black Radish
and Endive Salad in Shallot Vinaigrette (page 50) or
Strips of Roasted Red Pepper (page 263) and Black Olives

Gefilte Fish Quickly Steamed Between Cabbage Leaves (page 90)
or
Salmon Gefilte Fish Poached in Fennel-Wine Broth with Ginger-Beet Horseradish
(page 93)

Chicken Soup with Asparagus and Shiitakes, Served with Roasted Fennel
Matzoh Balls (page 316)

Braised Lamb with Artichokes, Lemon, and Fresh Herbs (page 321)
Toasted Matzoh Farfel with Wild Mushrooms and Roasted Garlic (page 330)
Fresh Spinach or Swiss Chard

Spring Compote (page 336) with Hazelnut Macaroons (page 334)

Matzoh
Huevos Haminados (page 314)

Fish in Tomato, Rhubarb, and Blood Orange Sauce (page 318)
or
Classic Chicken Soup (page 63) with Savory Herbed Matzoh Kleis (page 68)

Veronese Rolled Turkey Loaf (page 323)
or
If rice and legumes are eaten during Passover: Iranian Stuffed Chicken with
Fresh Green Herbs and Golden Soup (page 232)
Leek Croquettes from Rhodes (page 223) or Roasted Potatoes

Fresh Asparagus
Salad of Butterhead Lettuce and Minced Fresh Herbs with Lemon Vinaigrette

Hungarian Chocolate-Walnut Torte (page 337)
Ripe Pineapple with Fresh Mint and Floral Honey

Matzoh
Hard-boiled Eggs with Salt Water

Chopped Chicken Liver from the Rue des Rosiers (page 47)
Grated Black Radish and Endive Salad in Shallot Vinaigrette (page 50)

Egyptian Ground Fish Balls with Tomato and Cumin (page 96)

Beet-Braised Pot Roast with Horseradish and Potato Knaidlach (page 326)
or
Roasted Garlic–Braised Breast of Veal with Springtime Stuffing
(if rice is eaten during Passover) (page 121)

Salad of Mixed Greens

Spring Compote (page 336) with Toasted Almond–Coconut Macaroons (page 332)

Non-Seder Meals

Pastrami-Style Salmon (page 250) on Onion and Dill Matzoh (page 310)

Savory Artichoke Matzoh Brie (page 36) with Yogurt Cream (page 30)
or
Mozzarella in Matzoh Carrozza (page 344)

Crisp Hearts of Romaine with Vinaigrette

Spring Fruit Bowl: Mango, Banana, and Tangerine Slices Moistened
with Fresh Tangerine Juice
Honey–Ricotta Cheese Cake (page 361)

Chopped Eggs and Onions (page 312)
Cracked Pepper and Coarse Salt Matzoh (page 311)

Snapper Fillets in Pistachio-Matzoh Crust (page 342)
or
Oven-Fried Smoked Salmon Croquettes (omit mustard) (page 101)

Fresh Asparagus or Spinach
Baked Potato with Sour Cream and Dill

Hungarian Chocolate-Walnut Torte (page 337) with Fresh Whipped Cream

Ripe Melon Splashed with Red Wine
Rosemary Matzoh (page 310)
Lemon-Fried Chicken with Tart Salad Topping (page 340)
or
Fried Chicken Cutlets, Italian-Jewish Style (page 132) and Tossed Green Salad
Roasted White or Sweet Potatoes
Juicy-Ripe Apples or Pears with Toasted Pecans

Garlic Matzoh (page 310)
Rich Beef Broth from Flanken (page 108)

Flanken with Tart Greens (page 108)
Wild Mushroom—Potato Kugel (page 167)
Salad of Buttercrunch Lettuce, Avocado, and Red Onion with Vinaigrette Dressing

Mango and Sour Cherry Macaroon Crumble (page 346)
or
Pistachio-Ginger Macaroons (page 335)

Saturday Lunch

Salt and Pepper Matzoh (page 310)

Pastrami-Style Salmon (page 250) and Chopped Eggs and Onions (page 312)
or
Egyptian Ground Fish Balls with Tomato and Cumin (page 96)

Spinach-Cheese Squares (page 150)
Moroccan-Flavored Carrot Kugel (page 171)
Salad of Tart Greens

Old Country Cottage Cheese Cake (substitute very finely crushed
macaroons for cookie crumbs) (page 359)

SHAVUOT

Warm Shav with Salmon Kreplach (page 351)
or
Sorrel-Flavored Mushroom Barley Soup (page 73)
Fresh Corn-Rye or Pumpernickel Bread with Sweet Butter

Cheese Blintzes with Fresh Berried Fruit Compote (page 355)
or
Savory Cheese Blintzes (page 356)
or
Strawberry-Rhubarb Blintzes (page 141)

Yogurt Cream (page 30) or Sour Cream

Sliced Cucumbers Dressed with Fresh Dill, Coarse Salt, and Cider Vinegar
Salad of Boston or Bibb Lettuce with Chopped Summer Herbs and a Light Vinaigrette
(walnut or other nut oil or mild olive oil with raspberry or other fruit vinegar)

Turkish Silken Rice Pudding with Fresh Raspberry Sauce (page 357)
or
Old Country Cottage Cheese Cake (page 359)

Almond Challah (page 247)
Grandmother's Cold Fruit Soup (page 353)

Poached or Broiled Salmon with Green Olive Sauce (page 60)

Potato-Onion Kreplach, Pot Sticker Style (page 152)
or
Garlic Mashed Potato Knishes (page 154)

Buttered Garden Peas with Chopped Mint or Fresh Asparagus

Old Country Cottage Cheese Cake (page 359)
or
Rich Noodle Kugel Baked with Fresh Plums and Nectarines (page 186)

Sweet Ripe Melon Wedges

Fish in Tomato, Rhubarb, and Blood Orange Sauce (page 318)
or
Italian-Jewish Marinated Fried Fish (page 99)

Sautéed Chive Mamaliga with Feta-Yogurt Cream (page 156)
Roasted Red Peppers (page 263)
Salad of Fresh Tart Greens

Roseberry-Rhubarb Gelato (page 363)
Honey–Ricotta Cheese Cake (page 361)

LIFE-CYCLE BRUNCH (BAR OR BAT MITZVAH, BRIT MILAH, ETC.)

Hors d'Oeuvre: Miniature Garlic Mashed Potato Knishes (page 154)
Miniature Spinach-Cheese Squares (page 150)
or
Miniature Sorrel-Onion Noodle Kugel Squares (page 148)
Chard Stuffed with Artichokes and Rice (page 266)

Lentils "Hummus Style," with Pomegranate and Mint
and Toasted Za'atar Matzohs (page 53)
Italian-Jewish Marinated Fried Fish (page 99)
Roasted Red Peppers (page 263) Seasoned with Vinaigrette and Fresh Herbs
Smoked Whitefish and Fennel Salad (page 249)
Chopped Eggs and Onions (page 312)
Pastrami-Style Salmon (page 250)

Cream Cheese and Other Assorted Cheeses
Platters of Vine-Ripened Tomatoes, Sweet Onions, and Lemon Quarters
Almond Challah (page 247)
Fresh Onion Bialys and Bagels
Thinly Sliced Pumpernickel Bread

Rich Noodle Kugel Baked with Fresh Plums and Nectarines or Other Seasonal Fruit
(page 186)
Old Country Cottage Cheese Cake (page 359)
Caramel Rugelach (page 194)
Assorted Hamantaschen: Fresh Apple; Apricot, Date, and Pistachio; and Poppy Seed
Hamantaschen with Raisin-Walnut Filling (pages 300–304)
Platters of Melon Wedges, Grapes, and Fresh Strawberries or Other Seasonal Fruits

A GLOSSARY OF USEFUL TERMS

ADAFINA See *Dafina*.

APPETIZING STORE A Jewish institution, the appetizing store is a delicatessen specializing in foods other than meat, particularly smoked and pickled fish, barrels of pickles, dried fruit, and nuts. Many of the traditional appetizing stores expanded to purvey a cornucopia of foodstuffs. Perhaps the most famous of these is New York's Zabar's, which now sells everything from herring in sour cream sauce to fresh mesclun to fine Italian prosciutto.

ASHKENAZI, ASHKENAZIM (PLURAL) [from *Ashkenaz*, Germany, in Hebrew] Jews from Central and Eastern Europe and their descendants.

BAR MITZVAH Religious ceremony for a thirteen-year-old boy, after which he assumes the religious responsibilities and duties required of a Jewish man.

BAT MITZVAH Religious ceremony for a twelve- or thirteen-year-old girl, after which she assumes the religious responsibilities and duties required of a Jewish woman.

BLINTZ Very thin crepelike pancake rolled around a filling of cheese, fruit, vegetables, or meat, then fried or baked.

BRIT MILAH The ceremony of circumcision performed on the eighth day of a Jewish boy's life.

CHALLAH [ALSO HALLAH] A soft, eggy loaf of braided white bread traditionally served on Sabbath and various holidays. For holidays, *challah* is often formed into special shapes, like ladders, doves, circles, and so on.

CHOLENT A long-simmering Ashkenazi Sabbath stew, prepared on Friday and cooked overnight in a very slow oven, usually containing a savory combination of meat, beans, grains, vegetables, and sometimes, a dumpling.

CHOMETZ [ALSO HOMETZ] Food or drink forbidden during Passover because it is prepared from grain, or leaven other than ritually prepared matzoh products made from special Passover flour.

CHUTZPAH Unmitigated effrontery; incredible audacity.

DAFINA [from the Arabic, meaning *buried*, when the dish had to be buried to remain warm for the Sabbath; also called *adafina*, *t'fina*, and the Hebrew *hamin* and Moroccan *skhena*, meaning *hot*, as well as several other names] A well-seasoned, long-simmering Sephardi Sabbath stew, similar to the Ashkenazi *cholent*, prepared with a complex variety of meats, legumes, grains, vegetables, and often, eggs (huevos haminados) and sweet fruits, like dates and apricots.

DAIRY Any food containing milk or milk products (including butter and cheese), or the dishes, utensils, tablecloths, or dish towels used in preparing, serving and eating such foods. According to kashrut, no meat or meat products, like chicken fat, may be cooked or eaten with dairy foods. In a kosher kitchen, one set of dishes, utensils, tablecloths, etc., is reserved for use exclusively with dairy foods and one exclusively for meat foods.

DAYENU A Hebrew song chanted at the Passover seder.

DAY OF ATONEMENT See Yom Kippur.

DAYS OF AWE The Ten High Holy Days, beginning with Rosh Hashanah and ending with Yom Kippur. Also known as the Days of Penitence.

DESAYUNO [Ladino for breakfast] The meal eaten by Sephardim after returning home from morning synagogue services on Sabbath and festivals.

ERETZ ISRAEL The land of Israel.

FARFEL Egg noodle dough that has been grated into small bits (also called egg barley because the pieces of dough are the size of barley grains). On Passover it is prepared from matzoh.

FOUR QUESTIONS As part of the Passover seder, the youngest child present asks why this night is different from all other nights of the year in four ways: Why do we eat matzoh? Why do we eat bitter herbs? Why do we dip twice? Why do we recline at the table? The leader of the seder reads the answers from the Haggadah, beginning the story of the Exodus.

FRITADA Sephardi egg-based dish, similar to a *frittata*.

GEFILTE FISH Literally stuffed fish. Originally, a fish stuffed with ground fish (usually freshwater varieties, like carp, pike, and whitefish), bread or matzoh meal, eggs, onions, spices, etc., then poached or baked. Today the fish mixture is usually formed into patties and poached.

HAGGADAH The story of slavery in and the Exodus from Egypt, told at the Passover seder.

HAMANTASCH, HAMANTASCHEN [PLURAL] Three-cornered Purim cookie, usually filled with poppy seeds, apricot, prune, or raspberry preserves, dried fruit, or nuts.

HAMIN [from the Hebrew for hot] Long-simmering Sabbath stew (see *cholent* or *dafina*).

HANUKKAH [ALSO CHANUKAH] Known also as the Feast of Dedication or the Festival of Lights, this holiday celebrates the victory of the Maccabees over the Syrians, who tried to convert the Jews to Greek polytheism. It usually falls in December.

HAROSET [ALSO CHAROSET] One of the ritual foods on the seder plate, this pastelike mixture of fruit, nuts, wine, and spices symbolizes the mortar used to make Pharaoh's bricks by the Israelites during their slavery in Egypt.

HAVDALAH The Saturday evening ceremony that closes the Sabbath and marks the beginning of the new week. A benediction is recited over wine, fragrant spices, and a special candle.

HELZEL Stuffed poultry neck.

HIGH HOLY DAYS [ALSO KNOWN AS THE DAYS OF AWE AND DAYS OF PENITENCE] Beginning with Rosh Hashanah and ending with Yom Kippur, these ten days are marked by intense self-examination and atonement. Jews believe that God decides their fate for the coming year during this period.

HUEVOS HAMINADOS Eggs simmered with the Sabbath stew or cooked separately overnight, and served by Sephardim on Sabbath, holidays, and at life-cycle celebrations.

KABBALA The highly complex and esoteric main body of Jewish mysticism.

KASHA Literally any porridge, but now refers to roasted buckwheat groats. It is available whole or ground coarse, medium, or fine in most supermarkets and health food stores.

KASHRUT Jewish dietary laws that determine what is kosher, or ritually fit to eat.

KIDDUSH Prayer recited over wine before the start of the evening meal, sanctifying the incoming Sabbath or major holiday.

KNAIDL, KNAIDLACH [PLURAL] Dumpling, usually made of matzoh meal, but sometimes of potatoes or other starches.

KNISH Pastry pocket, filled with meat, cheese, kasha, potato, or other vegetables, then baked or fried.

KOSHER Ritually fit to eat, according to the Jewish dietary laws.

KREPL, KREPLACH [PLURAL] Triangular or square noodle dough, usually stuffed with meat or cheese. Like wontons or ravioli, it may be boiled and served in soup or fried and eaten as a side dish or main course.

KUGEL A baked sweet or savory pudding, containing eggs, usually a starch like noodles or potatoes, and sometimes other vegetables or fruits.

LADINO [ALSO CALLED JUDESMO AND JUDEO-SPANISH] The vernacular language spoken by Sephardim. It is based on medieval Castilian Spanish, mixed with Hebrew, Arabic, Turkish, Greek, and medieval French.

LATKE Pancake, especially the potato pancakes eaten on Hanukkah.

LOKSHEN Egg noodles.

MAH NISHTANAH [HA LILAH HA ZEH] Literally, "what is the difference?" Beginning words of the Four Questions asked at the Passover seder, meaning: "why is this night different?"

MAMALIGA Romanian cornmeal porridge (either fine or coarse meal is used, according to preference), prepared essentially like polenta, but served with different toppings.

MAROR Bitter herb, usually horseradish, on the seder plate, symbolizing the bitterness of slavery.

MATZOH Unleavened cracker made of flour and water, eaten instead of bread on Passover.

MATZOH MEAL Finely ground matzoh.

MENORAH A candelabrum. Usually refers to the eight-branched (nine including the *shammash*) candelabrum lit on Hanukkah.

MIPERI HA-ERETZ In Deuteronomy 8:8, the seven choice crops with which ancient Israel was blessed, namely: barley, date, fig, grape, olive, pomegranate, and wheat.

MITZVAH, MITZVOT [PLURAL] One of 613 commandments Jews are obligated to perform; also any good deed or kind act.

NOSH [Yiddish, from the German *nachen,* to eat on the sly; variants: *nashn, noshn*—verb, to nosh; *nasheray, nosheray*—foods to be noshed] A snack, a tidbit, a small portion.

ONGEPOTCHKEH Excessively and unattractively decorated or fussed with to the point of tackiness.

PAREVE Neutral; refers to foods made with neither meat nor milk products, that, according to Jewish dietary laws, may be eaten with either meat or dairy foods. Examples are: fish, eggs, grains, vegetables, and fruits.

PASSOVER Also known as the Festival of Freedom, this joyous spring holiday, occurring in March or April, commemorates the Exodus of the Jews from Egypt.

PHYLLO [ALSO SPELLED FILO OR FILLO] Paper-thin pastry leaves used to make both sweet and savory pastries. They are available fresh in some Greek and Arabic bakeries, and widely available frozen in supermarkets.

POTCHKEH To fuss with something.

PURIM The exuberant holiday in February or March that celebrates the Persian Jews' triumph over Haman's plot to exterminate them, as told in the Book of Esther.

ROSH HASHANAH The Jewish New Year; the first of the High Holy Days. The annual Day of Judgment, this solemn but joyous day usually falls in September or October.

ROSL Fermented beet juice.

SABBATH [ALSO SHABBAT] The Jewish Sabbath occurs from sundown on Friday to sundown on Saturday. This day of rest is a joyous interlude free not only from work but certain tasks, like cooking, as well.

SCHMALTZ Fat. Usually refers to rendered poultry fat.

SEDER The traditional home or community ceremony, including the evening meal, of Passover.

SEDER PLATE A special plate on the table at the seder containing symbolic foods connected with Passover.

SEPHARDI, SEPHARDIM [PLURAL] [from *Sepharad*, Spain in Hebrew] Jews and their descendants, expelled at the end of the fifteenth century from Spain and Portugal, who settled in Greece, the Middle East, England, Holland, the Americas, and parts of western Europe. The term is often used to refer to all Jews not of Ashkenazi background.

SHAMMASH [ALSO SHAMMES] The sexton of a synagogue; also the extra candle used to light the other candles on a Hanukkah menorah.

SHAV Sorrel soup.

SHAVUOT Also known as the Festival of Weeks, commemorates the covenant made between God and Israel on Mount Sinai, when Moses received the Law (the Torah). Occurring in May or June, it celebrates the arrival of the first fruits of the summer harvest.

SHEHEHEYONU Name of a prayer recited over the special, happy, noneveryday occurrences in life, e.g., the first day of holidays, eating the first fruits of the season at Rosh Hashanah, etc.

SHOFAR Special ram's horn blown in the synagogue on Rosh Hashanah and Yom Kippur. It is a reminder of Abraham's sacrifice, since the ram was sacrificed for his son Isaac.

SHTETL Village in pre–World War II Eastern Europe where most, and in some cases all, of the inhabitants were Jewish.

SIMCHAT TORAH The last day of Sukkot, when the weekly readings in the Torah are completed (with the end of Deuteronomy) and then commenced again (with the beginning of Genesis).

SUKKAH [ALSO SUCCAH] A booth of temporary shelter erected out-of-doors for Sukkot. The stars must be visible through the roof and the sukkah should be decorated with fruits, vegetables, flowers, and branches from the early autumn harvest. During Sukkot the family eats in the sukkah, weather permitting.

SUKKOT [ALSO SUCCOS] Originally an autumn harvest festival of thanksgiving, this holiday, known as the Festival of Tabernacles or Feast of Booths, commemorates the period of wandering in the Sinai desert, when the Israelites lived in booths (sukkot). Meals are eaten in the sukkah.

TALMUD A massive collection of writings, comprising the Mishnah, commentaries, interpretations, and reinterpretations by scholars of the Torah; and the Gemara, commentaries on and interpretations of the Mishnah. The Talmud contains not just exegeses of Holy Scripture, but reflections on a huge array of subjects, like theology, diet, ethics, jurisprudence, mythology, philosophy, medicine, and so on. Two Talmuds exist: the Jerusalem or Palestinian Talmud (completed around the fifth century A.D.), in which the Gemara was the work of the scholars of the Palestinian academies; and the Babylonian Talmud (finished around the sixth century A.D.), whose Gemara was produced by the Babylonian academicians. The influence of the Babylonian Talmud has been far greater and is the one to which most scholars refer.

TALMUDIC TIMES Period of Jewish chronological history, from about 70 to 500 A.D.

TORAH Handwritten on a parchment scroll, the Torah is the first five books in the Bible: Genesis, Exodus, Leviticus, Numbers, and Deuteronomy. It is also known as the Law and The Five Books of Moses. A portion of the Torah is read in the synagogue every morning on Sabbaths, Mondays, Thursdays, and festivals; completing the entire Torah cycle takes one year.

TREYF Ritually unfit to eat.

TSIMMES A sweetened, baked, or stewed mixture of vegetables and fruits. It often contains meat as well.

VARENIKES Noodle dough usually filled with fruit or meat.

VARNISHKES Noodles.

YIDDISH Almost 1,000 years old, this vernacular spoken by Ashkenazi Jews of Eastern and Central Europe mainly comprises old German, but includes elements of Hebrew, various Slavic and other European languages, French, and English. It is written with Hebrew characters.

YOM KIPPUR Solemn prayer and fasting marks this holiest day of the Jewish calendar. Known also as the Day of Atonement, it is the tenth and last of the High Holy Days, occurring in September or October.

SELECTED BIBLIOGRAPHY

Most of the works previously cited at the end of each quotation and in the text are not included here.

Abrahams, Israel. *Jewish Life in the Middle Ages.* New York: Meridian Books/Jewish Publications, 1958 (reprint of 1896 edition).

Agnon, Shmuel Yosef. *Days of Awe.* New York: Schocken Books, 1948.

Ausubel, Nathan. *A Treasury of Jewish Folklore.* New York: Crown, 1948.

Baron, Salo Wittmayer. *A Social and Religious History of the Jews.* 2nd edition. New York: Columbia University Press, 1983.

Bennett, Alan D., ed. *Journey Through Judaism: The Best of Keeping Posted.* New York: UAHC Press, 1991.

Brandes, Francesca. *Veneto Itinerari ebraici: I luoghi, la storia, l'arte.* Venice: Marsilio Editori, 1995.

Chiche-Yana, Martine. *La Table Juive: Recettes et traditions de fêtes.* Aix-en-Provence: Edisud, 1990.

———. *La Table Juive (Tome 2): Recettes et traditions du cycle de vie.* Aix-en-Provence: Edisud, 1994.

Cooper, John. *Eat and Be Satisfied.* Northvale, New Jersey, and London: Jason Aronson, 1993.

Dobrinsky, Herbert C. *A Treasury of Sephardic Laws and Customs.* New York: Ktav Publishing, 1986.

Encyclopedia Judaica. Jerusalem: Keter Publishing, 1978.

Encyclopedia Judaica (CD-Rom Edition). Jerusalem: Judaica Multimedia, 1997.

Gaster, Theodore. *Festivals of the Jewish Year.* New York: W. Sloane Associates, 1953.

Goodman, Philip. *The Purim Anthology.* Philadelphia: Jewish Publication Society of America, 1949.

———. *The Rosh Hashanah Anthology.* Philadelphia: Jewish Publication Society of America, 1992.

The Jewish Encyclopedia. New York and London: Funk and Wagnalls, 1903.

Levin, Schmarya. *Childhood in Exile* (trans. Maurice Samuel). New York: Harcourt, Brace and Co., 1929.

Root, Waverly. *Food.* New York: Simon & Schuster, 1980.

Rosten, Leo. *The Joys of Yiddish.* New York: McGraw Hill, 1960.

Rubenstein, Jeffrey L. *The History of Sukkot in the Second Temple and Rabbinic Periods.* Atlanta, Georgia: Scholars Press, 1995.

Schauss, Hayyim. *The Jewish Festivals from Their Beginnings to Our Own Day.* Cincinnati: Union of American Hebrew Congregations, 1938.

Schwartz, Oded. *In Search of Plenty: A History of Jewish Food.* London: Kyle Cathie, 1992.

Shosteck, Patti. *A Lexicon of Jewish Cooking.* Chicago: Contemporary Books, Inc., 1979.

Tigay, Alan M. *The Jewish Traveler.* Northvale, New Jersey: Jason Aronson, 1987.

Universal Jewish Encyclopedia. New York: Universal Jewish Encyclopedia, Inc., 1939/40–43.

Waskow, Arthur I. *Seasons of Our Joy: A Handbook of Jewish Festivals.* Toronto and New York: Bantam Books, 1982.

Zborowski, Mark, and Elizabeth Herzog. *Life Is with People.* New York: Schocken Books, 1978.

COOKBOOKS

There are hundreds of excellent Jewish cookbooks. The following sampling combines some particularly interesting recent titles with personal favorites covering both familiar and less-well-known cuisines.

Angel, Gilda. *Sephardic Holiday Cooking.* Mount Vernon, New York: Decalogue Books, 1986.

Ascoli Vitali-Norsa, Giuliana, ed. *La cucina nella tradizione ebraica.* 2nd edition. Padua: Edizione dell'Adei Wizo, 1979.

Benbassa, Esther. *Cuisine judeo-espagnole.* Paris: Editions du Scribe, 1984.

Engle, Fannie, and Gertrude Blair. *The Jewish Festival Cookbook.* New York: David McKay Company, 1954.

Fischer, Leah Loeb, with Maria Polushkin Robbins. *Mama Leah's Jewish Kitchen.* New York: Macmillan, 1990.

Goodman, Hanna. *Jewish Cooking Around the World.* Philadelphia: Jewish Publication Society of America, 1973.

Greenberg, Betty D., and Althea O. Silverman. *The Jewish Home Beautiful.* New York: The National Women's League of the United Synagogues of America, 1941.

Koronyo, Viki, and Sima Ovadya. *Sefarad Yemekleri.* Istanbul: Published for Society of Assistance to Old People, 1990.

Levy, Esther. *Jewish Cookery Book.* Philadelphia: W. S. Turner, 1871. [Facsimile edition published by Pholiota Press, Inc., 1982.]

Levy, Faye. *Faye Levy's International Jewish Cookbook.* New York: Warner Books, 1991.

Liebman, Malvina W. *Jewish Cookery from Boston to Baghdad.* Miami: E. A. Seemann Publishing, 1975.

Machlin, Edda Servi. *The Classic Cuisine of the Italian Jews.* Croton on Hudson, New York: Giro Press, 1981.

———. *The Classic Cuisine of the Italian Jews II.* Croton on Hudson, New York: Giro Press, 1992.

Marks, Copeland. *Sephardic Cooking.* New York: Donald I. Fine, 1992.

Marks, Gil. *The World of Jewish Cooking.* New York: Simon & Schuster, 1996.

Nathan, Joan. *The Jewish Holiday Kitchen.* New York: Schocken Books, 1988.

————. *Jewish Cooking in America.* New York: Alfred A. Knopf, 1994.

Roden, Claudia. *The Book of Jewish Food.* New York: Alfred A. Knopf, 1996.

Roukhomovsky, Suzanne. *Gastronomie juive et patisserie de Russie, d'Alsace, de Roumanie et d'Orient.* Paris: Flammarion, 1968.

Sternberg, Robert. *The Sephardic Kitchen.* New York: HarperCollins, 1996.

————. *Yiddish Cuisine: A Gourmet's Approach to Jewish Cooking.* Northvale, New Jersey: Jason Aronson, 1993.

ACKNOWLEDGMENTS

All books are collaborations, and I am fortunate to have completed this one with the help of many generous and talented people.

I know that I never would have written the book without my extraordinary agents, Elise and Arnold Goodman. I am deeply grateful to them for their astute advice, boundless enthusiasm, and abiding support. It was Elise who recognized that the seeds of this book had taken root deep within me even before I did and encouraged me to bring it to life.

Goodman Associates found a superb home for the manuscript at Scribner with my brilliant editor, Maria Guarnaschelli. Maria has been passionately committed to the project from the start, and enriched it with her keen intelligence, insightful objectivity, and vast knowledge of food. Generous and nurturing, she is a food writer's dream editor, fervently respecting my freedom of expression and creativity, while always guiding and pressing me to go further. Special thanks to production editor M. C. Hald, for her scrupulous attention to detail, and to Matt Thornton for his always patient good humor. Also at Scribner my great appreciation to publisher Susan Moldow and associate publisher Roz Lippel for believing in this book, and to my indefatigable publicist Mary Ellen Briggs, Maria's assistant, Anne Kemper, and copyeditor Pamela Mitchell.

Creative Abby Weintraub, with her exquisite design, art director John Fontana, and design director Erich Hobbing have made this book a thing of beauty. I thank them deeply.

Many thanks to great friend Lilyan Aloma, who photographed me for the book jacket, and to Mary Koneval, for on-the-spot assistance par excellence.

I would like to thank Zanne Early Stewart, Senior Food Editor at *Gourmet*, who published the article that inspired this book.

I turned to many people during the several years I spent writing—and eating—my way through this labor of love. To paraphrase Ecclesiastes, there are no completely new recipes under the sun. The infinite world of Jewish cuisines and traditions from which I borrowed freely for this book has been over five thousand years in the making, and I owe an enormous debt to those who shared their heirloom recipes and brought alive their traditions as well as those who opened the doors and orchestrated meetings with them. In addition to the people I mention in the text, I would particularly like to thank my cousins Herbert and Jerry Robinson, brother-in-law Joseph Schindelheim, Rabbi Fabian Schonfeld, Vivian Ellner, Honorable Sukru Elekdag, Farhad Eshaghpour, Edward Kabak, Arnold Kaye, Larry

Kaye, Tammy Koppel, Georgie London, Susan Dwyer Metzger, Amiel Rossabi, Leyla Schick, and Christina Sidoti. In Italy, Lia Hassan, Tina Ottolenghi, Ester Silvana Israel, and Rafi D'Angeli, and in Paris, Arlette and Claude Lustyk generously shared glimpses of their Jewish worlds. Many thanks to Giorgio Scattolin, Segretario Generale della Biblioteca Internazionale "La Vigna" in Vicenza, Italy, for all his help in poring through books on Italian-Jewish cooking. Rivka Wakslak gave me invaluable information on kashrut. And I am immensely grateful to the hundreds of Jewish cookbook writers who preceded me: I list just a small sampling in the bibliography.

I spent innumerable hours at the Dorot Jewish Division of the New York Public Library. Michael Terry and Eleanor Yadin were especially helpful to me there. Warm thanks go to Dr. Lucille Roussin for allowing me to use her personal photographs.

My dear friend and excellent baker, Dr. Mary McLarnon, graciously and patiently helped to perfect some of the pastry recipes.

I am blessed with a remarkable sister and brother. Sami Schindelheim not only heard me out, encouraged and pushed me on, but also tirelessly sought out recipes and information for me through her exceptional network of family and friends in the Orthodox community. Steven Cohen tasted and listened and kept me going with his inimitable humor, my special comfort when my father passed away.

My husband and soulmate Howard Spiegler was truly always there for me. No matter what the demands of his hectic law practice, he always made time to hear a new paragraph, taste another brisket, coddle and cosset and urge me on when I was sure I could go no further. I am eternally grateful for his unerring judgment, sound but always gentle criticism, and most important, fathomless love and support.

Ever since she was a toddler, my darling daughter and biggest booster, Alex, has had an eager and adventurous palate, always ready to try any of my experiments. I thank her for tasting every one of these recipes, many, many times. Her sophisticated opinions, unbridled enthusiasm, always helpful hands, and computer-savvy have been a personal joy during the several years I spent working on this project.

And many thanks to my terrific in-laws, the Stein family, my Schindelheim family, close friends Ed Kabak, the Metzgers, Compton/Lee, Delson/Ginsburg and Brown families, and all my other beloved, intrepid tasters.

*When an index entry has more than one reference, the page number in **boldface**
refers to the recipe itself; other page numbers refer to additional information.*

INDEX

The illustrations and photographs reproduced in this book were provided with the kind permission and courtesy of the following:

Jewish Museum, NY/Art Resource, NY:
    page 32: S0144841 F4072. Gift of Dr. Harry G. Friedman.
    page 39: S0084334. Munich State Library, Munich, Germany.
    page 49: S0072909 1985-170A, B. Cast, hammered, punched, applique.
    page 70: S0008860 F2378. 19 x 14 ½ in.
    page 95: S0144847 S815. 4 ¾ in. Gift of Mr. and Mrs. William Tasch.
    page 102: S0064860 JM45-58. Gift of Mr. Samuel B. Cohn.
    page 127: S0144845 F42. 4 ¾ x 6 ⅞ in. Gift of Dr. Harry G. Friedman.
    page 172: S0136253.
    page 177: S0144827 M446. Cast. 29 ¾ x 26 ½ x 13 ¾ in. The Rose and Benjamin Mintz
        Collection.
    page 193: S0144824 S1004.
    page 207: S0060537 F1779. Master Johann Georg Stenglin or Johann Gottfried Schleissner. 4 ½ in.
        Gift of Dr. Harry G. Friedman.
    page 255: S0014408 F502. Gift of Dr. Harry G. Friedman.
    page 285: S0144829 F5228. Gift of Dr. Harry G. Friedman.
    page 297: S0144816 F5181.
    page 335: S086948 1986-121C. Colored lithograph on paper, 10 ¾ x 10 in.

The Dorot Jewish Division, The New York Public Library; Astor, Lenox and Tilden Foundations:
    page 315.

From the Archives of the YIVO Institute of Jewish Research: page 224.

Collection of Dr. Lucille A. Roussin: page 55.

Collection of the author: pages 110, 145, 362.

The following recipes have been adapted from material previously published by the author in
Gourmet, September 1993:
    Egyptian Ground Fish Balls with Tomato and Cumin; Leek Croquettes from Rhodes; Syrian
Apricot-Stuffed Meat Rolls with Tart-Sweet Cherry Sauce; Egyptian Black-Eyed Peas with Cori-
ander; Hungarian Plum Tart; Pumpkin and Sweet Potato Soup with Sweet Potato Knaidlach.